Macroeconomics

GRADE BOOSTER SERIES

ELIJAH M. JAMES PhD

8TH HOUSE PUBLISHING

First Edition

Published worldwide by 8th House Publishing
www.8th House Publishing.com

Front Cover Design by 8th House Publishing

Set in Raleway, Adobe Garamand Pro and Adobe Caslon Pro.

ISBN 978-1-926716-45-9

'Macroeconomics - Grade Booster Series' by Elijah M. James Ph.D.

LIBRARY AND ARCHIVES CANADA CATALOGUING IN PUBLICATION DATA
A catalog record of this book is available from Library and Archives Canada.

BabalonBOOKS is a division of 8th House Publishing, Montreal, Canada.
www.8thHousePublishing.com

8th House Publishing
Montreal, Canada

Macroeconomics

GRADE BOOSTER SERIES

Dedicated to my dear friend and colleague, the late Dr. Matlub Hussain, without whose assistance and insistence, this book might never have been written.

PREFACE

The idea of a grade booster series in economics originated with my own observation of my students. I noticed that on numerous occasions, students obtained low grades, not so much because they were unfamiliar with the relevant material, but more so because of their inability to utilize the information they had to solve problems and answer questions. Discussions with colleagues quickly confirmed that they too were witnessing the same phenomenon. It was clear then, that if students could be taught how to harness the information they possess and use it to answer questions and solve problems, their grades would improve significantly.

The main purpose of the Grade Booster Series (GBS)—Macroeconomics is to help you, the student taking an introductory course in macroeconomics, improve your grade. By studying the problems contained in the Grade Booster Series, you will acquire confidence in attacking problems, your fear of economics will diminish, you will better understand the principles and concepts discussed in your textbook, you will be able to apply them in different circumstances, and you will learn how to answer economic questions and solve problems in tests and examinations.

Through the GBS—Macroeconomics, you will learn to properly organize economic information into answers to questions; you will learn a step-by-step procedure to solving economic problems; you will develop the ability to think clearly; and all these will translate into a better grade in your macroeconomics course.

The GBS—Macroeconomics gives you access to more than 1,500 economics problems/questions with full answers and explanations, including:

415 Essay problems
431 Multiple-choice questions
375 True/False questions
291 Completion questions

Pedagogical Features

The GBS—Macroeconomics is loaded with pedagogical features, including the following:.

1. *The Essay Questions:* Not only do we provide answers to the essay questions, but we provide a section referred to as ***Requirement and Clue*** under which we point out what is required for a good answer or solution, and give some hints as to how you should proceed.
2. *Multiple-choice Questions:* After indicating the correct choice, we provide a *reason* for making that choice.
3. *True-False Questions:* If a statement is false, we provide an *explanation* as to why it is false.

So, if you want to boost your grade in macroeconomics, the GBS—Macroeconomics is what you need. Welcome to the Grade Booster Series—Macroeconomics

Keyed to Your Textbook

The *Grade Booster Series (GBS)—Macroeconomics* is designed to be used with any traditional textbook in introductory macroeconomics. For the convenience of students taking an introduction to macroeconomics course, we have provided this key to some of the major macroeconomic textbooks. It would be impractical to list all the major textbooks used in macroeconomics courses, so only a sample is represented.

Using the *Key* is rather simple. For example, if you are studying Monetary Policy and you are using Colander, the relevant chapter is Chapter 29 (Monetary Policy). This is Module 15 (Monetary Theory and Monetary Policy) in the GBS. What if your textbook is not listed? Not a problem! Note the title of the chapter you are studying, turn to the index of the GBS and see which module matches the material you are studying. It's that simple.

GBS	BA	CA	COL	HUB	JAM	MAN	MCC	MIL	RAG	SAY
Mo1	1	1	1	1	1	2	1	1	1	-
Mo2	-	-	2A	1A	1A	2A	-	-	2	TK
Mo3	3	2	-	2	2	2	1	2	1	1
Mo4	-	-	3	2	-	-	2	-	-	-
Mo5	4	3,4	4,5	3	3	4	3	3	3	2,3
Mo6	5	5,6	25	8	4,5	5	6,7	8	19,20	3
Mo7	13	11	27	13	7	7	12	10	23-25	5
Mo8	10	15	-	-	-	8	-	12	-	-
Mo9	14	8	26	12	9	-	11	12	21	6
Mo10	8	7	33,34	9	6,16	9,16	9	7	29,30	4
Mo11	-	-	24	10	12	-	9	-	30	-
Mo12	16	9	32	16	11	15	13	13	31	7
Mo13	11	10	28	14	13	10	14	15	26	8
Mo14	11	10	28	14	14	10	14	15	26	8
Mo15	12,17	-	29	15	15	15	16	16	27,28	9
Mo16	19	19	35	19	18	12	21	33	34	11

Key:

GBS = *Grade booster series*; **Mo** = *Module*; **Tk** = *Toolkit*

BA = Robin Bade & Michael Parkin, *Foundations of Macroeconomics*, 8th Edition, Pearson, 2018

CA = Karl E. Case, Ray C. Fair, and Sharon E. Oster, *Principles of Macroeconomics,* 12th Edition, Pearson, 2017

COL = David Colander, *Macroeconomics*, 10th Edition, McGraw Hill, 2017

HUB = R. Glen Hubbard & Anthony Patrick O'Brien, *Macroeconomics*, 6th Edition, Pearson, 2017

JAM = Elijah M. James, *Macroeconomics*, 2nd Edition, Pearson, 2012

MAN = N. Gregory Mankiw, Ronald D. Kneebone, & Kenneth J. McKenzie, *Principles of Macroeconomics*, 7th Edition, Nelson, 2017

MCC = Campbell McConnell, S. Brue, and S. Flynn, *Macroeconomics*, 20th Edition, McGraw Hill, 2015

MIL = Roger LeRoy Miller, *Economics Today: The Macro View*, 19th Edition, Pearson, 2018

RAG = Christopher T. S. Ragan, *Macroeconomics*, 15th Edition, Pearson, 2017

SAY = John Sayre and Alan Morris, *Principles of Macroeconomics*, 8th Edition, McGraw Hill, 2015

Look for the ***Grade Booster Series****--Microeconomics!*

ACKNOWLEDGEMENTS

A work of this magnitude is not usually accomplished by any single individual. In the case of the Grade Booster Series (GBS)—Macroeconomics, I have received a great deal of help and support from many different quarters. My dear friend and colleague, the late Dr. Matlub Hussain, to whom I have dedicated this volume, was a staunch advocate of student success. He read an earlier draft of the manuscript and made many suggestions for improving it. Dr. Alaka Ganguli with whom I share an office, was always available for discussions, and gave freely of her time and expertise. Alaka, I am greatly indebted to you. I must thank the members of the Department of Economics at Dawson College for creating a friendly environment that fosters scholarship.

My children Ted, Jennifer, Andrea, Kapil, and my niece Bernadette have encouraged me throughout the entire process of preparing the manuscript. They have served as sounding board for my ideas.

I owe a debt of gratitude to my students at McGill University, Concordia University, John Abbott College, and Dawson College who opened my eyes to some of the problems that students face in their study of economics.

Finally, I would like to thank Mr. Emery Moreira and his hard-working staff at 8th House Publishing for the excellent job they have done in transforming my manuscript into such a fine product.

I thank you all.

TOPIC

1 THE SUBJECT MATTER OF ECONOMICS

SYNOPSIS

An understanding of economics is extremely important in any modern society. It is a fact that many of the critical problems and issues that members of society face are somehow related to economics. The decisions that consumers, businesses, and the various levels of government make determine how society uses its scarce resources.

Economics is the discipline that studies how a society uses its scarce resources to satisfy the unlimited wants of its customers. Because it studies a particular aspect of human behavior, economics is considered a **social science** in the same sense that social psychology, sociology, and political science are social sciences.

Human wants are unlimited while the means available to satisfy those wants are limited. This problem of **scarcity** is the fundamental economic problem. We must find ways of using our scarce resources to satisfy as many wants as possible.

Economists employ the scientific method. They construct models and use them to help them understand how the economy works. **Positive statements** are factual. They deal with what is, was, or will be. **Normative statements** are opinions or value judgements. They deal with what ought to be. **Positive economics** is concerned with how the economy actually works, while **normative economics** is concerned with how the economy ought to function. Economists are more likely to disagree over the normative aspects of economics than over the positive aspects.

A **variable** is anything that can assume different values. **Endogenous variables** are those whose values are determined in the model, whereas the exogenous variables are those whose values are determined by factors outside the model. The **exogenous variables** affect the endogenous. A **flow** (or flow variable) has a time dimension while a **stock** (or stock variable) does not have a time dimension.

The *post hoc ergo propter hoc* fallacy is the false conclusion that a cause-effect relationship exists because events may occur in sequence. The ***ceteris paribus*** (other things being equal) assumption is important in economics. It allows the economist to isolate the effects of certain variables. The assumption allows the economist to hold other factors constant while he or she examines the effects of the variable that is of current interest.

The two main branches into which economics is divided are *microeconomics* and *macroeconomics*. **Microeconomics** studies the behaviour of individual economic units, while **macroeconomics** studies the behavior of broad economic aggregates. A good understanding of how the economy functions requires a knowledge of both microeconomics and macroeconomics.

LEARNING OBJECTIVES

In connection with this module, you should be able to:

1. Formulate an adequate definition of economics.
2. Discuss the subject matter of economics.
3. Discuss the importance of economics.
4. Identify and classify the resources of the economy.
5. Discuss the incomes derived from various resources.
6. Explain what economists do in terms of employment.
7. Discuss the nature of scientific inquiry.
8. Explain economic methodology.
9. Distinguish between positive and normative economics.
10. Explain why economists sometimes disagree.
11. Distinguish between microeconomics and macroeconomics.

DEFINITIONS & CONCEPTS

You should be able to define the following terms and concepts:

social science
scarcity
scientific method
economic goods
free goods
producer goods
consumer goods
capital goods
scientific method
hypothesis
model
definitions
assumptions
ceteris paribus
positive economics
normative economics
variable
endogenous variable
exogenous variable
stock variable
flow variable
resources
rent
profit
wages and salaries
interest & dividends
land
labour
capital
entrepreneurial services
microeconomics
macroeconomics
positive statement
normative statement

1 THE SUBJECT MATTER OF ECONOMICS

Concepts, Definitions & Problems

Problem 1-1

Distinguish between absolute scarcity and relative scarcity. Why does scarcity exist?

Requirement and Clue: *Recognize that this is a two-part problem. Your solution should address both parts. The two concepts are different and it is your task to illustrate that difference.*

Solution:

Economists distinguish between *absolute* scarcity and *relative* or *economic* scarcity. Ordinarily, when we say that something is scarce, we mean that only a small quantity of it exists, or that it is difficult to obtain. For example, one may say that fresh vegetables are scarce during a drought, or that a 1945 coin is scarce or rare, meaning that it is seldom seen. That concept of scarcity is referred to as *absolute scarcity*. However, when economists talk about scarcity, they mean the extent of availability of something in relation to how much of it is wanted. This is the concept of *economic* or *relative* scarcity. The following table illustrates the difference.

Absolute scarcity versus relative scarcity

Situation	Amount available	Amount wanted	Condition
A	60	40	No economic scarcity
B	100	150	Economic scarcity

Let us look first at absolute scarcity. In situation A, 60 units of an item are available, while in situation B, 100 units are available. In an absolute sense, the item is scarcer in situation A than in situation B. Absolute scarcity can be determined solely by looking at the amounts available.

Let us now look at relative scarcity. In situation A, 60 units of an item are available, but only 40 units are required. In this situation economic scarcity does not exist since more of the item is available than is wanted. In situation B, 100 units of the item are available but 150 units are wanted. The amount that is wanted exceeds the amount that is available. In this situation, the item is relatively scarce. Relative scarcity is determined by comparing the amount available with the amount that is wanted.

Scarcity exists because quantities of goods and services are limited while desires for these goods and services are unlimited.

Problem 1-2

What is the meaning of the term scarcity in economics? Does scarcity really exist?

Requirement and Clue: *This is a two-part problem. The first part is definitional. You are required to demonstrate that you understand the concept of scarcity as it is used in economics. You are not asked to write an essay or a term paper on scarcity. Just say what scarcity means in economics. The second part of the problem requires a demonstration of the existence of scarcity.*

Solution:

In economics, scarcity is the condition that exists when the goods and services available are insufficient to satisfy our wants for them. Thus in economics, scarcity is always relative—the quantities available in relation to wants. Quantities of most goods and services are limited, whereas wants or desires for those goods and services are unlimited.

By definition, scarcity is a reality. It does exist. A few goods, such as air and sunlight (in most circumstances) are not scarce. But in the vast majority of cases, scarcity is a fact of life. We just don't have enough resources to enable us to produce all the goods and services that we want.

Problem 1-3

What is the difference between "economic goods" and "free goods"? Give examples of each.

Requirement and Clue: *Say what economic goods are and what free goods are. Your examples should support your definitions.*

Solution:

Economic goods are goods that are relatively scarce, that is, they are not available in sufficiently large quantities to satisfy people's wants for them. Such goods are produced using scarce resources and therefore have a positive price. Examples of economic goods are oil, computers, hospital beds, and automobiles.

Free goods, on the other hand, are goods that are readily available in sufficiently large quantities to satisfy people's wants for them. Free goods are not the result of the use of scarce resources. Even at a price of zero, there are sufficient quantities of free goods to satisfy all wants. Examples of free goods are air, sunlight, and sea water.

Problem 1-4

Explain each of the following terms:

(a) *Free good*

(b) *Producer good*

Requirement and Clue: *You are expected to define each concept clearly. Although the problem does not specifically ask for examples, you should provide them nonetheless.*

Solution:

(a) A free good is a good that is so plentiful that no one has to pay for it. If you were on a river and you wanted water to wash your hands, you would not have to pay for the water since there would be so much of it available. In this case, the water would be a free good. Note that a free good in one situation may not be a free good in another situation. For example, the water that flows out of the faucet in your bathroom is not a free good. If a government provides elementary education "free of charge", it does not mean that elementary education is a free good. Although the recipients do not pay for it directly, it is paid for out of taxation.

(b) A producer good is any good that is used by the producer in the process of production. They are the inputs or factors of production that producers use to produce their output of goods and services. They are distinguishable from consumer goods in that consumer goods are not intended for further processing. Examples of producer goods are raw material, fuel, equipment and plant.

Problem 1-5

What is the difference between consumer goods and capital goods? Can a good be both a consumer good and a capital good?

Requirement and Clue: *Notice that this is a two-part problem. Address each part in order. Your solution should include examples of consumer goods and capital goods. For the second part of the problem, think of a good that is used by both consumers and producers.*

Solution:

Consumer goods are goods that are intended to satisfy the wants of consumers directly. They are the goods that consumers buy for final use. Examples of consumer goods are clothing, home computers, television sets, food, furniture, and kitchen appliances. Capital goods on the other hand, are goods that are produced and used to produce other capital goods and consumer goods. Capital goods satisfy consumer wants only indirectly. Examples of capital goods are farm implements, machine tools, printing presses, and factories.

It is possible for the same item to be both a consumer good and a capital good. For example, a farmer may use his pickup truck to haul produce to market and for personal and family transportation. When the truck is used to haul produce it is a capital good, and when it is used for personal or family transportation it is a consumer good. Similarly, a personal computer in a business office is a capital good, but when it is used at home by a student it is a consumer good.

Problem 1-6

Economics is often defined as a social science. Sociology, psychology, and political science are also social sciences. How does economics differ from each of the social sciences listed above?

Requirement and Clue: *Say why these disciplines fall into the category of social science. Mention what each deals with and how economics differs from them.*

Solution:

Economics, sociology, psychology, and political science are all social sciences because each studies some aspect of human behavior. Economics studies how society uses its scarce resources to satisfy unlimited wants; sociology studies the development, organization, and functioning of a society and its institutions; psychology studies the mental characteristics or attitude of an individual or group to understand behavior; and political science studies the processes, principles, and structure of government and of political institutions.

Economics differs from these other social sciences in that none of the others deals specifically with how society uses its limited resources to satisfy its unlimited wants.

Problem 1-7

Why is it important for people to have an understanding of the economy and society?

Requirement and Clue: *Stress the importance of the economy and society to our lives.*

Solution:

An understanding of the economy and society enables us to improve the performance of the economy and make our society better. We will then be in a better position to deal with many of the problems that we encounter in life. The economy is such an important part of society that it is virtually impossible to understand society without a basic knowledge of economics. Our relationships with one another, our environment, the manner in which our collective wealth is distributed, the types of work we do, our ability to develop and maintain a viable health care system, and the amount of money we earn are all related to our economy. Our lives are shaped by the myriad economic decisions that have been made in the past by others and that are being made by us today. A decision to put more resources into the production of warplanes instead of using them to provide more educational and health facilities will affect our society not only today but also for a long time in the future. The better our understanding of our economy and our society, the better will be the control that we are likely to have over our own destiny.

Problem 1-8

What do professional economists do?

Requirement and Clue: *The solution to this problem requires a statement about occupations for economists. Think of employment situations that require decisions about the use of scarce resources.*

Solution:

Economists are engaged in a wide variety of activities. Some teach in high schools, colleges and universities. Large corporations like Wal-Mart, Ford Motor Company, Imperial Oil, or a public utilities company, might hire economists to estimate the demand for their products or services or to figure out the economic impact of price changes, or to increase the efficiency of their operations. A bank might employ economists to forecast interest rates or the demand for loans. A government might hire economists to determine the effects of certain taxes on its revenue and on the level of economic activity. A union might employ economists to study matters relating to wages and employment. Professional economists serve as presidents, vice-presidents, general managers, and executives of a wide variety of organizations. They also sit on the boards of many companies directing their affairs. Many economists work on their own as independent consultants.

Problem 1-9

What are resources and how can they be classified?

Requirement and Clue: *This is a two-part problem. Answer each part in order. Briefly define each category.*

Solution:

Resources are the things that are used to produce the goods and services that the society requires. They are productive agents such as trees, waterways, roads, oil, factories, air, buildings, tools, and human effort. They are also referred to as *factors of production.*

Economists usually classify them into four categories as follows:

Land: all natural resources such as minerals, rivers, lakes, wildlife, forests, and oil.

Labour: the physical and mental efforts that people contribute to the production process.

Capital: any manufactured item that can be used to produce goods and services. They include buildings, highways, equipment, and manufacturing plant.

Entrepreneurship: the organization of land, labour, and capital for the purpose of production. Entrepreneurship or entrepreneurial services include managerial skills, risk-taking, organizational skills, innovative skills, leadership, and decision-making skills.

Problem 1-10

Indicate whether each of the following should be classified as land (T), labour (L), capital (C), or entrepreneurial services (E).

a. The oil sands in a country
b. A ferry that takes passengers from point A to point B
c. The services provided by technicians employed by a telephone company
d. Deer in the ABC Public Park
e. Forests in North America and Western Europe
f. Lake Erie
g. A park in Australia
h. The services provided by Mavis Grant in securing funds and establishing her small bread and breakfast business
i. The services provided by your economics professor
j. The cranes used in constructing a multi-level parking facility

Requirement and Clue: *This is a test of your knowledge regarding the classification of resources. Before you answer, think of the meaning of each category.*

Solution:

a. The oil sands in a country (T)
b. A ferry that takes passengers from point A to point B (C)
c. The services provided by technicians employed by a telephone company (L)
d. Deer in the ABC Public Park (T)
e. Forests in North America and Western Europe (T)
f. Lake Erie (T)

g. A park in Australia (T)
h. The services provided by Mavis Grant in securing funds and establishing her small bread and breakfast business (E)
i. The services provided by your economics professor (L)
j. The cranes used in constructing a multi-level parking facility (C)

Problem 1-11

What do economists mean by land?

Requirement and Clue: *Recognize that "land" is an economic jargon with its own peculiar meaning. Provide illustrative examples.*

Solution:

"Land" is one of those economic terms that have a meaning that is different from its meaning in ordinary English language. Ordinarily, when we talk of land, we refer to the solid portion of the earth on which one can erect a building or grow crops. In economics also, land refers to the solid portion of the earth but the concept includes more than that. Any non-human resource that is made available by nature is called land in economic jargon. Thus land includes minerals embedded in the earth; fish in the seas; rivers, and lakes; the vast expanse of oceans; the natural waterfalls; wildlife; oxygen in the air; and even the space within which economic activity takes place. In economics, land is synonymous with "natural resources".

Problem 1-12

What is the economic definition of labour?

Requirement and Clue: *Provide examples in your answer.*

Solution:

Simply stated, labour is human effort. It consists of all human abilities or talents that may be employed in the production of goods and services. This definition includes both physical and mental abilities or talents. Examples of labour are the work of physicians, economic professors, movie actors, sales people, as well as farmers, mechanics, and material handlers.

Economists now generally exclude from the economic definition of labour one particular type of mental ability, that is, entrepreneurial ability which is classified as a separate resource category.

Problem 1-13

Distinguish between real capital and money capital.

Requirement and Clue: *Think of the usage of these terms in economics. Recognize that for most people, capital is money. Provide examples of real capital.*

Solution:

In economics, a distinction is made between real capital and money capital or financial capital. Real capital refers to any produced factor of production that can be used to produce other capital goods or consumer goods. Some examples of real capital are machines, tools, equipment, buildings, railroad tracks and highways. Money capital or financial capital, on the other hand, is defined as funds available to purchase real capital. Since money itself is not used as a factor of production until it is exchanged for real capital, economists focus on real capital and generally do not include money in their definition of capital.

Problem 1-14

What particular types of income are generated by the factors of production?

Requirement and Clue: *Recall that each category of resource generates a particular type of income. Be careful with capital and entrepreneurial services.*

Solution:

Land, labour, capital, and entrepreneurial services generate incomes for their owners. Owners of land receive *rent*, and owners of capital receive *interest and dividend* income. Those who provide labour services receive *wages and salaries*, and individuals who provide entrepreneurial services earn *profits*.

Problem 1-15

In the following table, the left-hand column shows factors of production while the middle column shows earning/income types that are incorrectly matched with the factors of production. In the right-hand column enter the correct income categories that match the factors of production.

Factors of production and their earnings

Factors of production	Earning/Income	Corrected income category
Land	Interest and dividends	
Labour	Rent	
Capital	Profits	
Entrepreneurial services	Wages and salaries	

Requirement and Clue: *You are required to demonstrate that you know which income type is associated with each resource category. Again, be careful with capital and entrepreneurial services.*

Solution:

Factors of production	Earning/Income	Corrected income category
Land	Interest and dividends	*Rent*
Labour	Rent	*Wages and salaries*
Capital	Profits	*Interest and dividends*
Entrepreneurial services	Wages and salaries	*Profits*

Problem 1-16

Indicate whether each of the following types of income would be classified technically as rent (R), wages and salaries (W), interest and dividends (i), or profit (π).

a. *The income that executive officers receive for their services*
b. *The money Mr. Jenkins (a landlord) collects each month from his tenants*
c. *The income that a student receives from a college as payment for her part-time tutoring services*
d. *The annual amount that Bell Canada Enterprises (BCE) pays out to its shareholders for their investment in the company*
e. *The income received by parking assistants for their services*
f. *The net earnings of Mr. Edwards, the proprietor of a parking lot business*
g. *The income that Mr. Peters receives monthly from Mr. Edwards for the use of his parking lot*
h. *The net revenue received by an inventor for developing and marketing a space-saving device*

Requirement and Clue: *You need to figure out which resource category generates the income indicated and then assign the appropriate income type.*

Solution:

a. The income that executive officers receive for their services (W)
b. The money Mr. Jenkins (a landlord) collects each month from tenants in his building (i)
c. The income that a student receives from a college as payment for her part-time tutoring services (W)
d. The annual amount that Bell Canada Enterprises (BCE) pays out to its shareholders for their investment in the company (i)
e. The income received by parking lot assistants for their services (W)
f. The net earnings of Mr. Edwards, the proprietor of a parking lot business (π)
g. The income that Mr. Peters receives monthly from Mr. Edwards for the use of his parking lot (R)
h. The net revenue received by an inventor for developing and marketing a space-saving device (π)

Problem 1-17

In what sense can economics claim to be a science?

Requirement and Clue: *Ask yourself, "What does science mean in this context?" You are expected to show that economics follows the scientific approach and thus qualifies as a science.*

Solution:

To qualify as a science, a discipline must follow certain procedures. Scientists, in attempting to explain certain phenomena, construct theories or models. In so doing, they must carefully define words and phrases so as to avoid confusion. They make certain assumptions that describe the conditions under which the theory is meant to apply. Then they specify the relationships that exist between the variables under consideration, i.e. they make certain hypotheses. Scientists also proceed to test their theories to see how well they predict or explain events. Scientists must relate their theories to empirical evidence. This is the scientific procedure. Any discipline that follows this method of enquiry earns the right to be called a science.

The discipline of economics follows the procedure outlined above, so economics can claim legitimately to be a science. It must be pointed out however, that economics is not an *exact* science like physics, or chemistry, for example. What distinguishes economics and other social sciences from the so-called exact or hard sciences is the difficulty that social scientists face in conducting experiments. Physicists, for example, can enter their laboratories and create the ideal condition for their experiments. Economists, on the other hand, cannot conduct any such controlled experiments. Their laboratory is the real world and their subjects of investigation are people. The variables with which the economist works are constantly changing so exact measurement is often not possible.

Problem 1-18

How has the use of mathematical tools and econometrics affected the scientific element in economics?

Requirement and Clue: *Think of the precision of mathematical tools and of the importance of measurement in science.*

Solution:

The increasing use of mathematical tools in economics has helped economists to be more scientific in that economists are forced to specify clearly and concisely their assumptions and the relationships among the variables with which they are working. The development of econometrics has also helped economists in testing their theories, and in encouraging economic theorists to formulate their theories in a testable manner.

Problem 1-19

Economics has been categorized as a social science. What is science?

Requirement and Clue: *The emphasis here is on the meaning of science. Briefly discuss this.*

Solution:

Science refers to a particular method of acquiring knowledge that includes observation, measurement, and testing. Science can be defined as a branch of study, especially one concerned with facts, principles, and methods. Science refers not only to a method of acquiring knowledge but also to the knowledge produced by the approach. Science, as in the scientific approach is the systematic investigation and observation of phenomena and the formulation of general laws and tendencies there from, after testing and verifying hypotheses.

Problem 1-20

What is a hypothesis?

Requirement and Clue: *Provide a clear definition of "hypothesis" and give an example that clarifies the meaning of the concept.*

Solution:

The process of observation often leads to ideas, hunches, or guesses about relationships among the variables observed. A hypothesis is a statement of suspected relationships among two or more variables. It does not state some fact that is already known but something to be tested. For example, consider the following two statements:

> A: *The average weight of economics professors in North America is 175 pounds.*
>
> B: *Students who have a strong mathematical background get better grades in economics than those without a strong background in mathematics.*

Statement **A** is not a hypothesis; it merely expresses a fact that is already known, perhaps from a previous study. Statement **B,** however, is a hypothesis because the statement expresses a relationship between students' grades in economics and their mathematical backgrounds. Hypotheses should be stated in a verifiable manner so that they can be confirmed or rejected on the basis of test results.

Problem 1-21

Does economics follow the scientific approach?

Requirement and Clue: *Briefly outline the scientific approach and then show that the methods of economics are scientific.*

Solution:

The scientific approach involves observation and measurement, the formulation of hypotheses, and verification through testing of hypotheses. Economics deals with human behaviour and therefore cannot conduct experiments in traditional laboratories. No laboratory instruments can measure human behaviour with any degree of precision. Nevertheless, economics follows the scientific procedure as faithfully as do the natural sciences such as physics, chemistry and biology. In attempting to explain economic phenomena, economists follow the scientific approach. They gather information, analyze it, and select what they consider to be the most relevant facts. They formulate and test hypotheses and thus arrive at general statements or laws concerning economic phenomena.

Problem 1-22

Describe the methodology used by economists in studying economic phenomena.

Requirement and Clue: *The focus here is on model building. Define a model and discuss its ingredients.*

Solution:

The factors involved in studying real-world economic events are often quite complex. The economist comes to grips with these complexities by constructing economic models. An economic model is a simplification of the real economy or some aspect of it, and it consists only of the factors that appear to pertain most to what is being studied. Details that do not pertain directly to the question or problem being studied are simply stripped away in the model.

In constructing economic models, economists use definitions, assumptions, hypotheses and predictions. Definitions serve to identify the variables in the model so that measurement can be facilitated; assumptions state the conditions under which the model is supposed to work and greatly reduce the complexities of the real economy; hypotheses are statements about how the variables are related. They are usually cause-effect statements such as, "if people earn more money, they will buy more goods and services." Predictions are the outcome of testing hypotheses. If a certain relationship is suspected to exist between two variables and a test confirms the suspicion, then the economist can make prediction. For example, if it is confirmed that people buy more goods and services when their incomes rise, then economists can predict that an increase in income will cause an increase in spending.

Problem 1-23

How does economic methodology differ from that of natural sciences? Does the economist have any advantage over the natural scientists in studying phenomena?

Requirement and Clue: *This is a two-part problem. In your solution, address each part in order. Briefly state what makes it necessary for economists to construct models. Explain why economists might have an advantage over natural scientists.*

Solution:

Economic methodology differs from that of the natural sciences mainly in that the economist cannot generally conduct controlled experiments, whereas the natural scientist usually can. Economics is concerned with the behavior of human beings engaged in various types of economic activities. These activities are influenced by a variety of factors over which the economist has little or no control, and these uncontrollable factors often do exert considerable influence on the variable(s) that might be of interest to the economist. This difficulty forces the economist to construct models in which restrictions can be placed on some variables. By contrast, natural scientists are usually able to isolate the phenomena they are studying under laboratory conditions in which all extraneous factors have been excluded or held at some controlled level.

The economist does have an advantage over the natural scientist in that the natural scientist cannot place himself or herself in the place of the object that is being studied. He or she cannot meaningfully ask the question: "What would I do if I were platinum being examined?" Economists, on the other hand, can make generalizations about human actions from introspection since they can put themselves in the place of their subjects and ask, "What would I do if I were given a Christmas bonus of $1500.00?" Economists can do this because they have approximately the same makeup, motives, and abilities as the subjects of their inquiry.

Problem 1-24

What are some of the dangers of using models in economics?

Requirement and Clue: *Recognize that models are simplifications of reality and as such, there are short comings. Point out these.*

Solution:

Although models are extremely useful in studying economics, there are some dangers associated with their use. First, there is the danger that in determining which facts are most relevant, the economist might strip away too many of the relevant facts, thus severely limiting the applicability of the model. For example, in studying demand and supply of oranges during a particularly good harvest year, the economist might neglect to include the weather as a variable in his or her model. In this case, the model will work well as long as the weather is favourable for orange production. It will not work well in a drought year.

Another danger of using models is that it becomes very easy to forget that they are simplifications of reality and so people may rely too heavily on them. Referring to the example above about the demand and supply of oranges, fifteen successive years of weather that is favourable to orange production could lull economists into forgetting that they have excluded the weather from their model, so that when unfavourable weather does occur, they may be unable to account for changes in the orange market.

Finally, in using economic models, economists must keep in mind that they are purely *positive* as opposed to *normative*. They state simply what is, not what ought to be.

Problem 1-25

"Economic theories are abstractions from reality. That makes them practically useless in real life." Is this statement true or false? Defend your answer.

Requirement and Clue: *Recall that if any part of a statement is false, then the entire statement is false. In your solution, stress the advantages of models.*

Solution:

The statement is false. Economists are confronted with a massive volume of facts when studying the economy. In formulating useful theories of the behavior of the economy, they must extract the most relevant facts, and eliminate the less relevant ones. If nothing were stripped away, then the theory would prove to be too unwieldy for practical use. It would accurately describe the reality of a particular situation, but it would be so encumbered by the enumerable details of the situation that it would be useless if any of the details changed. Prediction with such a theory would be practically impossible and one would not learn much about the economy using such a theory.

By weeding out the less relevant data, and focusing on the most relevant facts, economists formulate theories that are more useful in explaining/predicting economic phenomena. The basis of a good theory is its foundation in facts. A theory that ignores the facts is worse than one that tries to include too many irrelevant facts.

Problem 1-26

How is the "goodness" of an economic model determined?

Requirement and Clue: *Focus on the purpose of an economic model and the extent to which it (the model) accomplishes its purpose.*

Solution:

The whole purpose of an economic model is to use it to explain some aspect of economic reality or to predict certain economic outcomes. An economic model that does this well is a good model. If model A explains and predicts economic phenomena better than the competing model B, then model A is judged to be better than model B. If an economic model fails to explain what we observe in the real world, then it may be rejected. The "goodness" of a model should be based primarily on its ability to explain or predict reality.

Problem 1-27

What is the role of assumptions in economic models?

Requirement and Clue: *First define assumptions and then state their roles. Provide examples.*

Solution:

Assumptions are statements of the conditions under which a particular economic model is expected to work. Basically, economists make two types of assumptions. One type relates to what motivates economic behavior. For example, economists assume that consumers are motivated by the desire to maximize their satisfaction, whereas businesses are motivated by the desire to maximize their profits. The other type of assumption that economists make is aimed at simplifying the complexities of the actual economy so that the task of the economist is made much easier. For example, if economists are not currently concerned with how government spending and taxes affect the economy, they may simplify their analyses by *assuming* that the government neither spends nor taxes. Such abstractions are necessary because of the complexities of the actual economy. Admittedly, economic assumptions are sometimes quite unrealistic, but often what is lost in realism is more than compensated for in understanding.

Problem 1-28

What is the importance of the "ceteris paribus" assumption in economic analysis?

Requirement and Clue: *Define the "ceteris paribus" assumption and discuss its importance by stating how economists use it.*

Solution:

"*Ceteris paribus*" is a Latin phrase meaning "other things being equal." This assumption allows economists to investigate the effects of one variable while assuming that others remain constant. Suppose we are interested in finding out the effect of a fall in the price of smart phones on the quantity of smart phones that university students will buy. Some of the factors, in addition to the price of smart phones that will affect the quantity of smart phones that students will buy include their incomes, their preference for smart phones over ordinary cell phones, and the prices of textbooks. We can hypothesize that if the price of smart phones falls, students will buy more of them. If we observe that a fall in the price of smart phones is accompanied by an increase in the quantity purchased, can we then conclude that the increase in quantity purchased results from a fall in price? It is possible that the increase in quantity purchased results from an increase in income or from a fall in the prices of textbooks that leaves students with more money to spend on smart phones, or from an increase in the prices of ordinary cell phones or some other reason.

To determine how a change in one factor affects other factors, economists must find some way of isolating the effects of other factors. In the above example, economists must isolate students' income, preference, the prices of textbooks, and other factors other than the price of smart phones that can affect the quantity of smart phones that students will purchase. Economists accomplish this task by using the *ceteris paribus* assumption. This assumption allows them to keep other factors constant while they examine the effects of the variable that currently interests them. Thus they can investigate how a change in price affects the quantity purchased by assuming that income, preference, and all other factors except the price of smart phones remain unchanged.

Problem 1-29

Differentiate between positive statements and normative statements. Give one example of each.

Requirement and Clue: *It's a good idea to define positive statements and normative statements. Recognize that positive statements are not necessarily true. Don't forget the examples.*

Solution:

Positive statements are expressions about what is, was, or will be. They are statements about facts and can be verified. Positive statements may be true or false. *Normative statements*, on the other hand, are expressions about what ought to be. They are statements about opinions and value-judgments and cannot be empirically verified.

An example of a positive statement is, "The price of oil is $100 a barrel." An example of a normative statement is, "The price of oil should be lowered."

Problem 1-30

Categorize each of the following as either a positive (P) or a normative (N) statement:

a. *One way of increasing the number of units of air conditioners sold is to reduce their prices.*
b. *If the prices of air conditioners rise, people will buy more of them.*
c. *The government should control the prices of essential items such as electricity and gasoline and basic foodstuff.*
d. *Cigarettes and alcohol should be banned.*
e. *Lower interest rates on credit cards will encourage people to spend more.*
f. *The current interest charges on credit cards are much too high.*
g. *Lower interest rates across the board will have a positive impact on job creation.*
h. *Higher interest rates on loans will result in more consumption and more investment spending.*

Requirement and Clue: *Does it talk about what is, was, or will be or does it talk about what ought to be? It is important to remember that positive statements may be true or false.*

Solution:

a. One way of increasing the number of units of air conditioners sold is to reduce their prices. (P)
b. If the prices of air conditioners rise, people will buy more of them. (P)
c. The government should control the prices of essential items such as electricity and gasoline and basic foodstuff. (N)
d. Cigarettes and alcohol should be banned. (N)
e. Lower interest rates on credit cards will encourage people to spend more. (P)
f. The current interest charges on credit cards are much too high. (N)
g. Lower interest rates across the board will have a positive impact on job creation. (P)
h. Higher interest rates on loans will result in more consumption and more investment spending. (P)

Problem 1-31

If economics is a science, why do economists disagree?

Requirement and Clue: *Science is not determined by the amount of agreement or disagreement. State that natural scientists sometimes disagree. Then discuss reasons for disagreement among economists.*

Solution:

Disagreement among economists has nothing to do with whether or not economics is a science. Physics and chemistry are sciences yet physicists disagree, and chemists disagree. Economists disagree for different reasons. First, economists have different values, and they judge economic situations and events differently. When economists are asked to express their opinions about some economic action, they may try to be objective, but their objectivity might be coloured by their own moral sentiments. One economist might argue that wearing a seat belt prevents injuries in a collision, and therefore severe fines should be levied on people caught without wearing seatbelts in their cars. Another economist might take the position that the compulsory use of seatbelts is an unnecessary infringement of people's rights, and it's entirely their business if they don't want to wear seatbelts. Therefore the government has no business levying fines on people who do not wear seatbelts.

But it is not only on such normative issues that economists disagree. They disagree also on positive issues. Different explanations exist as to how the economy actually operates, and it is not always clear which explanation is best. That is, economists may disagree over the appropriate model of the economy, and the available data might not be such as to allow for definitive conclusions so the disagreement persists.

Economists may disagree even though they use the same economic model. They may agree on the qualitative aspects but disagree on the quantitative aspects. For example, two economists might agree that a fall in interest rates will result in an increase in the level of investment. They might disagree, however, over the magnitude of the increase, one claiming that the increase will be negligible, and the other claiming that the increase will be significant. This type of disagreement can be prolonged because of the inadequacy of relevant data.

Problem 1-32

What is the difference between an endogenous variable and an exogenous variable?

Requirement and Clue: *Recall that "en" means inside or within and the "ex" means outside. Give grief definitions of the concepts with examples.*

Solution:

An endogenous variable is one whose value is determined within a model, while an exogenous variable is one whose value is determined outside a model. The difference can be illustrated by the following example. Suppose we are trying to determine the quantity of gasoline that people will buy in a week. We could say that the quantity of gasoline depends on the price of gasoline, suggesting that the lower the price of gasoline, the more of it people will buy. In this case, the quantity of gasoline and the price of gasoline are endogenous variables. We know, however, that the quantity of gasoline that people will buy also depends on their income. In this case, income will be an exogenous variable.

Problem 1-33

Distinguish between stocks and flows. Give an example of each.

Requirement and Clue: *Notice that this is a two-part problem. Address each part in order. Define each concept. Remember to use the time dimension as a distinguishing feature.*

Solution:

A stock (or stock variable) is the amount of anything existing *at a particular time* while a flow (or flow variable) is the change in a stock *during a period of time.* A noticeable feature of these concepts is that a stock does not need a time dimension (per day, per hour, per year) but a flow does. Examples of stocks are the quantity of books in your school and the amount of money you have in your purse or wallet. Examples of flows are the amount of gasoline you purchase each week and the amount of money you earn each month.

Problem 1-34

Indicate whether each of the following variables is a stock (S) or a flow (F).

A. *The current balance on your credit card*
B. *The amount you spend each semester on books*
C. *The number of students in your economics class*
D. *The amount invested to start a business*
E. *The amount allocated each year to maintain a company's plant and equipment*
F. *The estimated amount of oil in an oil well*
G. *The amount of oil extracted from an oil well each month*
H. *The total amount of taxes collected by the government each year*
I. *The total amount of taxes collected by the government on April 30, 2013*
J. *The amount of money a family spends on groceries each month*
K. *The number of a particular type of car produced by General Motors on October 7*
L. *The number of CDs you currently own*

Requirement and Clue: *Check for the existence of a time dimension.*

Solution:

A. The current balance on your credit card (S)
B. The amount you spend each semester on books (F)
C. The number of students in your economics class (S)
D. The amount invested to start a business (S)
E. The amount allocated each year to maintain a company's plant and equipment (F)
F. The estimated amount of oil in an oil well (S)
G. The amount of oil extracted from an oil well each month (F)
H. The total amount of taxes collected by the government each year (F)
I. The total amount of taxes collected by the government on April 30, 2013 (S)
J. The amount of money a family spends on groceries each month (F)
K. The number of a particular type of car produced by General Motors on October 7 (S)
L. The number of CDs you currently own (S)

Problem 1-35

A seller of a particular type of computers wanted to know how a change in the price of her computers would affect the quantity of computers sold. So she lowered her price slightly and noticed that the quantity sold increased. On the basis of the result of this experiment, can she conclude that the increase in the quantity sold was due to the lower price?

Requirement and Clue: *This could be a "Post Hoc" fallacy. Recognize that the increase in quantity sold could be the result of a change in some factor other than the lower price.*

Solution:

This question is related to the "Post Hoc" fallacy. The fallacy lies in thinking that because event A precedes event, then event B must have been caused by event A. In the case of the computer seller, it could very well be that the increase in the quantity of computers sold had more to do with an increase in income, an increase in the prices of competing types of computers, or an increase in people's interests in computers resulting from a successful advertising campaign than with a fall in the price of this particular type of computers.

Problem 1-36

Define and distinguish between macroeconomics and microeconomics.

Requirement and Clue: *It is clear from the problem that it is not enough simply to define both concepts. You must also highlight the difference between them. Examples of microeconomic and macroeconomic problems would be helpful in showing the difference.*

Solution:

Macroeconomics is the study of broad economic aggregates (totals) such as inflation, unemployment in the economy as a whole, total production, and economic growth. The focus of macroeconomics is the economy as a whole. For example, one concept with which macroeconomics deals is gross domestic product (GDP) which is an aggregation or summing up of the total output of goods and services produced by all economic units and treating it as a single whole. A typical macroeconomic problem would be to determine the effect of a tax change on the overall level of activity within an entire economy.

In contrast to macroeconomics, microeconomics is the study of the behavior of the individual components of the economy, such as firms and households, and the economic relationship among them. Basic to the study of microeconomics is the efficiency with which scarce resources are allocated among various uses. Microeconomics focuses upon individual, rather than aggregate economic data. A typical microeconomic problem would be to determine the price that a firm should charge in order to maximize its profits.

Problem 1-37

Indicate whether each of the following falls under microeconomics (Micro) or macroeconomics (Macro):

a. *A study of the major causes of the 2007-2009 recession*
b. *A theory explaining why the prices of personal computers has declined over the years*
c. *A model explaining the effect of an increase in wages on the overall level of employment*
d. *An explanation of how a tax on cigarettes affects the price of cigarettes*
e. *A theory that explains the economic role of banks in a society*
f. *A theory explaining the price that firms should charge in order to maximum their profits*
g. *An explanation of how consumers should spend their income in order to maximize their satisfaction*
h. *A study of how an economy allocates its scarce resources among competing ends*
i. *A model showing that when interest rates fall, total consumer and investment spending both increase*
j. *A theory that explains how minimum wage legislation affects employment in an economy*

Requirement and Clue: *This problem is designed to test your understanding of the difference between micro and macro issues. It's macro if it deals with the whole economy; otherwise, it's micro.*

Solution:

a. A study of the major causes of the 2007-2009 recession (Macro)
b. A theory explaining why the prices of personal computers has declined over the years (Micro)
c. A model explaining the effect of an increase in wages on the overall level of employment (Macro)
d. An explanation of how a tax on cigarettes affects the price of cigarettes (Micro)
e. A theory that explains the economic role of banks in a society (Macro)
f. A theory explaining the price that firms should charge in order to maximum their profits (Micro)
g. An explanation of how consumers should spend their income in order to maximize their satisfaction (Micro)
h. A study of how an economy allocates its scarce resources among competing ends (Micro)
i. A model showing that when interest rates fall, total consumer and investment spending both increase (Macro)
j. A theory that explains how minimum wage legislation affects employment in an economy (Macro)

Multiple-Choice

In each case, circle the letter that corresponds with the correct answer.

1. Having an understanding of economics is important because:

a. it guarantees a good job with a good salary
b. it insulates you against any type of unemployment
c. it helps you to think logically
d. everyone agrees that it is by far the most important subject to study

Answer: c

Reason: Economics is analytical and it develops a particular way of thinking and making decisions. Economics helps to develop the science and art of logical thinking.

2. One of the main disadvantages of understanding economics is that:

a. it gives one a false view of world affairs
b. although it helps one to understand the economy, it does not help one to understand society

c. it is an extremely difficult subject and studying it does tend to reduce personal satisfaction

d. none of the above

Answer: d

Reason: One would be hard pressed to find a single disadvantage of understanding economics. That's why it is compulsory in many college and university programs.

3. A knowledge of economics is important because:

a. it guarantees perpetual employment

b. it helps us to understand many of the issues that affect our lives directly and indirectly

c. it ensures that we will always make decisions that are in our own self interest

d. all of the above

Answer: b

Reason: Many of the issues facing us today are of an "economic" nature.

4. Economists are employed:

a. only in profit-seeking companies

b. only by the government

c. only in international organizations, such as the United Nations and the World Bank

d. in all of the above

Answer: d

Reason: Economists are employed in a vast number of private and public organizations, both domestic and international.

5. Scarcity gives rise to:

a. Unnecessary waste

b. Inefficient methods of production

c. the necessity to choose

d. full employment of resources

Answer: c

Reason: Because of scarcity, society cannot have all the goods and services that it would like to have. Society is therefore forced to choose.

6. Choice is a direct result of:

a. pride　　b. extravagance

c. scarcity　　d. all of the above

Answer: c

Reason: Had it not been for scarcity, society would not have to choose.

7. By scarcity economists mean:

a. low stocks of goods

b. limited availability in the face of unlimited wants

c. limited wants in the face of unlimited resources

d. limited resources as well as limited wants

Answer: b

Reason: Economic or relative scarcity relates the amount available to the amount required. It exists when resources are insufficient to produce all the goods and services required to satisfy human wants.

8. Which of the following statements is true?

a. Scarcity would not exist if society were more efficient in its production of goods and services

b. Scarcity would not exist if society as a whole were more efficient in its use of available resources

c. Scarcity is totally unrelated to a society's resources

d. Scarcity would exist even if society used its available resources as efficiently as possible

Answer: d

Reason: The efficient use of resources would not make resources sufficient to produce all the goods and services that people want.

9. Scarcity exists:

a. Even in relatively rich countries like Canada and the United States

b. Only in underdeveloped countries like Haiti and Afghanistan

c. Only in countries ruled by dictators

d. Only in countries with limited resources

Answer: a

Reason: Even in Canada and the United States, people's wants far outstrip the economy's ability to produce enough goods and services.

10. Which of the following statements is correct?

a. Canada and the United States do not have to worry about scarcity because their citizens enjoy high standards of living

b. Democracy and the Rule of Law prevent Canada, the United States, and the United Kingdom from experiencing scarcity

c. As long as citizens of a country have limited resources and unlimited wants, they will experience scarcity

d. None of the above

Answer: c

Reason: This is the very essence of scarcity.

11. Because of scarcity:

a. individuals, not society, are forced to choose

b. society, not individuals, has to choose

c. neither society nor individuals have to choose

d. both society and individuals have to choose

Answer: d

Reason: The existence of limited resources coupled with unlimited wants (scarcity) is an individual and collective problem, forcing all to choose.

12. Economics is a social science because:

a. its variables are all measureable

b. economists like to socialize

c. ultimately, it all boils down to economics

d. it deals with human behaviour

Answer: d

Reason: Any discipline that studies human behaviour is a social science. Economics does this.

13. Which of the following is *not* a social science?

a. Chemistry　　b. Psychology

c. Political science　　d. Sociology

Answer: a

Reason: Chemistry does not study human behavior.

14. Which of the following disciplines studies the origin and development of humans as social beings?

a. Biology b. Anthropology

c. Economics d. All of the above

Answer: b

Reason: That is the definition of anthropology.

15. Economics deals with:

a. how people make decisions about the use of scarce resources to satisfy their wants

b. the mental characteristics associated with a particular kind of behavior

c. the nature and functions of the state and the way we are governed

d. the study of human social behavior, society and its institutions

Answer: a

Reason: Choices b, c, and d define psychology, political science, and sociology respectively. Choice "a" defines the subject matter of economics.

16. Which of the following definitions of economics is preferable?

a. The study of buyers and sellers in markets exchanging goods and services

b. The study of how a government organizes production activities

c. The study of how people use scarce resources to satisfy their wants

d. The study of all the factors that contribute to human happiness

Answer: c

Reason: No "preferred" definition of economics can omit the use of scarce resources to satisfy wants. This is the heart of economics.

17. A social science is:

a. any discipline that is socially acceptable

b. any discipline that studies human behavior

c. any discipline that avoids the use of mathematics

d. none of the above

Answer: b

Reason: Social science is the study of human behavior.

18. The government owns a quarry. It hires workers with pickaxes, shovels, and electric drills to extract stones from the quarry. The stones are loaded on to trucks and taken to a site where a road is being built. In this case:

a. the quarry, the shovels, the pickaxes, and the drills are all examples of capital

b. the quarry is land, the stones in it are capital, and the quarry workers are labour

c. the quarry and the stones in it are land, and the shovels, pickaxes, and drills are capital

d. the trucks are capital but the workers and the shovels, pickaxes, and drills represent labour

Answer: c

Reason: All natural resources (the quarry and the stones) are classified as land. Any human-made resources (shovels, pickaxes, and drills) are classified as capital.

19. Factors of production are:

a. the costs involved in using resources to produce goods and services

b. all the factors that must be considered when producing resources

c. things that can be used to produce goods and services

d. things like sunlight and air that we cannot produce

Answer: c

Reason: They are the resources (land, labour, capital, and entrepreneurial services) used to produce goods and services.

20. Alcohol and cigarettes are:

a. bads because they are harmful

b. bads because society frowns on their use

c. goods because they satisfy wants

d. goods because their sale is not illegal

Answer: c

Reason: Goods are tangible things that give satisfaction.

21. Illegal substances and chemicals, and items smuggled into a country, are classified as:

a. bads because taxes are not paid on them

b. bads because they are illegal

c. goods because someone wants them

d. goods because they are produced

Answer: c

Reason: They give satisfaction; therefore they are defined as goods.

22. The difference between a good and a service is that:

a. a good is tangible while a service is not

b. a service is tangible while a good is not

c. a good gives satisfaction while a service does not

d. a service gives satisfaction while a good does not

Answer: a

Reason: Both goods and services give satisfaction. Goods have physical substance. They can be touched. Services have no physical substance. They cannot be touched.

23. Bads are:

a. things like garbage and pollution that are unwanted and give no satisfaction

b. things like cigarettes, alcohol and guns that hurt people

c. items whose use is declared to be illegal

d. all of the above

Answer: a

Reason: Bads are undesirable. People are willing to pay money to get rid of bads.

24. An economy produces:

a. goods but not bads

b. both goods and bads

c. bads always as a result of people's wants for them

d. none of the above

Answer: b

Reason: An economy does not make a point of producing bads; but in the process of producing goods, some bads are also produced.

25. Which of the following statements about resources is true?

a. All resources are scarce

b. Some resources such as air and sunlight in most circumstances are not scarce

c. All resources command a price in the market

d. None of the above

Answer: b

Reason: All economic resources are scarce in an economic sense. Some resources, however, such as sea water in the ocean, are not scarce.

26. Resources are also referred to as:

a. consumer goods and services

b. goods generating agents

c. factors of production

d. all of the above

Answer: c

Reason: Resources are the factors used to produce things, hence the name.

27. The various types of resources can be grouped into the following four categories:

a. Goods, services, natural, and manufactured

b. Capital, human, scarce, and desired

c. Land, labour, capital, and entrepreneurship

d. Land, natural resources, capital, and man-made resources

Answer: c

Reason: This is the four-way classification normally used by economists.

28. In economics, land refers to:

a. real estate

b. the solid portion of the earth only

c. the solid portion of the earth and water only

d. all natural resources

Answer: d

Reason: Economists group all "gifts of nature" into this category called land.

29. In economics, forests, lakes, oil, and minerals are classified as a resource category called:

a. land b. wealth producers

b. capital d. none of the above

Answer: a

Reason: These are all examples of natural resources that economists categorize as land.

30. Which of the following is an example of labour?

a. The work produced by a machine to replace human effort

b. The services provided by a stand-up comedian

c. A plow that prepares a field for planting

d. None of the above

Answer: b

Reason: Labour is human resources.

31. In economics, capital refers to:

a. any produced means of production

b. anything that can be used to produce goods and services

c. items such as land, coal mines, and crops that can be sold for money

d. the income that people earn for their labour services

Answer: a

Reason: Capital is any manufactured factor of production.

32. Entrepreneurship is:

a. any act of production for money

b. the organization of land, labour, and capital into the production process

c. is just another name for marketing services which involves bringing goods and services from producers to consumers

d. the use of the most sophisticated method of production

Answer: b

Reason: Entrepreneurship includes the functions of managing, coordinating, leading, and risk-taking necessary for the production of goods and services.

33. Entrepreneurial skills include:

a. innovative skills

b. risk-taking

c. leadership skills

d. all of the above

Answer: d

Reason: The skills listed are all required to perform the entrepreneurial function.

34. The income generated by natural resources is called:

a. land b. natural money

c. rent d. profit

Answer: c

Reason: Land (or natural resources) earns rent.

35. Capital generates a type of income called:

a. profit income

b. rental income

c. wages and salaries

d. interest and dividends

Answer: d

Reason: Interest and dividends are earned by capital.

36. For their services, entrepreneurs earn a type of income called:

a. salaries b. profit

c. interest income d. rent

Answer: b

Reason: The reward for entrepreneurial services is called profits.

37. If someone is paid wages or salaries at the end of a certain period, we know that he or she provided:

a. entrepreneurial services
b. labour services
c. real capital
d. natural resources

Answer: b

Reason: Wages and salaries are the reward for labour services.

38. The sum of wages and salaries, rent, interest and dividends, and profit can be correctly called:

a. total income
b. total factor earnings
c. both a and b
d. neither a nor b

Answer: c

Reason: The items listed constitute the total earnings from the factors of production.

39. The main elements of the scientific approach include:

a. argumentation, realistic assumptions, and mathematics
b. mathematics, estimation, and statistics
c. educated guesses, estimation, and judgement
d. observation and measurement, hypotheses, and verification

Answer: d

Reason: The scientific procedure involves data collection and observation, measurement, the formation of hypotheses, and finally testing for the purpose of verifying or rejecting the hypothesis.

40. A hypothesis is:

a. a statement of known facts
b. a statement of suspected relationships among variables
c. an assumption that simplifies a complicated relationship
d. a conclusion that is drawn from facts that cannot be observed

Answer: b

Reason: It is an "if...then..." statement relating cause and effect. It states how variables are believed to be related until refuted or verified by testing.

41. An economic model is:

a. an exact replication of an economy with all its features intact
b. a simplification of a real economy with irrelevant details stripped away
c. is a vivid portrayal of what an economy ought to look like
d. none of the above

Answer: b

Reason: An economic model or theory is a simplified representation of a real economy or of some part of it.

42. Which of the following statements is correct?

a. An economic model can be expressed verbally, mathematically, or graphically
b. Only models expressed mathematically can be used to explain economic reality
c. Economic models that are expressed verbally should always be chosen in preference to those expressed graphically
d. An economic model cannot be expressed verbally

Answer: a

Reason: Those are the various forms that can be used to present economic models. Usually, more than one form is used to present the same model.

43. The components of an economic model are:

a. definitions, assumptions, hypotheses and predictions
b. equations, questions and answers, and solutions
c. ceteris paribus and normative statements
d. positive statements and ceteris paribus

Answer: a

Reason: The elements listed in choice "a" are the constituent parts of an economic model.

44. *Ceteris paribus* means:

a. all is well
b. nothing else matters
c. other things being equal
d. certain to occur

Answer: c

Reason: This is the Latin phrase used to hold all other influences on a variable constant in order to examine the effect of a single variable on some other.

45. Statements of the conditions under which a model is supposed to work are called:

a. hypotheses
b. predictions
c. assumptions
d. definitions

Answer: c

Reason: Assumptions specify the "rules of the game" so to speak. The model is expected to work well provided that certain conditions are fulfilled.

46. Statements about suspected cause-effect relations among variables are called:

a. assumptions
b. hypotheses
c. definitions
d. ceteris paribus

Answer: b

Reason: A hypothesis is a statement about cause and effect.

47. Positive statements:

a. are statements about facts
b. can be verified
c. can be true or false
d. all of the above

Answer: d

Reason: Positive statements are statements about what is, was, or will be. They can be true or false and can be verified or falsified by referring to the facts.

48. Normative statements:

a. are statements about facts
b. are statements of opinions

c. can be easily verified

d. generate the best hypotheses

Answer: b

Reason: Normative statements are subjective statements about what ought to be. They are value judgments and opinions.

49. Economists may disagree because:

a. they have different values

b. they use different models of the economy

c. neither a nor b

d. both a and b

Answer: d

Reason: Major reasons for disagreement among economists are differences in values, the use of different models, and differences about the severity of the impact of one variable on another.

50. A variable whose value is determined within a model is called:

a. an endogenous variable

b. an exogenous variable

c. a stock variable

d. a flow variable

Answer: a

Reason: The prefix "en" means within or inside. An endogenous variable is one whose value is determined inside a model.

51. The branch of economics that studies the behavior of individual economic units and focuses on resources allocation is called:

a. independent economics

b. econometrics.

c. microeconomics

d. macroeconomics

Answer: c

Reason: Microeconomics deals with the study of the individual units that make up the economy and focuses on the allocation of resources.

52. Macroeconomics studies:

a. the allocation of scarce resources among competing ends and is also called price theory

b. the economy as a whole and analyzes such topics as inflation, unemployment, and economic growth

c. group behavior and institutions in a social setting

d. all of the above

Answer: b

Reason: Macroeconomics studies the behavior of broad economics aggregates such as the topics mentioned in choice b.

True or False

Determine whether each of the following statements is true or false.

1. As important as economics may be, economic analysis sheds no light on the more serious issues that face society today.

Answer: False

Explanation: Some of society's most pressing issues are "economic" in nature.

2. One of the most important reasons for studying economics is that it develops a particular way of thinking and making decisions.

Answer: True

3. Economists find employment everywhere except as government employees.

Answer: False

Explanation: Economists are employed at all levels of government.

4. Scarcity is the situation that exists when resources are inadequate to produce all the goods and services that people want.

Answer: True

5. The means available to satisfy all society's wants are severely limited.

Answer: True

6. Advanced countries such as Canada, the United States, Sweden, and the United States are lands of plenty, well endowed with resources, so they do not have the problem of scarcity.

Answer: False

Explanation: With all their resources, these countries still cannot produce all the goods and services that would be required to satisfy all human wants.

7. Scarcity and the necessity to choose are both facts of life, but the two are unrelated.

Answer: False

Explanation: The necessity to choose is a direct result of scarcity.

8. Particular individuals in a society may be confronted with scarcity but society as a whole does not face scarcity.

Answer: False

Explanation: Because society's resources are limited (scarce), the society cannot produce all the goods and services required to satisfy everyone's wants.

9. Economics is a social science by virtue of the fact that economists are social beings.

Answer: False

Explanation: Economics is a social science because it studies human behavior, not because of any characteristics that economists may possess.

10. Resources are the things that are needed to produce the items needed to satisfy our wants.

Answer: True

11. In economics, resources are referred to as factors of production.

Answer: True

12. The essential difference between goods and services is that goods are intangible while services are tangible.

Answer: False

Explanation: *Goods are tangible while services are intangible.*

13. Our society is now so sophisticated and cares so much about human well-being that the economy no longer produces bads.

Answer: False

Explanation: *Although serious efforts may be made to reduce the production of bads, the economy cannot avoid producing bads.*

14. One of the fundamental teachings of economics is that all resources are scarce.

Answer: False

Explanation: *Some resources such as sunlight and air are not scarce.*

15. Economists generally classify resources into land, labour, capital and entrepreneurial services.

Answer: True

16. In economics, land includes only the solid portion of the earth.

Answer: False

Explanation: *Land includes all natural resources, including the solid portion of the earth.*

17. In economics, land includes minerals embedded in the earth, fish in the seas, oxygen in the air, and lakes.

Answer: True

18. In our modern society, the only capital of importance is money.

Answer: False

Explanation: *Although money is important and may be considered to be capital by some people, we cannot underestimate the importance of real capital: highways, buildings, machinery, etc.*

19. Human capital is the total amount of money owned by human beings and is also referred to as human wealth.

Answer: False

Explanation: *Human capital does not include money. It refers to education, training, skills and health possessed by humans.*

20. Human capital refers to the education, training, skills, health, and so on, that improve the quality of labour.

Answer: True

21. Entrepreneurial skills include managerial skills, organizational skills, decision-making skills, innovative skills, leadership skills, and risk-taking.

Answer: True

22. Capital generates a type of income known as profit.

Answer: False

Explanation: *Capital generates interest and dividends; entrepreneurship generates profits.*

23. Interest and dividends are a type of income earned by entrepreneurs.

Answer: False

Explanation: *Entrepreneurs earn profits; capital earns interest and dividends.*

24. Wages and salaries are the compensation for labour services.

Answer: True

25. Economics is not a science; therefore the scientific approach cannot be applied to it.

Answer: False

Explanation: *In their study of the economy and economic phenomena, economists do follow the scientific procedure.*

26. The scientific approach involves observation and measurement, the formulation of hypotheses, and verification.

Answer: True

27. An example of a hypothesis in economics is: "By the end of the year, the rate of unemployment will fall to 5%.

Answer: False

Explanation: *A hypothesis expresses a cause-effect relationship among variables. The statement given is a forecast.*

28. An economic model is a presentation of an economy at its best—an economy that is worthy of imitating.

Answer: False

Explanation: *An economic model is just a simplified economy with many details omitted.*

29. The ceteris paribus assumption allows economists to ensure that all the factors that can affect a given situation are allowed to change.

Answer: False

Explanation: *On the contrary, the ceteris paribus assumption ensures that only the factor being considered is allowed to change. All other factors are assumed to remain constant.*

30. An economic prediction and an economic forecast are one and the same thing.

Answer: False

Explanation: *An economic prediction is an "if...then..." statement. A forecast simply assigns a future value to a variable.*

31. The following is an example of an economic prediction: "If interest rates rise, people will tend to save more."

Answer: True

32. The following is an example of an economic prediction: "In the next six months, the price of gasoline will be no more than \$1.33/litre.

Answer: False

Explanation: The statement is an example of an economic forecast.

33. The goodness of a model can only be judged by the realism of its assumptions.

Answer: False

Explanation: *The goodness of a model should be judged primarily by its predictive ability.*

34. A statement cannot be positive unless it is true.

Answer: False

Explanation: A positive statement may be true or false.

35. Normative statements are value judgments or statements of opinions about what ought to be.

Answer: True

36. Economists can never disagree because economics is a science.

Answer: False

Explanation: The scientific nature of any discipline is unrelated to agreement among its practitioners. Scientists do disagree.

37. An exogenous variable can never become an endogenous variable, and an endogenous variable can never become an exogenous variable.

Answer: False

Explanation: Any variable can be endogenous or exogenous. It all depends on the particular model.

38. Stocks and flows are both variables.

Answer: True

A stock is a constant while a flow is a variable.

Answer: False

Explanation: Stocks and flows are both variables.

39. A significant difference between a stock and a flow is that a flow needs a time dimension while a stock does not.

Answer: True

40. A stock needs a time dimension while a flow does not.

Answer: False

Explanation: A flow needs a time dimension, not a stock.

41. If A increases when B decreases, we know that the increase in A is caused by the decrease in B.

Answer: False

Explanation: Not necessarily. This could be a case of the post hoc fallacy.

42. The *post hoc fallacy* is another name for *ceteris paribus*.

Answer: False

Explanation: They are distinct concepts.

43. The sequential fallacy is the erroneous conclusion that one event causes another simply because it precedes the other.

Answer: True

44. Microeconomics studies the behavior of individual economic units and focuses on the allocation of resources.

Answer: True

45. Microeconomics is concerned with what determines the composition of total output and analyzes such topics as the behavior of consumers and firms, the determination of relative prices, and the distribution of the economy's output among various groups.

Answer: True

46. Macroeconomics studies individual economic units rather than the economy as a whole.

Answer: False

Explanation: The statement would be true with respect to microeconomics.

47. A thorough understanding of the operation of the economic system requires only a good understanding of microeconomics.

Answer: False

Explanation: Much of the operation of an economic system has to do with macroeconomics.

48. A thorough understanding of the operation of the economic system requires only a good understanding of macroeconomics

Answer: False

Explanation: Microeconomics is also important for understanding the operation of the economic system.

49. A thorough understanding of the operation of the economic system requires knowledge of both microeconomics and macroeconomics.

Answer: True

Completion

Fill in the blanks

Use each word or combination of words from the list exactly once.

*(**Hint**: Proceed by elimination)*

Word list

Assumptions - Bads - Bads - Capital - Ceteris Paribus - Dividends - Econometrics - Economic Model - Economic Prediction - Endogenous - Exogenous - Entrepreneurial Services - Goods - Services - Human Capital - Hypotheses - Interest - Labour - Labour - Land - Land - Macroeconomics - Microeconomics - Positive - Post Hoc - Profit - Real - Salaries - Scarcity - Social Science - Social - Scarce - Stock - Flow - Stock - Wages

Questions

1. Economics is the __________ science that studies how people use __________ resources to satisfy their unlimited wants.
2. __________ is the situation that exists when resources are inadequate to produce all the goods and services that people want.
3. A __________ is any discipline that studies human behavior.
4. __________ are tangible things that satisfy wants; __________ are intangible things that satisfy wants.
5. __________ are things that are unwanted and do not give any satisfaction. Toxic waste and environmental pollution are examples of __________.
6. Economists classify the various types of resources into __________, __________, __________, and __________ __________.
7. __________ __________ refers to the education, training, skills, health, and so on, that improve the quality of labour.
8. The services rendered by sales representatives, lawyers, teachers, doctors, musicians, and actors are all classified under the category of __________.
9. __________ capital includes power tools, equipment, buildings, and machinery.
10. Labour earns __________ and __________; capital earns __________ and __________; __________ earns rent; and entrepreneurial services earn __________.
11. An __________ __________ is a simplification of the real economy or some aspect of it, and it consists only of the factors that appear to pertain most to what is being studied.
12. __________ are statements of the conditions under which a model is supposed to work.
13. The assumption by which an economist isolates the effect of an economic variable in a situation is the __________ __________ assumption.
14. Statements of suspected relationships among variables are referred to as __________.
15. An __________ __________ is a statement about the general direction of an economic variable resulting from the fulfilment of certain conditions.
16. The branch of economics that deals with the use of statistical methods to test economic hypotheses is called __________.
17. __________ economics explains or describes how the economy actually works and the behaviour of economic units. It attempts to explain what will happen under certain conditions, but it does not explain what the economic situation ought to be.
18. An __________ variable is one whose value is determined within a model while an __________ variable is one whose value is determined by factors outside the model.
19. A __________ variable is the quantity of anything existing at a particular time, while a __________ variable is a measure of the change in the __________ over time.
20. A severe drought destroys the pumpkin crop in a country one year. The seeds that farmer McDonald intends to plant the following spring are affected, without his knowledge, by radiation that causes each plant to produce twice as many pumpkins. Upon seeing his bumper crop the following fall, farmer McDonald concludes that a drought one year will cause a bumper crop the next. This is an example of the __________ __________ fallacy.
21. __________ studies the behaviour of individual economic units such as households and firms and focuses on the allocation of resources.
22. __________ studies the behaviour of broad economic aggregates such as total income and overall unemployment.

Solutions

1. Social, Scarce
2. Scarcity
3. Social, Science
4. Goods, Services
5. Bads, Bads
6. Land, Labour, Capital, and Entrepreneurial Services— In Any Order
7. Human Capital
8. Labour
9. Real
10. Wages, Salaries; Interest, Dividends; Land; Profit
11. Economic Model
12. Assumptions
13. Ceteris Paribus
14. Hypotheses
15. Economic Prediction
16. Econometrics
17. Positive
18. Endogenous, Exogenous
19. Stock, Flow, Stock
20. Post Hoc
21. Microeconomics
22. Macroeconomics

2 FUNCTIONS, GRAPHS & SLOPES

SYNOPSIS

To a large extent, the study of economics involves the study of relationships among variables. The *functional notation* is a very convenient way of expressing relationships among variables. For example, the notion that consumption depends on income and on the rate of interest may be conveniently expressed by the functional notation as:

$$C = C(Y,r)$$

Where C represents consumption, Y income, and r t he rate of interest. In this expression, consumption is the **dependent** variable while income and the rate of interest are **independent** variables.

Graphs are also used extensively in economics to show relationships among variables. An upward-sloping curve illustrates a **direct** relationship while a downward-sloping curve illustrates an inverse relationship. It is difficult to use graphs in cases where more than two variables are involved.

The **slope** of a line is the vertical distance divided by the horizontal distance. A declining line has a negative slope while a rising line has a positive slope. A 45-degree line through the origin has a slope of 1. The slope of a non-linear curve at a point on the curve is the slope of the line drawn tangent to the curve at the particular point.

LEARNING OBJECTIVES

In connection with this module, you should be able to:

1. use symbols and the functional notation to express relationships among variables
2. distinguish between dependent and independent variables
3. use graphs to represent certain relationships
4. explain and calculate slopes

DEFINITIONS & CONCEPTS

You should be able to define the following terms and concepts:

functional notation
function
dependent variable
independent (explanatory) variable
graphs
direct relation
inverse relation
slope
negative slope
positive slope
slope of a non-linear curve

2

FUNCTIONS, GRAPHS & SLOPES

Concepts, Definitions & Problems

Problem 2-1

What is the functional notation and what is its main use in economics?

Requirement and Clue: *This is a two-part problem. Answer each part in order and do so as directly as possible. Think of occasions when you can use the functional notation in economics.*

Solution:

The functional notation is a way of expressing relationships among variables. A large part of economics is concerned with examining relationships among variables. The main use of the functional notation in economics is to express these relationships in a very compact way. For example, we can express the idea that an individual's income depends on his or her level of education. If we use the letter y to represent income and the letter e to denote the level of education, we can express the idea as follows:

$$y = f(e) \quad \text{or } y = y(e)$$

which means simply that income depends on (or is a function of) the level of education.

Problem 2-2

Use the functional notation to express each of the following statements:

a. *If the level of income (Y) changes, spending on consumer goods and services (C) will also change.*
b. *Changes in interest rates (r) cause changes in the amount of saving (S).*
c. *The quantity of cell phones purchased (Q) depends on the price (P) of cell phones.*
d. *Attendance at the movies (A) is a function of the price of movie tickets (P).*
e. *Attendance at the movies (A) is a function of the price of movie tickets (P) and the weather (W).*
f. *Changes in interest rates (r) and the level of income (Y) affect the quantity of automobiles purchased (Q).*
g. *The amount of vacation (V) that people take depends on their income (Y) and the price of gasoline (P)*
h. *If the price of gasoline (P) changes, people will tend to change the number of automobile trips (T) taken.*

Requirement and Clue: *For this solution you must carefully determine which variable is dependent and which is independent.*

Solution:

C= C(Y)	e. A = A(P,W)
S = S(r)	f. Q = Q(r,Y)
Q = Q(P)	g. V = V(Y,P)
A = A(P)	h. T = T(P)

Problem 2-3

What is the difference between a dependent variable and an independent variable?

Requirement and Clue: *You are required to define each concept. Provide examples to illustrate the difference between them.*

Solution:

In a relationship among variables, the dependent variable is the variable that we are trying to explain, while the independent variable is the one that provides the explanation. An example will help to illustrate the difference. Consider the statement: "A family's grocery bill depends on the size of the family and on the family income." In this case, the family's grocery bill (what we are trying to explain) is the dependent variable, while the size of the family and family income (the variables that do the explaining) are independent variables.

Problem 2-4

What is the purpose of graphs in economics?

Requirement and Clue: *Think of graphs as illustrative pictures. Focus on relationships among variables.*

Solution:

For the most part, economics discusses relationships among variables, such as the relationship between income and consumption; interest rates and investment; saving and income; investment and economic growth, etc. Graphs are an effective way of showing relationships among variables, and since economics consists of so many of these relationships, economists find it useful to use graphs. Graphs add clarity to ideas that we try to express—they can actually *show* the changes that take place. For example, we can use graphs to show the growth in total production of goods and services within a country during a period of time. This type of graphic, visual presentation brings economic concepts to life. No wonder that graphs are used so pervasively in economics!

Problem 2-5

What methods or tools do economists use to express economic relationships? Give examples.

Requirement and Clue: *Graphs and tables will probably come to mind. Remember that words are tools also. Don't forget to give examples.*

Solution:

Economists use four methods of expressing economic relationships: verbal expressions (words), equations (functions), tables, and graphs. For example, the concept of total expenditure may be viewed in various ways. First, total expenditure may be expressed verbally as:

> *"Total expenditure equals price times quantity purchased."*

We can also state that: "Total expenditure is a function of quantity purchased."

Second, we can express the idea using an equation:

TE = f(Q) where TE is total expenditure and Q denotes quantity purchased. This equation is saying that if quantity changes, total expenditure will change.

Third, the relationship can be expressed using a table. For example, if we know that the price of the item is $3.00, we can show the relationship in a table as follows:

Quantity	Total Expenditure
10	30
20	60
30	90
40	120

The fourth method of expressing the relationship is the graph shown below.

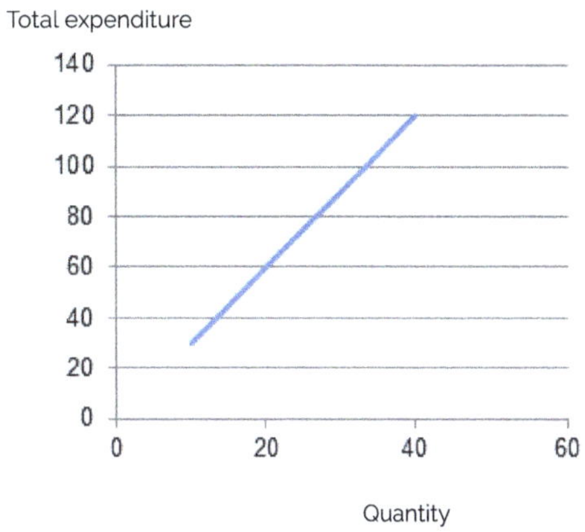

This graph shows the value of total expenditure for all possible quantities purchased. The graph makes certain information immediately apparent. For example, because the graph is upward-sloping, it is obvious that the relationship between quantity bought and total expenditure is positive.

Problem 2-6

Below are four graphs showing relationships between X and Y.

a. *In which of these graphs is the quantity of Y unrelated to the quantity of X?*

b. *In which of these graphs is the quantity of Y directly related to the quantity of X?*

c. *In which of these graphs are Y and X inversely related?*

d. *In which of these graphs is the quantity of X unrelated to the quantity of Y?*

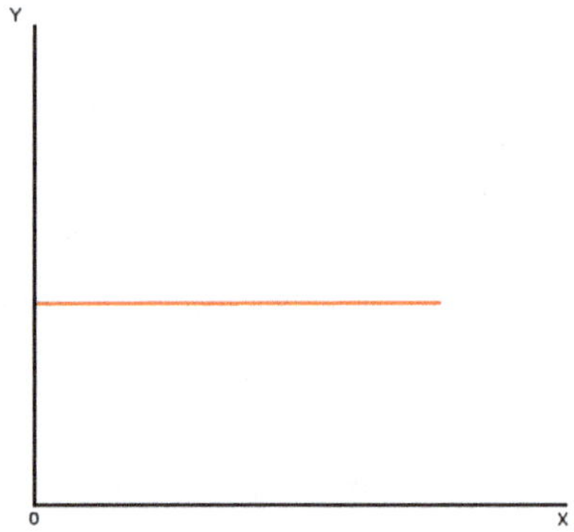

DIAGRAM 1

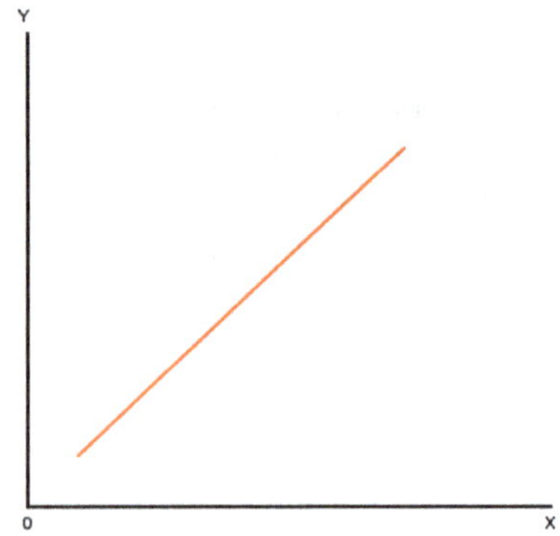

DIAGRAM 2

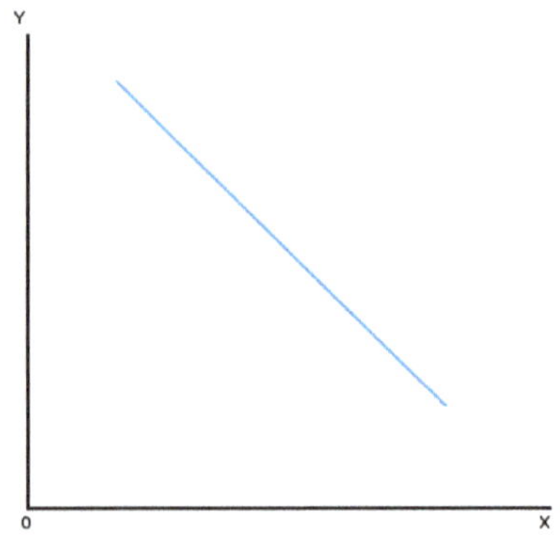

DIAGRAM 3

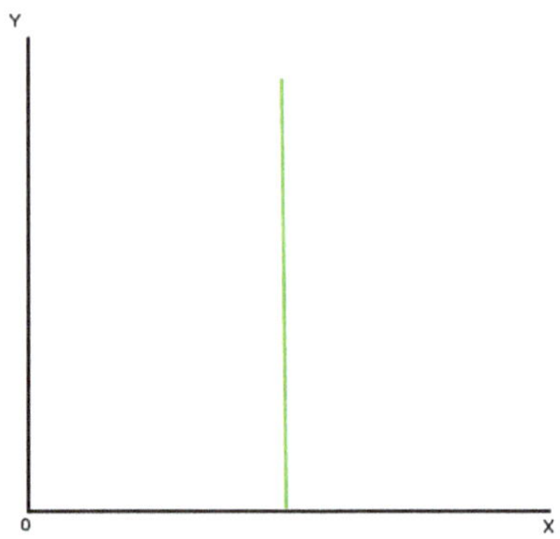

DIAGRAM 4

Requirement and Clue: *Think of direct and inverse relationships and how graphs can depict such relationships.*

Solution:

The quantity of Y is unrelated to the quantity of X in Diagram 1. No matter what value X takes, Y will remain the same.

a. The quantity of Y is directly related to the quantity X in Diagram 2. As X increases, Y also increases, and as X decreases, Y also decreases. These two variables move together in the same direction.

b. The quantity of Y is inversely related to the quantity of X in Diagram 3. As X increases, Y decreases. The two variables move in opposite directions.

c. The quantity of X is unrelated to the quantity of Y in Diagram 4. Here, X remains the same regardless of changes in Y.

Problem 2-7

Use words to express the idea contained in the following functional notations:

a. *C = C(Y,r,t) where C is consumption, Y is the level of income, r is the rate of interest, and t is time.*

b. *QMd = f(Y,r) where QMd is the quantity of money demanded, Y is the level of income, and r is the rate of interest.*

Requirement and Clue: *Recognize that the functional notation is nothing more than an idea expressed in the form of a mathematical function. You will need to identify the dependent and independent variables when using words.*

Solution:

a. *C = C(Y, r,t)* is read: Consumption is a function of the level of income, the rate of interest, and time, and it means that if either the level of income, the rate of interest, or time changes, consumption will also change.

b. *QMd = f(Y,r)* is read: The quantity of money demanded is a function of the level of income and the rate of interest, and it means that changes in the level of income or the rate of interest will cause changes in the quantity of money demanded.

Problem 2-8

In each of the following statements, identify the dependent and independent variables:

a. *The level of saving (S) depends on the level of income (Y).*

b. *If the level of income (Y) changes, the demand for money (Md) will change.*

c. *If the money supply (Ms) changes, the rate of interest (r) will also change.*

d. *Changes in the demand for money (Md) will cause the rate of interest (r) to change.*

e. *Changes in income (y) and the rate of interest (r) will cause the level of investment (I) to change.*

Requirement and Clue: *Recall that the dependent variable is the one* *we are trying to explain and the independent is the one that is doing the explaining.*

Solution:

a. *S* is the dependent variable and *Y* is the independent variable.
b. *Md* is the dependent variable and *Y* is the independent variable.
c. *r* is the dependent variable and *Ms* is the independent variable.
d. *r* is the dependent variable and *Md* is the independent variable.
e. *I* is the dependent variable and *y* and *r* are the independent variables.

Problem 2-9

Assume that the price of an item is $5.00.

a. *Construct a table to show total revenue (i.e. price times quantity) for quantities 1, 2, 3, 4, 5, 6 units sold.*
b. *Plot the information from your table on a graph with quantity on the horizontal axis and total revenue (TR) on the vertical axis.*

Requirement and Clue: *You require a two-column table: quantity for one and total revenue for the other. Your total revenue curve should be an upward-sloping straight line.*

Solution:

a.

Quantity	Total Revenue ($)
1	5
2	10
3	15
4	20
5	25
6	30

b.

Problem 2-10

Draw graphs to illustrate the relationship you would expect to find between the following pairs of variables, and indicate whether the relationship is direct or inverse.

a. *The price of apples and the quantity of apples bought in a month.*
b. *The level of income and the frequency of eating out in restaurants.*
c. *The rate of interest and the frequency of credit card use.*
d. *The price of gasoline and the frequency of automobile trips.*
e. *The number of students and government spending on education.*

Requirement and Clue: Consider whether the variables move together in the same direction (direct—upward sloping graph) or in opposite directions (inverse—downward sloping graph).

Solution:

a. The higher the price of apples, other things being equal, the smaller the quantity that will be bought. This inverse relationship is shown by a downward-sloping curve as shown in Diagram A.

DIAGRAM A

b. It is reasonable to expect that the higher the level of income, the more frequently people will tend to eat at restaurants. This direct relationship is shown by the upward sloping curve in Diagram B.

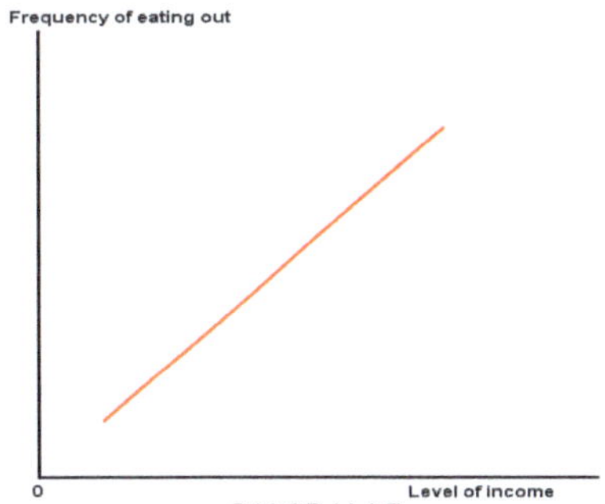

DIAGRAM B

c. Lower interest rates will tend to encourage credit card use, while high interest rates will tend to deter credit card use. This inverse relationship is shown by the downward sloping curve in Diagram C.

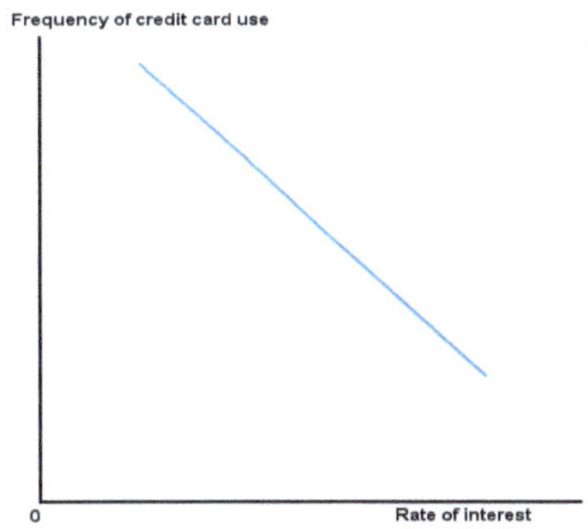

DIAGRAM C

d. People will tend to reduce the number of automobile trips when gasoline prices rise and to increase automobile trips when gasoline prices fall. This inverse relationship is shown by the downward sloping graph in Diagram D.

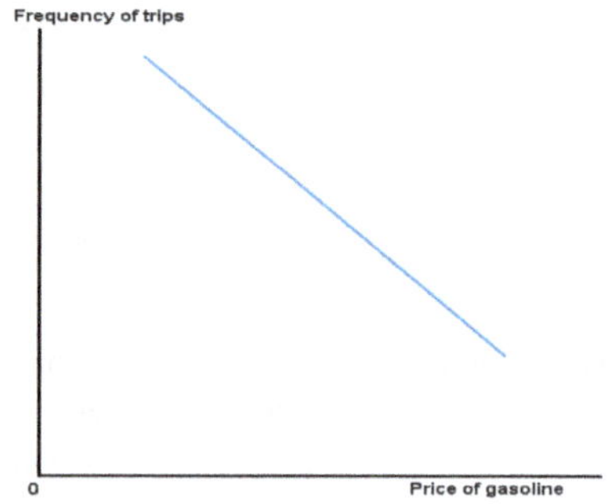

DIAGRAM D

e. Other things being equal, the greater the number of students, the more money the government will spend on education and vice versa. This direct relationship is shown by the upward sloping curve in Diagram E.

f.

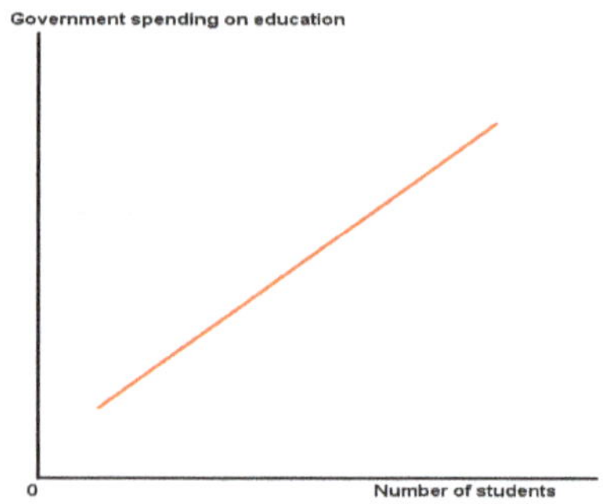

DIAGRAM E

Problem 2-11

What is the difference between a concave and a convex curve?

Requirement and Clue: *Illustrate with diagrams.*

Solution:

Concave and convex curves are used frequently in economics to illustrate behaviour of certain variables. A concave curve is bowed outward, as shown in Diagram A. A convex curve, on the other hand, is bowed toward the origin, as shown in Diagram B.

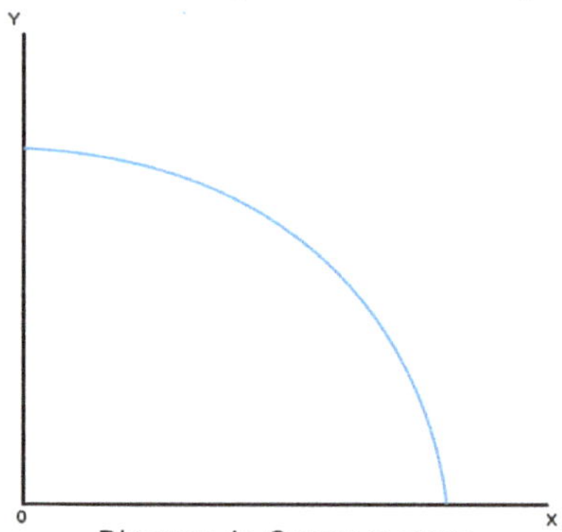

Diagram A: Concave curve

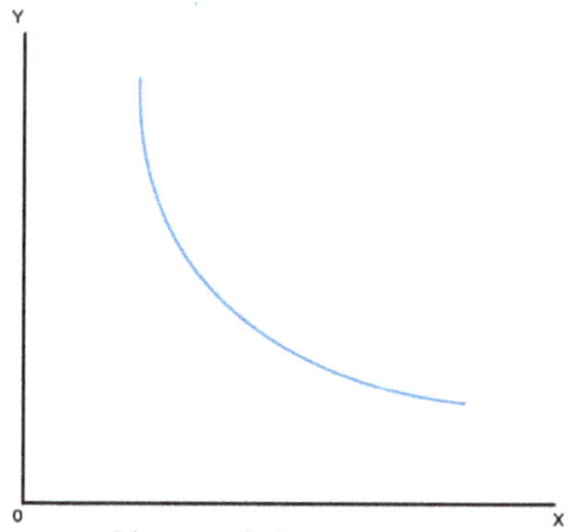

Diagram B: Convex curve

Problem 2-12

What kind of graph would you use to illustrate each of the following?

a. *The monthly sales for a company in 2013*
b. *The distribution of earnings among five banks*
c. *The growth in population over a 10-year period*
d. *The rates of inflation in 12 countries in 2012*
e. *The percentage of total sales attributable to five different products sold by a company*

Requirement and Clue: *Your choices are line graph, pie chart, bar chart. It's a good idea to justify your choice.*

Solution:

a. The monthly sales for a company in 2013 could be illustrated well using a bar chart. This chart makes it easy to compare one month's sale with another month's sale.

b. Since there are only five banks, a pie chart could be used effectively to illustrate the distribution of earnings among them. It would facilitate comparison of the earnings of one bank with that of any other bank.

c. A line graph would be appropriate to illustrate the growth in population since growth is continuous over the period.

d. The rates of inflation in 12 countries could be illustrated using a bar chart. The difference among the rates of inflation in the various countries would be seen at a glance.

e. Since there are only five products, a pie chart would be appropriate here for effective illustration.

Problem 2-13

What are the limitations to the use of graphs in economics?

Requirement and Clue: *Think, for example, of the difficulty of drawing and using graphs of more than two dimensions.*

Solution:

Although graphs are very useful in economics, some limitations exist. First, the use of graphs is limited to cases where there are only few variables. As the number of variables increases, one's ability to graph relations among them decreases rapidly. How would one graph the idea that the quantity of smart phones that people will buy varies with current income, the rate of interest, and buyers' expectations? Second, many students have been "turned off" graphs before they begin their study of economics. Thus, the use of graphs may be intimidating for some students.

Problem 2-14

Why is the concept of slope important in economics?

Requirement and Clue: *Relate your solution to rates of change.*

Solution:

The slope of a curve refers to its steepness or flatness. Economists are interested not only in changes in certain variables, but also in the rate of change of these variables. For example, it is important to know that income is rising or falling, but it may be even more important to know how fast it is rising or falling. The *slope* of a curve provides this information.

Problem 2-15

The following table contains information on combinations of As and Bs that can be bought for a given sum of money.

Quantity of A	Quantity of B
0	12
1	10
2	8
3	6
4	4
5	2
6	0

a. With A on the horizontal axis and B on the vertical axis, draw a graph showing the various combinations of A and B that can be bought.

b. Calculate the slope of your graph.

Requirement and Clue: *Recall that the slope is the change in the value on the vertical axis divided by the change in the value on the horizontal axis.*

Solution:

a.

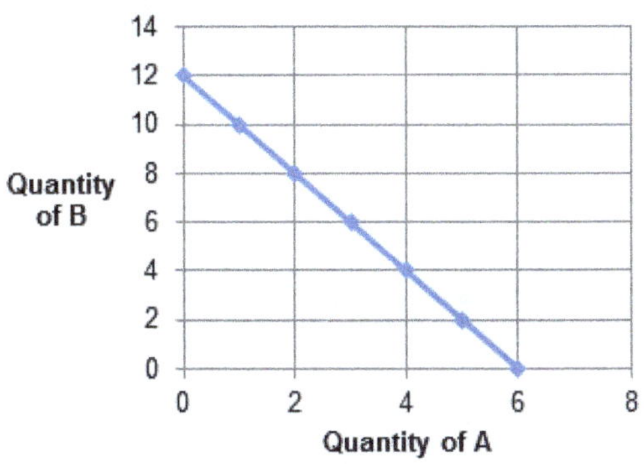

b. The slope is (Vertical distance) / (Horizontal distance) and so applying the formula we have,

(Vertical distance) / (Horizontal distance) = (-2) / 1 = – 2

Multiple-Choice

In each case, circle the letter that corresponds with the correct answer.

1. A mathematical function:

a. is an expression of the kind of work that a particular variable is designed to perform

b. expresses a relationship among two or more variables

c. is designed to prevent the use of sophisticated mathematics in economics

d. must be presented graphically to be meaningful

Answer: b

Reason: *A mathematical function is an equation that expresses a relationship among variables. It deals with how a change in one variable affects some other variable or variables.*

2. The functional notation:

a. is a mathematical tool for expressing relations among variables

b. is very useful in mathematics but not in economics

c. is very useful in economics but not in mathematics

d. can be used only by those who have significant mathematical training

Answer: a

Reason: *The functional notation is the use of mathematical symbols to express how variables are related.*

3. Relationships among variables can be expressed:

a. only verbally

b. only by using the functional notation

c. by using words, graphs, tables, or functions

d. by using graphs but not tables

Answer: c

Reason: *The various forms given in choice c can be used to express relationships among variables.*

4. The first step in using the functional notation is:

a. to eliminate all symbols that may be contained in the statement

b. to identify the work performed by each exogenous variable and then ignore the endogenous variable

c. discard all traces of mathematics

d. use symbols instead of words

Answer: d

Reason: *The functional notation is a symbolic expression of a concept.*

5. The idea that when hotel rates (r) change, the number of people taking vacations (V) in foreign countries also changes can be expressed as:

a. r = V

b. r = r(V)

c. V = V times r

d. V =V(r)

Answer: d

Reason: The dependent variable is the number of people taking vacations in foreign countries while the independent variable is hotel rates.

6. If I denotes investment, y denotes income, and r denotes the rate of interest, then the expression *I = I(y,r)* means that:

a. investment is the product of income and the rate of interest
b. income and the rate of interest are constant but investment varies
c. investment will change if either income or the rate of interest changes
d. changes in income and the rate of interest are due to changes in investment

Answer: c

Reason: Investment is a function of income and the rate of interest. Changes in the independent variables (income and the rate of interest) will cause the dependent variable (investment) to change.

7. In the expression c = c(y,i):

a. c is the dependent variable while y and i are independent variables
b. c is the independent variable while y and i are dependent variables
c. the value of c can be determined by multiplying y and i
d. dependent and independent variables cannot be determined unless the variables are defined

Answer: a

Reason: The expression can be read as c depends on y and i. Therefore c is dependent while y and I are independent.

8. Which of the following statements is correct?

a. The dependent variable is the variable that we are trying to explain while the independent variable is the variable that provides the explanation
b. The dependent variable is the variable that provides the explanation while the independent variable is the variable that we are trying to explain
c. Dependent and independent variables can be interchanged without changing the relationship among variables
d. The dependent variables is the variable whose value is known while the independent variable is the variable whose value is unknown

Answer: a

Reason: The independent variable or the explanatory variable is the variable that is used in a relationship to explain or predict changes in some other (dependent) variable.

9. Graphs are useful in economics because:

a. most students these days are comfortable with graphs
b. they are effective in illustrating relationships among variables
c. they elevate economics to the status of science
d. all of the above

Answer: b

Reason: Economics deals a great deal with relationships among variables and graphs do this well.

10. A graph showing a direct relationship between two variables is:

a. horizontal
b. vertical
c. upward sloping
d. downward sloping

Answer: c

Reason: A graph with a positive slope shows a direct relationship.

11. A graph showing an inverse relationship between two variables is:

a. horizontal
b. vertical
c. upward sloping
d. downward sloping

Answer: d

Reason: If two variables are inversely related, the graph will be negatively sloped.

12. Which of the following statements is correct?

a. Concave curves are used in economics, but not convex
b. Convex curves are used in economics but not concave
c. Both concave and convex curves are used in economics
d. Neither concave nor convex curves are used in economics

Answer: c

Reason: Economics deals with a wide variety of relationships among variables; thus curves of all shapes are used, including concave and convex curves.

13. Which of the following statements is correct?

a. A concave curve is bowed outward while a convex curve is bowed toward the origin
b. A concave curve is bowed toward the origin while a convex curve is bowed outward
c. Concave and convex curves are both bowed toward the origin
d. Concave and convex curves are both bowed outward

Answer: a

Reason: Choice "a" correctly describes the shapes of concave and convex curves.

14. A bar chart can be effectively used to show:

a. inflation rates in various countries
b. unemployment rates in various countries
c. investment levels in various countries
d. all of the above

Answer: d

Reason: Bar charts are a good way to show relative magnitudes, such as those mentioned in the choices.

15. The use of graphs is:

a. ineffective in illustrating relationships among variables in economics
b. ineffective in showing changes in variables
c. limited to cases with few variables
d. more effective as the number of variables increases

Answer: c

Reason: The ability to use graphs decreases as the number of variables increases.

16. If a change in one variable has no effect on another variable, a graph showing the relationship between them will be:

a. impossible to draw
b. a straight line through the origin though not necessarily at 45 degrees
c. drawn cutting both axes
d. either vertical or horizontal

Answer: d

Reason: If the variables are x and y with x on the horizontal axis and y on the vertical axis, a change in x that has no effect on y will be a horizontal straight line; a change in y that has no effect on x will be a vertical straight line.

17. Graphs enable us to show:

a. inverse relations but not direct relations
b. direct relations but not inverse relations
c. both direct and inverse relations
d. dependent but not independent variables

Answer: c

Reason: An upward sloping curve shows a direct relationship between two variables, while a downward sloping curve shows an inverse relationship.

18. The concept of slope helps economists to:

a. understand the rate at which a variable changes
b. work with curves but not straight lines
c. work with straight lines but not curves
d. none of the above

Answer: a

Reason: Slope gives information about the rate of change.

19. A downward sloping curve means that the variables are:

a. inversely related   b. directly related
c. not closely related   d. none of the above

Answer: a

Reason: A curve showing an inverse relationship between two variables has a negative slope.

20. When income rises, people consume more goods and services. This relationship between consumption and income would be shown on a graph as:

a. an upward sloping curve
b. a downward sloping curve
c. a vertical line
d. a horizontal line

Answer: a

Reason: A direct relationship exists between variables that move in the same direction. This direct relationship is shown by an upward sloping curve.

21. The slope of a straight line can be measured by:

a. the ratio of the horizontal distance to the vertical distance
b. the ratio of the vertical distance to the horizontal distance
c. taking the sum of the vertical and horizontal distances
d. the horizontal distance minus the vertical distance

Answer: b

Reason: The slope is the change in the y coordinate divided by the change in the x coordinate.

22. A curve with a negative slope is:

a. upward sloping   c. downward sloping
b. vertical   d. horizontal

Answer: c

Reason: A downward sloping curve has a negative slope.

23. A curve with a positive slope is:

a. upward sloping   c. downward sloping
b. vertical   d. horizontal

Answer: a

Reason: An upward sloping curve has a positive slope.

24. The slope of a non-linear curve at a particular point:

a. cannot be determined because slopes exist only for straight lines
b. cannot be determined because there are various slopes at any particular point
c. is the slope of any straight line drawn through the origin
d. is the slope of the straight line drawn tangent to the curve at that particular point

Answer: d

Reason: At the point of tangency, slopes are equal.

True or False

Determine whether each of the following statements is true or false.

1. Even the most elementary course in economics requires a relatively high level of mathematics.

Answer: False

Explanation: Although mathematics is important in economics, a high level is not required in most introductory courses.

2. The functional notation is used only when a complicated mathematical operation is to be performed.

Answer: False

Explanation: The functional notation is just a way of expressing relations among variables.

3. A mathematical function describes in detail the work that a variable is expected to perform.

Answer: False

Explanation: It is only an expression of relationship among variables.

4. The functional notation is a useful tool in economics because economics deals substantially with relations among variables.

Answer: True

5. The expression R = R(P,S), means that P and S will change only when R changes.

Answer: False

Explanation: It means that changes in P or S will cause R to change.

6. The expression R = R(P,S) means that R will change if P or S changes.

Answer: True

7. In the expression R = R(P,S), R is the dependent variable while P and S are independent variables.

Answer: True

8. The dependent variable is the variable that we are trying to explain and the independent variable is the variable that does the explaining.

Answer: True

9. It is quite impossible to draw graphs from data contained in tables. That's why economists use both graphs and tables.

Answer: False

Explanation: It is often quite possible and even easy to draw graphs from data contained in tables.

10. When variables move up and down together, we say that there is a direct relation between them.

Answer: True

11. When variable *A* rises we observe that variable *B* falls. We can therefore conclude that *A* and *B* are directly related.

Answer: False

Explanation: Variables that move in opposite directions like A and B in the statement are inversely related.

12. If an inverse relationship is established between the price of gasoline and the number of miles travelled by automobiles, we know that if the price of gasoline rises, the number of miles travelled by automobiles will fall.

Answer: True

13. Because graphs are often difficult to understand, only straight line graphs are used in economics.

Answer: False

14. A concave curve is bowed outward while a convex curve is bowed toward the origin.

Answer: True

15. A bar graph is a vertical or horizontal graph with categories on one axis and the value assigned to each category measured along the other axis.

Answer: True

16. A pie chart is a circular graph whose pieces add to 100%.

Answer: True

17. As the number of variables increases, our ability to graph relations among them also increases.

Answer: False

Explanation: It becomes more difficult, not easier.

18. The slope of a line is the change in the x value divided by the change in the y value when y is on the vertical axis and x is on the horizontal axis.

Answer: False

Explanation: It's the change in the y value divided by the change in the x value.

19. A downward sloping curve has a negative slope while an upward sloping curve has a positive slope.

Answer: True

20. The slope of a non-linear curve at a particular point is the slope of the straight line drawn tangent to the curve at that particular point.

Answer: True

Completion

Fill in the blanks

Use each word or combination of words from the list exactly once.
*(**Hint**: Proceed by elimination)*

Word list

Direct x 2 — Upward — Bar — Chart — Concave — Convex — Dependent x 2 — Negative— Positive — Q = QP — Downward — Function x 2 — Function — Graph — Graphs — Horizontal — Independent x 2 — Independent — Inverse x 2 — Pie — Tables — Vertical

Questions

1. If changes in income affect the level of consumption, we can say that consumption is a ____________ of income. In this case, consumption is the ____________ variable while income is the ____________ variable.
2. The idea that the quantity (Q) of grapes bought depends on the price (P) of grapes can be expressed by the ____________. (Q = Q(P)
3. In the equation P = P(t,m), t and m are the ____________ variables while P is the ____________ variable.
4. Economists use the concept of a ____________ to express relationships among variables.
5. Relations among variables can be expressed using words, ____________, ____________, and equations or functions.
6. Two variables move together in the same direction if there is a(n) ____________ relationship between them. Two variables move in opposite directions if there is a(n) ____________ relationship between them.
7. A graph showing a direct relationship between two variables is ____________ sloping, while a graph showing an inverse relationship is ____________ sloping.
8. A downward-sloping curve has a ____________ slope, while an upward-sloping curve has a ____________ slope.
9. A ____________ curve is bowed outward, while a(n) ____________ curve is bowed toward the origin.
10. A ____________ ____________ is a vertical or horizontal graph with categories on one axis and the value assigned to each category measured along the other axis.
11. A ____________ ____________ is a circular graph whose pieces add up to 100%.
12. The slope of a straight line is measured by the ____________ distance divided by the ____________ distance.
13. If two variables have a(n) ____________ relation, the slope of the curve showing that relationship will be negative.
14. If two variables have a(n) ____________ relation, the slope of the curve showing that relationship will be positive.

Solution

1. (function, dependent, independent)
2. (Q = Q(P)
3. (independent, dependent)
4. (function)
5. (tables, graphs)
6. (direct, inverse)
7. (upward, downward)
8. (negative, positive)
9. (concave, convex)
10. (bar graph)
11. (pie chart)
12. (vertical, horizontal)
13. (inverse)
14. (direct)

3 THE ECONOMIC PROBLEM: SCARCITY & CHOICE

SYNOPSIS

Because resources are limited and human wants are unlimited, society cannot produce all the goods and services that its members want. It must therefore choose. When a choice is made, something has to be given up or sacrificed. Opportunity cost is the term used to describe the alternative that is sacrificed.

Production possibility schedules and production possibility curves are used to show various combinations of goods and/or services that an economy can produce if it uses all its resources, assuming that technology is constant. A linear production possibility curve illustrates constant opportunity cost, while a concave production possibility curve illustrates increasing opportunity cost.

A point below the production possibility curve represents unemployment of resources. A point on the curve represents full employment, while a point above the curve represents a combination of goods/services that is unattainable. A change in technology or a change in the quantity or quality of resources will shift the production possibility curve.

LEARNING OBJECTIVES

In connection with this module, you should be able to:

1. establish a relationship between scarcity, choice and opportunity cost.
2. explain the concept of opportunity cost.
3. explain the usefulness of the concept of opportunity in decision making.
4. explain and use the concepts of production possibility schedules and production possibility curves.
5. discuss the factors that can cause the production possibility curve to shift.

DEFINITIONS & CONCEPTS

You should be able to define the following terms and concepts:

scarcity and choice
opportunity cost (alternative cost)
production possibility schedule
production possibility curve
economic growth

3

THE ECONOMIC PROBLEM: SCARCITY & CHOICE

Concepts, Definitions & Problems

Problem 3-1

"Every act of choosing involves a sacrifice." Discuss this statement.

Requirement and Clue: *View choice as giving up something rather than as taking something. Illustrate with examples.*

Solution:

The statement is true. Because of scarcity, we are forced to choose. In exercising choice, we must give up or sacrifice something. More steaks might mean fewer movies; an extra car might mean fewer vacations; and a new ipad might mean giving up the printer that I was planning to purchase. If nothing was sacrificed, then choice was not exercised. If I have the means to acquire both A and B and took them both, then I did not choose. One cannot choose without giving up something.

Problem 3-2

What do economists mean by opportunity cost and how can it be measured?

Requirement and Clue: *This is a two-part problem. Solve each part in order. Define opportunity cost and give examples. Say how it can be measured.*

Solution:

Opportunity cost can be defined as the next best alternative that is sacrificed when a choice is made. In a situation of economic scarcity, a decision to produce one good or service involves an opportunity cost represented by the good or service that might have been produced instead. The idea behind the concept of opportunity cost is that when we use funds to purchase goods and services, we are also deciding not to purchase some other goods or services. Similarly, when an economy uses resources to produce certain goods and services, it is also making a decision not to produce some other goods and services. What we decide not to purchase is the opportunity cost of what we do purchase; and what we decide not to produce is the opportunity cost of what we do produce. Suppose a manufacturer has material suitable for producing computer cases or briefcases. If he or she produces computer cases, the opportunity cost of the computer cases is the briefcases that could have been produced instead.

The discussion in the previous paragraph leads to the conclusion that the opportunity cost of what we get is equal to what we give it. If an economy gives up 2 units of apples for 1 unit of butter, then the opportunity cost of the unit of butter is the 2 units of apples given up. Opportunity cost, then, can be measured by the ratio of what is given up to what is obtained.

Problem 3-3

Establish a relationship among scarcity, choice and opportunity cost.

Requirement and Clue: *The basic idea is that we choose because of scarcity and choosing involves a sacrifice—a cost.*

Solution:

Scarcity means that society does not have sufficient resources to enable it to produce all the goods and services wanted, thus, society must choose. If scarcity did not exist, everyone would have as much of everything as he or she wants. Choice then, is a direct result of scarcity. Whenever a choice is made, something has to be given up. Whatever is given up or sacrificed is the opportunity cost of what was chosen. The following relationship has been established among scarcity, choice, and opportunity cost: scarcity forces us to choose, and choice results in opportunity cost.

Problem 3-4

Briefly define the coast-benefit approach to decision-making.

Requirement and Clue: *A clear and precise definition is required.*

Solution:

In any decision, there are benefits and costs. The cost benefit approach to decision-making is the comparison of the costs and benefits associated with a decision. If the benefits of taking a certain course of action outweigh the cost, then take the action; otherwise, don't.

Problem 3-5

For each of the following, name a possible opportunity cost.

a. *You decided to take a summer job.*
b. *You attended a concert on the night before a major test.*
c. *You took a couple of courses in summer school.*
d. *You decided to treat your friend to a restaurant meal.*
e. *Your family went on a one-week cruise to Alaska.*

Requirement and Clue: *Your solution to this problem will determine the extent to which you understand the concept of opportunity cost. Focus on the alternative that was sacrificed.*

Solution:

Opportunity cost is whatever is given up when a choice is made.

a. The opportunity cost of taking a summer job could be a summer course that you could have taken instead or a summer vacation in Mexico.
b. A possible opportunity cost of attending a concert on the night before a major test could be studying and getting a higher grade on the test.
c. The opportunity cost of these courses could be a summer job that you could have taken instead
d. A possible opportunity cost of treating your friend to a restaurant meal is a DVD that you could have bought instead.
e. The opportunity cost of the cruise to Alaska could be the repairs that could have been done on the house or the entertainment set that could have been purchased instead.

Problem 3-6

The following table contains information about an economy that produces only cups and hand bags with its available resources.

Combinations	Cups x (1000)	Handbags x (1000)
A	0	10
B	1	9
C	2	7
D	3	4
E	4	0

a. *If the economy is producing only handbags and then decides to produce 1,000 cups, what is the opportunity cost of the 1,000 cups in terms of handbags?*
b. *On the basis of the data contained in the table, draw the economy's production-possibility (p-p) curve.*
c. *On your diagram, indicate a point of productive inefficiency with the letter I.*
d. *Indicate a point of full employment with the letter E.*
e. *Indicate an unattainable combination of cups and handbags with the letter U.*

Requirement and Clue: *Note that opportunity cost is whatever is given up. Recall that a point of inefficiency would lie below the curve. A point of full employment would be on the curve, and an unattainable combination would be beyond (above) the curve.*

Solution:

a. In order to produce 1,000 cups, the economy would have to divert resources from the production of handbags and use them to produce cups. The output of handbags would fall from 10,000 to 9,000. The economy would thus give up 1,000 handbags for 1,000 cups. Therefore, the opportunity cost of 1,000 cups would be 1,000 handbags.

b. (See below)

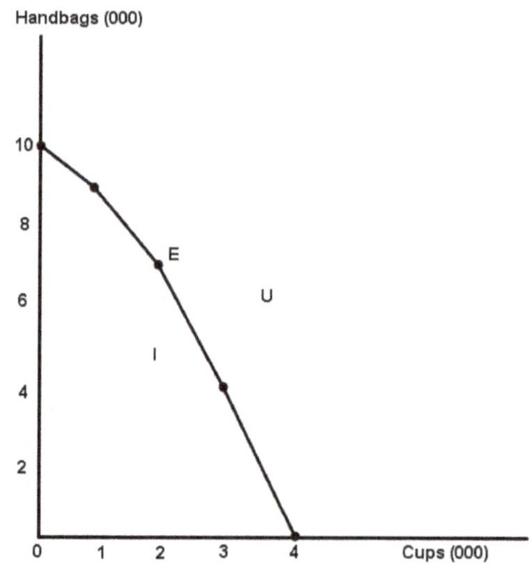

c. A point of productive inefficiency would lie below the production-possibility curve. See *I* on the graph above.

d. A point of full employment would lie on the production-possibility curve as shown by *E* on the graph above.

e. An unattainable combination of cups and handbags would lie above (beyond) the production-possibility curve as shown by *U* in the graph above.

Problem 3-7

The city of Courtland (a factitious city) hires 10 previously unemployed workers and pays them $500 per week each. What is the opportunity cost to Courtland of the extra output produced by the 10 new workers? If the 10 workers were employed elsewhere in Courtland, what would be the opportunity cost to the city of hiring them under the same payment conditions?

Requirement and Clue: *Recognize that there is no opportunity cost associated with unemployed resources. There is a cost associated with transferring workers, that is, the loss of output from where they were previously employed.*

Solution:

The opportunity cost would be the loss of output in Courtland caused by hiring the new workers. Since the 10 workers were unemployed, there is no loss of output associated with hiring them. Therefore the opportunity cost to Courtland is zero. If the 10 workers were employed elsewhere in Courtland, the opportunity cost of the extra output they produce for the city would be the loss of output that they were previously producing.

Problem 3-8

The following table shows production possibilities for a hypothetical economy producing only two goods: lap top computers and telephones.

# lap top computers x (1000)	# of telephones x (1000)
0	15
1	14
2	12
3	9
4	5
5	0

a. *What is the table called?*

b. *With telephones on the vertical axis and lap top computers on the horizontal axis, draw a graph from the data contained in the table. What is the graph called?*

c. *From your graph, determine whether the economy faces constant opportunity cost or increasing opportunity cost.*

Requirement and Clue: *Think of production possibility schedule and production possibility curve. Consider the meaning/significance of concave and linear production possibility curves.*

Solution:

a. The table is a production-possibility schedule or production-possibility table.

b. See graph below. The graph is a production-possibility curve. It is also called a production-possibility frontier or production-possibility boundary.

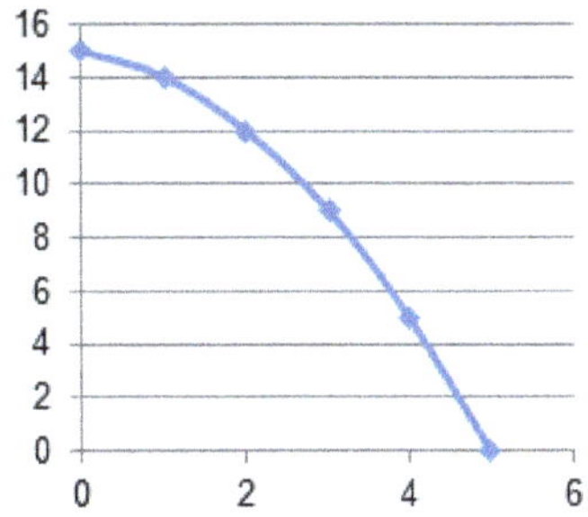

c. Because the production-possibility curve is concave, we can conclude that the economy faces increasing opportunity cost.

Problem 3-9

Use production-possibility graphs to show the immediate effect of each of the following events on a country's production-possibility curve.

a. *A significant number of people immigrate into the country.*

b. *The country embarks on a successful training program for all workers.*

c. *The country discovers a new and more efficient method of using its resources, but decides to delay the use of the new method for a year*

d. *The economy hires workers who were previously unemployed.*

Requirement and Clue: *Ask whether or not the event suggests a change in the quantity or quality of resources, or a change in technology.*

Solution:

If a significant number of immigrants enter the country, it will experience an increase in its human resources and its ability to produce goods and services will immediately increase. This means that its production-possibility (p-p) curve will shift to the right as shown in the following diagram.

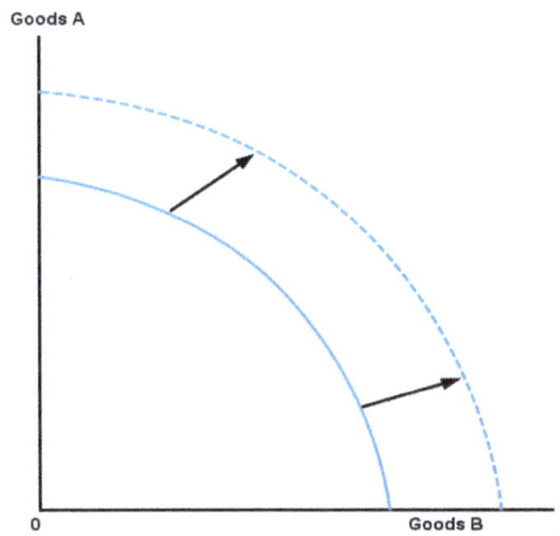

a. A successful training program for all workers will improve the quality of the country's human resources and will increase its productive capacity. Its p-p curve will shift outward to the right as shown in the following diagram.

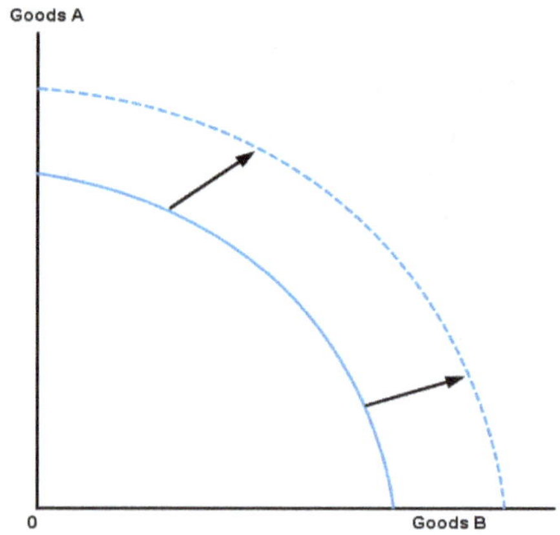

b. A new and more efficient method of using resources represents an improvement in technology. This will increase the country's ability to produce goods and services and will shift its p-p curve outward to the right as shown in the following diagram.

Note that although there is a delay in the use of the new method, its existence immediately increases the economy's potential to produce goods and services, so the curve shifts to the right.

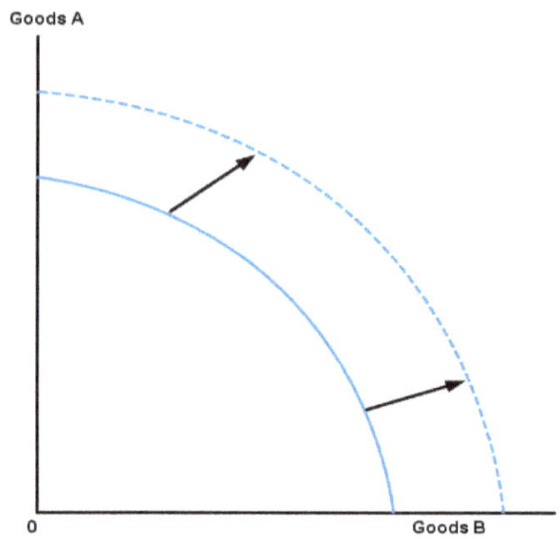

c. If the economy hires workers who were previously unemployed, there is no change in the quantity of human resources because they were already there. There is no change in the country's ability to produce goods and services so the p-p curve remains unchanged as shown in the following diagram.

Problem 3-10

It is observed that classes scheduled for 8:00 a.m. are less crowded than those scheduled for 11:30 a.m. Can the concept of opportunity cost be used as a possible explanation for this phenomenon?

Requirement and Clue: *Compare the opportunity cost of attending an 8:00 a.m. class with that of attending an 11:30 a.m. class.*

Solution:

Opportunity cost is the alternative that is given up when a choice is made. Some of the costs of attending an 8:00 a.m. class may include contending with rush-hour traffic, missing breakfast, and extra sleep. These costs may not be associated with attending an 11:30 a.m. class. It is possible that because of the lower opportunity cost involved in attending the 11:30 scheduled class, more students opt for this option.

Problem 3-11

Give a practical example of the use of the concept of opportunity cost in real life.

Requirement and Clue: *Numerous examples should come to mind. Almost every decision involves a choice and choosing involves giving up something.*

Solution:

Our daily lives are filled with decisions. Should I buy a car and drive to school or should I take public transportation? Should I live on campus while attending university or should I commute? Should we buy a new car or should we carry out extensive renovations on our home? Should I attend the concert tonight or should I use the time to study for my economics test? These are typical decisions that people make all the time. Some are major while others are minor. The concept of opportunity cost is used regularly in real life. Suppose Jane has arrived at school this morning. She is deciding whether or not she should attend her economics class. She attends classes because she believes that she will derive certain benefits from doing so. But attending class also has costs associated with it. These may include spending time with friends, visiting a mall, or doing some work on a psychology paper that is due in a couple of days. These are what Jane will give up by attending the class. They are the opportunity cost of going to the class.

To make the decision, Jane weighs the benefits against the costs. If, in her own subjective evaluation, the benefits of going to the class outweigh the costs, then she will decide to attend the class. If not, she will decide not to attend class. The costs referred to here are opportunity costs.

Problem 3-12

John Green has just graduated from a junior college where he earned his college diploma. He has been offered a job for $25,000 a year. He would like to go to university to obtain his bachelor's degree in business. This is a two-year program since he already holds a diploma from the junior college. Tuition, books, transportation, supplies and other things directly *related to his university education will cost $35,000 for the two-year period.*

a. *On the basis of this information, what is the full cost to John of a degree?*

b. *How should John decide whether or not to go for the degree?*

Requirement and Clue: *This is another two-part problem. Answer each part in order. Be careful not to omit opportunity cost. John could base his decision on a comparison of costs and benefits.*

Solution:

a. If John bases his decision only on the $35,000, he would severely underestimate his cost. The full cost of his degree must include the $25,000 a year (or $50,000 for the two-year period) that he could have received as salary from his employment. That is the opportunity cost. Thus the full cost of the degree is ($35,000 + $50,000) = $85,000.

b. To decide whether or not to go for the degree, John must consider the benefits of having the degree. These may include a higher-paying job, better working conditions, greater job security, and the prestige of having a university degree. If these benefits outweigh the $85,000 cost, then John would sacrifice the job and attend university. Otherwise, he would take the job for $25,000 a year.

Problem 3-13

What is the difference between a production-possibility schedule and a production-possibility curve?

Requirement and Clue: *The technical difference between the two concepts must be noted. An example of each would be helpful.*

Solution:

Although the terms "production-possibility schedule" and "production-possibility curve" are sometimes used interchangeably, there is a technical difference between them. A production-possibility schedule is a table showing *various* combinations of goods and services that can be produced with full utilization of all resources and a given state of technology. A production-possibility curve, on the other hand, is a graph showing *all* combinations. The following table is a production-possibility schedule showing various combinations of x and y that can be produced. When the information shown in the table is plotted on a graph and the points are connected as in the following graph, the result is a production-possibility curve.

Production-possibility schedule

Combinations	Quantity of y	Quantity of x
A	12	0
B	10	1
C	8	2
D	6	3
E	4	4
F	2	5
E	0	6

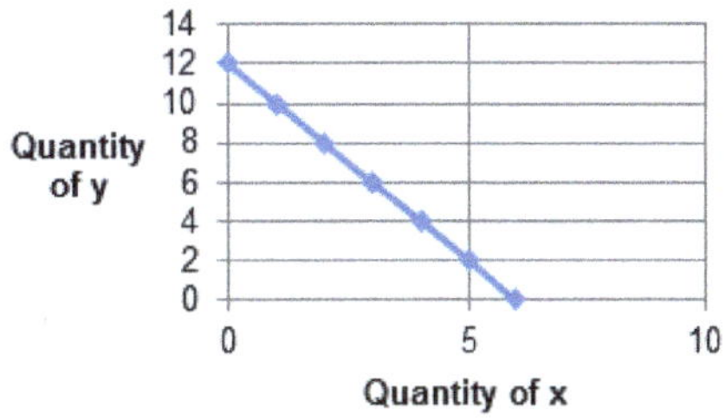

Production-possibility curve

Problem 3-14

Answer the following questions:

(a) *What is the production possibility curve?*

(b) *What can you conclude about an economy that is operating at a point on its production-possibility curve?*

(c) *What can you conclude about an economy that is operating at a point below its production-possibility curve?*

Requirement and Clue: *This is a three-part problem. Answer each part in order. Consider the significance of a point on the curve and a point below the curve.*

Solution:

(a) The production-possibility curve is a graph that shows all combinations of goods and services that an economy can produce with a given technology, using all its resources. Since it defines the limits of what an economy can produce, it is also referred to as the production-possibility boundary or production-possibility frontier. The following diagram shows a production-possibility curve.

The economy cannot produce any combination of goods and services that lies above this curve.

(b) If an economy is operating at a point on its production-possibility curve, it means that the economy is using all its resources efficiently. In such a situation, the economy cannot produce more of one good without producing less of some other good. Thus, a point on the production-possibility curve represents efficient production. The following diagram illustrates the point.

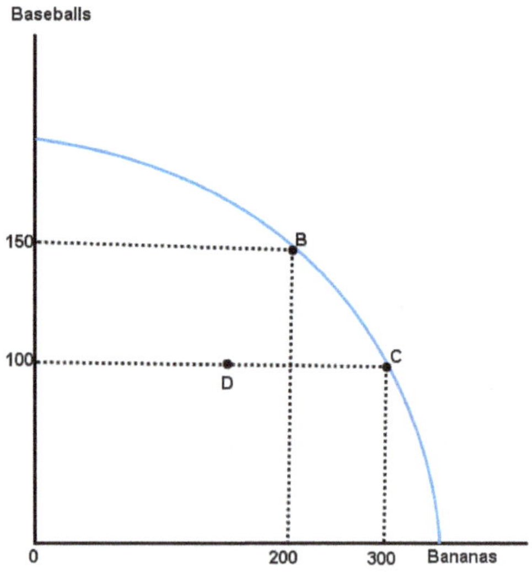

If the economy is operating at point B, producing 150 baseballs and 200 bananas, it can move to point C, producing 300 bananas only by producing 100 baseballs instead of 150, thus sacrificing 50 baseballs.

(c) If an economy is operating at a point below its production-possibility curve, such as point D in the diagram, it means that the economy is not using all its resources or is not using them efficiently. This economy can produce more baseballs by moving vertically from D toward the curve, without sacrificing the production of any bananas, or more bananas by moving horizontally from D toward C, without sacrificing the production of any of baseballs. It can produce more baseballs and more bananas by moving diagonally from D towards a point on the curve such as B.

Problem 3-15

Are production-possibility (p-p) curves likely to be linear or concave?

Requirement and Clue: *Explore the conditions for linear and concave p-p curves.*

Solution:

A straight line (linear) p-p curve means that opportunity cost is constant. This would be the case only if all resources were equally efficient in all uses. A concave p-p curve means that opportunity cost is increasing. This would be the case if resources were not all equally efficient in all uses. In reality, however, some resources are more suitable for some uses than for others. For example, some human resources are better equipped to be teachers than mechanics, and some natural resources are better suited for building sites than for cultivation. Moreover, land, labour, and capital are certainly not substitutable. We can conclude, therefore, that p-p curves are more likely to be concave than linear.

Problem 3-16

How can a production-possibility curve be used to show economic scarcity?

Requirement and Clue: *Say what economic scarcity is and consider why an economy cannot operate at a point beyond its production possibility curve.*

Solution:

Economic scarcity exists when available resources are insufficient to produce all the goods and services required to satisfy human wants. The existence of economic scarcity can be well illustrated by the production-possibility curve which shows all the choices available to society in terms of the combinations of goods and services that it is capable of producing, using all its resources with given technology. Consider the following graph.

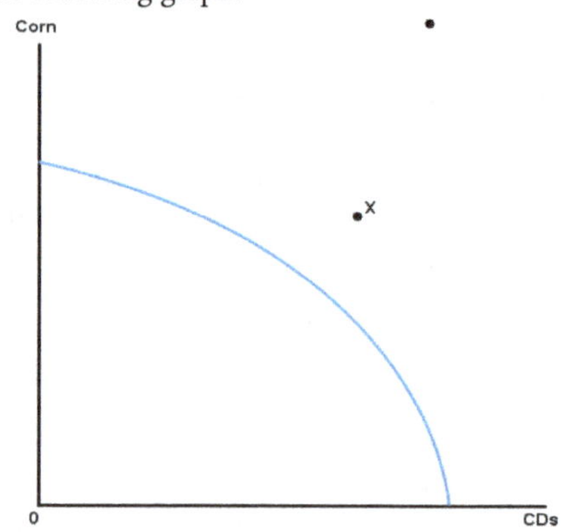

Each point on the production-possibility curve represents some maximum output of any two goods, corn and compact discs (CDs), for example. Society must choose which combination it desires; more corn means fewer CDs and more CDs means less corn. The fact that society cannot have more corn *and* more CDs at the same time means that scarcity exists. Moreover, consider point X. Society would like to have a combination of corn and CDs represented by this point; but this is not possible. Why? Because the resources and technology available do not permit that combination of goods. That is economic scarcity.

Problem 3-17

An economy produces only two goods, computers and cellular telephones. Like all economies, its economic resources are limited, so in order to produce more computers it must divert resources from cell phone production. Therefore, in order to produce more of one good, it must produce less of the other. The following table shows maximum quantities of computers and cell phones that the economy can produce.

Prod. Possibilities	Cell phones	Computers
A	100	0
B	90	10
C	70	20
D	40	30
E	0	40

Use the data in the table to construct a production-possibility curve for this economy.

Requirement and Clue: *This is just a matter of plotting the points and connecting them to get the production possibility curve.*

Solution:

With the quantity of computers on the vertical axis and the quantity of cell phones on the horizontal axis, we can plot the points as shown in the graph.

Problem 3-18

In the production-possibility diagram below, which points indicate full employment and which points indicate underemployment?

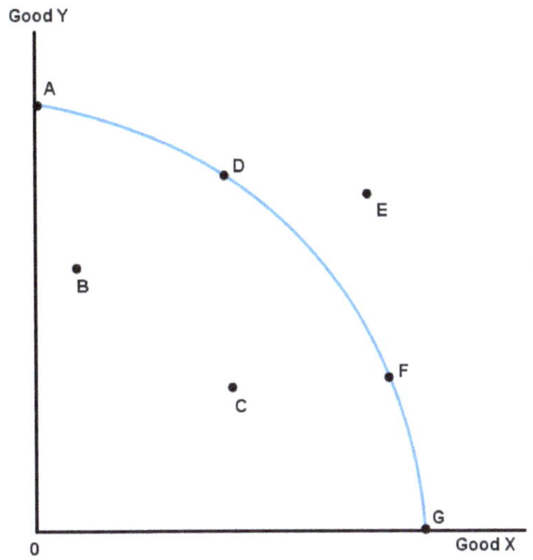

Requirement and Clue: *Consider the significance of points on the p-p curve and points below it.*

Solution:

Any point on the production-possibility curve represents full employment; therefore points A, D, F and G indicate full employment. Any point below the production-possibility curve represents underemployment or unemployment. Therefore points B and C indicate underemployment.

Problem 3-19

The following is the production-possibility curve for a hypothetical economy that produces books and bread.

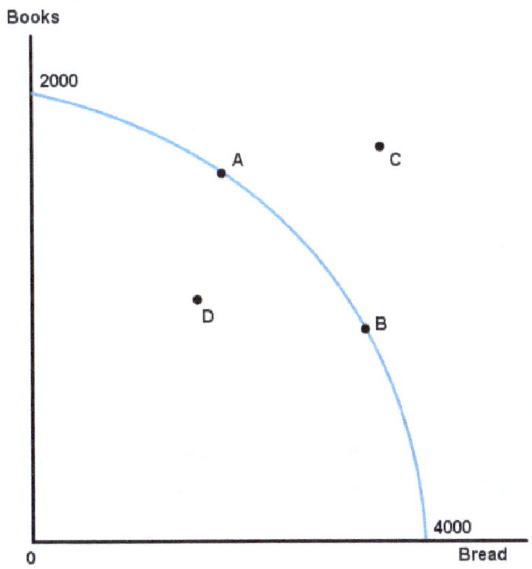

(a) *What is the maximum number books that this economy can produce?*

(b) *What is the maximum amount of bread that this economy can produce?*

(c) *Which points represent maximum use of resources?*

(d) *Which point represents unemployment?*

(e) *Which point is impossible to attain?*

Requirement and Clue: *This requires familiarity with the production possibility curve and the significance of points below, on, and above the curve.*

Solution:

(a) If this economy uses all its resources in the production of books, it will be able to produce a maximum of 2,000 books.

(b) If the economy produces no books but uses all its resources to produce only bread, it will be able to produce a maximum of 4,000 loaves of bread.

(c) Maximum use of resources is represented by points on the production-possibility curve. In this case, points A and B represent maximum use of resources.

(d) Any point below the production-possibility curve represents unemployment. Point D is such a point.

(e) The production-possibility curve defines the limit of what an economy can produce. Point C represents a combination of bread and books that this economy cannot attain.

Problem 3-20

Describe two ways by which an economy's production-possibility curve can be made to shift outward.

Requirement and Clue: *Focus on changes in resources and technology. Use a diagram to illustrate.*

Solution:

An outward shift of an economy's production-possibility curve occurs when the economy's productive capacity increases. This increase in productive capacity can occur if (a) there is an increase in the quantity and/or quality of resources available to the economy and (b) there is an improvement in technology. Either or both of these occurrences can shift the production-possibility curve outward.

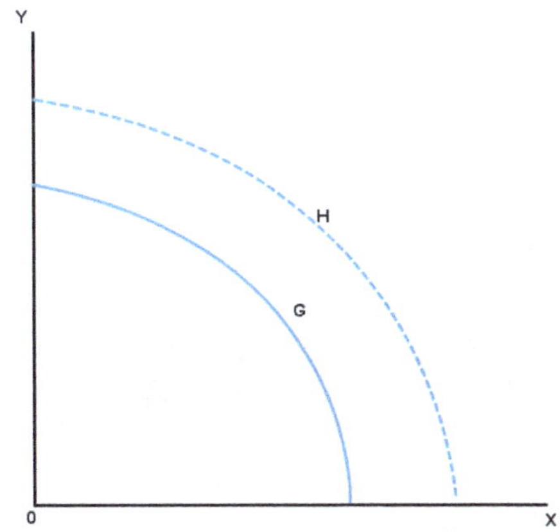

In the diagram above, *G* is the original production-possibility curve.

An increase in the quantity of human resources through immigration or an improvement in labour quality through education and training will cause the production-possibility curve to shift outward from production-possibility curve *G* to production-possibility curve *H* as shown in the diagram. An increase in the quantity or quality of any other factor of production will have a similar effect.

An improvement in technology means that a given quantity of resources can now produce more goods and services than before, or that fewer resources can now produce the same quantity of goods and services as before. For example, the discovery of a more efficient method of producing automobiles or airplanes will shift the production-possibility curve outward.

Problem 3-21

The economy of Wadidla (a fictitious country) produces only two goods: potatoes and wooden carvings. Over a two-year period, technological advance occurred in the wood carving industry but not in potato production. Show how Wadidla's production-possibility curve would be affected by the technological advance.

Requirement and Clue: *You are required to use a production possibility diagram to show the effects of technological advance in one industry but not in the other.*

Solution:

This particular technological advance positively affects the economy's potential to produce wooden carvings, but its impact on the ability to produce potatoes is nil. In the following graph, the old technology is shown. The new p-p curve resulting from technological advance in the wooden carving industry only would look like the p-p curve labeled new technology.

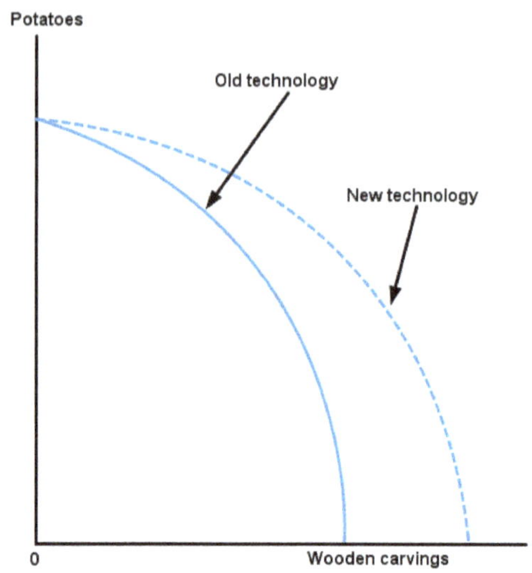

Problem 3-22

Briefly discuss the fundamental questions of microeconomics.

Requirement and Clue: *You should demonstrate that you are familiar with the fundamental questions of microeconomics: What, How and for whom.*

Solution:

The fundamental questions of microeconomics are usually stated as What?, How?, and For whom?

"What?" refers to what goods and services will the economy produce and in what quantities. Because of scarcity, society cannot have all the goods and services that are needed. It has to decide what will be produced and what will be sacrificed, knowing that more of one good or service means less of some other good or service.

"How?" refers to how the goods and services will be produced—the method of production. It's a question about the technology that will be used to produce the goods and services that society decides will be produced. The society must decide how the factors of production will be combined to produce its output of goods and services.

"For whom?" refers to who gets the goods and services that the economy produces. This is a question about the distribution of the economy's output of goods and services. Society must decide on the mechanism that will be used to distribute goods and services to its members.

Problem 3-23

What is the relationship between the fundamental microeconomic question, "What to produce?" and economic scarcity?

Requirement and Clue: *The central point here is that scarcity prevents the economy from producing all the goods and services necessary to satisfy human wants. A decision therefore has to be made with regard to what will be produced.*

Solution:

Had it not been for the existence of economic scarcity, society would simply produce all the goods and services necessary to satisfy all human wants. But economic scarcity is a fact of life and every economy must decide whether to produce more of A and less of B. Producing more automobiles might mean producing fewer miles of highway; producing more classrooms might mean producing fewer hospital beds; and producing more entertainment sets might mean producing fewer tons of wheat. Since economic scarcity limits society's ability to produce goods and services, society must decide what goods and services it will produce and in what quantities. What to produce and economic scarcity are integrally related.

Problem 3-24

"The fundamental microeconomic questions, What?, How? and For whom are essentially questions of allocation." Discuss.

Requirement and Clue: *The following points should be noted. Resources have to be allocated to whatever the economy decides to produce. The method of production involves allocating resources. The distribution of the output deals with allocating the output.*

Solution:

The fundamental microeconomic questions refer to what goods and services the economy will produce and in what quantities, what method of production will the economy use to produce its output of goods and services, and how the economy's output of goods and services will be distributed among the members of society. The question of what to produce is an allocation problem in the sense that resources have to be allocated to whatever goods and services the society decides it will produce. The question of how to produce is also an allocation question. If a decision is made to produce wheat, for example, will the production be done using a labour-intensive method or a capital-intensive method? In other words, how will resources be allocated to the production of wheat? Finally, the question of for whom to produce is also an allocation problem. Whereas the questions of what to produce and how to produce involve the allocation of resources or inputs, the question of for whom to produce is a question of the allocation of output. The question refers to how the society's output of goods and services will be allocated among the members of society. Thus we see that the fundamental microeconomic questions are really questions of allocation.

Multiple-Choice

In each case, circle the letter that corresponds with the correct answer.

1. When we choose:

a. we necessarily give up something
b. we don't necessarily give up something but we must take something
c. there is no cost involved unless the choice costs us money
d. we always incur a monetary cost

Answer: a

Reason: *Choice always involves giving up something.*

2. Choice is:

a. always without a cost because we have freedom of choice
b. always associated with a cost
c. a problem that is faced only by poor people
d. identical to taking

Answer: b

Reason: *Choice involves giving up something, and whatever is given up is a cost.*

3. The term used for the next best alternative that is sacrificed when a choice is made is:

a. sacrificial cost b. next-best cost
c. opportunity cost d. all of the above

Answer: c

Reason: *Opportunity cost is whatever is given up when a choice is made.*

4. Opportunity cost of an item is:

a. the monetary price of an item
b. the monetary cost of producing the item
c. the monetary cost of an opportunity that is missed
d. whatever is given up in order to obtain the item

Answer: d

Reason: *Opportunity cost is whatever is sacrificed when a choice is made.*

5. Opportunity cost can be measured by:

a. what we get when we give up something
b. what we give up divided by what we get
c. what we give up minus what we get
d. what we get minus what we give up

Answer: b

Reason: *A measure of opportunity cost is the ratio of what we give up to what we get.*

6. In order to get 5 more bananas, you have to give up 10 erasers. From this we can conclude that the opportunity cost of bananas is:

a. 2 erasers b. 50 erasers
c. 5 erasers d. none of the above

Answer: a

Reason: *You give up 10 erasers and you get 5 bananas. Opportunity cost is what you give up (10 erasers) divided by what you get (5 bananas): 10/5 = 2*

7. The cost-benefit approach:

a. is useful only in making business decisions
b. involves comparing costs and benefits
c. is a method of minimizing production costs
d. is a sure way of eliminating costs

Answer: b

Reason: *A rule of thumb in decision making is to compare benefits and costs.*

8. The cost-benefit approach is applicable:

a. only when costs can be measured in monetary terms
b. only when benefits can be measured in monetary terms
c. only when both costs and benefits can be measured in monetary terms
d. none of the above

Answer: d

Reason: *The cost-benefit approach is applicable whether or not cost and benefits can be measured in monetary terms.*

9. Cost-benefit analysis can be used:

a. to determine whether or not to take a vacation in France
b. to decide whether or not to attend a particular class
c. to choose between going to university or taking a full-time job
d. all of the above

Answer: d

Reason: *Coast-benefit analysis can be used in all the circumstances listed in the choices.*

10. A production-possibility schedule is:

a. a graph that shows possible combinations of goods that are available to consumers

b. a curve that separates the possible from the impossible

c. a table that shows various combinations of goods and services that can be produced under certain conditions

d. all of the above

Answer: c

Reason: *Unlike the p-p curve that is a graph, the p-p schedule is a table that shows production possibilities, given the quantity and quality of resources and the state of technology.*

11. A production possibility curve is:

a. A graph that shows all combinations of goods and services that an economy can produce under certain conditions

b. drawn on the assumption that resources and technology are constantly changing

c. applicable only small countries with underdeveloped economies

d. always upward-sloping because of increasing opportunity cost

Answer: a

Reason: *Unlike the p-p schedule that is a table, the p-p curve is a graph that shows all production possibilities, given the quantity and quality of resources and the state of technology.*

12. A linear (straight line) production possibility curve for an economy means that:

a. a constant amount of goods and services can be produced with given resources

b. all resources must always be used at a constant rate in the economy

c. the economy faces constant opportunity cost

d. all resources are not equally efficient in all uses

Answer: c

Reason: *A situation of constant opportunity cost is represented by a downward sloping linear p-p curve.*

13. If an economy is facing increasing opportunity cost, then we know that its production-possibility (p-p) curve will be:

a. upward sloping b. horizontal
c. downward sloping but linear d. concave

Answer: d

Reason: *A situation of increasing opportunity cost is represented by a concave p-p curve.*

14. Production-possibility curves are usually drawn concave because:

a. of the law of scarcity and resource use

b. all resources are limited

c. not all resources can be used equally efficiently in all uses

d. of an agreement among economists to use concave curves

Answer: c

Reason: *Increasing opportunity cost occurs because resources are not all equally efficient in all uses. Concave p-p curves illustrate increasing opportunity cost.*

15. The production-possibility curve illustrates the fundamental fact that:

a. an economy's productive capacity increases with the passage of time

b. if an economy is using all its resources and technology is given, it can produce more of one good only by producing less of some other good

c. an economy will always operate at the highest level of efficiency

d. the quantities of goods and services that an economy can produce are limited only by people's imagination

Answer: b

Reason: *This is the scarcity issue. Because of limited resources, we can produce more of one thing only by producing less of something else.*

16. A point below a production-possibility curve means that:

a. the economy is deliberately and consciously saving resources for future use

b. the economy is not using all its resources or is not using them efficiently

c. the economy is operating at more than full employment

d. the economy is using all its resources in an efficient manner

Answer: b

Reason: *A point on the curve means that the economy is using all its resources. A point below (inside) the curve means that it is not using all its resources.*

17. The following diagram is the production-possibility curve for Betterland (a fictitious country). With reference to the diagram, which of the following is true?

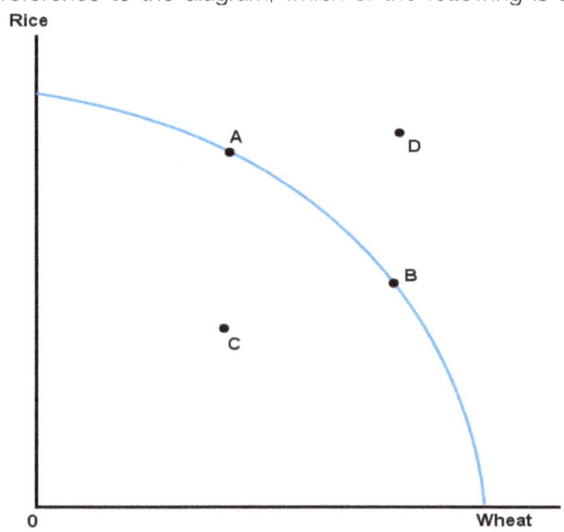

a. Betterland cannot move from point A to point B without an increase in available resources or an improvement in technology.

b. Betterland can move from point C to point B with no increase in the quantity of resources available or in its technology.

c. Betterland can move from point D to point A if it

ceases to produce rice.

d. At point C, Betterland can produce either more rice or more wheat, but not more of both.

Answer: b

Reason: *At point C, Betterland has idle resources that it can employ to move to point B.*

18. Which of the following will cause an economy's p-p curve to shift outward, other things being equal?

a. An increase in demand for all goods and services
b. A more intensive use of available resources
c. The acquisition of more resources or better technology
d. All of the above

Answer: c

Reason: *An increase in the quantity or quality of resources or an improvement in technology will enhance the economy's productive capacity.*

19. Which of the following is not illustrated in a production-possibility curve?

a. Opportunity cost   b. Choice
c. Economic scarcity   d. Price

Answer: d

Reason: *The p-p curve tells us nothing about price.*

20. A *free lunch*:

a. refers to the additional output produced by an economy without sacrificing the production of some other good or service
b. can occur if an economy is operating below its production-possibility curve
c. is possible if an economy is not using all its resources
d. all of the above

Answer: d

Reason: *The concept of a free lunch is getting something for nothing. If the economy has idle resources, it can use them to produce goods and services. This use of idle inputs does not result in a loss of output elsewhere in the economy.*

21. An outward shift of the production-possibility curve is often referred to as:

a. economic growth   b. a production shift
c. graph expansion   d. all of the above

Answer: a

Reason: *Economic growth can be defined as an increase in the economy's ability to produce more goods and services. This is represented by an outward shift in the p-p curve.*

22. An outward shift of an economy's production-possibility curve means that:

a. the economy is actually producing more goods and services
b. the economy is capable of producing more goods and services
c. the economy is using its resources efficiently
d. all of the above

Answer: b

Reason: *An economy's p-p curve gives information about what the economy is capable of producing. It speaks to the economy's potential in terms of production.*

23. The following diagram shows the production-possibility (p-p) curve for a hypothetical economy.

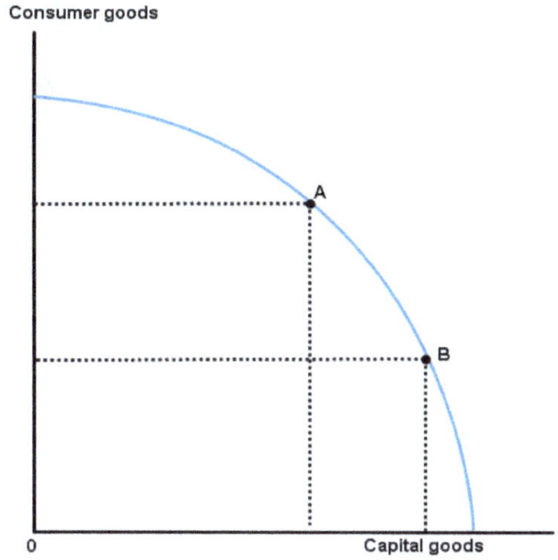

If the economy shifts production from point A to point B:

a. it will have no effect on the p-p curve in the future
b. it will cause the p-p curve to shift towards the origin
c. it will cause the p-p curve to shift outward in the future
d. none of the above

Answer: c

Reason: *By shifting production from A to B, the economy would increase its production of capital goods, which will enable it to produce more capital and more consumer goods in the future.*

24. The fundamental microeconomic questions are:

a. What to produce, how to produce it, and who gets what is produced
b. How large the population should be and what kind of economic system is best
c. Why are resources limited and how can the quantity be increased
d. How can unemployment and inflation be controlled

Answer: a

Reason: *Because of scarcity, every economy has to decide what goods and services it will produce, the method of production that it will use, and how to distribute the output that is produced.*

25. The fundamental microeconomic questions must be addressed by:

a. only developing economies
b. only economies in transition
c. only advanced economies
d. all economies

Answer: d

Reason: *No matter how the economy is organized, it has to decide what, how, and for whom.*

True or False

Determine whether each of the following statements is true or false.

1. One cannot choose without giving up something.

Answer: True

2. If economic scarcity did not exist, one would not have to choose.

Answer: True

3. Opportunity cost is the name given to the monetary cost of production.

Answer: False

Explanation: *It is an alternative that is sacrificed and may have nothing to do with production cost.*

4. The opportunity cost to a farmer of producing more wheat is the corn that he or she could have produced instead.

Answer: True

5. Opportunity cost can be defined as the next best alternative that is sacrificed when a choice is made.

Answer: True

6. Opportunity cost can be measured by what we give up divided by what we get in its place.

Answer: True

7. If you have to give up 8 CDs in order to get 4 more Blu-ray movies, then the opportunity cost of a Blu-ray movie is 2 CDs.

Answer: True

8. Economic scarcity forces us to choose, but we can choose without incurring any opportunity cost.

Answer: False

Explanation: *Choosing always involves a cost in terms of what is given up.*

9. A production possibility curve is a graph that shows all combinations of goods and/or services that an economy is currently producing with all its resources, using the available technology.

Answer: False

Explanation: *The graph shows what the economy is capable of producing, not necessarily what it is producing.*

10. Other names for the production possibility curve are the transformation curve, the production possibility boundary, and the production possibility frontier.

Answer: True

11. If the production possibility curve for an economy is linear and downward sloping, we know that the economy is facing decreasing opportunity cost.

Answer: False

Explanation: *This would be a case of constant opportunity cost.*

12. If the production possibility curve for an economy is linear, we know that the economy is facing constant opportunity cost.

Answer: True

13. An economy that is facing increasing opportunity cost will have an upward sloping production possibility curve.

Answer: False

Explanation: *Upward sloping p-p curves don't make any economic sense. If the economy is facing increasing opportunity cost, its p-p curve will be concave.*

14. A country's production possibility curve will be linear (i.e. a straight line) if all its resources are equally efficient in all uses.

Answer: True

15. Production possibility curves are likely to be concave because of the law of increasing opportunity cost.

Answer: True

16. Because resources are not all equally efficient in all uses, production possibility curves are likely to be concave.

Answer: True

17. A point below a production possibility curve indicates unemployment; a point on the curve indicates full employment; and a point above the curve indicates an unattainable combination of output.

Answer: True

18. An economy can never be in a situation where it can produce more of one good without producing less of some other good.

Answer: False

Explanation: *It can if it has unemployed resources. By using unemployed resources, it can produce more of one good without producing less of some other good. Recall the case of a "free lunch."*

19. A production possibility curve shows the maximum output that an economy can produce; therefore the curve can never shift to the right.

Answer: false

Explanation: *The curve can shift to the right if the economy obtains more or better resources or if technology improves.*

20. A greater quantity and better quality of resources or an improvement in technology will shift the production possibility curve to the right.

Answer: True

21. In a modern economy that is well organized, a production possibility curve cannot shift downward to the left.

Answer: False

Explanation: *A p-p curve can shift to the left if the economy loses resources through a flood or forest fires, for example.*

22. The production possibility curve will shift to the right if the country uses idle resources that were previously unemployed.

Answer: False

Explanation: Using resources that the economy already has will not affect its capacity to produce and will therefore not shift the curve.

23. The production possibility curve gives information about what the economy is actually producing, not what it is capable of producing.

Answer: False

Explanation: The p-p curve is about the economy's productive capacity.

24. A decision to reduce current consumption by investing in capital goods will shift the production possibility curve to the right in the future.

Answer: True

25. Referring to the fundamental microeconomic questions, What and How are essentially questions of allocation of resources while the question of For whom is a question of the allocation of output.

Answer: True

Completion

(Fill in the blanks)

Use each word or combination of words from the list exactly once.
*(**Hint**: Proceed by elimination)*

Word list

Concave x 2 — Constant — Cost x 2 — Cost-Benefit — Economic — For Whom — Free — Graph — Growth — How — Increasing — Linear — Lunch — Opportunity x 2 — Produce — Resources — Right —Technology x 2 — Underemployment — Unemployment — What

Questions

1. Choice involves giving up something, and whatever is given up is ____________ ____________.
2. The ____________ approach to decision making involves comparing benefits and costs.
3. The next best alternative that is sacrificed when a choice is made is referred to as ____________ ____________. (opportunity cost)
4. A country's production possibility curve is a ____________ that shows all combinations of goods and services that the country can____________ if it uses all its resources and if technology is constant.
5. A production possibility curve represents the maximum amount of goods and services than an economy can produce with a given level of ____________ and ____________.
6. A linear production possibility curve indicates ____________ opportunity cost, while a concave production possibility curve indicates ____________ opportunity cost.
7. The production possibility curve for a country facing increasing opportunity cost will be ____________.
8. Because resources are not all equally efficient in all uses, production possibility curves are more likely to be ____________ than ____________.
9. The additional output produced without sacrificing the production of any other good or service is called a ____________ ____________.
10. An outward shift of a country's production possibility curve is sometimes referred to as ____________ ____________.
11. A country's production possibility curve will shift to the right if it acquires more or better resources or if its ____________ improves.
12. A country's production possibility curve will shift to the ____________ in the future if it reduces current consumption and invests in capital goods.
13. The fundamental microeconomic questions are ____________ to produce, ____________ to produce it, and ____________ to produce.
14. A point below the production possibility curve means that the economy is experiencing either ____________ or ____________.

Solutions

1. (opportunity cost)
2. (cost-benefit)
3. (opportunity cost)
4. (graph, produce)
5. (resources, technology)
6. (constant, increasing)
7. (concave)
8. (concave, linear)
9. (free lunch)
10. (economic growth)
11. (technology)
12. (right)
13. (what, how, for whom)
14. (unemployment, underemployment)

4 A MARKET-ORIENTED ECONOMIC SYSTEM

SYNOPSIS

An economic system comprises households, firms, and government authorities who make decisions about the use of the economy's resources. Economic systems may be classified loosely as free enterprise and socialist economic systems. In a free enterprise economic system, most economic decisions are made by households and firms responding to the market forces of demand and supply. Consequently, free enterprise economies are often called **market-oriented economies**. In a socialist economic system, the state dominates most economic decisions. Consequently, socialist economic systems are often called **command economies**. In practice, all economies are mixed economies where decisions are made by households, firms, and government.

Every economic system, no matter how it is organized, must deal with the fundamental economic problem of scarcity. It must decide *what* goods and services will be produced, how they will be produced, and *for whom* they will be produced. In addition, an economic system is expected to provide economic stability, economic security, and economic growth.

The role of government in a market economy includes the protection of individual freedom, the protection of property rights and the enforcement of contracts, the prevention of the abuse of monopoly power, the promotion of economic stability and an equitable distribution of income.

The three basic sectors of the economy are the consumer sector (households), the business sector (producers or firms), and the government sector. Consumers provide resources to firms, and they purchase a large part of the output of the economy. The business sector purchases resources mainly from households and other firms, and produces goods and services. The government engages in production, and in a number of regulatory activities.

LEARNING OBJECTIVES

In connection with this module, you should be able to:

1. describe economic systems and their functions
2. explain the role of households in a market economy
3. explain the role of firms in a market economy
4. explain the role of government in a market economy
5. construct a simple circular flow model of a market-oriented economy

DEFINITIONS & CONCEPTS

You should be able to define the following terms and concepts:

economic systems
command economy
free enterprise system
mixed economy
market mechanism
consumer sovereignty
household sector
business sector
government sector
factor market
product market

4

A MARKET-ORIENTED ECONOMIC SYSTEM

Concepts, Definitions & Problems

Problem 4-1

What is a market-oriented economic system?

Requirement and Clue: *What is required here is demonstration of your knowledge of what a market-oriented economy is. You are not required to write a thesis on a market-oriented economic system. Just say what it is and provide an example, if you can.*

Solution:

A market-oriented economic system is one in which the fundamental economic questions of what, how and for whom are made by private individuals and groups through the market forces of demand and supply. In such an economic system, most of the economy's resources are owned and controlled privately rather than by the government. Consumers are free to maximize their satisfaction and firms are free to maximize their profits by working through markets. Such an economic system is often referred to as a *free enterprise* economic system. Examples of countries with a market-oriented economic system are Canada, the United Kingdom, and the United States.

Problem 4-2

What are the main advantages of a market-oriented economic system?

Requirement and Clue: *Although it may be tempting to discuss the disadvantages as well as the advantages or benefits, and to compare a market-oriented economic system with some alternative, the question requires only that you state the main advantages of a market-oriented economic system. You may briefly define the system and then state its main advantages.*

Solution:

A market-oriented economic system is one in which most economic decisions are made by individuals and firms acting through free markets to achieve their economic objectives.

One of the most important advantages of a market-oriented economic system is the freedom of choice that individuals enjoy. Because individuals and groups are free to use their resources to advance their own interests, a market-oriented economic system provides initiative and incentive for people to pursue their economic objectives and improve their economic well-being. Under a market-oriented economic system, every individual has an opportunity to use his or her talents and resources for his or her own benefit.

Another major advantage of a market-oriented economic system is that the goods and services that consumers want are produced without any deliberate coordinated decision-making. The system works automatically for the most part and is therefore relatively efficient. There is no need to make any special arrangement with a grocery store to provide you with milk today. If you wanted to, you could go to the grocery store and buy milk. Under this system, you don't have to make any arrangements with the college cafeteria for breakfast on any particular morning, yet you are quite confident that you will be able to obtain breakfast any morning. The system works in such a way that it does not require a great deal of coordination for a market-oriented economy to produce the goods and services that consumers want.

Problem 4-3

Does a market-oriented economy have any weaknesses? If so, what are they?

Requirement and Clue: *The question is designed to determine whether or not you are familiar with the weaknesses of a market-oriented economy. The solution requires that you focus on the weaknesses. Notice that the problem has two parts. You are expected to address both.*

Solution:

Despite major advantages, a market-oriented economic system does have some notable weaknesses. If left to itself, it often produces results that are quite socially unacceptable; and that's why the government often intervenes so that the system gives results that are more acceptable.

First, a market-oriented economic system does not automatically generate full employment. There are many people who genuinely want to work but are unable to find jobs. After you have completed your studies, there is a good chance that you will find a job where you can use the training and skills that you have developed, but the system does not guarantee it. Associated with the problem of unemployment is the problem of economic instability. A market-oriented economic system is susceptible to wide fluctuations in economic activity, sometimes with serious economic consequences.

Second, under a market-oriented economic system, certain goods and services may not be produced at all, or may be produced only in vastly inadequate quantities. A market-oriented economic system tends to produce goods and services that are wanted by those members of the society who can pay for them. Some goods and services, such as sanitation and defence, which benefit the entire society, may not be produced by private businesses since it is difficult for private firms to exact a payment from all members of the society. Such goods, known as public goods, are better provided collectively through the government.

Third, a market-oriented economic system, with its emphasis on private property, may not provide adequate protection to the environment. Resources such as rivers, lakes, and the air are common property, owned by everyone but by no one in particular. Often, no price is charged for the use of common property with the result that the environment becomes a dumping ground for all types of pollutants. This is a serious weakness of a market-oriented economic system.

Fourth, the promotion of self-interest, a feature of a market-oriented economic system, may result in a very inequitable distribution of income, which may be socially unacceptable. Critics of the market-oriented economic system charge that under this system, the rich get richer and the poor get poorer. When this occurs, government intervention may be necessary to deal with the problem.

Finally, a market-oriented economic system does not guarantee the competition that is necessary to ensure the efficient allocation of resources. Under a market-oriented economic system, the production of certain goods may be controlled by one seller or a few sellers who may take advantage of the opportunity to exploit other members of the society.

Problem 4-4

What is the main identifying feature of a free enterprise economic system?

Requirement and Clue: *Simply defining a free enterprise economic system will not be adequate for a solution to this problem. Although it would do no harm to briefly define a free enterprise economic system, the emphasis should be placed on indicating its main identifying feature.*

Solution:

A free enterprise economic system is one in which economic decisions are made by individuals and firms responding to a system of prices and markets—the system in which prices are used to allocate resources and goods and services.

The main identifying feature of a free enterprise economic system is the right of private persons and private groups to own property—a concept known as the institution of private property. In this type of economic system, people are free, not only to own resources, but also to use them in whatever way they choose, subject to certain legal limitations designed to safeguard society. In this kind of economic system, individuals enjoy freedom of choice. Consumers are free, within certain legal and social constraints, to use their income to purchase the goods and services that they want to maximize their satisfaction. They are also free to use the resources at their disposal to maximize their income. Businesses also have freedom of choice. They are free to use their resources in such a way as to maximize their profits.

Problem 4-5

Discuss the role of government in a market-oriented economy.

Requirement and Clue: *The problem recognizes that government plays a role in a market-oriented economy. Your job is to discuss that role.*

Solution:

In a market-oriented economy, most economic decisions are left to private individuals acting in response to the market forces of demand and supply. However, the market system does not perform some tasks satisfactorily and the government therefore enters the market to assist the system to produce results that are in accordance with the goals of society.

The government plays an important role in a market-oriented economy. First, government intervention in a market-oriented economy is often necessary to protect individual freedom, to protect the institution of private property, to enforce contracts, and to regulate economic activity. Thus, laws and regulations and public policies exist to ensure that these objectives are net.

Second, government intervention is often necessary to ensure that social problems do not arise from a socially unjust distribution of income. For example, under a market-oriented economy, individuals who own large quantities of valuable resources and who use them where they make sizeable contributions to the economy's output will likely receive huge incomes, while those individuals who happen to be in less fortunate circumstances may hardly be able to afford the bare necessities of life. In this case, government may intervene to achieve what is considered to be social justice.

Finally, government may intervene in a market-oriented economy to ensure that the environment is protected from abuse that will harm society. The enacting and enforcement of a law forbidding the dumping of waste into the environment is an example of the role of government intervention into a market-oriented economy.

Problem 4-6

In many countries, government provides free elementary and secondary education. How can such use of public funds be justified?

Requirement and Clue: *What is required here is an argument that society benefits from a more educated population.*

Solution:

Education provides benefits not only to the recipient directly, but also to society as a whole. A better educated population implies a better educated labour force and generally a more productive economy. It can also be argued that a more educated population benefits society by creating better informed and socially involved citizens. Since the entire society benefits from education, then public expenditure on education is justified.

Problem 4-7

How does a free enterprise economy system answer the question, "What to produce"?

Requirement and Clue: *You are required to explain how the workings of a free enterprise economic system result in a decision regarding what goods and services will be produced and in what quantities. A brief definition of a free enterprise economic system may be included, but it is not necessary. It is expected that you show some awareness of the meaning of the question, "What to produce"?*

Solution:

A free enterprise economic system is one in which most economic decisions are made by private individuals and firms interacting in a system of markets and prices to achieve their economic objectives. What to produce refers to what goods and services will the economy produce and in what quantities.

Firms in a free enterprise economic system engage in production because they hope to make a profit by selling the product at a price that exceeds the cost of production. It follows then, that firms will produce what consumers want to buy. Consumers express their wants by their behaviour in the market. Firms respond by producing those goods and services that receive the highest number of dollar votes. Suppose a manufacturing company decides to produce a certain product called *asitis*, and then find out that consumers are unwilling to spend their money on that particular product. The firm will soon discover that the production of *asitis* is not profitable and would put its resources into some other venture. By their decision not to purchase *asitis,* consumers have communicated effectively to the manufacturing company that they do not want *asitis* produced.

Problem 4-8

What is meant by consumer sovereignty?

Requirement and Clue: *This is a definitional problem. There is no need to write all you know about the concept of consumer sovereignty. You are not even required to explain how it works. All that is required is a clear statement of the meaning of the term.*

Solution:

Consumer sovereignty refers to the role of consumers in determining what goods and services will be produced in an economy and in what quantities. It refers to the idea that consumers, by their buying behaviour, that is, by their dollar votes, have the power to determine ultimately what is produced.

Problem 4-9

How does a free enterprise economic system determine how goods and services are produced?

Requirement and Clue: *Your task here is to explain how the decision regarding the method of production to be used is made in a free enterprise economic system.*

Solution:

The economic system must have a way of organizing its productive resources in order to provide the members of the society with appropriate quantities of goods and services. A mechanism must exist for shifting resources away from uses that contribute less to consumers' satisfaction and toward uses that contribute more to consumers' satisfaction.

In a free enterprise economic system, individual producers decide on the methods of production (that is, the technology to be used) but their decisions are guided by the system of prices and markets. If the goal of a producer is to earn as large a profit as possible, then the producer will use the method of production with the lowest cost; that is, the producer will use an efficient method of production.

Problem 4-10

How does a free enterprise economic system answer the question of the distribution of output among members of the society?

Requirement and Clue: *This question tests your understanding of the "For whom" question in microeconomics and your knowledge of how the free enterprise system addresses the problem. People's ability to buy depends on their income. How is income determined in a free enterprise economic system? Here is where your focus should lie.*

Solution:

In a free enterprise economic system, the task of distributing the economy's output among members of the society is accomplished mainly through the market system. The share of the total output that individuals receive depends mainly on their abilities to purchase goods and services. The ability of any individual to purchase goods and services depends on the individual's income, which in turn depends on the quantity and quality of human and physical resources over which that individual has control. If the market places a high value on particular resources, their owners will receive large payments for their use and will be able to obtain a large share of the total output of goods and services. Individuals who own very few resources that are poorly employed will receive low incomes and consequently, only small portions of the total output. Thus, the distribution of the economy's total output in a free enterprise economic system depends largely on the distribution of income, which in turn depends on the distribution of resources among the members of society.

Problem 4-11

How does a free enterprise economic system answer the three basic questions of microeconomics?

Requirement and Clue: *Before you can answer this question, you need to know what a free enterprise economic system is and the three basic microeconomic questions. Having settled that in your head, you must now consider how these three questions are solved through the workings of a free enterprise economic system.*

Solution:

A free enterprise economic system is one in which most economic decisions are made by private individuals and firms interacting in a system of markets and prices to achieve their economic objectives. The three basic questions of microeconomics are: (1) what goods and services will be produced and in what quantities, (2) how the economy's inputs (resources) will be used to produce those goods and services, and (3) who will get the goods and services that the economy produces.

What to Produce

Firms in a free enterprise economic system engage in production because they hope to make a profit by selling the product at a price that exceeds the cost of production. It follows then, that firms will produce what consumers want to buy. Consumers express their wants by their behaviour in the market. Firms respond by producing those goods and services that receive the highest number of dollar votes.

How to produce

In a free enterprise economic system, individual producers decide on the methods of production (that is, the technology to be used) but their decisions are guided by the system of prices and markets. If the goal of a producer is to earn as large a profit as possible, then the producer will use the method of production with the lowest cost; that is, the producer will use an efficient method of production.

For whom to produce

The free enterprise system solves the question of the distribution of the economy's output by determining, in markets, the value of resources and the incomes that they generate. . If the market places a high value on particular resources, their owners will receive large payments for their use and will be able to obtain a large share of the total output of goods and services. Individuals who own very few resources that are poorly employed will receive low incomes and consequently, only small portions of the total output. Thus, the distribution of the economy's total output in a free enterprise economic system depends largely on the distribution of income, which in turn depends on the distribution of resources among the members of society.

Problem 4-12

In most countries, there are no laws forcing authors to write books; yet, when you register for your courses, you are confident that there will be textbooks in the bookstores for your courses. Why?

Requirement and Clue: *This is an application problem. By carefully examining it, you will see that it is referring to the problem of what to produce. Essentially, you are required to explain how a market-oriented economy decides to produce textbooks for students.*

Solution:

Authors know that students are willing to purchase textbooks, so in a free enterprise economic system, they write them in the hope of finding publishers who are willing to publish them and pay royalties to the authors. The publishers, on the other hand, publish the books in the hope of making a profit in the process. Although there is no direct command to authors or publishers to produce books, they respond to market signals, which indicate to them that writing and publishing textbooks can be a profitable undertaking.

Problem 4-13

What is meant by a "mixed economy"?

Requirement and Ckue: *This is a definitional problem. There is no need for you to write a term paper on mixed economies. That would be far beyond the requirements of this question. Simply define a mixed economy and give examples. A brief mention of a completely free market economy and a command economy for comparison may be helpful but not absolutely necessary.*

Solution:

In contrast to an entirely free market enterprise economy where private individuals and firms exercise total control over the economy's resources, and a totally planned economy where all resources and owned and controlled by the government, a mixed economy is one where public and privately owned enterprises exist. The *mixture* is one of government and private enterprises.

In the real world, all economies are "mixed" to some extent. But the economies of the United States, Canada, the United Kingdom and Germany are examples of major mixed economies.

Problem 4-14

Briefly define the circular flow model.

Requirement and Clue: *The word "briefly" is underlined for emphasis. You cannot ignore it. All that you are required to do here is to provide a clear definition of the circular flow model.*

Solution:

The circular flow model is an economic model—a simplification of a real economy—showing the flow of resources, goods and services, expenditures, and income between sectors of the economy.

Problem 4-15

Define each of the following terms:

a. *Market*
b. *Product market*
c. *Factor market*
d. *Real flows*

Requirement and Clue: *You are required just to state what each of the terms is, giving examples if you can. You are not asked to write an essay on the terms or concepts.*

Solution:

a. A market is a mechanism that facilitates the buying and selling of goods and services and resources.
b. A product market is a market in which goods and services are bought and sold. An example of a product market is the market for shoes.
c. A factor market is the market in which factor of production or resources are bought and sold. An example of a factor market is the market for steel.
d. Real flows are flows of physical goods and services and of resources. An example of a real flow is the flow of goods and services from firms to households.

Problem 4-16

What is meant by real flows and money flows in a simple circular flow model?

Requirement and Clue: *What is required here is the identification of real and money flows in a simple circular model.*

Solution:

Real flows are flows of resources and goods and services. In a simple circular flow model, resources such as land, labour, and capital flow from households to firms, and finished goods and services flow from firms to households. These are the real flows.

Money flows are the flows of money that result from purchasing resources and finished goods and services. Payments made by firms to households for resources, and payments made by households to firms for finished goods and service are examples of money flows in the circular flow model.

Problem 4-17

Clearly describe the two types of markets in the simple circular flow model.

Requirement and Clue: *Before you can describe the markets in question, you must know what they are. Think of the simple circular model and identify the two markets in your head and then provide the solution. Note that the solution involves a little more than simply defining the markets.*

Solution:

The two types of markets in the simple circular flow model are the product market and the factor market. The product market is the market in which firms sell finished goods and services to households. Money is used to effect the transfer of goods and services from firms to households. The market for ipods is an example of a product market. In this market, the buyers are the households while the sellers are the firms.

The factor market (also called the resource market) is the market in which households sell resources (land, labour, capital, and entrepreneurial services) to firms. Money is used to effect the transfer of resources (factors of production) from households to firms. The market for labour services is an example of a factor market. In this market, the buyers are the firms while the sellers are the households.

Problem 4-18

Use a simple circular flow diagram to illustrate the flows of resources, goods and services, and money in an economy.

Requirement and Clue: *Essentially, you are to draw and explain a simple circular flow diagram.*

Solution:

Below is a simple circular flow diagram. It shows households and businesses, product and resource markets, and flows of resources, finished goods and services, and money.

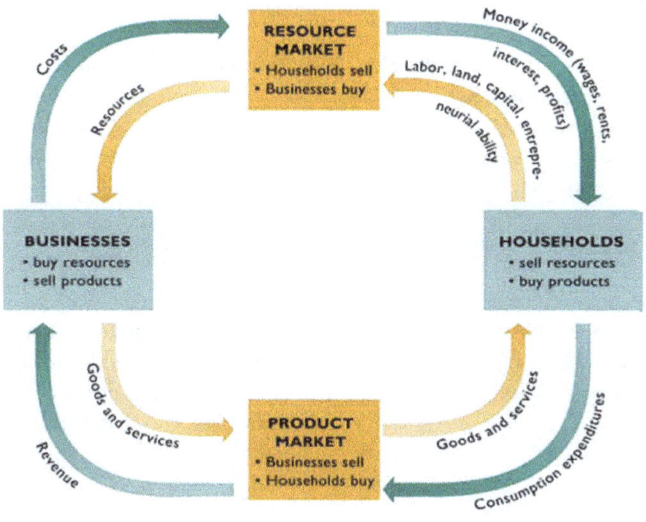

There is a flow of resources from the households to the resource market and a flow of money/costs from the business sector to the resource market. Households sell and businesses buy resources in the resource market. After the transaction, there is a flow of resources from the resource market to the businesses and a flow of money (income) from the resource market to the households. Firms/ businesses use the resources to produce goods and services which are sold in the product market. Thus there is a flow of goods and services from the firms to the product market. Households buy and firms sell goods and services in the product market. Thus, there is a flow of money from households to the product market. After the transaction, there is a flow of goods and services from the resource market to the households and a flow on money from the product market to the firms.

Problem 4-19

In the simple circular flow model, the roles of households and firms are reversed in the factor and product markets. Explain.

Requirement and Clue: *This problem is designed to test your understanding of the roles of the key actors in the circular flow model. The solution calls for a statement of the roles of households and firms in the factor and product markets.*

Solution:

Most people probably think of households as buyers of goods and services and firms as sellers of goods and services. That, of course, is true of the product market. Firms sell their output of goods and services in that market and households buy finished goods and services in that market. But in the factor market, the roles of households and firms are reversed. In this market, firms are buyers while households are sellers. Firms buy resources and households sell resources in this market. Thus we see that households and firms are both buyers and sellers.

Problem 4-20

How is labour accounted for in the circular flow model?

Requirement and Clue: *The solution requires you to determine where labour fits into the circular flow model. To do this you must know whether labour is a factor of production or a finished product. Having decided that labour is a resource, then it will be accounted for in the factor market.*

Solution:

Labour is a factor of production—a resource that is used along with other factors of production to produce finished goods and services and other resources. In the circular flow model, households provide labour by selling labour services in the factor market to firms. Firms then use the labour services to produce finished goods and services to be sold in the product market to households.

Problem 4-21

What set of transactions that normally occur in a real economy are omitted from the simple circular flow model?

Requirement and Clue: *The problem is testing your familiarity with transactions in a real economy and with the limitations of the simple circular flow model. You are expected to identify transactions that are, for simplicity, omitted from the circular flow model, even though they are normal in a real economy.*

Solution:

One of the limitations of the simple circular flow model is its exclusion of transactions between firms and between individuals. In a real economy, firms do buy goods and services from other firms, and consumers do carry our transactions between each other. However, these types of transactions are not captured in the simple circular flow model. The simple circular flow model also assumes no economic role for the government. In reality however, there are transactions between firms and the government and between individuals and the government. For example, private firms provide aircrafts and road construction services to the government, and the government engages the services of households in a wide range of employment activities.

Problem 4-22

Indicate whether each of the following is true or false as it relates to the simple circular flow model with only households and firms:

a. *Households sell resources to the firms.*
b. *Firms purchase finished goods from the households.*
c. *Households' income includes wages, rent, and interest.*
d. *Firms sell their products in the factor market.*
e. *Households buy resources in the factor market and sell goods and services in the product market.*
f. *Households operate only in the product market, buying goods and services.*
g. *Households and firms operate in both product and factor markets.*
h. *Firms earn dividends for their entrepreneurial services.*

Requirement and Clue: *You should read each statement carefully and then determine whether it is true or false. Remember to consider the solution as it relates to the simple circular flow model.*

Solution:

a. True
b. False
c. True
d. False
e. False
f. False
g. True
h. False

Multiple-Choice

In each case, circle the letter that corresponds with the correct answer.

1. An economic system is:

a. the same as a political system

b. not necessary for production and distribution of goods and services

c. a set of laws, institutions and customs whereby a society accomplishes the task of producing goods and service

d. a mechanism for ensuring economic freedom, equitable distribution of wealth, fair competition, and social justice

Answer: c

Reason: *It is the function of an economic system to produce and distribute goods and services to satisfy consumers' wants.*

2. A market-oriented economy is one where:

a. money is the most important thing for every member of society

b. most economic decisions are made by households and firms responding to market forces

c. the government forces all individuals and firms to comply with the dictates of capitalism

d. there is a tendency for markets to develop but their development is prevented because of the disadvantages of market-determined decisions

Answer: b

Reason: *A market-oriented economy is one in which a system of prices and markets dictates the flow of resources and goods and services.*

3. All modern economies are:

a. mixed economies
c. capitalistic

b. socialistic
d. command economies

Answer: a

Reason: *All real world economies combine private ownership and decision making and public enterprise.*

4. An advantage of a free enterprise economic system is:

a. the ability to generate full employment at all times

b. freedom of choice by consumers

c. government assurance of huge profits for businesses

d. guarantee of an equitable distribution of income

Answer: b

Reason: *One of the greatest advantages of a free enterprise economy is that consumers enjoy freedom of choice.*

5. A major weakness of a market-oriented economy is that:

a. it does not guarantee full employment

b. government intervention tends to be pervasive

c. choices of individuals and firms are severely limited

d. it is relatively inefficient

Answer: a

Reason: *Because individuals enjoy freedom of choice regarding the use of their resources in a market-oriented economy, the economy may fail to generate full employment.*

6. Features of a free enterprise economic system include:

a. the right of private individuals and groups to own property

b. freedom of enterprise

c. reliance on the price system

d. all of the above

Answer: d

Reason: *The features listed in choices a, b, and c are all characteristics of a free enterprise economic system.*

7. Which of the following is a distinguishing feature of a free enterprise economic system?

a. Private ownership of economic resources

b. Limited use of money

c. Use of capital as opposed to labour

d. Pervasive government intervention

Answer: a

Reason: *Private ownership and control of resources is a feature of a free enterprise economy.*

8. An example of a market-oriented economic systems:

a. the economy of the United States

b. the Canadian economy

c. the economy of the United Kingdom

d. any of the above

Answer: d

Reason: *The economies listed are all market-oriented economies.*

9. The economies of Cuba and the People's Republic of China are examples of:

a. pure capitalism

b. centrally planned economies

c. market-oriented economies

d. free enterprise economies

Answer: b

Reason: *Cuba and China are classified as centrally planned economies.*

10. Which of the following is a weakness of a free enterprise economic system?

a. It may produce economic instability

b. It may not encourage the production of public goods

c. It may not distribute income equitably

d. All of the above

Answer: d

Reason: *The issues cited in choices a, b, and c all apply to a free enterprise economic system.*

11. A mixed economy is:

a. one that has difficulty deciding what to produce and how to produce it

b. one that is mandated to produce a wide mixture of

goods and services

c. one that allows both private and public ownership and control of the means of production

d. one where the government decides on the mix of output that should be produced

Answer: c

Reason: *In a mixed economy, there is a combination (mixture) of private enterprise and public ownership of resources.*

12. Which of the following functions the price system does not perform?

a. Informing producers of consumers' wants

b. Determining the most efficient method of production

c. Conserving the use of scarce resources

d. Redistributing income among the owners of the factors of production

Answer: d

Reason: *The price system does not redistribute income; public policy may do that.*

13. Under a free market economic system, the government does not:

a. set all wages and prices

b. enforce contracts

c. allow the institution of private property

d. play any role in society

Answer: a

Reason: Under a free market economy, the system of prices and markets sets wages and prices.

14. Which of the following statements is true of a market-oriented economy?

a. It solves the problem of what to produce but not how to produce

b. It solves the problem of how to produce but not what to produce

c. It solves the problem of how to produce, what to produce, but not for whom to produce

d. It solves the problem of what to produce, how to produce, and for whom to produce

Answer: d

Reason: *In a market-oriented economy, the fundamental economic problems of what, how, and for whom are dealt with by the system of prices and markets.*

15. A free enterprise economic system solves the question of what to produce by:

a. conducting monthly surveys of consumer wants and preferences

b. allowing the government to make the decision

c. paying attention to what consumers are buying, that is, consumer sovereignty

d. none of the above

Answer: c

Reason: *Wanting to earn a profit, firms in a free enterprise economic system produce the goods and services that consumers indicate willingness and an ability to buy.*

16. Consumer sovereignty exists when:

a. consumers can do whatever they want without fear of being prosecuted

b. consumers ultimately determine what goods are produced by their dollar votes in markets

c. consumers are forced to abandon their preferences and purchase whatever firms produce and offer for sale

d. none of the above

Answer: b

Reason: *Consumer sovereignty is the concept that firms produce what consumers indicate by their buying behaviour they want firms to produce.*

17. The flow of resources, goods and services, expenditures, and income between households and firms is called:

a. the circular flow

b. producers' circle

c. consumer sovereignty

d. none of the above

Answer: a

Reason: *The circular flow describes the flow of resources, income, goods and services, and expenditures between households and firms.*

18. Which of the following is a true statement?

a. The product market is the market in which firms sell resources

b. The factor market is the market in which firms buy goods and services

c. The product market is the market in which households buy resources

d. The factor market is the market in which firms buy resources

Answer: d

Reason: *Firms buy factors of production (resources) in the factor market from households. They use these resources to produce goods and services.*

19. Flows of income and expenditures are:

a. real flows

b. money flows

c. normative flows

d. none of the above

Answer: b

Reason: *Income and expenditures are in monetary terms, as opposed to resources and goods and services that are in real terms.*

20. In the simple circular flow model, the flow of income from the factor market to households:

a. consists of wages, rent, interest & dividends, and profit

b. represents payment for factors of production

c. is a money flow as opposed to a real flow

d. all of the above

Answer: d

Reason: *Choices a and b amount to the same thing, and the flow of income is in monetary terms.*

True or False

Determine whether each of the following statements is true or false.

1. An economic system is characterized by a set of laws, institutions, and customs by means of which a society is governed.

Answer: False

Explanation: *The statement describes a political system, not an economic system.*

2. An economic system is a set of mechanisms—laws, institutions, and customs—by means of which the society accomplishes the task of producing goods and services.

Answer: True

3. Economic decision makers can be classified into households or consumers, firms or producers, and government authorities.

Answer: True

4. In all free enterprise economic systems, most of the economy's resources are privately owned.

Answer: True

5. Examples of market-oriented economies are the United States, Canada, the United Kingdom and Germany.

Answer: True

6. The economies of the People's Republic of China and Cuba are examples of market-oriented economies.

Answer: False

Explanation: *The economies listed are centrally planned economies.*

7. The economies of the People's Republic of China and Cuba are examples of centrally planned economies.

Answer: True

8. The basis of a free enterprise economic system is the institution of private property.

Answer: True

9. In a free enterprise economic system, consumers are free, within certain legal and social constraints, to use their income to purchase the goods and services that maximize their satisfaction.

Answer: True

10. In a free enterprise economic system, the government intervenes to ensure that all members of society get an equal share of the economy's output of goods and services.

Answer: False

Explanation: *In a free enterprise economic system, there is little or no government intervention, and certainly not to ensure equal distribution of output.*

11. The freedom of choice that is characteristic of the free enterprise economic system more often than not results in chaos.

Answer: False

Explanation: *Order and not chaos results from freedom of choice.*

12. The free enterprise economic system ensures that the goods and services that consumers want are those that are produced.

Answer: True

13. One advantage of a free enterprise economic system is that the goods and services that consumers want are produced without any deliberate coordinated decision-making.

Answer: True

14. One of the advantages of a free enterprise economic system is that it guarantees the production of public goods such as education and general sanitation.

Answer: False

Explanation: *A disadvantage is that it may not produce sufficient public goods.*

15. A major weakness of a free enterprise economic system is that it has no way of dealing with the fundamental economic questions of what, how and for whom.

Answer: False

Explanation: *It's a strength that the free enterprise economic system deals with the questions in a relatively efficient manner.*

16. A mixed economy is one in which the government forces producers to produce a good blend of public and private goods.

Answer: False

Explanation: A mixed economy is one in which there is a mixture of private and public ownership of resources.

17. In practice, all economies are mixed economies with varying degrees of government intervention.

Answer: True

18. The free enterprise economic system distributes more goods and services to those individuals and groups with more dollar votes.

Answer: True

19. Government intervention is never warranted and cannot be justified in a market-oriented economic system.

Answer: False

Explanation: *Government intervention is justified in some cases.*

20. In a simple circular flow model, households exchange factors of production for income, and firms exchange goods and services for revenue.

Answer: True

21. The circular flow model shows flows of resources and flows of goods and services but not flows of money.

Answer: false

Explanation: It does show money flows as well.

22. The factor market is the market in which goods and services are traded while the product market is the market in which resources are traded.

Answer: False

Explanation: Goods and services are sold in a product market while resources are bought and sold in the factor market.

23. In the simple circular flow model with money as the means of exchange, only money flows are shown.

Answer: False

Explanation: Real as well as money flows are shown.

24. In the circular flow model, money flows represent the monetary values of the real flows.

Answer: True

25. One of the advantages of the simple circular flow model is that it shows clearly how the prices of individual goods and services are determined.

Answer: False

Explanation: One of the disadvantages of the simple circular flow model is that it does not show how prices are determined.

Completion
(Fill in the blanks)

Use each word or combination of words from the list exactly once.
*(**Hint**: Proceed by elimination)*

Word list

Consumer — Economic — Economy — Factor / Resource x 2 — Free — Free Enterprise / Market-Oriented x 2 — Government — Interest and Dividends — Market — Mixed — Money — Price System — Private — Product — Profit — Property — Public or Government — Real — Rent — Resources — Resources / Factors Of Production — Show / Does Not Show x 2 — Sovereignty — System — Wages

Questions

1. A(n) ____________ ____________ is a set of mechanisms by means of which a society accomplishes the task of producing goods and services.
2. In a(n) ____________ enterprise economic system, most of the factors of production are owned privately. (free)
3. The economies of the United States, Canada, and Great Britain are examples of ____________ ____________ economies.
4. The basis of a ____________ ____________ economic system is the right of private persons and private groups to own property.
5. The right of private individuals and private groups to own property is referred to as the institution of ____________ ____________
6. A free enterprise economic system is essentially a(n) ____________ ____________ because a system of prices and markets coordinates the allocation of resources.
7. In practice, all economies are ____________ economies.
8. In a market-oriented economic system, consumers ultimately determine what to produce. This idea is known as ____________ ____________.
9. In a free enterprise economic system, consumers and firms play major roles in determining the allocation of scarce resource, while the ____________ plays a minor role.
10. A mixed economy is one in which both private and ____________ ownership of resources exists.
11. In a free enterprise economic system, the incentive to coordinate the use of resources in production and consumption is facilitated by the ____________ ____________.
12. The circular flow model shows the flows of income, expenditures, goods and services, and ____________.
13. In the circular flow model, households sell ____________ in the ____________ market.
14. In the circular flow model, firms buy resources in the ____________ market and sell finished goods and services in the ____________ market.
15. The flow of income from the factor market to households consists of ____________, ____________, ____________, and ____________.
16. In the circular flow model, the flows of resources and goods and services are ____________ flows, while the flows of income and expenditures are ____________ flows.
17. The simple circular flow model without a government sector ____________ (shows, does not show) transactions between firms.
18. The circular flow model ____________ (shows, does not show) how the prices of goods and services are determined.

Solution

1. (economic system)
2. (free)
3. (free enterprise / market-oriented)
4. (free enterprise / market-oriented)
5. (private property)
6. (market economy)
7. (mixed)
8. (consumer sovereignty)
9. (government)
10. (public or government)
11. (price system)
12. (resources)
13. (resources or factors of production, factor or resource)
14. (factor or resource, product)
15. (wages, rent, interest and dividends, and profit [in any order])
16. (real, money)
17. (does not show)
18. (does not show)

5

DEMAND & SUPPLY

LEARNING OBJECTIVES

In connection with this module, you should be able to:

1. define demand
2. distinguish between demand and quantity demanded
3. identify the factors affecting quantity demanded
4. define supply
5. distinguish between supply and quantity supplied
6. identify the factors affecting quantity supplied
7. explain market price determination
8. use demand-supply analysis to solve simple economic problems

DEFINITIONS & CONCEPTS

You should be able to define the following terms and concepts:

demand schedule	supply curve
law of demand	substitutes
market-size effect	complements
income effect	joint products
substitution effect	supply shifters
demand curve	surplus
normal good	shortage
inferior good	equilibrium price
independent good	equilibrium quantity
demand shifters	price floor
supply schedule	price ceiling
law of supply	black market

SYNOPSIS

Demand and supply play important roles in a market-oriented economy. **Demand** is the term used to refer to the various quantities of a good or service that people will be willing and able to purchase at various price during a period of time. Demand may be represented by a **demand schedule,** a **demand curve,** or a **demand function.**

The **law of demand** states that as the price of a product falls, other things being equal, the quantity demanded increases; and as the price of a product rises, other things being equal, the quantity demanded decreases. This inverse relationship between price and quantity demanded exists because as the price falls, (1) more people are drawn into the market, (2) the real income or purchasing power of the buyers rises, and (3) people will substitute the cheaper product for a more expensive product.

Factors affecting quantity demanded include:

- the price of the product
- the incomes of buyers
- prices of complements and substitutes
- tastes and preferences
- the number of buyers
- expectations

A change in the price of a product will cause a change in quantity demanded (i.e., a movement along the demand curve). A change in a determinant other than the price of the product will cause a change in demand (i.e., s shift of the demand curve).

Supply refers to the various quantities of a good or service that sellers will be willing and able to offer for sale at various prices during a period of time. The **law of supply** states that as the price of a product falls, other things being equal, the quantity offered for sale decreases; and as the price of a product rises, other things being equal, the quantity offered for sale increases.

Factors other than price that affect the quantity offered for sale include:

- the number of sellers
- prices of related goods (production complements and substitutes)
- technology
- production costs
- expectations

A change in the price of a product causes a movement along the supply curve while a change in a non-price determinant causes a shift of the supply curve.

Equilibrium price and **equilibrium quantity** occur at the point of intersection of the demand and supply curves. When the market is in equilibrium, neither a **shortage** nor a **surplus** exists. An increase in demand, other things being equal, will raise equilibrium price and equilibrium quantity. A fall in demand, other things being equal, will lower equilibrium price and equilibrium quantity. An increase in supply, other things being equal, will lower equilibrium price and increase equilibrium quantity. A fall in supply, other things being equal, will raise equilibrium price and reduce equilibrium quantity.

A **price floor** will generally result in a surplus while a **price ceiling** will generally result in a shortage. A price ceiling may also result in a **black market**.

5

DEMAND & SUPPLY

Concepts, Definitions & Problems

Problem 5-1

What do economists mean by a market? What are the requirements for a market to exist?

Requirement and Clue: *The problem has two parts, both of which must be answered. The solution requires that you understand and can demonstrate what a market is, as understood by economists. You are then required to state the elements without which there can be no market.*

Solution:

Economists think of a market as a mechanism or institution that facilitates exchange by bringing buyers and sellers together. Although it may be a specific geographical area, the spatial condition is not necessary for a market to exist. To economists, a market exists as long as buyers and sellers are in contact to do business.

The existence of a market requires four things. First, there must be at least one *buyer*. Buying and selling are the fundamental activities in markets. There can be no buying unless there is at least one buyer. Second, there must be at least one *seller*. Exchange—a market fundamental—suggests the existence of at least one seller. Third, there must be something to buy or sell, something to trade. That "something" is a good, service, or resource, or even a idea. It is a *product* without which, there can be no market. Finally, buying and selling (trading) requires a *price* at which exchange takes place. Price is often a deciding factor in whether or not exchange does take place.

Problem 5-2

Briefly define the market process.

Requirement and Clue: *Your task is to state clearly what the market process is. You must resist the temptation to write reams about the market. A simple straightforward definition is sufficient. Be careful not to confuse the market process with a market. Do not ignore the request for brevity.*

Solution:

Buyers and sellers are the players in the market. The buying and selling decisions of the players are reflected in their behaviour in the marketplace. The market process is the process by which buyers and sellers exchange goods and services. In this process, prices play a crucial role in determining the flow of goods and services between market players.

Problem 5-3

Give a brief definition of the concept of demand.

Requirement and Clue: *Although many people may have different ideas of what constitutes demand, you are expected to define demand as used in economics.*

Solution:

Demand refers to the various quantities of a good or service that people will be willing and able to buy at various possible prices during a period of time.

Problem 5-4

What methods do economists use to illustrate demand?

Requirement and Clue: *This problem is designed to test your knowledge of the tools used to show demand. Think of all the ways that demand may be represented.*

Solution:

Economists use a variety of methods/tools to depict concepts. They use words (a verbal statement of the concept), demand schedules (tables that show the relationship between price and quantity), demand curves (graphs that show the relationship between price and quantity) and demand functions (equations that express the relationship between price and quantity).

Problem 5-5

Distinguish between demand and quantity demanded.

Requirement and Clue: *Think of an effective way to illustrate the difference between these two concepts.*

Solution:

The difference between demand and quantity demanded is not just a matter of semantics. There is, in fact, a real difference. Demand is a *relationship* between price and quantity demanded. It refers to a whole range of prices with the various quantities associated with them. Quantity demanded, on the other hand, is just one quantity that will be bought *at some specific price.*

A demand schedule can be used to illustrate the difference. Consider the following table showing a relationship between the price of an item and the quantity demanded.

Price	Quantity demanded
10	60
9	70
8	80
7	90
6	100

The entire table, a demand schedule, represents demand. But quantity demanded is represented by any of the numbers in the right hand column. For example, 70 is the quantity that will be demanded at a price of $9, and 100 is the quantity that will be demanded at a price of $6.

A demand curve can also be used to illustrate the difference between demand and quantity demanded. Consider the following diagram.

The entire curve represents demand whereas quantity demanded is represented by a point such as A on the demand curve.

Problem 5-6

What do economists mean by "demand" and what is a demand curve?

Requirement and Clue: *This is a two-part problem and each part must be addressed. You must provide a clear statement of the meaning of demand and then proceed to describe a demand curve.*

Solution:

Demand refers to the various quantities of a good or service that people are willing and able to buy at various prices during a period of time. The desire for a good does not by itself constitute demand for that good. The ability to buy it must also be present.

A demand curve is a graphical representation of the various quantities of a good or service that people will be willing and able to buy at various prices during a period of time. The demand curve is drawn on the assumption that influences other than the price of the item being considered—factors such as income, prices of related goods, number of buyers, etc.)—remain constant.

The curve below labelled DD, illustrates a demand curve.

Note that the curve is downward sloping depicting the inverse relationship between price and quantity demanded.

Problem 5-7

Explain what economists mean by "demand" and give an example to illustrate the concept.

Requirement and Clue: *You must know that demand has a specific meaning in economics. You are required to demonstrate that knowledge. You are also required to give an example to support your knowledge of the concept.*

Solution:

Demand refers to the various quantities of a good or service that people are willing and able to buy at various prices during a period of time. The desire for a good does not by itself constitute demand for that good. The ability to buy it must also be present.

For example, perhaps people are willing and able to buy 1,000 smart phones per week when the price per smart phone is $400 each; 1,050 when the price is $350; 1,100 when the price is $300; 1,150 when the price is $250; 1,200 when the price is $200; and 1,250 when the price is $150. This information is shown in the following table which is called a demand schedule, representing the demand for smart phones.

Price ($)	Quantity demanded per week
400	1,000
350	1,050
300	1,100
250	1,150
200	1,200
150	1,250

This same information can be plotted on a graph known as a demand curve (shown below) which is also a way of illustrating demand.

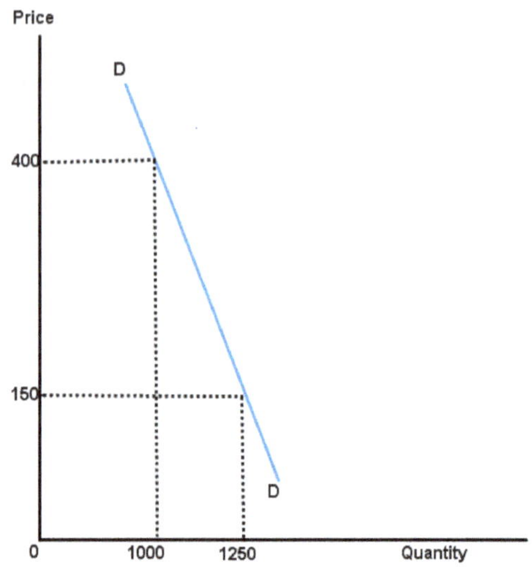

Problem 5-8

The following table represents the demand schedule for cornflakes for a one-week period. Construct the demand curve for cornflakes.

Price ($)	Quantity of boxes demanded per week
5.50	70,000
5.00	80,000
4.50	90,000
4.00	100,000
3.50	110,000
3.00	120,000
2.50	130,000
2.00	140,000

Requirement and Clue: *This problem is straightforward. With price on the vertical axis and quantity of the horizontal axis, you are to plot the data from the table on a graph. This graph will be the demand curve for cornflakes.*

Solution:

See graph below.

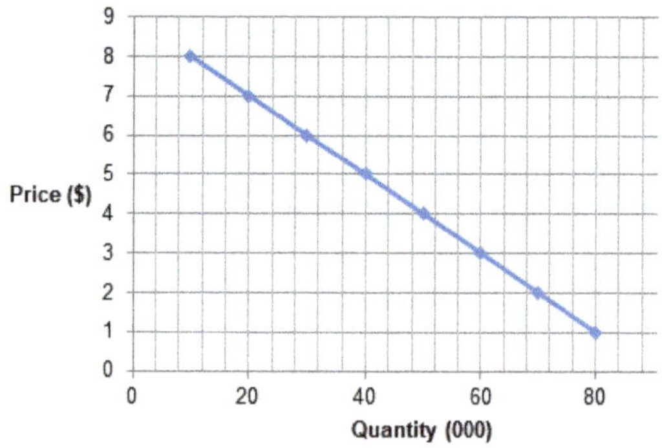

Problem 5-9

The following demand curve is given for novels for a particular period of time.

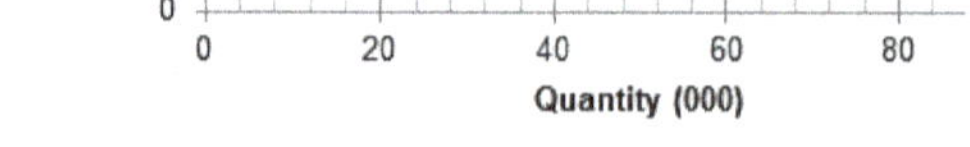

(a) *If the price of a novel was $4, how many novels would people buy?*

(b) *Why wouldn't they buy 60,000 at a price of $4?*

(c) *Given that people bought 70,000 novels, what was the price?*

(d) *Why wouldn't the price have been $3 when they bought 70,000?*

Requirement and Clue: *This problem is associated with one's ability to read graphs. For each price, there is a unique quantity that is associated with it, and for each quantity demanded, there is a unique price associated with it. Your task is to use the graph to locate any unique given price-quantity pair.*

Solution:

(a) According to the graph, the quantity that is associated with a price of $4 is 50,000. Thus we know that people will buy 50,000 novels when the price is $4.

(b) The point representing a quantity of 60,000 and a price of $4 lies off this demand curve and is therefore not a valid combination. The price that is associated with 60,000 novels is $3. Therefore the price would have to be $3 for 60,000 novels to be bought.

(c) The graph shows that the only price associated with a quantity of 70,000 is $2.

(d) The point representing a quantity of 70,000 and a price of $3 is not on this demand curve. If the price were $3, only 60,000 novels would have been bought.

Problem 5-10

Carefully state the law of demand.

Requirement and Clue: *What is required here is a clear statement of the relationship between price and quantity demanded. Remember to include the "ceteris paribus" assumption.*

Solution:

The law of demand states that as the price of a good or service falls, other things being equal, the quantity demanded increases; as the price of a good or services rises, other things being equal, the quantity demanded decreases. In other words, an inverse relationship exists between the price of an item and the quantity of that item demanded.

It is important to note that the law does not say that if the price of an item falls, the quantity demanded will rise, and vice versa. It says that if the price falls and nothing else changes (other things being equal), then the quantity demanded will rise. So if the price of an item falls, and consumers' incomes also fall, the quantity demanded may not increase. This would not be a violation or negation of the law of demand, because other things did not remain constant.

Problem 5-11

What explanation can you give for the observation that people tend to buy more of an item when its price falls and less of it when its price rises?

Requirement and Clue: *Basically, you are being asked to explain the law of demand, that is, the inverse relationship between price and quantity demanded.*

Solution:

There are three explanations for the inverse relationship between price and quantity demanded: (1) the market –size effect, (2) the real income effect, and (3) the substitution effect.

As the price of an item falls, more and more people are drawn into the market. In other words, as the price falls, the size of the market increases, thus the quantity demanded increases. More people buy the item *as its price falls*. This is the market-size effect.

When the price of an item falls, other things being equal, the people who buy that item experience an increase in purchasing power or real income even if there is no change in their money income, so they buy more—they buy more as the price falls. This is the real income effect.

When the price of an item falls, some people will switch from other items that they were previously purchasing but that have now become relatively more expensive. That is, some people will substitute the cheaper item for a more expensive substitute. This is the substitution effect.

Problem 5-12

What are the major determinants of demand?

Requirement and Clue: *You are to discuss important factors that affect the demand for a good or service. It is crucial not to include the price of the good or service as a determinant of demand. The price of the good or service will affect the quantity demanded, not the demand. Think of factors other than the price of the item that will exert significant influence of the quantity demanded. In other words, think of factors that will shift the demand curve.*

Solution:

Some of the important determinants of demand are consumers' income, prices of related goods, consumers' tastes and preferences, consumer expectations of future prices and future incomes, and population.

Consumers' income: If consumers' incomes increase, they will tend to buy more goods and services because they will be able to afford to buy more, other things being equal. If their incomes decrease, they will tend to buy fewer goods and services. This will be the case for normal goods. For inferior goods, they will buy less as their incomes increase.

Prices of related goods: If the price of a substitute for a certain good increases, the demand for the good will increase as some people will switch from the substitute to the now relatively cheaper good. If the price of a substitute for a good or service decreases, the demand for the good will tend to decrease as some people will switch from the good to the relatively cheaper substitute. For example, if people consider limes and lemons to be substitutes and the price of lemons rises, they will tend to buy more limes, thus the demand for limes will increase.

If the price of a complement for a certain good rises, the demand for the good will decrease. Since they will buy less of the complement, they will also buy less of the good. If the price of a complement for a certain good falls, the demand for the good will increase. Since they will buy more of the complement, they will also buy more of the good. For example, if people consider french-fries and ketchup to be complements and the price of french-fries falls, they will buy more french-fries *and* more ketchup, thus the demand for ketchup will increase.

Tastes and preferences: People will tend to buy more of something for which they have a liking. If people's preference or taste for vegetarian food increases, their demand for vegetarian food will increase. If their liking decreases, their demand for vegetarian food will fall.

Expectations: People's expectations regarding the course of future prices will affect present demand for goods and services. If people expect the price of an item to rise, they are likely to increase their purchases of that item now to avoid paying the expected higher price in the future. On the other hand, if they expect the price of an item to fall, they will attempt to delay their purchases of that item now to take advantage of the lower future price.

People's expectations about future changes in their incomes will also influence the present demand for goods and services. If people expect substantial raises in their salaries sometime in the near future, they are likely to buy more goods and services even before the increase in income materializes. If people expect decreases in their incomes, they are likely to buy fewer goods and services. Thus, the demand for an item will tend to increase if future income is expected to rise and fall if future income is expected to fall.

Population: The more buyers there are to buy any item, the greater the demand for that item will be. The greater the population, the greater the number of potential buyers will be. Other things being equal, the demand for vegetables in a city with a population of 2,000,000 people will be greater than the demand for vegetables in a city with only 100,000 people. If the number of potential buyers increases, the demand for an item will likely increase.

Problem 5-13

What is the difference between:

(a) *normal goods and inferior goods?*

(b) *Substitutes and complements?*

Requirement and Clue: *First, you must know the meaning of these terms. Then you must state how normal goods differ from inferior goods and how substitutes differ from complements.*

Solution:

(a) Normal goods and inferior goods refer to people's responses to goods as their incomes change. If people buy more of a good when their incomes rise, and less when their incomes fall, then the good is a normal good. If they buy less of a good when their incomes rise then the good is an inferior good. These terms are not necessarily descriptions of the goods, but they provide information about people's responses to them as their incomes change. People tend to buy more of most goods when their incomes increase. This seems normal, hence the term "normal goods". If people's income rise, they tend to buy more new cars, more new furniture, more steaks, and more movie tickets. Such goods are normal goods. On the other hand, if people's incomes rise, they tend to buy fewer used furniture, fewer used clothing, fewer Kraft dinners, and fewer reconditioned (re-treaded) tires. Goods in this latter category are inferior goods.

(b) Substitutes are goods that can replace each other in use. For many purposes, lemons and limes, tea and coffee, pens and pencils, and milk and cream are substitutes. Complements, on the other hand, are goods that can be used together. If you buy more of one, you are likely to buy more of the other. Examples of complements are coffee and cream, cars and gasoline, computers and flash drives, and pillows and pillow cases.

Problem 5-14

What is the difference between a change in demand and a change in quantity demanded?

Requirement and Clue: *This problem is not just dealing with semantics. The two concepts are totally different and you are required to state that difference as clearly as possible.*

Solution:

A change in demand means that a different quantity is bought *at any given price* because of a change in a determinant of demand such as income, price of related good, expectations, population, etc. Note that a change in the price of the item being considered will not change the demand for the item.

A change in quantity demanded means that a different quantity of an item is demanded as the price of the item changes.

Graphically, a change in demand is illustrated by a shift of the entire demand curve, either to the right for an increase in demand as shown in the following diagram, from DD to D1D1, or to the left.

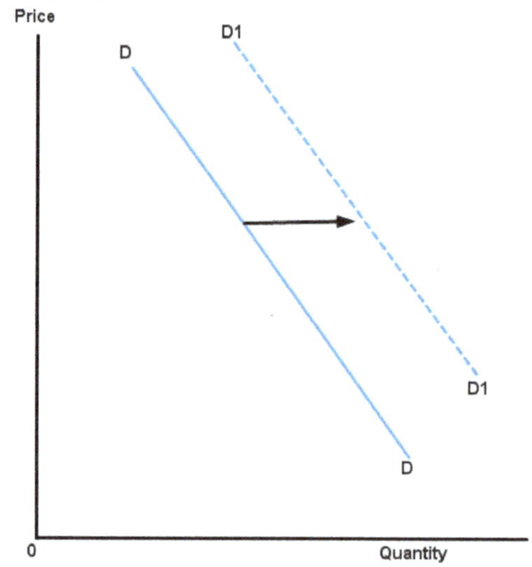

A change in quantity demanded is illustrated graphically by a movement along a given demand curve as shown as a movement from point A to point B on demand curve DD in the diagram below.

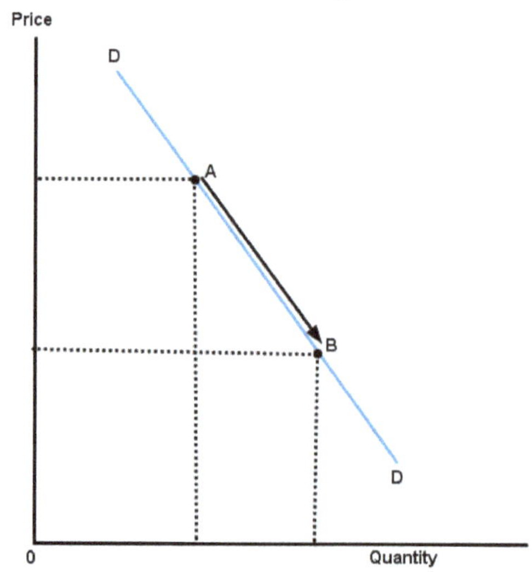

Problem 5-15

Determine whether each of the following represents a change in demand or a change in quantity demanded. In each case, indicate whether there is a shift in the demand curve or a movement along the demand curve.

a. *The price of eggs rises by 10 cents per dozen and consumers purchase fewer eggs.*
b. *The price of lap top computers falls and as a result, people buy more flash drives.*
c. *The price of electricity for heating purposes rises. As a result, homeowners turn down their thermostats to lower temperatures.*
d. *Households, on a whole, get income tax refunds and consequently take more frequent and longer vacations.*

Requirement and Clue: *This problem is designed to test your understanding of factors that change demand and those that change quantity demanded. The key is to determine whether the change is due to a change in the price of the item or to a change in one or more of the determinants of demand. If it's a price-induced change, then it's a change in quantity demanded represented by a movement along the demand curve. If it's a change in a determinant of demand, then it's a change in demand represented by a shift in the demand curve.*

Solution:

a. The increase in the quantity of eggs purchased is in response to a change in the price of eggs. Therefore, this is a change in quantity demanded. There will be a movement from one point on the demand curve to another.
b. The increase in the quantity of flash drives bought is due to a fall in the price of lap top computers. Since the change is not in response to a change in the price of flash drives, then this is a change in demand. The demand for flash drives increases so the demand curve shifts to the right.
c. In this case, homeowners are responding to an increase in the price if electricity. They purchase less (lower the thermostats) as the price rises. This is a change in quantity demanded which would be indicated by a movement along the demand curve.
d. Here, households are responding to a change in a variable other than the price of vacations. They buy more vacations because of an increase in their incomes caused by income tax refunds. This is an increase in demand which would be incicated by a shift in the demand curve.

Problem 5-16

One Tuesday afternoon you went to the grocery store to buy some oranges. Upon arriving at the store, you noticed that oranges were on sale at 20% below the regular price. Therefore, you bought more oranges than you intended to buy.

Did your demand for oranges increase?

Requirement and Clue: *Here, you must be careful not to confuse a change in demand with a change in quantity demanded. Yes, you bought more oranges, but that does not necessarily mean that your demand for oranges had increased. You must consider whether you bought more oranges because of the lower price or because of a change in a determinant of demand.*

Solution:

There is no indication here that income, tastes and preferences, prices of substitutes or complements, your expectations or any other determinant of demand had changed. Therefore, your demand for oranges did not change. What did change, however, is the quantity of oranges demanded in response to the change in the price of oranges. Expressed graphically, your demand curve did not shift, but there was a movement down the demand curve.

Problem 5-17

One week a grocer charged $2.99 for Sunkist oranges and sold 5,000 oranges. The next week, he brought in a stock of Navel oranges, raised the price to $3.99 and sold 6,000 oranges. Apparently, he sold more oranges when he raised the price. Is this a contradiction of the law of demand?

Requirement and Clue: *This solution requires that you pay careful attention to the law of demand. Did people buy more Sunkist oranges at a higher price? No. Did they buy more Navel oranges at a higher price? No. Did they buy more oranges at a higher price? This is what you need to explain.*

Solution:

According to the law of demand, as the price of <u>an item</u> rises, other things being equal, the quantity demanded will fall, and vice versa. In this problem, there are two items: Sunkist oranges and Navel oranges. On the surface, it may seem as if a greater quantity of the item (oranges) was bought as the price rose; but on closer examination, there are really two items being considered here: Sunkist oranges and Navel oranges. What is happening here is that there are two demand curves—one for Sunkist oranges and the other for Navel oranges. There is little doubt that if the price of Sunkist oranges had risen, other things being equal, the quantity demanded would have fallen; and if the price of Navel oranges had risen, the quantity demanded would have fallen, according to the law of demand. The law of demand remains intact.

Problem 5-18

Music Mack raised the price of a set of guitar strings from $10.99 to $12.99, informing his customers that guitar strings were in short supply. Expecting the price to rise even higher, Music Mack's customers bought more guitar strings at $12.99 than they bought at $10.99.

Is this a sign of an upward-sloping demand curve? Explain.

Requirement and Clue: *The question you need to ask is this: Did people buy guitar strings because Music Mack raised the price or because of the expectation of a higher price in the future? Clearly, the latter is the case. Your task then is to explain how an expected higher price led to an increase in demand for guitar strings.*

Solution:

People bought more guitar string not because of a rise in the price of guitar strings but because of the *expectation* of a higher price in the future. Their reasoning may have been along these lines. Since the price is expected to be higher in the future, it makes good sense to stock up on guitar strings now (they are not perishable) to avoid paying the future higher price. What we have here is a shift of a downward-sloping demand curve, not an upward-sloping demand curve.

Problem 5-19

What do economists mean by supply?

Requirement and Clue: *Although "supply" may be used in ordinary language to mean many different things, the term has a very definite meaning in economics. Your job is to provide the specific meaning of "supply" as used by economists.*

Solution:

As used by economists, supply refers to the various quantities of a good or service that sellers will be willing and able to sell at various prices during a period of time. It is an entire schedule of prices and their associated quantities. Supply must be distinguished from the quantity that will be offered for sale at some particular price, which is referred to as *quantity supplied.*

Problem 5-20

Define supply. What is a supply schedule?

Requirement and Clue: *This is another two-part problem. First, you must state precisely what supply is. Having done that, you proceed to a definition of a supply schedule. An example would be helpful here.*

Solution:

Supply refers to the various quantities of an item that sellers will be willing and able to offer for sale at various prices during a period of time.

A supply schedule is a tabular representation of the various quantities of an item that sellers will be willing and able to sell at various possible prices during a period of time. The following table is an example of a supply schedule.

Price *($)*	Quantity supplied per week *(000)*
10	60
15	80
20	100
25	120
30	140
35	160
40	180

The schedule shows that at a price of $10, the quantity supplied per week is 60,000. At a price of $15, the quantity supplied is 80,000; at a price of $20, the quantity supplied is 100,000, and so on.

Problem 5-21

What methods do economists use to illustrate supply?

Requirement and Clue: *This problem is designed to test your knowledge of the tools used to show supply. Think of all the ways that supply may be represented.*

Solution:

Economists use a variety of methods/tools to depict concepts. In the case of supply, they use words (a verbal statement of the concept), supply schedules (tables that show the relationship between price and quantity supplied), supply curves (graphs that show the relationship between price and quantity supplied) and supply functions (equations that express the relationship between price and quantity supplied).

Problem 5-22

What is the difference, if any, between supply and quantity supplied?

Requirement and Clue: *Think of an effective way to illustrate the difference between these two concepts.*

Solution:

There is an important difference between supply and quantity supplied. It is not just a matter of semantics. Supply is a *relationship* between price and quantity supplied. It refers to a whole range of prices with the various quantities associated with them. Quantity supplied, on the other hand, is just one quantity that will be offered for sale *at some specific price.*

A supply schedule can be used to illustrate the difference. Consider the table below showing a relationship between the price of an item and the quantity supplied.

The entire table, *a supply schedule*, represents supply. But *quantity supplied* is represented by any of the numbers in the right hand column. For example, 70 is the quantity that will be demanded at a price of $7, and 100 is the quantity that will be demanded at a price of $10.

Price	Quantity supplied
10	100
9	90
8	80
7	70
6	60
5	50
4	40
3	30

A supply curve can also be used to illustrate the difference between supply and quantity supplied. Consider the following diagram.

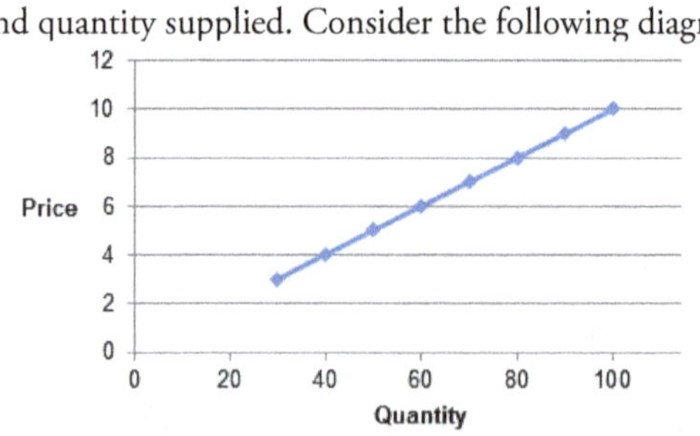

The entire curve represents supply whereas quantity supplied is represented by any point on the supply curve shown in the diagram.

Problem 5-23

Carefully state the law of supply.

Requirement and Clue: *The word "carefully" in the problem should not be ignored. It might just be a subtle reminder not to forget the ceteris paribus assumption.*

Solution:

According to the law of supply, a direct relationship exists between the price of an item and the quantity supplied. The law states that as the price of an item falls, *other things being equal*, the quantity offered for sale decreases; or alternatively, as the price of an item rises, *other things being equal*, the quantity offered for sale increases. Stated differently, the law says that sellers are motivated to offer more for sale at higher prices.

Problem 5-24

The following schedule represents the supply of a particular type of pen. Use the information to construct the supply curve for that kind of pen.

Price ($)	Quantity supplied (000)
0.40	100
0.50	120
0.60	140
0.70	160
0.80	180
0.90	200
1.00	220
1.10	240

Requirement and Clue: *Plotting the points in the supply schedule on a graph will give the supply curve. That's what you are required to do.*

Solution:

See graph below

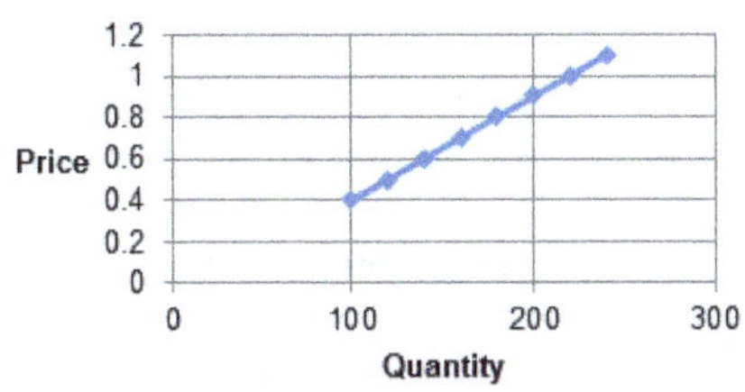

Problem 5-24

The following diagram shows the supply curve for CDs.

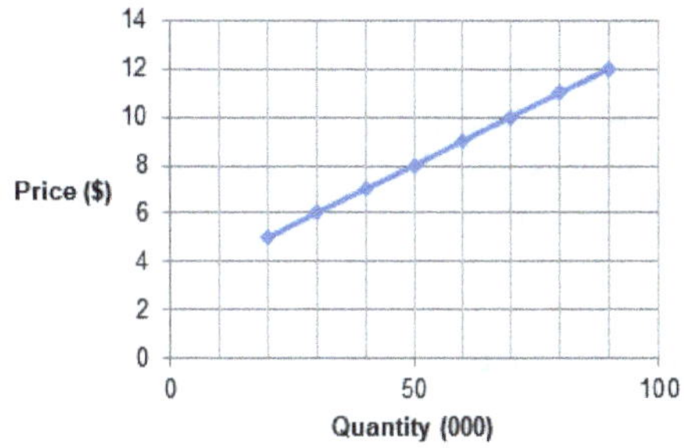

Use the graph to construct the supply schedule for CDs.

Requirement and Clue: *This problem is designed to test your ability to read information from a supply curve. Select each point on the graph and read its associated price and quantity. Record them on the supply schedule.*

Solution:

The table below is the resulting supply schedule.

Price ($)	Quantity supplied (000)
5	20
6	30
7	40
8	50
9	60
10	70
11	80
12	90

Problem 5-25

What are the major determinants of supply?

Requirement and Clue: *You are to discuss important factors that affect the supply of a good or service. It is crucial not to include the price of the good or service as a determinant of supply. The price of the good or service will affect the quantity supplied, not the supply. Think of factors other than the price of the item that will exert significant influence of the quantity offered for sale. In other words, think of factors that will shift the supply curve.*

Solution:

Some of the important determinants of supply are the number of producers/sellers, prices of related goods, technology, sellers' expectations of future prices, and prices of inputs.

Number of sellers:

As the number of sellers of an item increases, others things being equal, the greater the quantity that will be offered for sale at any given price; and as the number of sellers decreases, the quantity will also decrease.

Prices of related goods:

Consider lettuce and tomatoes which can be considered substitutes in production. If the price of lettuce increases, other things being equal, the supply of tomatoes will decrease as producers shift from tomato production to lettuce production. In general, if the price of a substitutable product increases, sellers will tend to reduce the supply of the substitute in question.

For goods that are complements in production, in general, if the price of a complement in production falls, the supply of the good in question will also fall. For example, if the price of beef falls, the quantity of beef supplied will also fall, but so will the quantity of hides as fewer cattle are slaughtered.

Technology:

An improvement in technology makes existing factors of production (inputs) more productive, and introduces new types of inputs that are more efficient than older types. Hence, an improvement in technology causes an increase in supply.

Expectations:

If producers expect prices to rise in the future, they might begin now to expand their productive capacity and thus increase their present output levels. If they expect prices to fall, they will likely switch resources into the production of items that have a more promising outlook, thus expectations of price decreases will tend to reduce supply.

Prices of inputs:

The costs of production reflect the prices of inputs. An increase in the prices of inputs (production costs) will result in a reduction in the supply of a product. A reduction in input prices will cause the supply to increase.

Problem 5-26

How will an increase in wages in the electronic components industry affect the supply of electronic components?

Requirement and Clue: *Think if there is any relationship between wages and any of the determinants of supply. It is easy to establish a relationship between wages and production costs. Once you've made that connection, the solution is clear.*

Solution:

An increase in wages in the electronic components industry will result in an increase in the cost of producing electronic components, other things being equal. This increase in cost will reduce produces ability to produce these components and therefore reduce supply of electronic components.

Problem 5-27

What is the difference between an increase in supply and an increase in quantity supplied? Illustrate graphically.

Requirement and Clue: *Here is another two-part problem. What does an increase in supply mean and what does an increase in quantity supplied mean? You are asked to demonstrate your knowledge of the difference verbally and then graphically.*

Solution:

An increase in supply means that at any given price, a greater quantity is supplied. If at a price of $5.00 sellers were placing 2,000 cups on the market for sale, and because of lower production costs, for example, they are willing and able to offer 2,200 cups for sale at the same price of $5, then supply has increased. If the price rises from $5 to $6 and as a result, sellers are willing and able to offer 2,300 cups for sale, then that's an increase in quantity supplied.

Graphically, an increase in supply is shown by a shift in the supply curve to the right as shown in the diagram below.

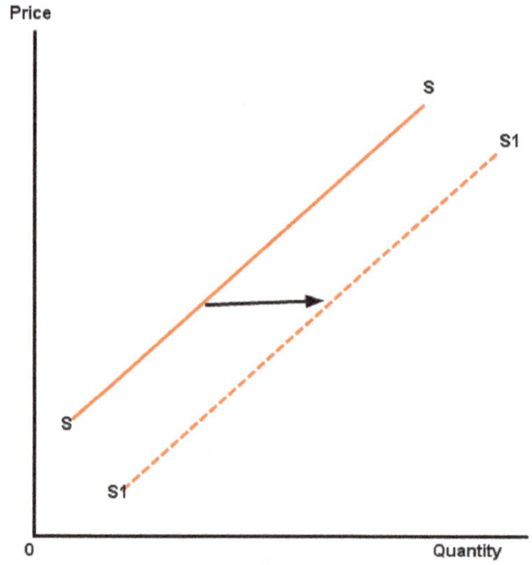

The initial supply is SS. With an increase in supply, the entire supply curve shifts from SS to S1S1.

An increase in quantity supplied is illustrated in the diagram below.

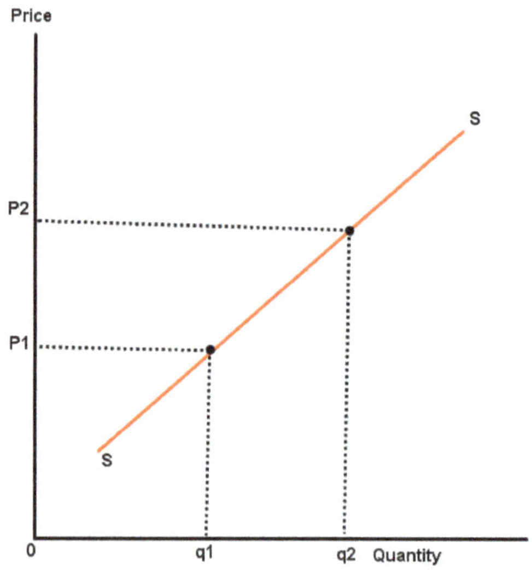

The supply curve is SS. At a price of p1, the quantity supplied is q1, corresponding to point A on the supply curve. An increase in price from p_1 to p_2 causes an increase in quantity supplied from q_1 to q_2—a movement along the supply curve from point A to point B.

Problem 5-28

Determine whether each of the following represents a change in supply or a change in quantity supplied. In each case, indicate whether there is a shift in the supply curve or a movement along the supply curve.

a. *The price of eggs rises by 10 cents per dozen and sellers offer more eggs for sale.*

b. *The price of lap top computers falls and as a result, sellers produce more flash drives.*

c. *The price of electricity for heating purposes rises. As a result, electricity providers increase their output of electricity.*

d. *Firms, on a whole, get tax incentives and consequently increase the production levels.*

Requirement and Clue: *This problem is designed to test your understanding of factors that change supply and those that change quantity supplied. The key is to determine whether the change is due to a change in the price of the item or to a change in one or more of the determinants of supply. If it's a price-induced change, then it's a change in quantity supplied represented by a movement along the supply curve. If it's a change in a determinant of supply, then it's a change in supply represented by a shift in the supply curve.*

Solution:

a. The increase in the quantity of eggs sold is in response to a change in the price of eggs. Therefore, this is a change in quantity supplied. There will be a movement from one point on the supply curve to another.

b. The increase in the quantity of flash drives produced is due to a fall in the price of lap top computers. Since the change is not in response to a change in the price of flash drives, then this is a change in supply. The supply of flash drives increases so the supply curve shifts to the right.

c. In this case, providers of electricity are responding to an increase in the price if electricity. They produce more as the price rises. This is a change in quantity supplied which would be indicated by a movement along the supply curve.

d. Here, firms are responding to a change in a variable other than the price of any item. They produce more goods and services because of the incentive provided by the tax. This is an increase in supply which would be indicated by a shift in the supply curve.

Problem 5-29

Use a supply schedule to illustrate the difference between supply and quantity supplied.

Requirement and Clue: *You need to know what a supply schedule is and how to construct one. Then you are required to construct a supply schedule and by referring to it, demonstrate your understanding of the difference between supply and quantity supplied.*

Solution:

A supply schedule is a table that shows the direct relationship between price and quantity supplied. The following is a supply schedule.

Price ($)	Quantity supplied (000)
14	140
12	120
10	100
8	80
6	60
4	40
2	20

Supply refers to the entire schedule—all the quantities with their associated prices. Quantity supplied, on the other hand, refers to a specific quantity that sellers will be willing and able to sell at a specific price. Thus, 100,000 is the quantity supplied at a price of $10; and 40 is the quantity supplied at a price of $4.

Problem 5-30

When the price of coffee falls from $1.10 per pound to $1.00 per pound, it is observed that coffee growers produce 25% less coffee. Does this signal a decrease in the supply of coffee?

Requirement and Clue: *This problem is designed to test your understanding of the difference between a change in supply and a change in quantity supplied. A decrease in the supply of coffee would occur only if a determinant of supply changed. Recall that the price of coffee is not a determinant of the supply of coffee.*

Solution:

The problem establishes a direct relationship between price and quantity supplied. When the price of coffee falls, coffee growers produce less coffee. The change in the quantity of coffee supplied is a direct result of the fall in coffee prices, all other influences on the quantity of coffee supplied being held constant. This is an example of movement along the supply curve rather than a shift in the supply curve. There is no change in the supply of coffee, only a change in quantity supplied.

Problem 5-31

Explain how each of the following is likely to affect the supply curve.

a. *The costs of production*

b. *Technology*

c. *The number of sellers*

d. *Taxes and subsidies*

Requirement and Clue: *Each of these is a non-price determinant of supply and will therefore shift the supply curve. Once you realize this, you have to state for each, whether it will shift the curve to the right or to the left.*

Solution:

a. *The costs of production:* A lowering of the costs of production will tend to increase supply. Lower production costs make it more profitable for firms to offer a larger quantity at each possible price. This will shift the supply curve to the right. An increase in the costs of production will reduce supply. This will shift the supply curve to the left.

b. *Technology:* An improvement in technology suggests a more efficient method of producing goods and services. With a better technology, producers are able to produce more with given resources. This will shift the supply curve to the right.

c. The number of sellers: Other things being equal, the larger the number of sellers, the greater will be the supply; and the smaller the number of sellers, the less will be the supply. A larger number of sellers will cause the supply curve to shift to the right while a smaller number of sellers will shift the supply curve to the left.

d. *Taxes and subsidies:* The imposition of taxes tends to increase the cost of production and thus reduce supply, causing the supply curve to shift to the left. Lower taxes tend to reduce the cost of production and this increase supply, causing the supply curve to shift to the right. Subsidies tend to reduce cost and thus increase supply, causing the supply curve to shift to the right. The elimination of reduction in subsidies tends to increase cost and thus reduce supply, causing the supply curve to shift to the left.

Problem 5-32

The following demand and supply schedules are given for apples.

Price ($)	Quantity demanded (000)	Quantity supplied (000)
12	40	120
11	50	110
10	60	100
9	70	90
8	80	80
7	90	70
6	100	60
5	110	50
4	120	40

On the basis of these schedules:

a. *What is the equilibrium price?*

b. *What is the equilibrium quantity?*

c. *If the government sets the price at $9, will there be a surplus or a shortage?*

d. *What action will the government have to take in order to maintain the price of $9?*

Requirement and Clue: *You must be familiar with the equilibrium condition and also with surpluses and shortages when price is fixed.*

Solution:

a. Equilibrium occurs when quantity demanded and quantity supplied are equal. The price that equates quantity demanded and quantity supplied as indicated in the schedule is $8. This is the equilibrium price.

b. The equilibrium quantity is the quantity that is traded (bought and sold) at the equilibrium price. In the schedule, this quantity is 80,000.

c. At a price of $9, the quantity supplied will be 90,000 while the quantity demanded will be 70,000. At $9 therefore, there will be a surplus of 20,000.

d. To maintain the price at $9, the government will have to purchase 20,000 at a price of $9.

Problem 5-33

Define each of the following terms and use demand and supply schedules to illustrate each.

a. *Equilibrium price*

b. *Surplus*

c. *Shortage*

Requirement and Clue: *This is another two-part problem. You must remember to answer both parts. You are required to state precisely what each term is. Then you should construct a table with demand and supply schedules and use it to illustrate each term.*

Solution:

a. Equilibrium price is the price at which quantity demanded equals quantity supplied.

b. A surplus is the amount by which quantity supplied exceeds quantity demanded at some particular price.

c. A shortage is the amount by which quantity demanded exceeds quantity supplied at some particular price.

Consider the following table.

Price ($)	Quantity demanded	Quantity supplied
10	60	100
9	70	90
8	80	80
7	90	70
6	100	60

The equilibrium price is $8 because at that price, the quantity demanded equals the quantity supplied.

At a price of $9, a surplus exists because the quantity supplied (90) exceeds the quantity demanded (70)

At a price of $7, a shortage exists because the quantity demanded (90) exceeds the quantity supplied (70).

Problem 5-34

Explain how the equilibrium price of a commodity is determined in a purely competitive market.

Requirement and Clue: *You must first demonstrate that you know what is meant by a purely competitive market. Then you must explain how the forces of demand and supply determine equilibrium price.*

Solution:

A purely competitive market is characterized by a large number of firms producing a homogeneous product. The output of each firm is such a small proportion of the total industry output that variations in the output of any firm will have no effect on the price at which the product is sold. Each producer can sell his entire stock at the existing price.

In this type of market, the price of a commodity is determined by the forces of demand and supply. We assume that as the price of a commodity rises, other things being equal, consumers will purchase less of that commodity, and as the price falls, they will purchase more of it. This gives the negatively (downward) sloping demand curve DD shown in the diagram below. We assume also that as the price of a commodity falls, sellers will want to offer less for sale, and as the price rises, they will want to offer more for sale. This gives the positively (upward) sloping supply curve SS shown in the diagram. The two curves intersect to give the equilibrium price of $2.

If the price were $3, sellers would wish to sell a larger quantity than that which consumers would wish to buy at that price: there would be a surplus in the market and price would be forced down.

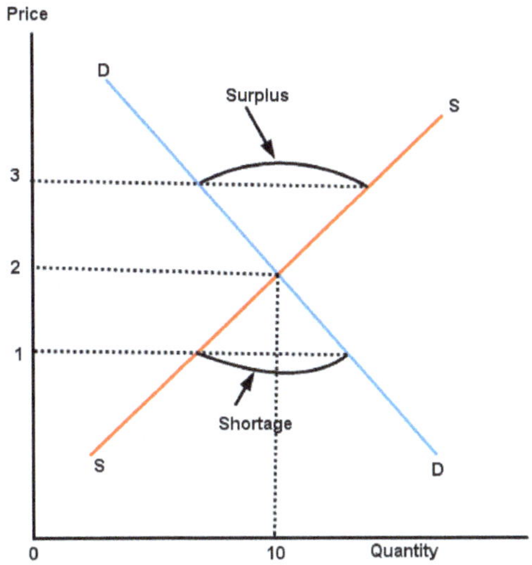

Also, if the price were $1, sellers would wish to sell a smaller quantity than that which consumers would be willing to buy at that price: there would be a shortage in the market and price would be forced up. The only price at which buyers and sellers are willing to trade the same quantity is $2. This is known as the equilibrium price. This price will be maintained unless some force disturbs the balance between quantity demanded and quantity supplied.

Problem 5-35

The first three columns of the following table show demand and supply for belts. Complete the last two columns. The first row is completed as an example.

Price ($)	Quantity Demanded (000)	Quantity supplied (000)	Market condition	Effect on price
12	60	140		
11	70	130		
10	80	120		
9	90	110		
8	100	100		
7	110	90		
6	120	80		
5	130	70		

Requirement and Clue: *The last two columns are the "Market conditions" and "Effect on price" columns. In the "Market conditions" column you are to indicate whether there is a shortage, surplus, or equilibrium in the market at each price. In the last column you are expected to indicate whether price will rise, fall, or whether there will be no effect.*

Solution:

Price ($)	Quantity Demanded (000)	Quantity supplied (000)	Market condition	Effect on price
12	60	140	*Surplus*	*Fall*
11	70	130	*Surplus*	*Fall*
10	80	120	*Surplus*	*Fall*
9	90	110	*Surplus*	*Fall*
8	100	100	*Equilibrium*	*None*
7	110	90	*Shortage*	*Rise*
6	120	80	*Shortage*	*Rise*
5	130	70	*Shortage*	*Rise*

Problem 5-36

Use a demand/supply graph to show the effect of an increase in demand on equilibrium price and quantity, other things being equal.

Requirement and Clue: *You are required to show the initial equilibrium price and quantity on a graph and then show the new equilibrium price and quantity following the increase in demand.*

Solution:

In the following diagram, DD and SS represent the initial demand and supply curves respectively.

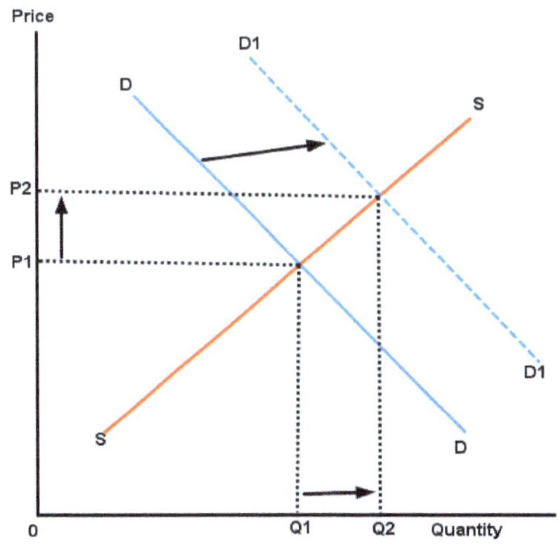

The equilibrium price is P1 and the equilibrium quantity is Q1. An increase in demand, other things being equal, shifts the demand curve from DD to D1D1. The new equilibrium price rises from P1 to P2 and the new equilibrium quantity rises from Q1 to Q2.

Problem 5-37

When the price of a corn is 35 cents, people will buy 50 but Pete the Grocer wants to sell 450. For every 5 cents fall in the price of corn, people want to buy 100 more while Pete wants to offer 100 less corn. What will be the equilibrium price of corn?

Requirement and Clue: *From the data given, you must try to construct a table showing demand and supply schedules for corn. From the table, you can then see the price that equates quantity demanded and quantity supplied.*

Solution:

The following demand/supply schedules can be constructed from the data provided in the problem.

Price ($)	Quantity Demanded	Quantity supplied
0.35	50	450
0.30	150	350
0.25	250	250
0.20	350	50

As can be seen from the table, at a price of \$0.25, consumers are willing and able to buy 250, while Pete is willing and able to offer 250 for sale. Thus, the equilibrium price is \$0.25.

Problem 5-38

Use graphs to show the effect of each of the following changes on the market for wheat, other things being equal.

a. *The demand for wheat increases*

b. *Bad weather results in a poor wheat harvest*

c. *The price of corn falls (consider corn and wheat to be substitutes)*

d. *Farmers expect wheat prices to rise*

e. *A group of agricultural scientists declare that wheat is beneficial to health*

Requirement and Clue: *Determine whether the change will affect demand or supply and how. Then show the result graphically. You are to state what will happen to the price and quantity of wheat in each case.*

Solution:

a. In the diagram below, DD and SS are the initial demand and supply curves for wheat. The equilibrium price is P1 and the equilibrium quantity is Q1.

As the demand for wheat increases, the demand curve shifts to the right from DD to D1D1 as shown in the graph above. This results in an increase in the equilibrium price from P1 to P2 and an increase in the equilibrium quantity from Q1 to Q2.

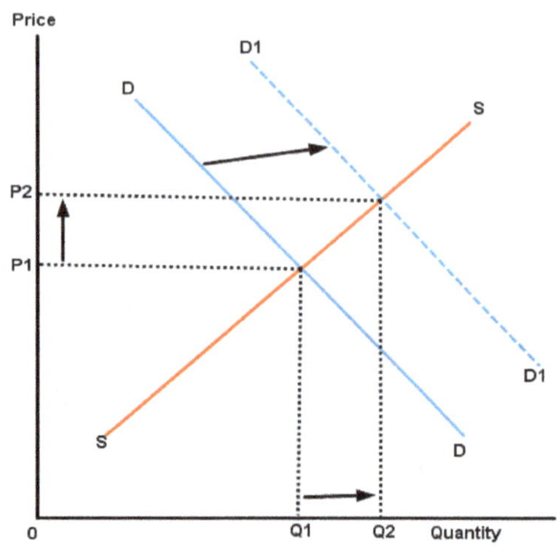

b. Initially, the demand and supply curves for wheat are DD and SS as shown in the following graph, and the initial equilibrium price and quantity are P and Q respectively.

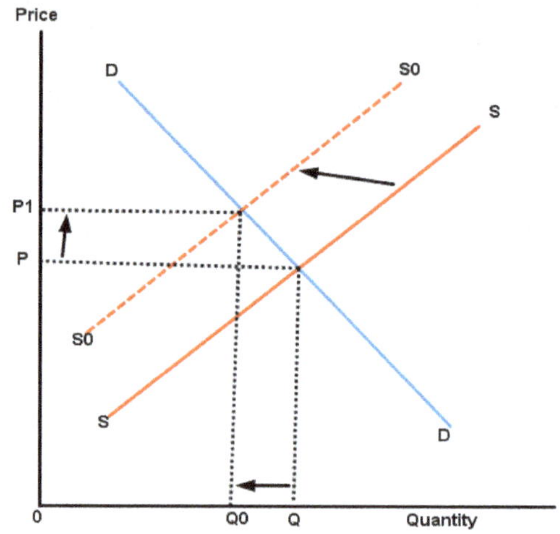

The poor wheat harvest means a reduction in the supply of wheat, so the supply curve shifts to the left from SS to S0S0.As a result, the equilibrium price rises from P to P1 and the quantity falls from Q to Q0.

c. The initial demand and supply curves for wheat are shown as DD and SS respectively in the diagram below. The equilibrium price and quantity are P and Q respectively.

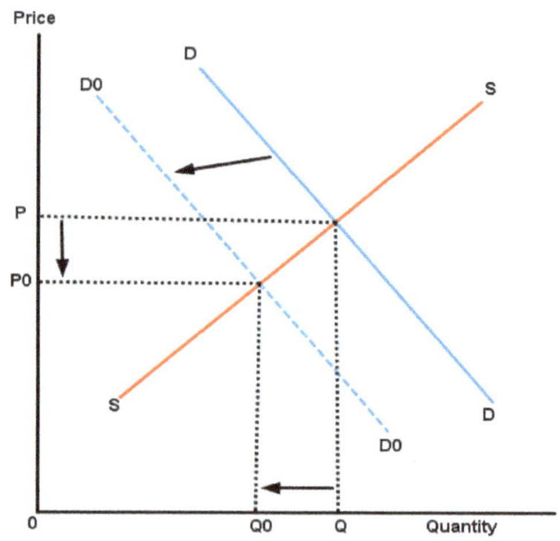

Since wheat and corn are substitutes, a fall in the price of corn will cause some consumers to switch from wheat to corn, thus reducing the demand for wheat. Consequently, the demand curve shifts to the left from DD to D0D0 as shown in the diagram, causing equilibrium price to fall from P to P0, and equilibrium quantity to fall from Q to Q0.

Alternatively, we can look at the problem from the producers' perspective. The diagram below shows the initial demand curve DD and the initial supply curve SS. The equilibrium price and quantity are P and Q respectively. A fall in the price of corn will cause growers to grow less corn and more wheat. Accordingly, the supply curve for wheat will shift to the right, lowering the price from P to P0, and increasing the quantity from Q to Q1.

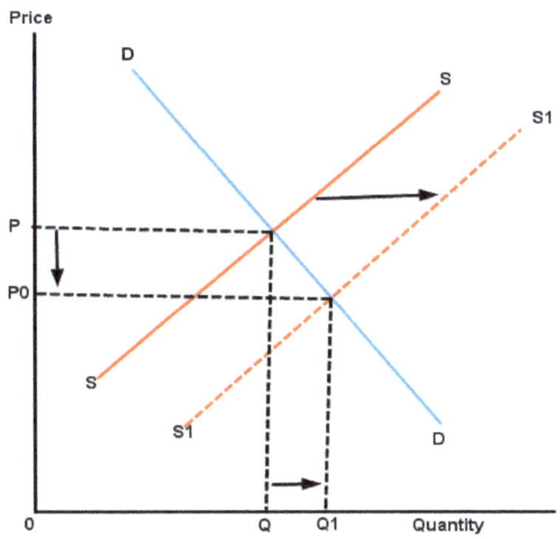

d. If farmers expect wheat prices to rise, other things being equal, they will produce more wheat. The following diagram illustrates the market for wheat. The initial demand and supply curves are DD and SS respectively, and the equilibrium price and quantity are P and Q.

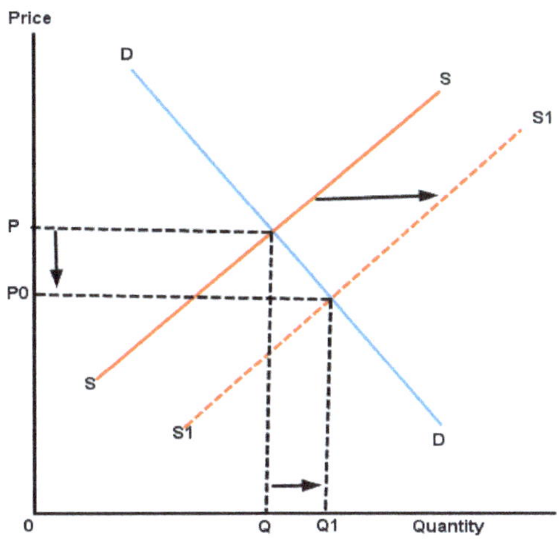

The production of more wheat by farmers shifts the supply curve from SS to S1S1 as shown in the graph. This causes a fall in price from P to P0, and an increase in quantity from Q to Q1.

e. The declaration by scientists that wheat is beneficial to health will increase the demand for wheat as more people try to take advantage of the health benefits. The following diagram shows the market for wheat.

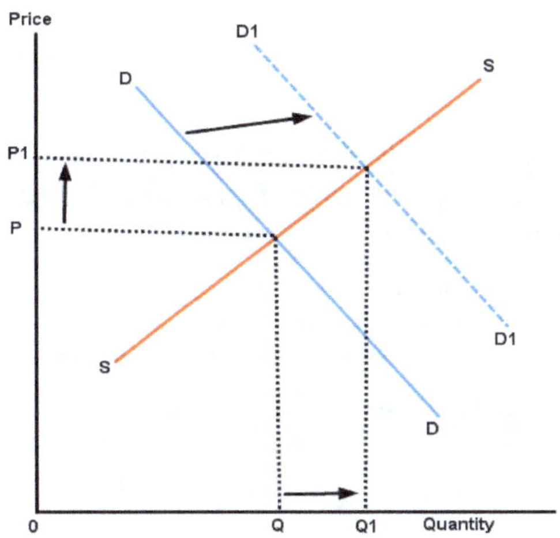

The initial demand and supply curves for wheat are DD and SS respectively. The initial equilibrium price and quantity are P and Q respectively. The demand curve shifts to the right from DD to D1D1 following the declaration; and the equilibrium price rises from P to P1, while the equilibrium quantity also rises from Q to Q1.

Problem 5-39

Parker runs a small hot dog stand. If a new amusement park opens up across the street from him, use demand/supply graphs to show what is likely to happen to the price that Parker can charge for his hotdogs?

Requirement and Clue: *You need to figure out how the opening of the amusement park will likely affect demand for Parker's hotdogs. An amusement park attracts people, and Parker will likely benefit from the greater traffic. You must graphically show the effect of the change in demand on price.*

Solution:

The following diagram shows the initial demand (DD) and supply (SS) for Parker's hotdogs. The equilibrium price and quantity are P and Q respectively. The opening up of the new amusement park across the street from Parker's hot dog stand will most likely increase the demand for Parker's hotdogs. The demand curve will shift to the right from DD to D1D1. This increase in demand will raise the equilibrium price from P to P_1.

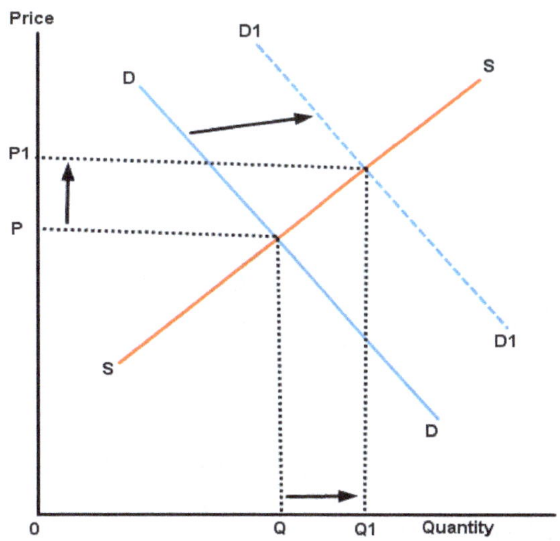

Problem 5-40

The development of a new technology increases the efficiency of ipad production. Show graphically how this development will affect the market for ipads.

Requirement and Clue: *This is clearly a supply-side shock. You are required to state the effect of this supply-side shock on the equilibrium price and equilibrium quantity of ipads.*

Solution:

The initial demand and supply curves for iPads are DD and SS in the following figure. The initial equilibrium price and equilibrium quantity are P and Q respectively.

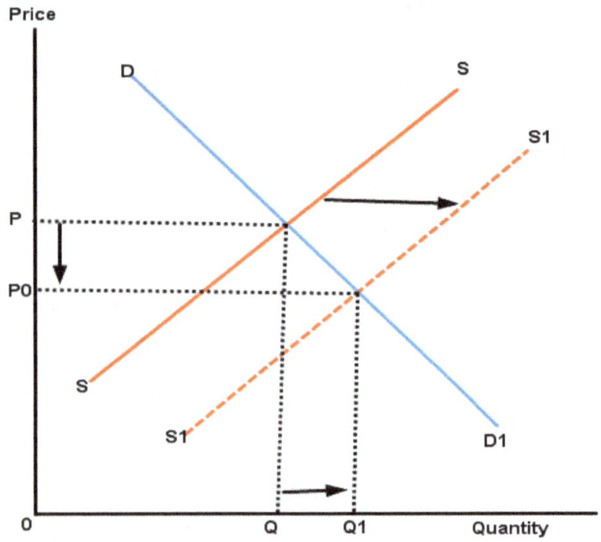

The new technology enables a greater quantity of iPads to be produced at every price. In other words, the new technology increases the supply of iPads. The increase in supply is shown by shifting the supply curve to the right from SS to S1S1. This results in a fall in the equilibrium price of iPads from P to P0 and an increase in the equilibrium quantity from Q to Q1.

Problem 5-41

It is observed that apples are inexpensive in the fall and that Christmas trees are quite cheap on December 26. Use demand and supply graphs to explain why this is so.

Requirement and Clue: *Think about the quantity of apples available in the fall as opposed to other seasons of the year. Thank also of the change in demand for Christmas trees between the day before Christmas and the day after Christmas. Use this information to analyse the markets for apples and Christmas trees at the times indicated.*

Solution:

First, let us consider the market for apples. In the diagram below, the demand and supply curves for apples are DD and SS respectively, and the equilibrium price and equilibrium quantity are P and Q respectively.

The fall is the usual harvest time for apples so their supply increases. The supply curve shifts from SS to S1S1 as shown in the diagram. This increase in the supply of apples causes a surplus of apples at the initial price which reduces the equilibrium price from P to P0.

Let us now consider the market for Christmas trees. In the diagram below, the demand and supply curves for Christmas trees are DD and SS respectively, and the equilibrium price and equilibrium quantity are P and Q respectively. Between December 25 and December 26, the demand for Christmas trees falls significantly.

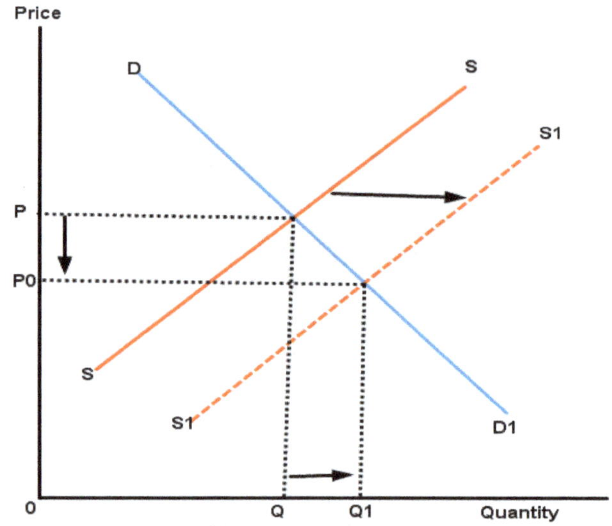

Very few people will be buying Christmas trees on Boxing Day. This drastic drop in the demand for Christmas trees is shown by shifting the demand curve to the left as shown in the diagram below. The price falls from P to P0.

Apples are inexpensive in the fall because the supply of apples increases during that time. Christmas trees are quite cheap on December 26 because of the drastic fall in demand for Christmas trees on December 26.

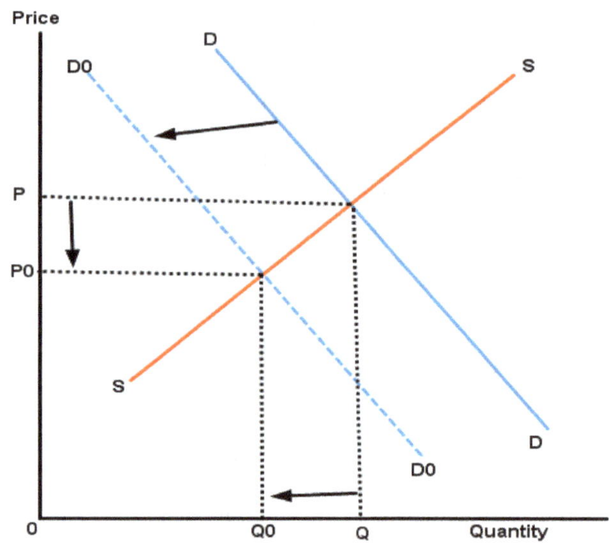

Problem 5-42

Explain with the help of demand/supply diagrams, the effect of a good banana crop on the price of apples, assuming that apples and bananas are substitutes in consumption.

Requirement and Clue: *There are two markets to consider here: the market for bananas and the market for apples. However, the problem requires you to state how the price of apples will be affected.*

Solution:

A good banana crop will increase the supply of bananas. Other things being equal, this will cause the price of bananas to fall as shown in Figure 1 below.

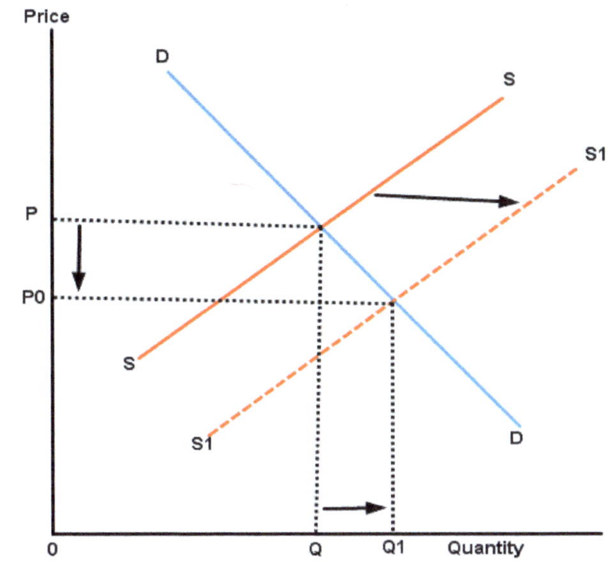

Figure 1

The original demand and supply curves for bananas are shown by DD and SS. The equilibrium price of bananas is P. The increase in supply caused by the good banana crop is shown by a shift in the supply curve from SS to S1S1, and the price is forced down from P to P0.

It is given that apples and bananas are substitutes, so as the price of bananas falls, consumers will switch from apples which are now relatively more expensive. This means that the demand for apples will fall and, other things being equal, this fall in demand will cause the price of apples to fall as shown in Figure 2. The original demand and supply curves for apples are DD and SS, and the price established by the market is P. The fall in demand is represented by a shift in the demand curve from DD to D0D0 in Figure 2.

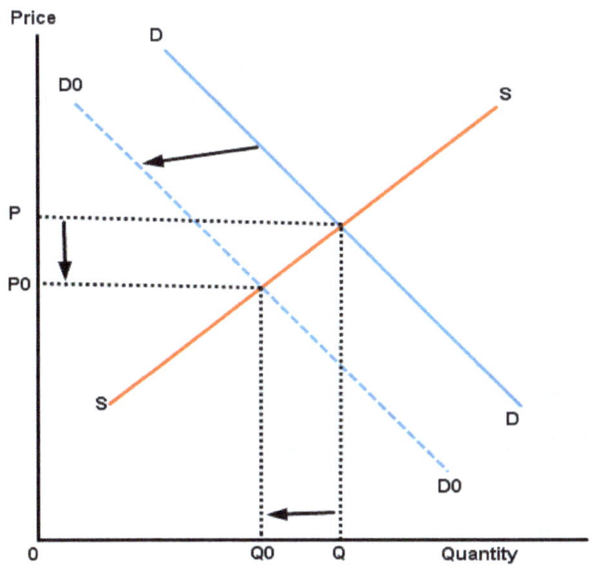

Figure 2

The decrease in demand causes the price to fall from P to P0. Thus, the good banana crop will cause the price of bananas to fall and this in turn will lower the price of apples. As a general rule, a fall in the price of a good will lower the price of a substitute.

Problem 5-43

Use demand and supply graphs to show that minimum wage legislation can cause unemployment.

Requirement and Clue: *This problem is an application of demand/supply analysis to the market for labour services. The problem requires an analysis of the effects of minimum wage legislation on the quantity of labour demand and on the quantity supplied.*

Solution:

The following graph shows the market for labour services. Weq is the equilibrium wage rate where the quantity of labour demanded equals the quantity supplied. The equilibrium quantity of labour (number of workers) is Neq.

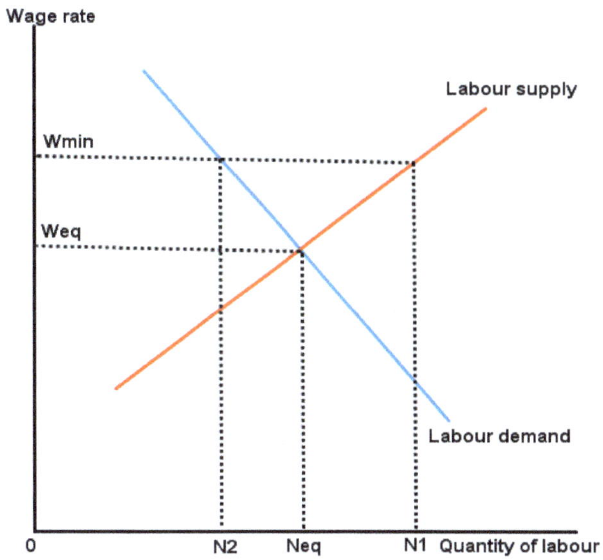

If the minimum wage is set below the equilibrium wage rate, it will have no effect. The equilibrium wage rate will prevail. However, if the minimum wage is set above the equilibrium wage rate (Wmin for example), the number of workers demanded by firms will be N2, while the number of workers offering to work will be N1. Thus, the number of workers who will not be hired is (N1 – N2). This represents unemployment that is due to the minimum wage legislation. Minimum wage legislation is an example of a price floor.

Problem 5-44

Explain, with the use of graphs, the effect of a price ceiling. Give an example of a price ceiling.

Requirement and Clue: *You should recognize the problem as an application of demand/supply analysis. You are expected to show your understanding of the concept of a price ceiling and your ability to use graphs in this particular case. Don't forget to give an example of a price ceiling.*

Solution:

A price ceiling is a point beyond which a price is not allowed to rise. Consider the diagram below. The demand and supply curves are DD and SS respectively, and the equilibrium price and quantity are \$500 and 5,000 respectively. Suppose a price ceiling of \$300 is established. Sellers may not charge more than \$300. At this price, sellers are willing and able to offer only 3,000 for sale as can be seen from the supply curve, while consumers are willing to purchase 7,000 as can be seen from the demand curve. Thus, a price of \$300 results in a shortage of 4,000. Quite often, a black market, in which the item is sold at a price above that prescribed by law, is the result of a price ceiling. A popular example of a price ceiling is rent control.

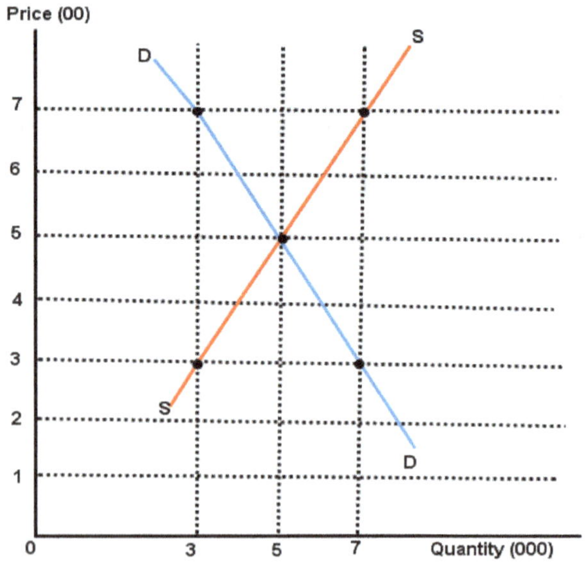

Problem 5-45

When the price of gold rises considerably, the price of silver also tends to rise. How might this occurrence be explained?

Requirement and Clue: *The problem suggests that a relationship exists between silver and gold. Silver and gold can be considered substitutes in consumption, perhaps as jewelry. Apply demand/supply analysis to the effect of a change in the price of a substitute.*

Solution:

A plausible explanation could be as follows. Gold and silver are substitutes. As the price of gold rises, people will tend to buy less gold, turning instead to silver, a relatively cheaper substitute. They may also substitute silver for gold in their investment portfolios. This increase in demand for silver results in an increase in the price of gold. This situation can be analyzed with the help of the diagram below.

The original demand and supply curves for silver intersect to determine an equilibrium price of P and an equilibrium quantity of Q for silver. When the price of gold increases significantly, people will switch from gold to a cheaper substitute such as silver. Therefore the demand for silver will rise. The demand curve shifts from DD to D1D1 as shown in the diagram. This increase in the demand for silver raises the price from P to P1 as shown in the diagram.

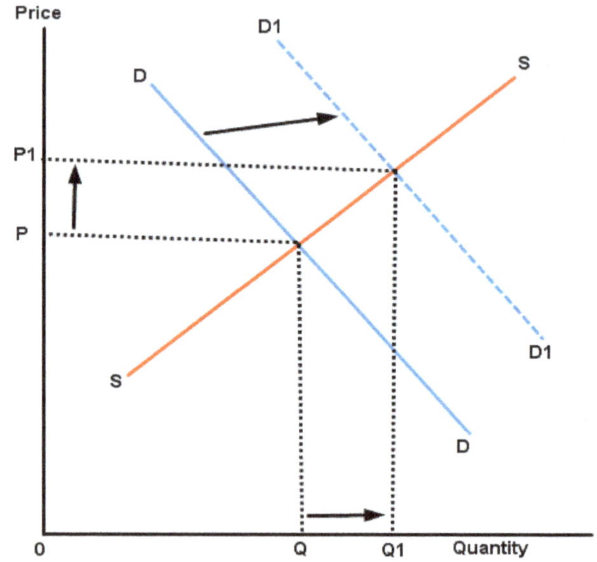

Problem 5-46

Use demand and supply graphs to analyze the effect of an excise tax on:

(a) *the price of the taxed item*
(b) *the quantity traded*
(c) *the consumers' share of the tax*
(d) *the producers' share of the tax*
(e) *the government's revenue from the tax*

Requirement and Clue: *Here is an example of the application of demand and supply analysis to a popular tax problem. You are expected to know what an excise tax is and to show (by graphs) how such a tax affects the indicated variables. You need to know how an excise tax affects the supply of the taxed item.*

Solution:

An excise tax is a tax levied on a domestically produced good or service. Let us assume, for this solution, that the government imposes a tax of \$1.00 on each gallon of gasoline sold. The following graph shows the demand curve DD and the supply curve SS before the imposition of the tax.

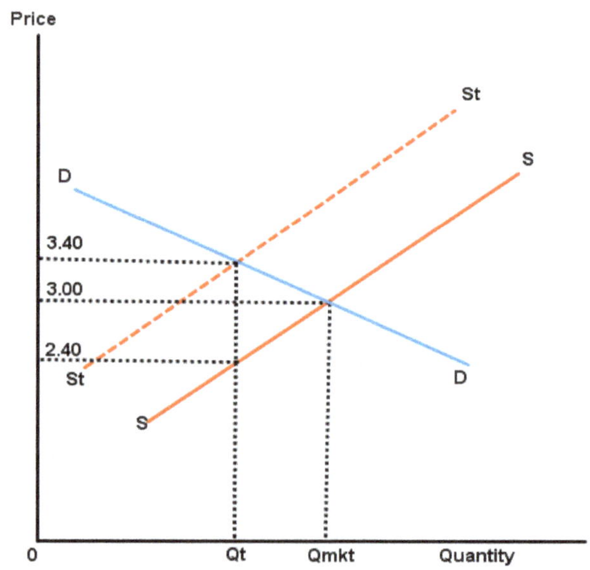

The equilibrium price of gasoline is \$3 and the quantity traded at that price is Qmkt which we assume to be 14,000 gallons. The tax causes production costs to rise by \$1.00 per gallon and this reduces supply. The supply curve shifts up by the amount of the tax, as shown by St, so the vertical distance between SS and StSt represents the tax. The new equilibrium price is now \$3.40 and consumers now buy Qt which we assume to be 12,000 gallons at that price.

(a) The price of the taxed item (gasoline in this example), has increased

(b) The quantity traded has fallen from 14,000 bottles to 12,000 gallons

(c) Consumers were paying \$3.00 before the tax. After the tax they are paying \$3.40 Therefore, their share of the tax is \$0.40

(d) The producers' share of the tax is \$0.60

(e) Since 12,000 gallons are sold and the tax is \$1 per gallon, the government's revenue from the tax is (12,000 × \$1) = \$12,000

Problem 5-47

Consider the demand and supply equations:

$$Q_d = 50 - 4P$$
$$Q_s = -10 + 8P$$

Find the equilibrium price and the equilibrium quantity.

Requirement and Clue: *We know that in equilibrium, Q_d and Q_s are equal. You are required to solve the equations for P and Q.*

Solution:

$$50 - 4P = -10 + 8P$$
$$12P = 60, \text{ so } P = 5$$

By substituting P = 5 in either the demand or the supply equation, we obtain Q = 30.

The equilibrium price is **\$5** and the equilibrium quantity is **30**.

Problem 5-48

You are given the following demand and supply equations:

$$Q_d = 130 - 3P$$
$$Q_s = -20 + 12P$$

Complete the following demand and supply schedules

Price	Quantity Demanded	Quantity supplied
5	130 – 3(5) = 115	–20 + 12(5) = 40
10	130 – 3(10) = 100	–20 + 12(10) = 100
15	130 – 3(15) = 85	–20 + 12(15) = 160
20	130 – 3(20) = 70	–20 + 12(20) = 220

(a) *From the schedules, determine the equilibrium price and equilibrium quantity*

(b) *Solve the demand and supply equations for P and Q and compare your answer with the answer obtained in part (b).*

Requirement and Clue: *Try to solve the problem in order suggested by the problem. To obtain the demand schedule, you need to plug each price into the demand equation; and to obtain the supply schedule, you need to plug each price into the supply equation. Once you have the demand and supply schedules, the equilibrium price and quantity can be easily determined by observing the price at which quantity demanded equals quantity supplied. Equating Q_d with Q_s you can solve for P and Q.*

Solution:

Price	Quantity Demanded	Quantity supplied
5	130 – 3(5) = 115	–20 + 12(5) = 40
10	130 – 3(10) = 100	–20 + 12(10) = 100
15	130 – 3(15) = 85	–20 + 12(15) = 160
20	130 – 3(20) = 70	–20 + 12(20) = 220

(a) At a price of 10, the quantity demanded (100) equals the quantity supplied (100). Therefore, the equilibrium price is **10** and the equilibrium quantity is **100.**

$$130 - 3P = -20 + 12P$$
$$15P = 150$$
$$\mathbf{P = 10}$$
$$Q = 130 - 3(10) = \mathbf{100}$$

The answer is the same as that obtained in part (b).

Problem 5-49

The market demand and supply equations are given as:

$$Qd = 18 - 2P$$
$$Qs = 3 + 5P$$

(a) *By selecting prices ranging from \$1 to \$6, construct the demand and supply schedules.*

(b) *Solve the equations for the equilibrium price and the equilibrium quantity.*

Requirement and Clue: *The demand and supply schedules can be constructed by plugging prices from \$1 to \$6 into each equation.*

Solution:

Price	Quantity Demanded	Quantity supplied
1	18 – 2(1) = 16	3 + 5(1) = 8
2	18 – 2(2) = 14	3 + 5(2) = 13
3	18 – 2(3) = 12	3 + 5(3) = 18
4	18 – 2(4) = 10	3 + 5(4) = 23
5	18 – 2(5) = 8	3 + 5(5) = 28
6	18 – 2(6) = 6	3 + 5(6) = 33

$$18 - 2P = 3 + 5P$$
$$7P = 15$$
$$P = 15/7 = \mathbf{2.14}$$
$$Q = 18 - 2(2.14)$$
$$Q = 18 - 4.28 = \mathbf{13.72}$$

Problem 5-50

The demand and supply equations are given as

$$Q_d = 28 - 2P$$
$$Q_s = 5P$$

What are the equilibrium price and quantity?

Requirement and Clue: You are required to solve the equations for P and Q. Remember that in equilibrium, $Q_d = Q_s$.

Solution:

$$28 - 2P = 5P$$
$$7P = 28$$
$$\mathbf{P = 4}$$
$$Q = 28 - 2(4) = \mathbf{20}$$

The equilibrium price is 4 and the equilibrium quantity is 20.

Multiple-Choice

In each case, circle the letter that corresponds with the correct answer.

1. The market process refers to:
   a. the methods used my merchants to take their products to market
   b. the various laws and regulations governing behaviour in markets
   c. the means by which a government sets the price of an item in the market
   d. the process by which buyers and sellers exchange goods and services.

Answer: d

Reason: A market exists for the buying and selling of goods and services. This process of buying and selling is the market process.

2. The existence of a market requires:
   a. at least one buyer
   b. a good or service
   c. at least one seller
   d. all of the above.

Answer: d

Reason: A market cannot exist without buyers, sellers, a product, and a price.

3. Which of the following is not necessary for a market to exist?
   a. A specific geographical location
   b. A price at which the product is sold
   c. A specific good or service
   d. At least one buyer and one seller.

Answer: a

Reason: A market is more of a mechanism that facilitates exchange than a particular place.

4. A market is:
   a. a point of contact between buyers and sellers
   b. a mechanism that facilitates exchange
   c. both a and b
   d. neither a nor b.

Answer: c

Reason: A market exists as long as buyers and sellers are in contact to exchange goods and services.

5. Demand refers to:
   a. the quantity that will be bought at a particular price
   b. the quantity that sellers place on the market for sale as a result of buyers' wants
   c. consumers wants and needs
   d. the various quantities that buyers will be willing and able to buy at various prices.

Answer: d

Reason: A set of prices with the associated quantities that people will be willing and able to buy constitutes demand. It is not a specific quantity that will be purchased at some stipulated price.

6. To the economist, demand refers to:
   a. the actual quantity purchased at a particular price
   b. the buyers' need for a product
   c. people's ability to buy a product
   d. none of the above.

Answer: d

Reason: Demand refers to the various quantities of an item that buyers will be willing and able to buy at various prices during a period of time.

7. A demand schedule is:
   a. a table that shows various quantities of an item that buyers will be willing and able to buy at various prices
   b. a downward sloping curve that shows various quantities of an item that will be bought at various prices
   c. a graph that shows the direct relationship between the price of an item and the various quantities that people will purchase
   d. a table that shows price increasing as demand increases.

Answer: a

Reason: Choice "a" defines a demand schedule. It differs from a demand curve in that the curve is a graph while the schedule is a table.

8. In a demand schedule, a price of \$6 is associated with a quantity of 100 units. This tells us that:
   a. the demand is 100 units
   b. the demand is \$6
   c. the product will be sold for \$6 per unit
   d. none of the above.

Answer: d

Reason: The quantity of 100 units associated with a price of $6 is referred to as the quantity demanded at $6.

9. Demand can be illustrated:

a. only by a demand curve
b. only by a demand schedule
c. only by a demand schedule or a demand curve
d. none of the above.

Answer: d

Reason: Demand can be illustrated by a demand schedule, a demand curve, or a demand function.

10. Demand is:

a. a stock concept
b. a flow concept
c. a combination of a stock and a flow
d. none of the above.

Answer: d

Reason: Demand occurs "during a period of time". This time dimension makes demand a flow concept.

11. If the demand curve for an item is downward sloping and its price falls from $5 to $4.75:

a. the demand will fall
b. the demand will rise
c. the quantity demanded will fall
d. the quantity demanded will rise.

Answer: d

Reason: A fall in the price of an item does not affect the demand for the item. It affects the quantity demanded. It will be reflected in a movement along the demand curve.

12. According to the law of demand:

a. demand and price are directly related
b. demand and price are inversely related
c. an inverse relationship exists between price and quantity demanded
d. if the price falls, quantity demanded with rise.

Answer: c

Reason: The law of demand states that, other things being equal, an increase in price will cause a decrease in quantity demanded and vice versa. The relationship between price and quantity demanded is inverse.

13. The law of demand states that:

a. price will fall as demand rises
b. price will rise as demand falls
c. quantity demanded will fall as price rises, other things being equal
d. people should buy only what they can afford.

Answer: c

Reason: The law of demand stipulates an inverse relationship between price and quantity demanded.

14. According to the law of demand:

a. the demand curve slopes downward
b. people will buy more of an item as its price falls, other things being equal
c. the variables in the demand schedule move in opposite directions
d. all of the above.

Answer: d

Reason: Choices a, b, and c are just different ways of saying the same thing.

15. The demand for a product is represented graphically by:

a. a point on the demand curve
b. the entire demand curve
c. the intersection of the demand curve and the price of the item
d. all of the above.

Answer: b

Reason: The entire curve represents demand while a point on the curve represents quantity demanded.

16. A downward sloping demand curve implies that:

a. demand will increase as price falls
b. a greater quantity will be bought as price falls
c. price and quantity demanded are positively (directly) related
d. a smaller quantity will be bought at any price.

Answer: b

Reason: A downward sloping curve illustrates an inverse relationship. Price and quantity demanded move in opposite directions.

17. Which of the following is likely to have the least effect on the quantity of a product that consumers will be willing and able to buy?

a. An increase in population
b. A decrease in the price of the product
c. A fall in consumers' total income
d. The state of technology.

Answer: d

Reason: All of the choices affect quantity demanded except technology.

18. Which is the following is unlikely to cause a change in the demand for steak?

a. An increase in the price of steak
b. Farmers launch a successful campaign extolling the benefit of steak
c. An announcement by scientists that beef consumption is injurious to health
d. A significant fall in the price of hamburgers.

Answer: a

Reason: The price of an item does not affect the demand for the item; it affects quantity demanded.

19. Which of the following explains the inverse relationship between price and quantity demanded?

a. the income effect
b. the substitution effect
c. both a and b
d. neither a nor b.

Answer: c

Reason: The income effect, the market-size effect, and the substitution effect all explain the inverse relationship between price and quantity demanded.

20. When the price of an item falls, more buyers are attracted to the market, so the quantity demanded rises. This phenomenon is known as:

a. the attraction effect
b. the falling price syndrome
c. the "quantity demanded" phenomenon
d. the market size effect.

Answer: d

Reason: *Note that the market-size is an explanation for the law of demand. It is related to a movement along the demand curve, not a shift of the curve.*

21. The demand curve shows:

a. the inverse relationship between price and income
b. the direct relationship between income and demand
c. the inverse relationship between income and demand
d. none of the above.

Answer: d

Reason: *The demand curve shows an inverse relationship between price and quantity demanded.*

22. The market demand curve is:

a. upward sloping
b. vertical in most cases
c. downward sloping
d. horizontal in most cases.

Answer: c

Reason: *The market demand curve is downward sloping signifying that as price moves in one direction, quantity demanded moves in the other direction.*

23. Which of the following is likely to increase the demand for a product?

a. A fall in the price of the product
b. An increase in total income
c. Expectations of a fall in the price of the product in the future
d. All of the above.

Answer: b

Reason: *An increase in income will cause people to buy more at any given price.*

24. Tide and Cheer are substitutes as laundry detergents. If the price of Cheer rises from $8 to $9.50, other things being equal:

a. the quantity of Cheer demanded will fall
b. the demand for Cheer will not be affected
c. the demand for Tide will increase
d. all of the above.

Answer: d

Reason: *An increase in the price of Cheer causes the quantity demanded to fall. A change in the price of Cheer will affect the quantity demanded, not the demand. As the price of Cheer rises, people will switch to a substitute, Tide; thus increasing the demand for Tide.*

25. In general, the market supply curve will be:

a. upward sloping
b. downward sloping
c. vertical
d. horizontal.

Answer: a

Reason: *There is an inverse relationship between price and quantity supplied, giving rise to an upward sloping supply curve.*

26. In economics, supply:

a. is everything that producers place on the market for sale
b. is the various quantities that sellers will be willing and able to offer for sale at various possible prices
c. refers to a specific quantity that sellers will actually sell at some specific price during a given period of time
d. all of the above.

Answer: b

Reason: Supply is a relationship between price and quantity supplied. That is implied in choice "b".

27. An increase in the price of steel is likely to:

a. increase the demand for cars
b. increase the supply of cars
c. decrease the supply of cars
d. have no effect on the market for cars.

Answer: c

Reason: *Steel is an input in the production of cars. An increase in the price of steel increases the cost of producing cars, which decreases the supply of cars.*

28. Which of the following is <u>not</u> a supply shifter?

a. The price of the item being considered
b. Technology
c. The prices of inputs used to produce the item
d. The number of producers of the item under consideration.

Answer: a

Reason: *A change in the price of an item causes a movement along the supply curve. It does not shift the curve.*

29. An increase in supply is shown graphically by:

a. a movement down the supply curve
b. a movement up the supply curve
c. an upward shift (to the left) in the supply curve
d. a downward shift (to the right) in the supply curve.

Answer: d

Reason: *An increase in supply means that a greater quantity is supplied at each price. This implies a rightward shift of the entire supply curve.*

30. Which of the following is likely to affect the supply of a product?

a. The cost of resources
b. Technology
c. Weather conditions
d. All of the above.

Answer: d

Reason: *Supply shifters include the number of producers, prices of related products, technology, expectations of future price changes, and production costs.*

31. All of the following will cause the supply curve for peaches to shift <u>except:</u>

a. an increase in workers' wages by 15%
b. a fall in the price of a complement
c. an increase in the market price of peaches from $1.05

to $1.15 per pound

d. a bountiful peach harvest

Answer: c

Reason: *An increase in the price of peaches will cause a movement along the supply curve, but the curve will not shift.*

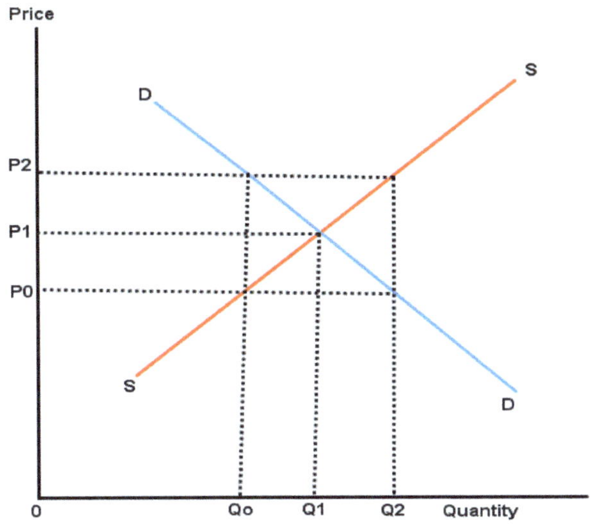

Diagram for questions 32-34

Questions 32, 33 and 34 refer to the preceeding diagram displaying the demand and supply curves for peanuts.

32. The equilibrium price and equilibrium quantity are:

a. P2 and Q2 because they are the highest

b. Po and Qo because consumers pay the least at that price

c. P1 and Q1 because at the price there is no shortage or surplus

d. Po and Q2 because at that price and quantity, buyers and sellers are doing their best

Answer: c

Reason: *Equilibrium occurs when the quantity demanded and the quantity supplied are equal. At that price, there is neither a shortage nor a surplus.*

33. We can notice that:

a. a shortage exists at Po

b. the equilibrium price is P2

c. a surplus exists at P1

d. the equilibrium quantity is Q2

Answer: a

Reason: *At Po, the quantity demanded exceeds the quantity supplied. A shortage exists.*

34. A surplus exists at:

a. P2

b. P1

c. Po

d. Q2

Answer: a

Reason: *At P2, the quantity supplied exceeds the quantity demanded. A surplus exists.*

35. If demand increases, other things being equal, we predict:

a. an increase in price and a decrease in quantity

b. an increase in price and an increase in quantity

c. a decrease in price and an increase in quantity

d. a decrease in price and a decrease in quantity.

Answer: b

Reason: *An increase in demand, other things being equal, shifts the demand curve to the right and causes a shortage which raises the price. The equilibrium quantity also increases.*

36. Assume that tea and coffee are substitutes. An increase in the price of tea is likely to have which of the following effects on the price of coffee?

a. An increase in the price of coffee

b. A fall in the price of coffee

c. No effect on the price of coffee

d. It is impossible to tell

Answer: a

Reason: *When the price of tea increases, some people will switch from tea to coffee, causing the demand for coffee to increase. This increase in the demand for coffee raises the price of coffee.*

37. A price floor will be effective:

a. if the minimum price is set below the market equilibrium price

b. if the minimum price is set above the market equilibrium price

c. regardless of the level at which the minimum price is set

d. only if the minimum price coincides with the equilibrium price.

Answer: b

Reason: *If the minimum price is set below the equilibrium price, it will be ineffective because the equilibrium price will prevail. To be effective, it must be set above the market equilibrium price.*

38. A price ceiling will most likely benefit:

a. consumers of the product

b. producers and sellers of the product

c. both producers and consumers

d. neither producers nor consumers

Answer: a

Reason: *In the absence of the price ceiling, consumers would pay a higher price.*

39. A black market is:

a. a market dominated by black people

b. a market in which stolen items are sold

c. often the result of price ceilings

d. none of the above.

Answer: c

Reason: *Price ceilings often result in black markets because some buyers are willing to pay the higher market equilibrium price.*

40. If the demand and supply equations are

$Q_d = 900 - 20P$ and $Q_s = -100 + 30P$, then the equilibrium price and quantity are:

a. P = 50 and Q = 10
b. P = 20 and Q = 500
c. P = 100 and Q = 40
d. P = 500 and Q = 20

Answer: b

Reason: *Equating quantity demanded and quantity supplied and solving for P and Q give P = 20 and Q = 500.*

True or False

Determine whether each of the following statements is true or false.

1. Demand refers to how much of an item consumers will buy at some specific price and can be represented by a demand schedule.

Answer: False

Explanation: *Demand can be represented by a demand curve, but the concept defined in the statement is quantity demanded, nit demand.*

2. Demand is defined as the various quantities of an item that consumers will be willing and able to buy at various prices during a period of time.

Answer: True

3. There is absolutely no difference between a demand schedule and a demand curve. They are just different names for the same thing.

Answer: False

Explanation: *They both represent demand, but the demand schedule is a table while the demand curve is a graph.*

4. A demand schedule is a table that shows the inverse relationship between price and quantity demanded, while a demand curve is a graph that shows the inverse relationship between price and quantity demanded.

Answer: True

5. A demand curve shows the inverse relationship between price and demand.

Answer: False

Explanation: *The relationship is between price and quantity demanded.*

6. The law of demand states that as the price of an item falls, the demand for it will rise.

Answer: False

Explanation: *First, a change in price affects the quantity demanded, not the demand. Second, the "other things being equal" condition must be included.*

7. According to the law of demand, as the price of an item falls, other things being equal, the quantity demanded will rise.

Answer: True

8. The market size effect, the substitution effect, and the income effect explain why people buy more of an item as its price falls.

Answer: True

9. The market size effect refers to the change in quantity demanded as the number of buyers changes in response to a change in price.

Answer: True

10. The market demand curve is downward sloping indicating that a greater quantity will be demanded as the price falls.

Answer: True

11. The demand curve will shift to the right when the price falls because a greater quantity will be bought.

Answer: False

Explanation: A greater quantity will be bought when the price falls, but this will be shown as a movement along the demand curve, not as a shift in the curve.

12. The market demand curve will shift to the right if the number of buyers increases or if buyers' incomes increase.

Answer: True

13. Changes in income, prices of related goods, the price of the item under consideration, population, and expectations will shift the demand curve and are therefore called demand shifters.

Answer: False

Explanation: *All of the variables listed in the statement, except the price of the item, will shift the demand curve. The price of the item being considered is not a demand shifter.*

14. Demand shifters include income, prices of related goods, population, tastes and preferences, and expectations.

Answer: True

15. All goods are normal goods because people buy more of all goods and services when their incomes increase.

Answer: False

Explanation: *People buy less inferior goods and their incomes increase.*

16. A good is said to be an inferior good if a smaller quantity of the good is bought as income increases.

Answer: True

17. A change in demand is shown by shifting the demand curve while a change in quantity demanded is shown by a movement along a demand curve.

Answer: True

18. Supply is expected to rise if the price of the item rises.

Answer: False

Explanation: If the price of an item rises, quantity supplied is expected to rise.

19. A supply schedule is an upward sloping graph that shows the direct relationship between price and supply.

Answer: False

Explanation: The relationship is between price and quantity supplied.

20. A supply schedule is a table that shows the direct relationship between price and quantity supplied.

Answer: True

21. The law of supply states that as the price of an item rises, the quantity supplied will also rise.

Answer: False

Explanation: The "other things being equal" condition is required to make the statement true.

22. According to the law of supply, as the price of an item falls, other things being equal, the quantity supplied will also fall.

Answer: True

23. The supply curve is an upward sloping curve showing the direct relationship between price and quantity supplied.

Answer: True

24. Factors that will shift the supply curve include a change in the price of the good or service and a change in the number of producers.

Answer: False

Explanation: A change in the price of the good or service will cause a movement along the supply curve. It will not shift it.

25. Factors affecting supply include the number of producers, technology, prices of inputs, prices of related products, and expectations.

Answer: True

26. A supply curve shifting to the left means that producers will offer a smaller quantity for sale at each price.

Answer: True

27. The equilibrium price is the highest price at which an item can be sold.

Answer: False

Explanation: The equilibrium price is the price that equates quantity demanded and quantity supplied.

28. Whenever a surplus exists, it will exert downward pressure on the price; and whenever a shortage exists, it will exert an upward pressure on the price.

Answer: True

29. An increase in the demand for product *A* will always raise the price of *A*.

Answer: False

Explanation: This will be true only if all other things remain equal.

30. Other things being equal, an increase in supply will cause a shortage that forces the price down.

Answer: False

Explanation: The increase in supply will cause a surplus, not a shortage.

31. A tax imposed on a product will tend to raise the price of the product by the full amount of the tax.

Answer: False

Explanation: The tax will increase the price but generally not by the full amount of the tax.

32. If demand and supply both increase, we know that the equilibrium quantity will increase, but we cannot be certain about the effect on the equilibrium price.

Answer: True

33. A price ceiling that is set above the equilibrium price is likely to be ineffective.

Answer: True

34. If carpets and vacuum cleaners are considered to be complementary goods, then an increase in the price of carpets will lead to a decrease in the demand for vacuum cleaners.

Answer: True

35. An increase in the minimum wage is likely to result in an increase in jobs for low-skilled workers.

Answer: False

Explanation: An increase in the minimum wage will make it more expensive for firms to hire low-skilled workers. Hence, a decrease in the number of jobs will likely result.

Completion

(Fill in the blanks)

Use each word or combination of words from the list exactly once.

*(**Hint**: Proceed by elimination)*

Word list

six — seven — five x 2 — Above — Below — Curve — Demand x 3 — Downward — Equilibrium x 2 — Expectations — Fall — Greater — Horizontal — Income x 2 — Increase x 2 — Left — Lower — Normal — Population — Prices Of Related Goods — Quantity Demanded x 2— Raise — Right — Schedule — Shortage x 3 — Substitutes/Complements — Substitution — Supply — Surplus x 2 — Tastes and Preferences

Questions

1. The various quantities that consumers will be willing and able to buy at various prices during a period of time constitute ______________. The quantity that will be bought at a specific price is referred to as ______________ ______________.

2. A(n) ______________ ______________ is a table showing various quantities that people will be willing and able to buy at various prices.

3. The increase in quantity demanded resulting from an increase in the buyers' real income as the price falls is known as the ______________ effect. The change in quantity demanded resulting from substituting one good for another when the price of a good changes is called the ______________ effect.

4. The law of demand states that if the price of an item rises, other things being equal, the quantity demanded will ______________.

5. On a demand/supply graph, economists usually place price on the ______________ axis and quantity on the ______________ axis.

6. A change in ______________ is shown by a shift in the demand curve; a change in ______________ is shown by a movement along the demand curve.

7. The major determinants of demand are ______________, ______________, ______________, ______________, and ______________.

8. The market demand curve slopes ______________, indicating that a ______________ quantity will be demanded as the price falls.

9. Electric guitars and guitar amplifiers would be considered to be ______________.

10. An increase in income, other things being equal, will cause the demand curve to shift to the ______________. A decrease in income will cause it to shift to the ______________.

11. Good *A* is a(n) ______________ good if people buy more of it as their incomes rise.

12. A graph showing the direct relationship between price and quantity offered for sale is called a(n)______________ ______________.

13. The intersection of the demand and supply curves determines the ______________ price and the ______________ quantity.

14. A(n)______________ exists when quantity demanded exceeds quantity supplied t some specific price; and a(n)______________ exists when quantity demanded is less than quantity supplied at some specific price.

15. A surplus will tend to ______________ the price while a shortage will tend to ______________ it.

Questions 16-19 refer to the following diagram.

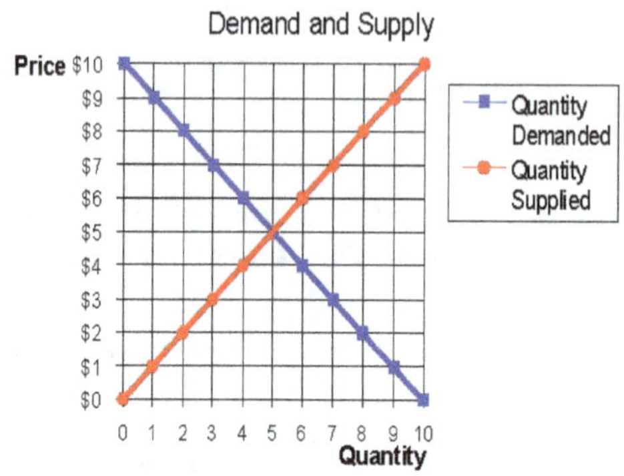

16. If the price is $8, there will be a surplus of ______________ units.

17. If the price is $2, there will be a(n) ______________ of 6 units.

18. The highest price that buyers will be willing and able to pay for 3 units of this product is $ ______________.

19. The equilibrium price and quantity as reflected in this diagram are $ ______________ and ______________ units.

20. Any price below the equilibrium price will result in a(n)______________ of the product. Any price above the equilibrium price will result in a(n)______________ of the product.

21. If demand increases, other things being equal, we predict a(n)______________ in price and a(n)______________ in quantity traded.

22. To be effective, a price ceiling must be set ______________ the equilibrium price. To be effective, a price floor must be set ______________ the equilibrium price.

Solution

1. (demand, quantity demanded)
2. (demand schedule)
3. (income, substitution)
4. (fall)
5. (vertical, horizontal)
6. (demand, quantity demanded)
7. (income, tastes and preferences, population, prices of related goods, expectations—in any order)
8. (downward, greater)
9. (complements)
10. (right, left)
11. (normal).
12. (supply curve)
13. (equilibrium, equilibrium)
14. (shortage, surplus)
15. (lower, raise)
16. (6)
17. (shortage)
18. (7)
19. (5, 5)
20. (shortage, surplus)
21. (increase, increase)
22. (below, above)

6 MACROECONOMICS & NATIONAL INCOME ACCOUNTING

SYNOPSIS

Macroeconomics is concerned with the total output of all goods and services in the economy, total employment, and movements in the price level. Macroeconomic behavior reflects the sum total of decisions made by individuals. A fruitful approach to studying macroeconomics is to consider its microeconomic foundations.

At the time of the Great Depression, there were no macroeconomic models to successfully explain the major macroeconomic problem of prolonged involuntary unemployment. The **classical models** failed to explain the widespread unemployment that existed during that period. A new direction was needed, and John Maynard Keynes developed a **macroeconomic model** to deal with the situation.

The great macroeconomics issues include unemployment, inflation, economic growth, the business cycle, and international economic problems. These topics form the core of macroeconomics. In fact, macroeconomic theory provides a basis for much of public policy.

The **gross domestic product (GDP)** is a measure of the value of the economy's total output of goods and services. The two main ways of measuring the GDP are the **income approach** and the **expenditure approach**.

Nominal gross domestic income figures can be deflated by appropriate price indexes to obtain **real** gross domestic income figures. Real gross domestic income figures are obtained by dividing the nominal figures by the price index and then multiplying by 100.

Many factors have to be taken into consideration when using GDP as a measure of economic well-being. The size of the population, the distribution of income, non-marketed goods and services, leisure time available, and the quality of life must all be taken into consideration when using GDP as a measure of well being.

LEARNING OBJECTIVES

In connection with this module, you should be able to:

1. differentiate between microeconomics and macroeconomics
2. discuss the origin of macroeconomics
3. identify the great macroeconomic questions
4. discuss the importance and relevance of macroeconomics
5. explain how macroeconomists study the economy
6. construct and describe a simple circular flow of the economy
7. explain the meaning of GDP
8. explain how to measure GDP
9. discuss the relationship between GDP and economic well-being

DEFINITIONS & CONCEPTS

You should be able to define the following terms and concepts:

microeconomics	fine tuning
fiscal policy	macroeconomics
economic policy	financial market
classical economic model	monetary policy
stagflation	invisible hand
incomes policy	deficit
Great Depression	product market
new classical economics	Keynesian economics
labour market	stocks (shares)
supply side	bonds (securities)
New Keynesian economics	Treasury bills
inflation	circular flow
unemployment	interest and dividends
international economy	transfer payments
economic growth	gross domestic product
business cycle	price index
net capital formation	double-counting
net domestic income	value added
intermediate product	final product
base year	capital consumption
underground economy	real GDP

6

MACROECONOMICS & NATIONAL INCOME ACCOUNTING

Concepts, Definitions & Problems

Problem 6-1

Discuss the importance of macroeconomics.

Requirement and Clue: *Focus on the use of macroeconomics by government, businesses, and private individuals.*

Solution:

Macroeconomic theory or macroeconomics provides a basis for public policy. It is now generally accepted that government spending and taxes can be used to regulate the economy. Fiscal policy (i.e., government spending and taxing decisions) is now an important tool that governments use to try to stabilize the economy. In addition, the government has some control over the quantity of money and credit in the economy to bring about certain desired economic conditions. The government also uses macroeconomics when it imposes direct controls on wages and prices—an instrument known as incomes policies.

Business decisions are made with consideration for the macroeconomic environment in which these businesses operate. A firm's profitability depends on the performance of the entire economy. For example, during a period of rapid economic growth, the demand for a firm's product might be expected to increase. The firm's decisions should reflect this possibility.

Macroeconomics is also important to private individuals. If an economy is expected to enter into a period of economic contraction, private individuals might be well advised to brace themselves for tough economic times. They might want to be more prudent in the way they spend their money, knowing that the probability of being unemployed will increase.

Problem 6-2

Give an account of the origin of Keynesian macroeconomics.

Requirement and Clue: *Focus on economic theory before Keynes. Consider the Great Depression and its influence on the development of economic thought.*

Solution:

In the period from 1929 to 1939, there was a severe economic contraction called the Great Depression. There were no macroeconomic models then to explain the phenomenon of the Great Depression. The only models available were microeconomic models, which were, nevertheless, applied to the macroeconomy. These classical economic models, as they are called, were incapable of explaining prolonged periods of involuntary unemployment.

The popular economic view at the time was as follows: Unemployment was a surplus of labour on the labour market. The excess quantity of labour supplied would cause the wage rate (the price of labour) to fall. As wages fell, employers would be willing to hire more workers at the new, lower, wage rate. Workers would be hired until the excess labour was absorbed by the market.

The classical model failed during the Great Depression. Unemployment was severe and prolonged. It was in this economic environment that modern macroeconomics was born. The obvious failure of classical economics led an economist named John Maynard Keynes to take a close look at classical economics. This resulted in the formulation of a new economic model that could explain the economic situation during the Great Depression. In his epic work, The General Theory of Employment, Interest, and Money, Keynes developed a framework that was to become the foundation of macroeconomics. Instead of focusing on wages and prices in the labour market, Keynes emphasized total spending as the major determinant of employment in the economy.

Problem 6-3

(a) Distinguish between microeconomics and macroeconomics.
(b) What is the "aggregation problem" in macroeconomics?

Requirement and Clue: *This is a two-part problem. Answer each part in order. Your solution to part (a) should clearly explain the difference between these two concepts. For part (b), you are expected to clearly define the concept, giving an appropriate example.*

Solution:

(a) The two major branches of modern economic theory are microeconomics and macroeconomics. Microeconomics, also called price theory, is concerned with the behavior of the individual units that constitute the economy. Microeconomics deals with the behavior of consumers, producers, and the determination of prices in various types of market structures. It explains the composition of output and the distribution of income among the various factor owners. It describes the allocation of resources among competing ends.

Macroeconomics, on the other hand, deals with the broad aggregates of the economy. Macroeconomics studies the behavior of variables such as total personal expenditures on consumer goods and services, total investment, and government spending. It attempts to explain the level of national income and changes in the general level of prices.

(b) Since macroeconomics deals with the behavior of broad economic aggregates, a large number of variables must be added together to obtain a single measure. For example, the macroeconomic concept of total consumption is the sum of all household consumption, and total business investment is the sum of the investments of all firms. Quite often, the individual units may not be directly conformable to addition. How, for example, do we add the various interest rates to obtain the macroeconomic variable called the interest rate? This is the problem referred to as the aggregation problem. Some procedure must be devised for aggregating a large number of variables into a single measure. Economists usually overcome the difficulty by using some kind of averaging procedure or by making appropriate assumptions which allow them to perform the aggregation.

Problem 6-4

Using P for the product market, L for the labour market, and F for the financial market, indicate the market in which each of the following exchanges is likely to occur.

	Exchange	***Market***
a.	*A firm sells computers to households*	____
b.	*The government buys paper from a firm*	____
c.	*A firm sells furniture to the government*	____
d.	*Firms borrow money from households for expansion*	____
e.	*The government hires 100 new civil servants*	____
f.	*Firms employ people to work as salesmen*	____
g.	*People deposit money in their bank accounts*	____

Requirement and Clue: *Think of the circular flow model and macroeconomic market interaction.*

Solution:

	Exchange	**Market**
a.	A firm sells computers to households	P
b.	The government buys paper from a firm	P
c.	A firm sells furniture to the government	P
d.	Firms borrow money from households for expansion	F
e.	The government hires 100 new civil servants	L
f.	Firms employ people to work as salesmen	L
g.	People deposit money in their bank accounts	F

Problem 6-5

"One cannot deny the importance of macroeconomics in the area of public policy. However, the importance of macroeconomics for business decision making is questionable. If the objective of firms is to maximize their profits, then what they need is knowledge of microeconomics. They need to know how much to produce and what price to charge. Knowledge of macroeconomics is unlikely to be helpful in making business decisions."

Comment on the above statement.

Requirement and Clue: *You should read the statement carefully to see if you can detect any errors. If you find any errors, you should note them and offer a solution. Focus on the nature of macroeconomics.*

Solution

It is erroneous to say that macroeconomics is not useful in business decision making. Decisions such as pricing and production levels are not made in a vacuum. The decision maker needs to know as much as possible about the economic environment within which businesses operate, and macroeconomics provides much of that information.

Businesses need both microeconomics and macroeconomics for good decision making.

Problem 6-6

Briefly explain the great macroeconomic questions?

Requirement and Clue: *You are expected to demonstrate that you know what the great macroeconomic questions are. State clearly what is involved in each of the great questions.*

Solution

The great macroeconomic questions are:

- Unemployment
- Inflation
- Fluctuations in aggregate output
- Economic growth
- The international economy

Unemployment

The unemployment rate is of interest to macroeconomists, governments, households and businesses. Economists are interested in knowing why there is so much more unemployment than what can be expected from normal business failures and from new workers entering the labour market.

Inflation

Inflation, defined as a sustained increase in the average level of prices over time, is a serious macroeconomic issue. Rapid inflation is a sign that the economy is not performing well. Inflation reduces purchasing power and often leads to a misallocation of the economy's scarce resources. Economists are constantly seeking a better understanding of the inflationary process.

Fluctuations in aggregate output

An economy's output of goods and services is important because our standard of living depends, to a great extent, on what we are able to produce. If a society can keep the total output of goods and services close to its potential, its citizens will be better off. Fluctuations in the output of goods and services produced are problematic. These fluctuations, known as business cycles, are of interest to economists. They are very much interested in understanding and being able to explain why such fluctuations occur.

Economic growth

Economic growth can be defined as an increase in a country's output per capita. Other things being equal, economic growth implies an increase in economic well being. Economists are interested in the drivers of economic growth. They are also concerned with an increase in the economy's productive potential.

The international economy

Over the past several years, the economies of the world have become more interdependent than ever. An understanding of how the macroeconomy functions requires an understanding of how the domestic economy is affected by economic events in the rest of the world. As a case in point, consider the effect of the 1987-88 recession in the United States on the world economy.

Problem 6-7

Explain briefly how macroeconomists study the economy.

Requirement and Clue: *The problem is a test of your understanding of macroeconomic methodology. You are required to discuss briefly macroeconomic methodology.*

Solution

Macroeconomists use models to study the behavior of economic aggregates. There are different models to explain different macroeconomic phenomena. Economists are not in agreement on which is the "best" model, but most modern macroeconomists try to explain macroeconomic behavior by focusing on three markets: the product market, the labour market, and the financial market. The three markets are related. Economists learn much about the major macroeconomic problems and issues by studying the interaction of demand and supply in each of these markets. Macroeconomists also base the study of macroeconomics on its microeconomic foundations.

Problem 6-8

Determine whether each of the following statements is a classical (C) or Keynesian (K) view of the economy:

a. *Unemployment will be short-lived of wages and prices are flexible.*
b. *Total expenditure is the main determinant of the level of output and employment*
c. *Unemployment will cause wages to fall.*
d. *Unemployment results from wages that are too high.*
e. *Unemployment results from a deficiency in total spending.*
f. *Governments can and should use fiscal policy to reduce unemployment and increase output.*

Requirement and Clue: *Focus on the assumptions and prescriptions of the classical and Keynesian models of the economy.*

Solution

a. Unemployment will be short-lived if wages and prices are flexible. (C)
b. Total expenditure is the main determinant of the level of output and employment. (K)
c. Unemployment will cause wages to fall. (C)
d. Unemployment results from wages that are too high. (C)
e. Unemployment results from a deficiency in total spending. (K)
f. Governments can and should use fiscal policy to reduce unemployment and increase output. (K)

Problem 6-9

In the circular flow model with a government sector, give a specific example of each of the following:

a. *A resource flowing from households to government*
b. *A resource flowing from households to firms*
c. *Payment from government to households*
d. *A flow from firms to households*
e. *A flow from households to firms*

Requirement and Clue: *This problem is designed to test you understanding of the various flows in the circular flow model. You are required to give a specific example of each of the flows indicated.*

Solution

a. Labour services are an example of a resources flowing from households to the government.
b. An example of a resource flowing from households to firms is an investment of $20,000 in a company.
c. Salaries of civil servants are an example of a payment from government to households.
d. An example of a flow from firms to households is furniture and appliances.
e. An example of a flow from households to firms is labour services.

Problem 6-10

(a) *Briefly define national income accounting.*
(b) *What is the importance of economic statistics?*

Requirement and Clue: This is a two-part problem. Answer each part in order. Your definition should be clear and precise. For part (b), focus on the users and uses of economic statistics.

Solution

(a) National income accounting is the process of collecting, measuring, and recording data on the output or income of a country. Examples of the data collected in the process are total output produced, unemployment rates, exports and imports, wages and salaries, and government purchases of goods and services.
(b) Economic statistics such as gross domestic product (GDP), the unemployment rate, interest rate trends, etc. provide much useful information about the patters of economic activity. These statistics are of great importance to economists and other researchers who are trying to explain economic and social phenomena. They are also important to economic decision and policy makers in government and industry who need to formulate good economic policies. They are also of great importance to individuals in making certain decisions. For example, individuals may consider taking out loans when interest rates are low or expected to fall.

Problem 6-11

What is double-counting in national income accounting? How can it be avoided?

Requirement and Clue: *This is a two-part problem. Answer each part in order. You are required to give a clear and precise meaning of the concept with an example. For the second part of the problem, focus on intermediate and final products.*

Solution:

In estimating the market value of all goods and services produced in an economy, each item should be counted once only. Double-counting is counting an item more than once. If we count the plastic produced by a plastic manufacturer and then count it again in the chairs made from the plastic and in plastic cups, we would be double-counting. To avoid double-counting, we should count only the final products and omit the intermediate products. An intermediate product is an output of one firm or industry that is used as an input by other firms or industries. An example of an intermediate product is plastic. A final product is a product that is bought for final use. An example of a final product is a plastic cup.

Problem 6-12

Define each of the following terms as they relate to national income accounting.

(a) *Double-counting*
(b) *Value added*
(c) *Intermediate product*
(d) *Final product*

Requirement and Clue: *This is a multi-part problem. Answer each part in order. You are asked merely to define each concept. You are not required to write an essay on any of them. Just give a clear and precise meaning of each concept. Examples will be helpful.*

Solution

(a) Double-counting, in national income accounting, is counting an item more than once. It occurs when items are counted as intermediate goods and again as final goods. An example of double-counting is counting flour produced by flour mills and then counting the flower again in bread, cakes, pastries, etc.
(b) Value added is the increase in the value of a firm's product resulting from enhancements by the firm to inputs bought from other firms. In other words, value added is the difference between the value of the firm's output and the cost of the inputs. For example, if a firm buys electronic parts for $250 and uses the parts to make an electronic device that is sold for $300, then the value added is $50.
(c) An intermediate product is an output of one firm or industry that is used as an input by another firm or industry. An example of an intermediate product is cardboard produced by one firm and sold to another firm to make book covers.
(d) A final product is a good that is intended for final use and not intended for resale or further processing. An example of a final good is a suit of clothes or a cup of coffee.

Problem 6-13

Briefly describe the two main approaches used to measure the gross domestic product (GDP). Why should the two approaches give the same result?

Requirement and Clue: *This is a two-part problem. Answer each part in turn. In order to solve this problem, you must know what the two main approaches are. You are expected to explain what is entailed in each method. Pay attention to the word "briefly" in the problem. Focus on the logic behind using each approach.*

Solution

There are two main methods or approaches used to measure the GDP: the income approach and the expenditure approach.

The income approach: The GDP can be measured by measuring the total income earned by those factors of production that contribute to the production of the total output. This would involve adding the incomes generated by the resources used in producing the total output. This is the income approach.

The expenditure approach: Alternatively, the GDP can be measured by measuring the total amount of money spent in purchasing the total output. This involves adding all the expenditures of the various groups that purchase the goods and services produced in the economy. This is the expenditure approach.

Each approach is measuring the same thing: the value of all goods and services produced in the economy. Logically then, the two approached should give the same result. All expenditures on the goods and services produced (total expenditure) are received as income by the owners of the resources used to produce the goods and services (total income). Thus, total expenditure equals total income.

Problem 6-14

What is capital consumption allowance? What role does it play in national income accounting?

Requirement and Clue: This is a two-part problem. Answer each part in turn. Give a clear and precise meaning of the concept. An example will be helpful. For the second part of the problem, focus on what happens to the income measure when capital consumption is added.

Solution

During any given period, the capital stock used to produce goods and services will suffer some loss of value because of the passage of time and wear and tear. This loss of value (depreciation) of the capital stock is referred to as capital consumption allowance. Capital consumption allowance then, is an allowance for the depreciation of the economy's capital stock during production. For example, if at the beginning of the production period, a firm's factory was valued at \$3.5 million, and at the end of the period it is valued at \$3.4 million, then capital consumption allowance on that building would be (\$3.5 – \$3.4) million = \$100,000.

En route to calculating the GDP, we must add capital consumption allowance to net domestic income at factor cost in order to obtain gross domestic income at factor cost. In other words, the addition of capital consumption allowance converts a net figure to a gross figure.

Problem 6-15

An accountant pays someone \$600 a season to cut his lawn. He also gives his daughter an allowance of \$600. Which of these payments should be included in the GDP? What is the difference?

Requirement and Clue: *This is a two-part problem. Answer each part in order. Focus on the definition of GDP.*

Solution

The gross domestic product is the market value of all final goods and services produced in an economy during a period of time. The \$600 paid to mow the lawn represents payment for services produced. The gardener produced lawn-mowing services valued at \$600. This should be included in the GDP. The daughter's allowance should not be included. The difference is that the allowance does not represent the value of any good or service produced. Only the value of goods and services produced during the period under consideration should be included in the GDP for that period. The daughter's allowance is a transfer of purchasing power from father to daughter.

Problem 6-16

(a) *Define each of the following terms with reference to the circular flow of income and expenditure:*

(i) *Injection*

(ii) *Leakage*

(b) *What is the effect of each on the level of income and expenditure?*

Requirement and Clue: *This is a two-part problem. Answer each part in order. For part (a), a clear and precise meaning of each concept is required. Note that the context is the circular flow model. For part (b), you are to state succinctly how each concept will change the level of income and expenditure.*

Solution

(a) (i) An injection is any income or expenditure that is pushed into the flow of income and expenditure in the circular flow model. Injections include investment spending, government purchases of goods and services, and exports of goods and services.

(ii)A leakage (also called a *withdrawal*) is any income or expenditure that is taken out of the flow of income and expenditure in the circular flow model. Leakages include savings, taxes, and imports.

(b) Other things being equal, injections will increase the level of income and expenditure in the circular flow. Leakages, on the other hand, will reduce the level of income and expenditure in the circular flow.

Problem 6-17

The following table contains data for a hypothetical economy in a certain year.

Item	*$million*
Personal expenditure on consumer goods & services	25, 280
Government current expenditure on goods & services	5,181
Indirect taxes less subsidies	4,587
Wages and salaries	20,141
Accrued net income of farm operators	1,026
Exports of goods and services	6,709
Capital consumption allowances	4,769
Gross investment	9,153
Corporation profits before taxes	3,946
Interest and miscellaneous investment income	1,174
Imports of goods and services	7,222
Net income of non-farm unincorporated business, incl. rent	3,458

On the basis of the data contained in the table above, compute each of the following:

(a) *Net domestic income at factor cost*

(b) *GDP, income-based*

(c) *GDP, expenditure-based*

(d) *Net investment*

Requirement and Clue: *This is an example of a typical problem on national income accounting. It's a four-part problem. Answer each part in order. You are required to know the components of GDP, income and expenditure based. It might be helpful to write down the formula for each measure to be computed.*

Solution

(a) Net domestic income at factor cost is the sum of the incomes earned by the factors of production. This measure consists of the following items:

Items	**$million**
Wages and salaries	20,141
Accrued net income of farm operators	1,026
Corporate profits before taxes	3,946
Interest & miscellaneous investment income	1,174
Net income of non-farm unincorporated business, incl. rent	3,458
Net domestic income at factor cost	**29,745**

(b) GDP income-based = Net domestic income at factor cost + capital consumption allowance + indirect taxes – subsidies. Thus, GDP income-based is:

29,745 + 4,769 + 4,587 = **$39,101million**

(c) GDP, expenditure-based is the sum of consumer spending (C), investment spending (I), government purchases (G), and net exports (X – M) where X is the value of exports and M is the value of imports. Thus,

GDP, expenditure-based is:

C + I + G + (X – M) = 25,280 + 9,153 + 5,181 + (6,709 – 7,222) = **$39,101 million**

(d) Net investment is gross investment minus capital consumption allowance. That is:

Net investment = (9,153 – 4,769) = **$4,384million**

Problem 6-18

To which component of aggregate expenditure does each of the following belongs? (Use C for consumption, I for investment, G for government purchases, X for exports, and M for imports).

(a) *The purchase of a new car made in Korea*

(b) *A sum of money paid by a household to a personal consultant for two hours work*

(c) *The construction of a wall around a playground*

(d) *The purchase of a new home*

(e) *The purchase of new office furniture to furnish city hall offices*

(f) *An increase in the stock of electronic components over last year's level.*

Requirement and Clue: *This is a multi-part problem. Answer each part in order. The question requires you to be able to identify the components of aggregate expenditure.*

Solution

(a) *The purchase of a new car made in Korea*---M

(b) *A sum of money paid by a household to a personal consultant for two hours work*---C

(c) *The construction of a wall around a playground*---I

(d) *The purchase of a new home*---I (Note: It is tempting to classify this as consumption, but it is classified as residential construction, which is investment)

(e) *The purchase of new office furniture to furnish city hall offices-*--G

(f) *An increase in the stock of electronic components over last year's level*---I (This is inventory investment).

Problem 6-19

In 2010, a car manufacturer produced a certain number of cars but was able to sell only 90% of them in 2010. The income generated by producing the cars was accounted for in GDP income-based for 2010. Since only 90% of the cars were sold in 2010, how would the 10% unsold cars be included in GDP expenditure-based for 2010?

Requirement and Clue: *Focus on the components of GDP expenditure-based and what each component measures. Perhaps the process of elimination will help you to arrive at the treatment of the unsold cars.*

Solution:

Even though 10% of the cars were not sold in 2010, they must be included in that year's GDP because they were produced in 2010. In national income accounting, the unsold cars would be treated as investment on the expenditure side. They would be treated as if the firm that produced the cars turned around and bought them. They would be considered to be inventory investment.

Problem 6-20

Under which heading in the national income accounts should the following transactions be included?

(a) *The purchase of a brand new sports utility vehicle (SUV) by a family*

(b) *Income paid by a firm to a TV repair technician for her services*

(c) *The purchase of a new book-binding machine by a book-binding company*

(d) *The purchase of new laptop computers by a public school board*

(e) *The purchase of new DVD players from a foreign country*

(f) *The sale of telecommunication devices to a buyer in a foreign country*

(g) *The payment of dividends to shareholders*

(h) *The payment for labour services provided to the government.*

Requirement and Clue: *This is a multi-part problem. Answer each part in order. Consider both income and expenditure items and focus on the various categories that constitute each account.*

Solution

(a) The purchase of a brand new sports utility vehicle (SUV) by a family should be included under personal expenditure on consumer goods and services in the expenditure account.

(b) Income paid by a firm to a TV repair technician for her services should be included under wages and salaries in the income account.

(c) The purchase of a new book-binding machine by a book-binding company should be included under investment in the expenditure account.

(d) The purchase of new laptop computers by a public school board should be included under government expenditure on goods and services in the expenditure account.

(e) The purchase of new DVD players from a foreign country should be included under imports of goods and services in the expenditure account.

(f) The sale of telecommunication devices to a buyer in a foreign country should be included under exports of goods and services in the expenditure account.

(g) The payment of dividends to shareholders should be included under interest and miscellaneous investment income in the income account.

(h) The payment for labour services provided to the government should be included under wages and salaries in the income account.

Problem 6-21

You are given the following data:

Consumption = *$5,400,000*

Personal saving = *$1,200,000*

Personal taxes = *$2,000,000*

Compute:

(a) *Personal income*

(b) *Disposable income*

Requirement and Clue: *This is a two-part problem. Answer each part in order. You are required to know the meaning and composition of the two concepts listed in the problem. This will help you to use the data provided to do the necessary computations.*

Solution

(a) Personal income is the total income of individuals from all sources before personal income taxes are paid. A part of it is used for consumption, a part is saved, and a part is used to pay personal taxes. Thus, personal income (PI) can be computed by using the following equation:

PI = Consumption + personal saving + personal taxes

PI = 5,400,000 + 1,200,000 + 2,000,000 = **$8,600,000**

(b) Disposable income (DI) is after tax income that can be used for consumption or saving. Thus, disposable income can be computed using the following equation:

DI = consumption + saving

DI = 5,400,000 + 1,200,000 = **$6,600,000**

Problem 6-22

The following data are available for a hypothetical economy.

Item	$million
Rents	120
Personal consumption expenditures	5,400
Indirect taxes less subsidies	815
Net exports	35
Corporate income taxes	325
Undistributed profits	90
Interest and dividends	585
Wages and salaries	5,140
Income from unincorporated business	485
Gross investment	1,200
Capital consumption allowances	900
Government purchases of goods and services	1,825

(a) *Calculate the GDP using*

(i) the expenditure method

(ii) the income method

(b) *Compute net domestic income at factor cost*

(c) *Compute net investment*

Requirement and Clue: *This is a three-part problem. Answer each part in order. Focus on the components of GDP expenditure-based and the components of GDP income-based. Be careful not to mix up income items with expenditure items. The standard relationship between gross and net should help with the solution for part (c).*

Solution

(a) (i) The expenditure method involves adding: consumer spending (C), investment (I), government purchases (G), and net exports (X – M).

C ....=	5,400
I .... =	1,200
G .... =	1,825
(X – M)... =	35
GDP...... =	**$8,460 million**

(ii)The income method involves adding all incomes along with capital consumption allowances and indirect taxes less subsidies. Corporate profits are distributed among corporate income taxes, undistributed profits, and interest and dividends. Thus, GDP by the income method is:

Rents	= 120
Indirect taxes less subsidies	= 815
Corporate income taxes	= 325
Undistributed profits	= 90
Interest and dividends	= 585
Wages and salaries	= 5,140
Income from unincorporated business	= 485
Capital consumption allowances	= 900
GDP	= **$8,460 million**

(b) Net domestic income at factor cost = GDP – Capital consumption – indirect taxes less subsidies. Thus net domestic income at factor cost is:

8460– 900 – 815 = **$6,745 million**

(c)Net investment is gross investment minus capital consumption allowances. Thus,

Net investment = 1,200 – 900 = **$300 million**

Problem 6-23

The following table gives data for a hypothetical economy.

Year	*Average level of prices*	*Quantity of output*
2000	*15*	*650*
2005	*20*	*1,000*
2010	*25*	*1,500*

(a) *Calculate the GDP for 2000, 2005, and 2010*

(b) *Using 2005 as the base year, give price indexes for 2000 and 2010.*

(c) *Using the price indexes calculated in (b), express GDP for 2000, 2005, and 2010 in constant (2005) dollars.*

Requirement and Clue: *This is a three-part problem. Answer each part in order. Recall that GDP is a price times quantity (P × Q) figure. The formula for the price index can be used part (b), and the formula for the real GDP will be useful for part (c).*

Solution

See the last column of the table below.

Year	Avg level of prices	Quant. of output	GDP
2000	15	650	9,750
2005	20	1,000	20,000
2010	25	1,500	37,500

(a) See table below. (The base year has an index of 100)

Year	Price Index
2000	**75**
2005	100
2010	**125**

(b) Real GDP (GDP in constant dollars) is as follows:

$$\text{Real GDP} = \frac{\text{GDP}}{\text{P}} \times 100; \text{ P is the price index.}$$

See the last column on the table below.

Year	Price index	GDP	GDP in constant $
2000	75	9,750	9,750 × 100 ÷ 75 = **13,000**
2005	100	20,000	20,000 × 100 ÷ 100 = **20,000**
2010	125	37,500	37,500 × 100 ÷ 125 = **30,000**

Problem 6-24

The following statistics are given for a hypothetical economy.

Item	*$million*
Consumption expenditure	*800*
Profits	*120*
Gross investment spending	*420*
Rental income	*250*
Government purchases	*300*
Imports	*140*
Wages	*1,100*
Exports	*160*
Interest and dividends	*70*

Use the data to compute the GDP by

(a) *The income method*

(b) *The expenditure method*

Requirement and Clue: This is a two-part problem. Answer each part in order. Focus on the components of both methods.

Solution

(a) The income method:

Item	$million
Wages	1,100
Rental income	250
Interest	70
Profits	120
GDP	**1,540**

(b) The expenditure method:

Item	$million
Consumption	800
Investment	420
Government purchases	300
Net exports (X – M)	20
GDP	**1,540**

Problem 6-25

You are given the following data for a hypothetical economy in a particular year.

Item	*$million*
Personal income	*800*
Net domestic income	*1,000*
Indirect taxes less subsidies	*140*
Imports of goods and services	*200*
Personal expenditure on consumer goods & services	*550*
Exports of goods and services	*210*
Government purchases	*450*
Gross domestic product	*1,200*

Compute:

(a) *Capital consumption allowances*

(b) *Net investment*

Requirement and Clue: This is a two-part problem. Answer each part in order. Note that it may not be necessary to use all the data provided.

Solution

(a) Gross domestic product = (Net domestic income + capital consumption allowances + indirect taxes less subsidies).

Hence 1,200 = (1,000 + capital consumption allowances + 140

Capital consumption allowances = 1,200 – 1,000 – 140 = 1,200 – 1,140 = **$60 million**

b) GDP = C + I + G + (X – M)

1200 = 550 + I + 450 + (210 – 200)

I = 1200 – 550 – 450 – 10 = 190 (This is gross investment)

Net investment = gross investment – capital consumption allowances

= 190 – 60 = **$130 million**

Problem 6-26

The following data are for a hypothetical economy.

	$million
GNP = GDP	700
Consumption	500
Personal saving	30
Personal taxes	60
Capital consumption	80
Indirect taxes	20

Compute:

(a) *Disposable income (DI)*

(b) *Personal income (PI)*

(c) *Net domestic income (NDI)*

Requirement and Clue: *This is a three-part problem. Answer each part in order. Focus on the definition of each concept and then use the data provided to arrive at the value.*

Solution

(a) Disposable income (DI) is the sum of consumption (C) and personal saving (S). That is:

DI = C + S = 500 + 30 = **$530 million**

(b) Personal income (PI) is the sum of disposable income (DI) and personal taxes (T). Thus,

PI = DI + T = 530 + 60 = **$590 million**

(c) Net domestic income (NDI) = GDP – capital consumption (D) – indirect taxes (Ti).

NDI = GDP – D – Ti

= 700 – 80 – 20 = **$600million**

Problem 6-27

As an economic statistician, you have collected the following economic data for a hypothetical economy.

	$billion
Profits	40
Income of unincorporated businesses	60
Net investment	60
Wages, salaries & other employees' compensation	400
Indirect business taxes	40
Net exports	2
Capital consumption allowances (Depreciation)	80
Interest	120
Rents	20
Consumption	480

Use the data to compute:

(a) *GDP*

(b) *Net domestic income*

(c) *Government purchases*

Requirement and Clue: This is a three-part problem. Answer each part in order. Look at the data carefully to see whether you can obtain GDP by the income method or by the expenditure method. Appropriate formulas will help you to compute the other concepts.

Solution

(a) Using the income method, GDP can be computed as follows:

GDP = Wages + rent + interest and dividends + profits + other income + depreciation (capital consumption) + indirect taxes.

Thus,

GDP = 400 + 20 + 120 + 40 + 60 + 80 + 40 = **$760 billion**

(b) Net domestic income = GDP – depreciation – indirect taxes. Thus:

Net domestic income = 760 – 80 – 40 = **$640 billion**

(c) Using the expenditure method, we know that:

GDP = C + I + G + (X – M)

760 = 480 + (60 + 80) + G + 2, hence

G = **$138 billion**

Problem 6-28

What is the difference between GDP and GNP?

Requirement and Clue: *Clearly, you must be familiar with the concepts to be able to state the difference between them. Carefully defining each concept will help to demonstrate their difference.*

Solution

Gross domestic product (GDP) is the market value of all final goods and services produced within the borders of a country, regardless of who owns the resources used to produce the output. Gross national product (GNP) on the other hand, is the market value of all final goods and services produced by the country's resources, regardless of where the resources are located. Goods and services produced outside a country by its resources that are outside the country are a part of the country's GNP but not a part of its GDP. Goods and services produced within a country by foreign owned resources are a part of its GDP but not a part of its GNP.

Problem 6-29

The following table gives data for a hypothetical economy. Fill in the blanks.

Year	Real GDP (2005 $)	GDP (current $)	Price Index (2005 = 100)
1995	300	-----	25
2000	-----	750	85
2005	1,500	-----	-----
2010	-----	3,000	200

Requirement and Clue: *This problem is a test of your knowledge of using price indexes to compute real and nominal GDP.*

Solution

The first thing we can do is to fill in the price index for 2005 which is the base year (index = 100).

Next, we know that Real GDP = GDP × 100 ÷ P where P is the price index. We can use this formula to fill in the real GDP for 2000 as follows:

Real GDP = 750 × 100 ÷ 85 = **882.35**

Next, we know that in the base year, the real GDP and the GDP in current dollars are the same. So we can fill in the current GDP for 2005.

Next, we can use the real GDP formula to fill in the real GDP for 2010 as follows:

Real GDP = GDP × 100 ÷ P

Real GDP = 3,000 × 100 ÷ 200 = **1,500**

Finally, we can use the GDP formula to fill in the current GDP for 1995 as follows:

GDP = Real GDP × P ÷ 100

GDP = 300 × 25 ÷ 100 = **75**

The table with the blanks filled is shown below.

Year	Real GDP (2005 $)	GDP (current $)	Price Index (2005 = 100)
1995	300	75	25
2000	882.35	750	85
2005	1,500	1,500	100
2010	1,500	3,000	200

Problem 6-30

Give three examples of non-marketed goods and services and explain how they affect GDP as a measure of economic well-being.

Requirement and Clue: *This is a two-part problem. Answer each part in order. Focus on items that are produced but not recorded in the GDP calculation.*

Solution

GDP is the market value of all goods and services produced so the measure includes goods and services sold in regular, recognized markets. However, many goods and services produced do not get counted in the GDP because they are not really sold. Three examples of these non-marketed goods and services are housework, home garden cultivation, and volunteer work. These goods and services do increase economic well-being but they are not captured in the GDP figure.

Problem 6-31

Given the information shown in the following table about a hypothetical economy, how much did real GDP grow between 1990 and 2000? How much did it grow between 2000 and 2010?

	1985	1990	1995	2000	2005	2010
Nominal GDP ($million)	800	1,100	1,500	2,500	3,500	5,000
Price index	100	120	160	250	300	420

Requirement and Clue: This is a two-part problem. Answer each part in order. You must convert nominal GDP to real GDP in order to solve this problem.

Solution

The real GDP for 1990 is: GDP × 100 ÷ price index.

Real GDP (1990) = 1,100 × 100 ÷ 120 = 916.67

The real GDP for 2000 is: GDP × 100 ÷ price index.

Real GDP (2000) = 2,500 × 100 ÷ 250 = 1,000

Therefore, between 1990 and 2000, real GDP grew from $916.67 million to $1,000 million—an increase of $(1,000 – 916.67) = **$83.33 million**. That's an increase of **9.09%.**

The real GDP for 2000 is: $1,000 million (see above)

The real GDP for 2010 is: GDP × 100 ÷ price index.

Real GDP (2010) = 5,000 × 100 ÷ 420 = 1,190.48

Therefore, between 2000 and 2010, real GDP grew from $1,000 million to $1,190.48 million—an increase of $(1,190.48 – 1,000) = **$190.48 million.** That's an increase of **19%.**

Problem 6-32

Explain what would happen to the GNP and GDP of a country if:

(a) *a number of foreign companies established subsidiaries in the country;*

(b) *some firms from the country relocated in foreign countries;*

(c) *there was a global increase in the productivity of all workers.*

Requirement and Clue: *This is a three-part problem. Answer each part in order. The solution requires an understanding of the difference between GNP and GDP. Keep the difference in mind as you solve this problem.*

Solution

(a) If a number of foreign companies established subsidiaries in a country, the GNP of the country would not be affected, but its GDP would increase.

(b) If some firms relocated in foreign countries, the GDP would fall, but the GNP would not be affected.

(c) If there was a global increase in the productivity of all workers, both the GNP and the GDP would increase.

Problem 6-33

Explain what would happen to the GDP of a country if:

(a) *all housekeepers decided to marry their employers;*

(b) *prostitution and illicit drug dealing were legalized;*

(c) *home-makers were paid for their services.*

Requirement and Clue: This is a three-part problem. Answer each part in order. Focus on the definition of GDP as the *market* value.

Solution

(a) If all housekeepers decided to marry their employers, their services would no longer be sold on the market; therefore the GDP would fall.

(b) If prostitution and illicit drug dealing were legalized, they would be sold on the market like any other good or service and would therefore be included in the GDP. This would cause GDP to increase.

(c) If home-makers were paid for their services, these services would then be included in the GDP and thus cause it to increase.

Problem 6-34

What is gross domestic product? Discuss some modifications that would have to be made in order to use gross domestic product as a measure of economic progress and human well-being.

Requirement and Clue: *This is a two-part problem. Answer each part in order. A clear and precise definition is required for the first part of the problem. For the second part of the problem, focus on what affects people's well-being. Consider what is omitted from GDP that adds to economic progress or human well-being.*

Solution

Gross domestic product (GDP) is defined as the market value of all final goods and services produced in an economy during a period of time. This measure of total production is often used as a measure of economic progress. An increase in total production means that we have more goods and services to consume and hence a higher standard of living.

In order to use GDP as an adequate measure of economic progress, we have to make a number of adjustments. The GDP can increase from year to year without any increase in the actual quantities of goods and services produced. This can happen of the prices of goods and services rise. To make meaningful comparisons, and to arrive at an estimate of changes in actual production, we must eliminate the effects of price changes from current GDP. This is done by deflating GDP by the implicit price deflator. This enables us to express values in constant rather than current dollars. GDP in constant dollars, or real GDP as it is called, is a better measure than GDP in current dollars for purposes of estimating economic progress.

If the real GDP of a country increases by ten percent in a year, then obviously more goods and services will be available. But what if the population also increases by tem percent? On an average, people will be no better off. Only if the rate of growth of GDP exceeds the rate of growth of the population will people be better off in terms of having more goods and services. The real GDP figure must therefore be adjusted by considering changes in the population. By dividing real GDP by the population we obtain a measure called real GDP per capita which is a better measure of economic progress. It must be noted however, that GDP per capita is only an average which tells us nothing about how total output is distributed among the population.

The GDP measures only those goods and services that actually pass through the market. But a number of goods and services actually produced do not get counted in GDP because they do not involve any monetary transactions. For example, if people paint their own houses, or do their own landscaping, their services are not counted in GDP; and the services rendered by homemakers in their own homes are not counted in GDP. Although these goods and services do not get counted in GDP, they nevertheless increase our standard of living.

Finally, GDP measures only the value of goods and services produced by the economy. There are other factors besides goods and services that are indicative of economic well-being. These include leisure, clean and un-crowded cities, unpolluted environments and safe highways—all of which contribute to the quality of life.

Problem 6-35

Distinguish between national income and national wealth. How are they related?

Requirement and Clue: *This is a two-part problem. Answer each part in order. A definition of each concept is in order. Focus on differences between the two concepts and state them. Don't forget to state how the concepts are related.*

Solution

National income refers to the total earnings of the owners of the factors of production from the services provided by those factors. It may be calculated by adding the amounts paid for the use of land, labour, capital and entrepreneurial services or by adding the incomes received by the owners of these factors of production. National wealth, on the other hand, refers to the nation's stock of buildings, machinery, land, equipment, natural resources, and other economic goods that it has accumulated.

An important distinction between national income and national wealth is that one is a flow variable while the other is a stock variable. National income is a flow while national wealth is a stock.

A national uses its stock of wealth to increase its flow of goods and services, or its income. The greater the national wealth, the greater is likely to be the national income. Also, the greater the national income, the greater is likely to be the nation's ability to add to its stock of wealth.

The distinction between national wealth and national income and also the relation between the two concepts can further be illustrated by considering a nation's manpower. The quantity and quality of the labour stock represents an important part of national wealth. The services provided by the nation's manpower yield a part of national income.

Problem 6-36

Differentiate between gross investment and net investment. How are these concepts related to gross domestic product?

Requirement and Clue: *This is a two-part problem. Answer each part in order. You should provide clear definitions of the concepts in a way that points out the difference between them. Familiarity with the gross domestic product will help to solve the second part of the problem.*

Solution

Gross investment is total expenditure on capital goods. A portion of this expenditure is used to keep the capital stock intact. During the production period, a certain part of the capital stock is used up and needs to be replaced. This type of investment which simply maintains the capital stock at its existing level is called replacement investment or capital consumption or depreciation. The part of gross investment which actually increases the capital stock is called net investment. Thus gross investment is the sum of net investment and replacement investment.

In calculating gross domestic product (GDP)—the market value of all goods and services produced by the economy—we can add total expenditures by all the spending units. Thus, GDP is the sum of consumption (C), investment (I), government purchases (G), and net exports (X – M). That is:

$$GDP = C + I + G + (X - M)$$

The investment variable in the equation above is gross investment. If replacement investment is subtracted from the GDP, the resulting figure is net domestic income (NDI). Moreover, if net investment is undertaken, we will be building up our stock of machines, buildings, equipment, etc. and so increase our capacity to produce a greater output of goods and services. On the other hand, if expenditure on capital is less than what is required to maintain the capital stock at its existing level, then we say we are disinvesting. In this case, we are actually reducing our capacity to producing goods and services. Thus, there is a close relationship between gross investment, net investment, and GDP.

Problem 6-37

What effect does illegal activity have on well-being?

Requirement and Clue: *The solution to this problem requires that a distinction be made between individual well-being and societal well-being. It is necessary also to focus on the nature of the illegal activity.*

Solution

The impact of illegal activity on well-being is somewhat subjective. It is debatable whether illegal activities increase well-being. The individuals who willingly engage in such activities must do so because they feel that they derive some net benefits. From the view point of the society as a whole, however, these activities may be considered as discommodities (i.e., bads rather than goods).

The case of under-the-table transactions is different. Each year, babysitters, dentists, private tutors, carpenters, accountants, and so on, provide a wide variety of services. Such services do increase the total amount of goods and services produced during the year and therefore add to our well-being. They are, however, not reflected in the national accounts if they are paid for under the table.

Multiple-Choice Questions

In each case, circle the letter that corresponds with the correct answer.

1. National income or product means:
   a. total wages of all workers in the nation
   b. the total amount of money in the nation
   c. the value of the flow of final goods and services during a period of time
   d. all of the above

   Answer: c

   Reason: *National income refers to the money measure of the overall flow of all final goods and services. This is consistent with choice c.*

2. National income accounting is:
   a. the accounting data collected and analyzed by all accountants for all businesses in the country
   b. the system devised by a nation's accountants to prepare financial statements for companies
   c. is the process used by national accountants to assist the government to collect income taxes
   d. none of the above

   Answer: d

   Reason: National income accounting is the process of collecting, measuring, and recording data on the economy's income and output

3. National income accounts are important to:
   a. economists and other researchers
   b. policymakers in government
   c. policymakers in industry
   d. all of the above

   Answer: d

   Reason: All of the groups listed use national income accounts for various reasons.

4. National income accounting involves:
   a. keeping records of the number of trips politicians make abroad
   b. accounting for all the goods and services produced in the country
   c. counting all the money distributed by banks
   d. keeping track of the number of hours worked by illegal immigrants

   Answer: b

   Reason: National income accounts measure the GDP and other related aggregates.

5. National income statistics serve only to:
   a. provide employment for economic statisticians
   b. provide jobs for government economists
   c. show the rest of the world how great a country we have
   d. none of the above

   Answer: d

   Reason: National income statistics serve a wide variety of purposes including providing valuable information upon which decisions can be based.

6. The total value of all goods and services produced within the borders of a country is that country's:
   a. total wealth
   b. gross domestic product (GDP)
   c. total annual sales
   d. volume of trade

   Answer: b

   Reason: The GDP is defined as the market value of all final goods and services produced in a country.

7. Which of the following is true about the GDP?
   a. It is a flow concept
   b. It is expressed in monetary terms rather than in real physical output
   c. It avoids double-counting
   d. All of the above

   Answer: d

   Reason: Choices a, b, and c all apply to the GDP.

8. GDP measures:
   a. the value of all intermediate goods produced domestically within a given period
   b. the value of all goods and services sold in an economy within a given period
   c. the value of all final goods and services produced domestically within a given period
   d. all of the above

   Answer: c

   Reason: Choice c is an accurate definition of GDP.

9. The value added in production is:
   a. the amount paid for productive inputs
   b. the price of the intermediate products
   c. the difference between the value of the output and the cost of the inputs
   d. the mark-up on the product so that the firm can earn a larger profit.

   Answer: c

   Reason: Value added is the value of a firm's output minus the value of the inputs that it purchases from other firms to product its output. This is consistent with choice c.

10. An intermediate product is:
   a. an output of one firm that is used as an input by other firms
   b. a product that is placed between two final products
   c. any output that is waiting to be sold
   d. intended for final use by the final consumer.

   Answer: a

   Reason: An intermediate product is a good that is used as an input into a further stage of production. This fits choice a.

11. Sales among firms:
   a. ensure that the GDP is as large as possible
   b. make total sales greater than GDP

c. make total sales less than GDP
d. reduce the value of the GDP

Answer: b

Reason: *Sales among firms involve intermediate products. GDP involves only sales of final goods and services. Total sales would include, among other things, sales of final goods and services and sales of intermediate products. Therefore total sales must exceed GDP.*

12. Which of the following transactions is not included in GDP?

a. The purchase of goods added to the inventories of firms
b. The purchase of stocks and bonds by households
c. The purchase of consumer goods and services
d. Government expenditures on salaries of civil servants

Answer: b

Reason: *The purchase of stocks and bonds does not represent expenditure on currently produced goods and services and is therefore excluded from the GDP.*

13. In national income accounting, double-counting is avoided by:

a. considering only the values added at each stage of production
b. counting the sales of each firm only once
c. considering only factor incomes and then adding all final sales
d. subtracting total sales of goods and services from total factor earnings and doubling the difference

Answer: a

Reason: *By dealing only in values added at each stage of production, there will be no double counting.*

14. GDP by the expenditure method adds together:

a. consumption, interest, government purchases, and net exports
b. consumption, government purchases, wages and salaries, and net exports
c. consumption, investment, government purchases, and net exports
d. wages and salaries, rent, interest and dividends, and profit

Answer: c

Reason: *GDP by the expenditure method is the sum of all expenditures on currently produced goods and services. Choice c is consistent with this.*

15. Which of the following is true about government transfer payments and private transfer payments?

a. Government transfer payments are included in the GDP but private transfer payments are not.
b. Private transfer payments are included in the GDP but government transfer payments are not.
c. Neither government transfer payments nor private transfer payments are included in the GDP.
d. Both government transfer payments and private transfer payments are included in the GDP.

Answer: c

Reason: *Transfer payments, whether government or private, do not represent payments for goods or services produced and therefore are not included in the GDP.*

16. Two main approaches to measuring the GDP are:

a. the statistical and the mathematical approaches
b. the income and expenditure approaches
c. the total sales and intermediate sales approaches
d. none of the above

Answer: b

Reason: *GDP can be measured by measuring the income generated in the process of production (the income method) or by measuring expenditures on the goods and services produced (the expenditure method).*

17. GDP by the income method is calculated by adding:

a. all expenditures during the year
b. wages and other factor incomes, and subtracting taxes
c. exports to total domestic expenditure
d. none of the above

Answer: d

Reason: *GDP by the income method is calculated by adding all the incomes generated by the factors of production, capital consumption allowance (depreciation) and indirect taxes less subsidies.*

18. Transfer payments include all of the following except:

a. federal government grants to students
b. social security payments
c. government assistance to farmers
d. government payment of teachers' salaries

Answer: d

Reason: *Government payment of teachers' salaries represents purchase of the services provided by teachers and that's not a transfer payment.*

19. An intermediate product is:

a. the same as a final product, but it is worth more
b. one that is expected to last from three to five years
c. a product that is intended for resale or further processing
d. none of the above

Answer: c

Reason: *An intermediate product is an output of one firm that is used as an input by some other firm. This is consistent with choice c.*

20. Net domestic income at factor cost is measured by:

a. Multiplying the quantity of each final good and service produced by its market price and then adding the total
b. Adding together the total of all expenditures on newly produced final goods and services
c. Adding together the total of all incomes earned from the factors of production
d. Subtracting the capital consumption allowance from GNP

Answer: c

Reason: *Net domestic income at factor cost refers to the costs of the factors of production which is the same as the income that they generate.*

21. Which of the following would **not** be included in GDP expenditure based for 2012?

a. The purchase of a new lawnmower in 2012

b. The purchase of a 1882 silver cup in 2012

c. The purchase of a movie ticket in 2012

d. All of the above would be included.

Answer: b

Reason: The 1882 silver cup was not produced in 2012 and should not be included in the GDP for 2012.

22. Which of the following would **not** be included when estimating GDP income-based?

a. Wages
b. Consumer spending
c. Rents
d. Profits

Answer: b

Reason: Consumer spending is an expenditure item; not an income item.

23. Net investment is:

a. the sum of capital consumption allowance (depreciation) and subsidies

b. the difference between GDP and net domestic income at factor cost

c. the difference between gross investment and depreciation

d. always greater than gross investment

Answer: c

Reason: Gross investment is made up of net investment and depreciation.

24. Which of the following would not be included in investment for an economy?

a. The addition of a new wing to a hospital

b. The purchase of a building previously used as a warehouse

c. An increase in a firm's inventories

d. The purchase of a new machine by manufacturing company

Answer: b

Reason: The purchase of a building previously used as a warehouse would not be included in investment because it was included when the warehouse was first built.

25. If all prices have doubled in the last ten years and all quantities have fallen to half their former levels, then:

a. real GDP is unchanged but nominal GDP has grown

b. nominal GDP is unchanged but real GDP has fallen

c. nominal GDP is unchanged but real GDP has grown

d. real GDP is unchanged but nominal GDP has fallen.

Answer: b

Reason: Price level changes do not affect real GDP; changes in quantity do.

26. Nominal GDP in 2005 in a certain economy was $500 million. By 2010, it had risen to $1,300 million. The GDP implicit price deflator, base 2007, rose from 80 to 130 during the same period (i.e., 2005 - 2010). Real GDP was:

a. $100 million in 2005 and $650 million in 2010

b. $400 million in 2005 and $650 million in 2010

c. $500 million in 2005 and $1,000 million in 2010

d. $625 million in 2005 and $1,000 million in 2010

Answer: d

Reason: By calculating the real GDP in 2005 and 2010, we obtain the results in choice d.

Use the following information to answer questions 27 and 28.

A wheat farmer sells wheat to a mill for 10 cents. The mill sells the flour to a bakery for 30 cents. The bakery sells the bread to a grocery store for 55 cents. The grocery store sells the bread to a poor economics student for 75 cents.

27. How much did this set of transactions add to GDP?

a. 20 cents
b. 65 cents
c. 45 cents
d. 75 cents

Answer: d

Reason: The total values added at each stage are equal to the value of the final product.

28. The value added by the bakery was:

a. 20 cents
b. 45 cents
c. 25 cents
d. 55 cents

Answer: c

Reason: The bakery bought the flour for 30 cents and sold the bread for 55 cents, thus adding value equal to 25 cents.

29. Which of the following is a non-marketed good or service?

a. Housework
b. Volunteer work
c. Garage chores
d. All of the above

Answer: d

Reason: Al though choices a, b, and c involve production of goods and services, they are not sold in the market place and are therefore categorized as non-marketed goods and service.

30. Which of the following reduces the accuracy of GDP as a measure of well-being?

a. The underground economy

b. Non-marketed goods and services

c. Environmental damage

d. All of the above

Answer: d

Reason: GDP does not take choices a, b, and c into consideration, but they do affect people's well-being, either positively or negatively.

True-False Questions

Determine whether each of the following statements is true or false.

1. National income accounting is of interest only to national governments to enable them to track certain economic aggregates such as unemployment and inflation rates.

Answer: False

Explanation: *National income accounts are of interest to a wide range of individuals and organizations, including researchers, governments, businesses, and private individuals.*

2. GDP is a measure of the value of all goods and services sold in the economy in a given year.

Answer: False

Explanation: *GDP is the value of all final goods and services produced in an economy during a period of time.*

3. National income accounting is the method used by governments to ensure that their books are balanced.

Answer: False

Explanation: *National income accounting is the process of collecting, measuring, and recording data on the economy's output.*

4. GDP is a stock concept rather than a flow concept.

Answer: False

Explanation: *GDP is a flow concept because it measures the economy's output of goods and services during a period of time.*

5. Double-counting is counting an item exactly twice when measuring the GDP.

Answer: False

Explanation: *The term is used to describe the error in counting an item more than once.*

6. The value added in production is the difference between the value of the output and the cost of the inputs.

Answer: True

7. An intermediate product is a product that is used to bridge the gap between inventories.

Answer: False

Explanation: *An intermediate product is a product that is intended for resale or further processing.*

8. In calculating GDP, one must add intermediate products and final products.

Answer: False

Explanation: *Adding intermediate products and final products will lead to the problem of double counting. Only the final products need to be considered.*

9. Government transfer payments are non-productive transactions and should be excluded from GDP calculations.

Answer: True

10. Government transfer payments should be included in GDP calculations but private transfer payments should be excluded.

Answer: False

Explanation: *Neither should be included because they do not represent the value of current production.*

11. Theoretically, the income approach and the expenditure approach to measuring the GDP should give different results because different things are being measured.

Answer: False

Explanation: *The two approaches should theoretically give the same results because they are not different ways of measuring the same concept—the GDP.*

12. Capital consumption allowance is a measure of the amount of consumption that takes place in the economy during a period of one year.

Answer: False

Explanation: *Capital consumption allowance is an allowance made for the wear and tear of the capital stock during production.*

13. Government current expenditure on goods and services does not include transfer payments.

Answer: True

14. In national income accounting, the purchase of a home is considered to be a consumption expenditure.

Answer: False

Explanation: *The purchase of a home is considered to be an investment, not consumption.*

15. Net investment is the difference between gross investment and indirect ytases less subsidies.

Answer: False

Explanation: *Net investment is the difference between gross investment and capital consumption allowance.*

16. GDP is a measure of the output produced domestically regardless of who owns the resources, while GNP is a measure of the output produced by resources owned by nationals of the country regardless of their location.

Answer: True

17. Nominal GDP is GDP expressed in current dollars while real GDP is GDP expressed in constant dollars.

Answer: True

18. In any year, nominal GDP divided by the GDP deflator and multiplied 100 equals real GDP.

Answer: True

19. If it cost $240 in 2010 to buy the same basket of goods that could have been bought in 2000 for $120, a consumer price index for 2010, using 2000 as base year, would have a value of 200.

Answer: True

20. Purely financial transactions that do not reflect current production are excluded from GDP.

Answer: True

21. Net domestic income at factor cost is always the same as gross domestic product at market prices.

Answer: False

Explanation: Indirect business taxes less subsidies, and capital consumption allowances must be added to net domestic income at factor cost to obtain gross domestic product at market prices.

22. If the average level of prices was stable, gross domestic product would be a perfect measure of economic and social well-being.

Answer: False

Explanation: Nominal GDP and real GDP would be identical but other issues such as the sige of the population, the distribution of output, non-marketed goods, the underground economy, etc. would still remain.

23. The existence of an underground economy results in an underestimation of the total value of goods and services produced as reported in the GDP.

Answer: True

24. Given that over time, the average level of prices has doubled and money income has also doubled, this means that real income has not changed.

Answer: True

Completion

(Fill in the blanks)

Use each word or combination of words from the list exactly once.
*(**Hint**: Proceed by elimination)*

Word list

accounting — allowance — capital — consumption x 2 — counting — current/nominal — depreciation — capital consumption — domestic x 2 — double — economy — expenditure x 2 — final — flow — GDP — government purchases — gross x 2 — income x 5 — index — intermediate — investment — national x 2 — net x 3 — net exports — nominal x 2 — payments — price — product — real — rise — transfer — underground — zero

Questions

1. The market value of all final goods and services produced in an economy during a period of time is called the ____________.
2. GDP minus depreciation minus indirect taxes less subsidies equals ____________ ____________ ____________ at factor cost.
3. The process of collecting, measuring, and recording data on the economy's output is called ____________ ____________ ____________.
4. GDP is a ____________ concept because it has a time dimension; that is, it is measured during a period. (flow)
5. The term used in national income accounting for including both intermediate and final products in the GDP is ____________ ____________.
6. Transfers of purchasing power from one individual or group to another for which no goods and services are produced are called ____________ ____________.
7. The two main approaches to measuring the total output of an economy are ____________ and the ____________ approaches.
8. The following items are included when using the ____________ method to calculate the GDP: wages and salaries, profits, interest and dividends.
9. An allowance made for the wear and tear of the capital stock during production is called ____________ ____________ ____________.
10. The items included in the ____________ method when calculating the GDP are government purchases of goods and services, investment, consumer spending, and net exports.
11. ____________ ____________ ____________ is the market value of all final goods and services produced by a country's resources, regardless of where the resources are located.
12. Goods produced for further processing and resale are called ____________ goods. Goods produced for final use are called ____________ goods.

13. Adding all the earnings of the factors of production located within the borders of a country gives ________ ________ ________ at factor cost.

14. GDP by the expenditure method is the sum of ________, ________, ________, and ________.

15. Investment in excess of that required to maintain the capital stock at its current level is called ________ investment. It may be computer by subtracting ________ from ________ investment.

16. GDP expressed in current dollars is called ________ GDP; expressed in constant dollars, it is called ________ GDP.

17. To arrive at constant GDP, we must deflate ________ by the ________ ________.

18. If prices rise and output remains the same, GDP will ________. Such a change in GDP will be ________, not real.

19. If the GDP increases by 10 percent and the population grows by 10%, then GDP per capita will grow by ________ percent.

20. Economic activities that are not reported to government and on which no taxes are paid form a part of the ________ ________.

Solution

1. (GDP)
2. (net domestic income)
3. (national income accounting)
4. (flow)
5. (double counting)
6. (transfer payments)
7. (income, expenditure; in any order)
8. (income)
9. (capital consumption allowance)
10. (expenditure)
11. (Gross national product)
12. (intermediate, final)
13. (net domestic income)
14. (consumption, investment, government purchases, net exports; in any order)
15. (net, depreciation [capital consumption], gross)
16. (nominal, real)
17. (current or nominal, price index)
18. (rise, nominal)
19. (zero)
20. (underground economy)

7 NATIONAL INCOME, PRICE LEVEL DETERMINATION, & ECONOMIC GROWTH

LEARNING OBJECTIVES

In connection with this module, you should be able to:

1. explain aggregate demand
2. explain aggregate supply
3. explain the determination of the equilibrium real output and the price level
4. analyze the effects of changes in aggregate demand
5. analyze the effects of changes in aggregate supply
6. discuss the policy implications of the AD-AS model
7. explain the basis of supply-side policies

DEFINITIONS & CONCEPTS

You should be able to define the following terms and concepts:

aggregate demand	intermediate range
aggregate demand curve	equilibrium real output
fallacy of composition	equilibrium price level
aggregate supply	fiscal policy
aggregate supply curve	monetary policy
Keynesian range (of AS curve)	marginal tax rate (MTR)
Classical range (of AS curve)	supply-side economics

SYNOPSIS

Aggregate demand refers to the various quantities of all goods and services that will be purchased at various price levels. **Aggregate supply** refers to the various quantities of all goods and services that will be produced at various price levels. Real output and the price level will be at their equilibrium levels where the aggregate demand and the aggregate supply curves intersect.

The effect of a change in aggregate demand depends on the shape of the aggregate supply curve. An increase in aggregate supply, other things being equal, will cause the price level to fall and real output to increase. A fall in aggregate supply, other things being equal, results in an increase in the price level and a fall in real output.

Supply-side economists argue that by stimulating aggregate supply, we can reduce inflation and unemployment. We can stimulate aggregate supply by lowering the **marginal tax rate (MTR),** reducing government deficit spending, deregulating industries, granting investment tax credits, and by lowering business taxes. The conclusion of supply-side economists, that tax cuts will provide an incentive for greater work effort, is based on the assumption that the economy is operating on the declining portion of the **Laffer curve**.

Critics of supply-side economics claim that supply-side policies have, at best, only limited effects on incentives to work, save, and invest. They claim further, that supply-side policies may result in recessions.

7

NATIONAL INCOME, PRICE LEVEL DETERMINATION, & ECONOMIC GROWTH

Concepts, Definitions & Problems

Problem 7-1

What is the difference between aggregate demand and aggregate expenditure?

Requirement and Clue: *The two concepts are closely related and some authors use them interchangeably. You are required to present each concept in such a way that their difference is highlighted.*

Solution

Aggregate demand refers to the various quantities of all goods and services that will be demanded in an economy at various price levels during a period of time. It is a relationship between the various quantities of real GDP demanded at various price levels. Aggregate expenditure, on the other hand, is total spending on the economy's output of goods and services, consisting of consumer spending, investment spending, government purchases, and net exports. It is often expressed as the familiar equation:

$$AE = C + I + G + (X - M)$$

where AE = aggregate expenditure, C = Consumer spending, I = Investment, G = government purchases, X = exports, and M = imports. (X – M) = net exports.

Problem 7-2

Carefully explain why the aggregate demand (AD) curve slopes downward.

Requirement and Clue: *Be careful not to give the same reasons that explain the downward slope of the market demand curve. The question to be addressed is this: Why do people buy more of the economy's output of goods and services when the price level falls and less when it rises?*

Solution

There are three reasons that explain the downward slope of the AD curve: the real wealth effect, the interest rate effect, and the foreign trade effect.

<u>The real wealth effect</u>

When the price level rises, other things being equal, holders of financial assets lose purchasing power. Their real wealth decreases. Thus their expenditures on consumer goods and services fall. This means that as the price level rises, the quantity of real output demanded falls.

<u>The interest rate effect</u>

As the price level rises, more money is demanded to purchase goods and services. This increase in the demand for money, other things being equal, results in an increase in interest rates. Higher interest rates reduce the amount of consumption and investment spending; thus the quantity of real output demanded falls when the price level rises.

The foreign trade effect

An increase in the price level in one country means that that country's goods have become more expensive in foreign countries and foreign goods have become less expensive. Thus imports into the country will increase while exports from the country will decrease, resulting in a fall in net exports. A fall in net exports means that a smaller quantity of the country's real output will be demanded as the price level rises.

For these three reasons, as the price level rises, the quantity of real output demanded decreases. This is just another way of saying that the aggregate demand curve is downward sloping as shown in the following diagram.

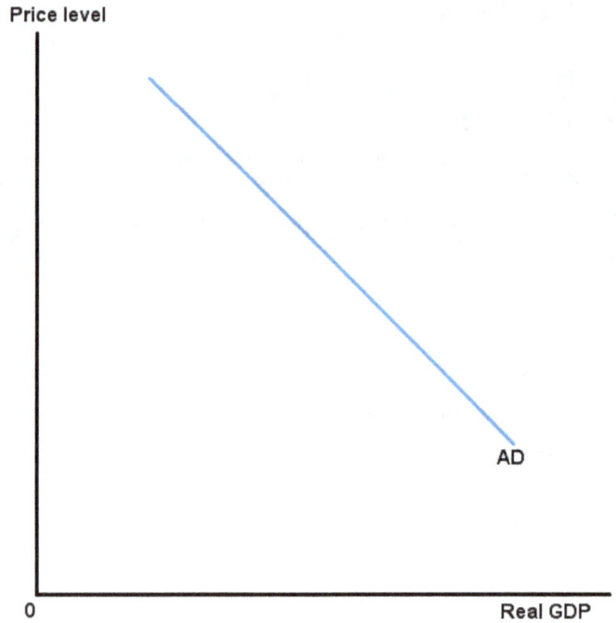

Problem 7-3

Use graphs to show the difference between an increase in the quantity of real output demanded and an increase in aggregate demand. Identify the variables that will shift the aggregate demand (AD) curve.

Requirement and Clue: *This is a two-part problem. Answer each part in order. Focus on a shift of the AD curve and a movement along the curve and what causes each.*

Solution

An increase in the quantity of real output demanded is shown by a movement along the aggregate demand curve as shown in Diagram 1 below. When the price level falls from P1 to P2, there is a movement along the AD curve from point A to point B.

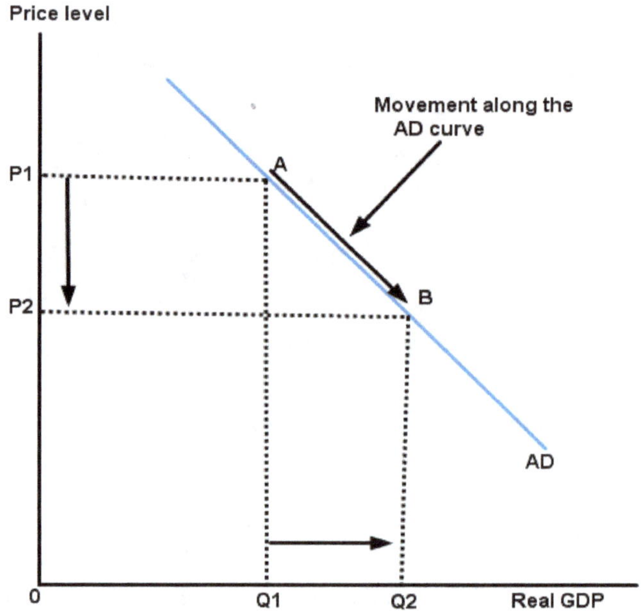

Diagram 1

The quantity of real output demanded increases from Q1 to Q2.

An increase in aggregate demand, on the other hand, is shown by a shift of the entire aggregate demand curve from AD to AD1 as shown in Diagram 2 below.

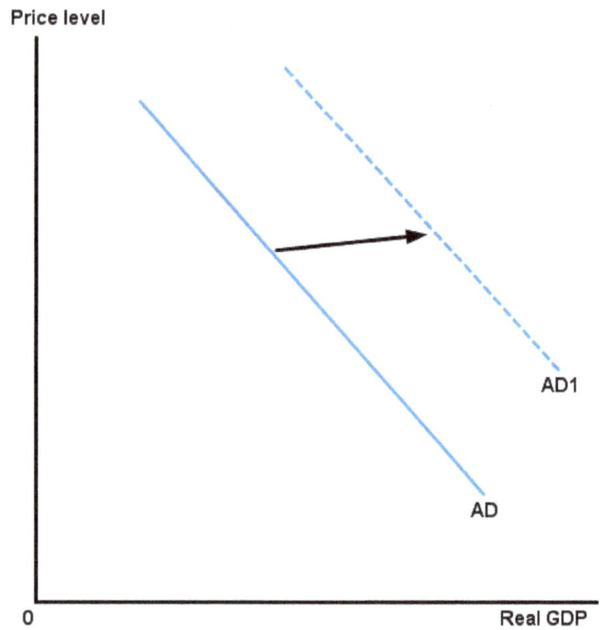

Diagram 2

The variables that that will shift the AD curve are the components of aggregate expenditure: Consumer spending (C), investment (I), government purchases (G), and net exports (X – M). A change in any of these variables will shift the AD curve.

Problem 7-4

Briefly discuss some of the main determinants of consumer spending?

Requirement and Clue: *Focus on factors that cause consumers to spend more or less. Three or four determinants should suffice. Do not ignore the word "briefly" in the problem.*

Solution

Some of the main determinants that will affect consumer spending are income, consumer wealth, interest rates, and taxes. Each of these is discussed below.

Income

Other things being equal, an increase in consumers' incomes will cause them to purchase a greater quantity of the total output of goods and services. Conversely, a fall in total income of consumers will cause them to purchase a smaller quantity of goods and services.

Consumer wealth

If consumers' assets increase in value, they will feel better off, other things being equal, and will therefore tend to purchase a greater quantity of goods and services. On the other hand, if the value of their assets falls, they will tend to reduce the quantity of goods and services bought.

Interest rates

Consumers typically purchase certain items on credit: automobiles, furniture, entertainment devices, etc.) When interest rates fall, consumers have an incentive to purchase such consumer items because lower interest rates mean lower interest cost. Conversely, higher interest rates tend to discourage consumer spending.

Taxes

A fall in personal income taxes increases disposable income. Other things being equal, with more disposable income, consumers are able to purchase more consumer goods and services. On the other hand, an increase in personal income taxes decreases disposable income and reduces consumers' ability to purchase goods and services.

Problem 7-5

How do interest rates, technological advance, and changes in income affect investment spending and aggregate demand?

Requirement and Clue: *You must be aware of the kind of spending that constitutes investment spending. Focus on how each of the concepts (in turn) affects investment and also aggregate demand.*

Solution

Investment is defined as the purchase of capital goods such as machinery, bridges, buildings, roads, etc.

Interest rates

Other things being equal, lower interest rates reduce the cost of acquiring investment funds and thus increase investment spending. More investment means greater aggregate expenditure, which means an increase in aggregate demand. Rising interest rates, conversely, will reduce investment and reduce aggregate demand.

Technological advance

Technological advances present new investment opportunities. For example, technological advances in communication have resulted in huge investment expenditures in that field. Such huge investment expenditures increase aggregate demand.

Changes in income

Other things being equal, an increase in income makes consumers better off so they tend to purchase more goods and services. This increase in the demand for goods and services will likely lead firms to invest more in production and technology. Aggregate demand will increase. By similar reasoning, a fall in income will reduce demand, lower investment spending, and reduce aggregate demand.

Problem 7-6

(a) *Define aggregate supply.*

(b) *Describe the three sections of the short-run aggregate supply curve.*

Requirement and Clue: *This is a two-part problem. Answer each part in order. For part (a) you are required to give a clear and precise meaning of the concept. A lengthy discussion is unnecessary. For part (b), a graph showing the three sections would be helpful.*

Solution

(a) Aggregate supply refers to the various quantities of real GDP that will be supplied at various price levels during a period of time.

(b) The three sections of the short-run aggregate supply curve are: (1) the Keynesian range, (2) the intermediate range, and (3) the classical range. The three sections are shown in the following diagram. Yf is the full-employment level of real GDP and SRAS is the short-run aggregate supply curve.

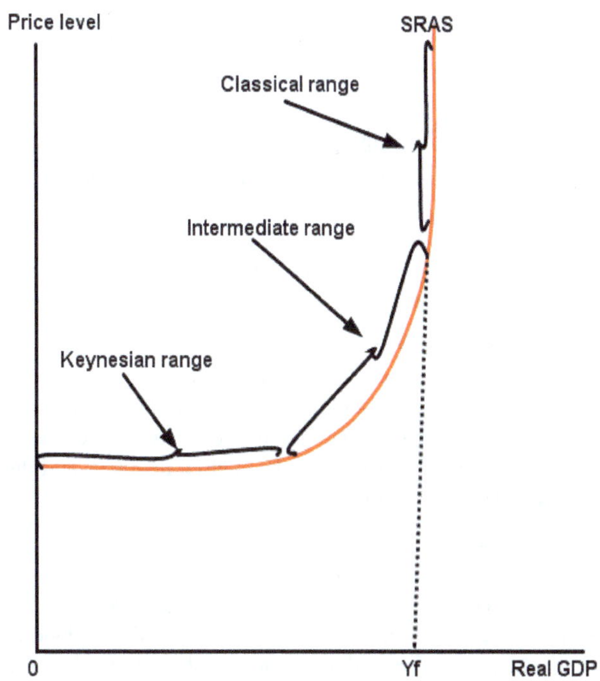

A description of each section follows:

The Keynesian Range

The horizontal section of the short-run aggregate supply curve is the Keynesian range or section. It represents a situation of unemployment and relatively low output.

The Intermediate Range

This is the upward sloping section of the SRAS curve that lies between the Keynesian (flat) section and the vertical section. Here the economy is neither experiencing severe unemployment nor severe inflation.

The Classical Range

This section of the SRAS curve is vertical at the full-employment level of GDP, indicated by Y_1 in the diagram. It is virtually impossible for real output to expand beyond this level.

Problem 7-7

Briefly discuss four factors that will shift the short-run aggregate supply (SRAS) curve.

Requirement and Clue: *Don't fall into the trap of thinking that the price level with shift the AS curve. Think of non-price level factors that affect the economy's ability to produce goods and services.*

Solution

Four factors that will shift the aggregate supply (AS) curve are: (1) the costs of production, (2) changes in the quantity or quality of resources, (3) Changes in technology, and (4) natural disasters.

1. The costs of production

Changes in the costs of production will cause the short-run supply curve to shift. For example, increases in important inputs such as wages or in the price of oil will increase production costs and will discourage firms from increasing production, shifting the SRAS curve to the left. Conversely, cost reductions will shift the SRAS curve to the right.

2. Changes in the quantity or quality of resources

If a country acquires more resources, the short-run aggregate supply curve will shift to the right. If, through training, the economy's labour force becomes more skilled and hence more productive, its short-run aggregate supply curve will shift to the right. If resources are destroyed, the short-run AS curve will shift to the left.

3. Changes in technology

Advances in technology enhance a country's ability to produce goods and services. If a country develops technologies that allow firms to use their resources more productively, then the economy will be able to obtain a greater volume of real output from given resources, and the SRAS curve will shift to the right.

4. Natural disasters

Hurricanes, earthquakes, volcanoes, floods, and other natural disasters can seriously affect an economy's ability to produce goods and services. Consider the effects of hurricane Sandy on parts of the Caribbean, New York, and New Jersey during late October in 2012. The devastation was enormous; resources were destroyed and many lives were lost. The storm wreaked havoc on those economies and shifted the SRAS curve to the left.

Problem 7-8

Explain the determination of the short-run equilibrium real GDP and the equilibrium price level.

Requirement and Clue: *Perhaps the easiest and most effective way to solve this problem is to use an aggregate demand/aggregate supply diagram.*

Solution

The short-run equilibrium real GDP and the equilibrium price level are simultaneously determined by the aggregate demand and aggregate supply curves as illustrated in the following diagram.

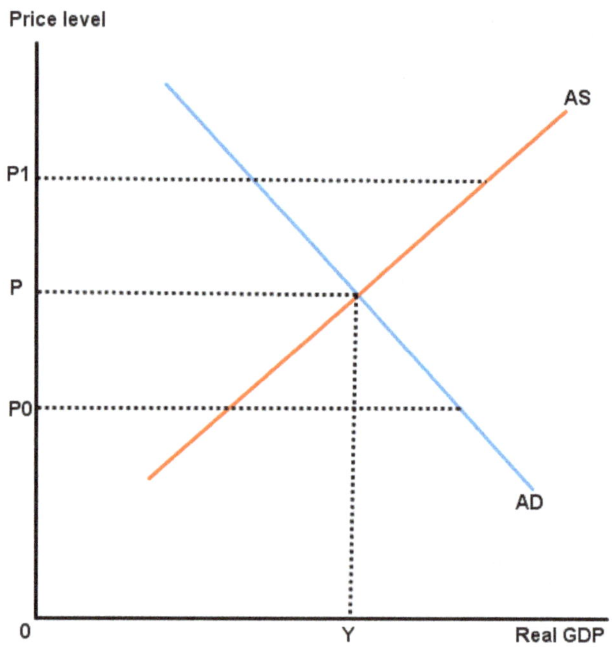

At a price level of P1, the quantity of all goods and services produced exceeds the total amount that will be demanded. Consequently, the price level and real GDP will fall. Any price level below P (P0, for example), will result in a lower level of production than the economy's customers are willing to purchase at that price level. Consequently, the price level and real GDP will rise. Only at a price level of P will the total amount of all goods and services that are demanded exactly equal the total amount of all goods and services that are supplied. Hence, P is the equilibrium price level and Y is the equilibrium level of real GDP. The equilibrium price level is the price level at which the total quantity of all goods and services demanded equals the total quantity supplied. There is no tendency for this price level to change. The equilibrium level of real GDP is the level of real GDP at which the AD and AS curves intersect.

Problem 7-9

Other things being equal, what is the effect on the equilibrium price level and real GDP of an increase in AD in each of the following ranges of the AS curve?

(a) *The Keynesian range*

(b) *The intermediate range*

(c) *The classical range*

Requirement and Clue: *This is a three-part problem. Answer each part in order. Clearly, a diagram would be of great help.*

Solution

(a) Diagram A below shows the effect of an increase in AD in the Keynesian range of the AS curve.

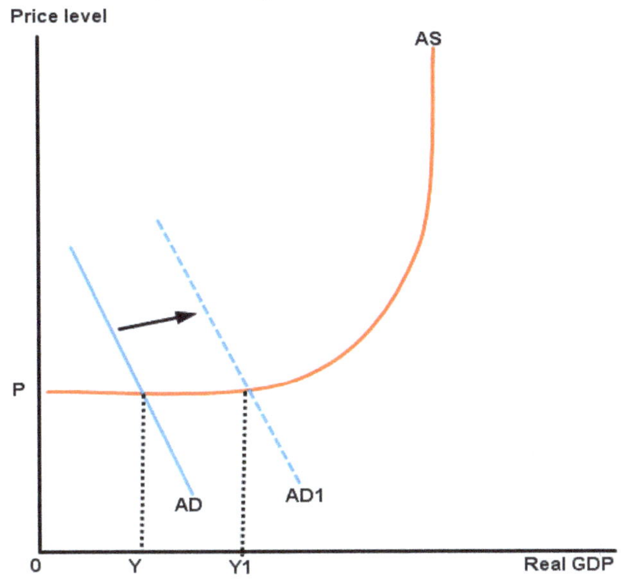

Diagram A

The initial equilibrium price level is P and the real GDP is Y where the AD and AS curves intersect. An increase in aggregate demand from AD to AD1 leaves the price level unchanged but increases real GDP from Y to Y1.

(b) Diagram B below shows the effect of an increase in AD in the intermediate range of the AS curve.

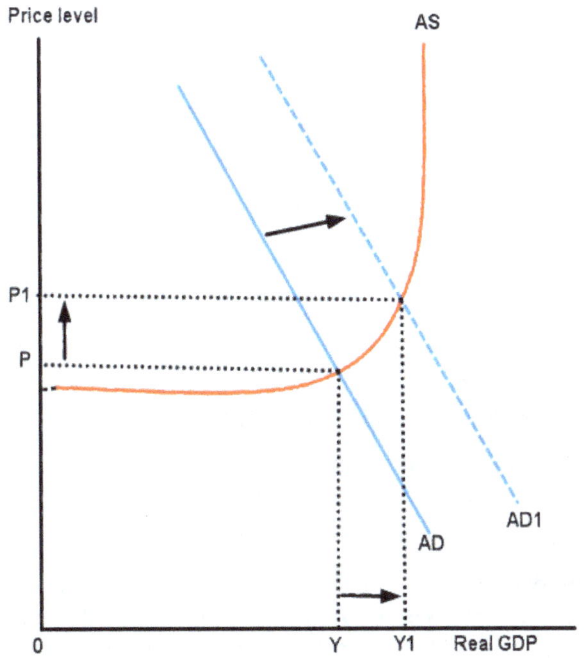

Diagram B

AD and AS are the initial aggregate demand and aggregate supply curves, respectively. The initial equilibrium price level is P and the equilibrium real GDP is Y. An increase in aggregate demand from AD to AD1 results in an increase in the price level from P to P1, and an increase in real GDP from Y to Y1.

(c) Diagram C below shows the effect of an increase in aggregate demand in the classical range of the AS curve.

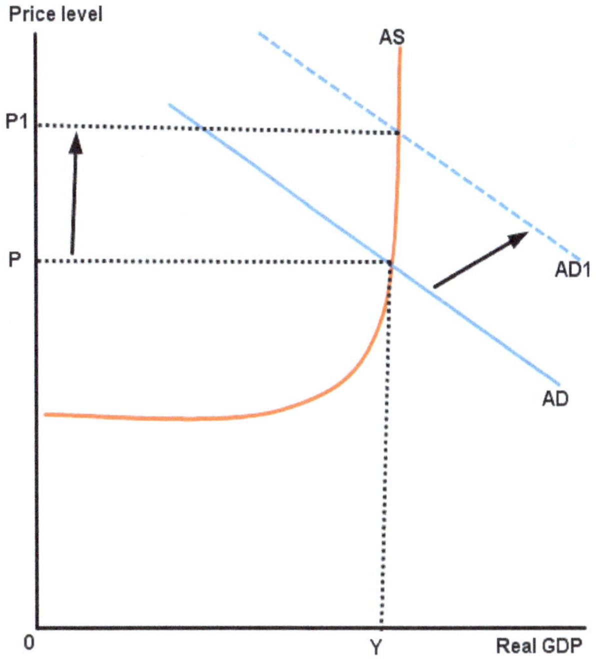

Diagram C

The initial aggregate demand and aggregate supply curves are AD and AS respectively. The initial equilibrium price level is P and the equilibrium real GDP is Y. An increase in aggregate demand from AD to AD1 leaves real GDP unchanged at the full-employment level of Y, but the price level rises from P to P1.

Problem 7-10

(a) *Define fiscal policy and monetary policy.*

(b) *How can these policies be used to reduce severe unemployment?*

Requirement and Clue: *This is a two-part problem. Answer each part in order. Part (a) is definitional. State clearly and precisely the meanings of the concepts. Just say what the concepts are without entering into a lengthy discussion. For part (b), a diagram will be helpful.*

Solution

(a) Fiscal policy is the deliberate use of government spending and taxes in order to influence economic activity. Monetary policy, on the other hand, is the manipulation of the money supply and interest rates by the central bank to influence economic activity.

(b) The problem suggests that the economy is operating at a level of output that is substantially below the full-employment level. Graphically, the economy is in the

Keynesian range of the short-run aggregate supply (SRAS) curve. See diagram below.

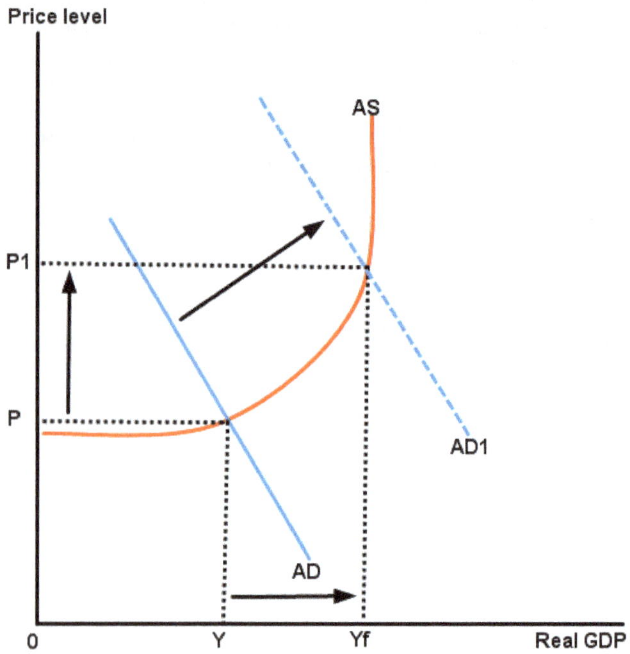

The economy is in equilibrium at a level of real output of Y which is far below the full employment level of Yf. The objective of macroeconomic policy (in this case fiscal policy and monetary policy) is to shift the aggregate demand curve from AD to AD1 where, ideally, the economy will be in equilibrium at full employment.

The government can achieve this objective by increasing its spending and/or lowering taxes—fiscal policy. This will increase total spending and shift the aggregate demand curve to the right as required. The Bank of Canada can achieve the same result by increasing the money supply and/or lowering interest rates—monetary policy.

Problem 7-11

Define each of the following concepts:

(a) *Supply-side policies*

(b) *Marginal tax rate*

(c) *Laffer curve*

Requirement and Clue: *This is a three-part problem. Answer each part in order. These are definitional so you are required to clearly state the meaning of each concept and give illustrative examples, if possible.*

Solution

(a) Supply-side policies are policies designed to influence real GDP at the price level. They affect aggregate supply by influencing incentives to work, save, and invest.

(b) The marginal tax rate is the ratio of the change in taxes to a change in income. Symbolically, the marginal tax rate (MTR) can be expressed as:

$$MTR = \frac{\Delta T}{\Delta Y}$$

where T represents taxes and Y represents income.

For example, if an increase in income of $100 million causes taxes to rise by $20 million, then the tax rate is 20/100 = 0.2 or 20%.

(c) The Laffer curve is a curve that shows the relationship between tax revenues and tax rates. According to the Laffer curve, at a zero tax rate, tax revenues will be zero. As the tax rate increases so do tax revenues. But after a point, higher tax rates only lead to lower tax revenues as high tax rates reduce work incentive. The following diagram illustrates the Laffer curve.

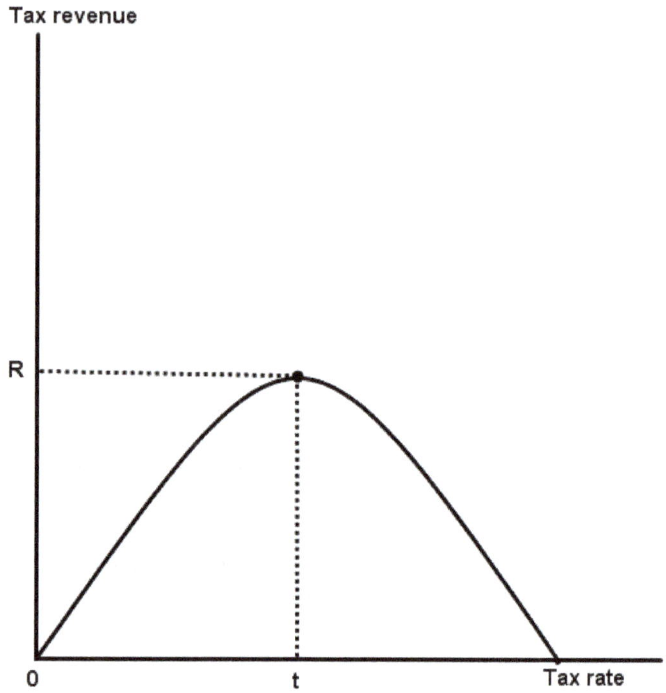

The diagram shows that as the tax rate rises from 0 to t, tax revenues increase from zero to a maximum of R. Any increase in the tax rate above t reduces tax revenues.

Problem 7-12

Use aggregate demand/aggregate supply diagrams to show the effect of each of the following events on the equilibrium price level and real output (GDP). In each case, assume that the economy is operating in the intermediate range of the aggregate supply (AS) curve.

(a) *A wave of technological advance hits various industries across the country*

(b) *Firms invest in new machinery and buildings*

(c) *The central bank increases the money supply and reduces interest rates*

(d) *The government conducts an expansionary fiscal policy.*

Requirement and Clue: This is a multiple-part problem. Answer each part in order. Focus on which curve will be affected by the change and how it will be affected. Remember that the AS curve Make sure you explain your diagrams.

Solution

(a) A wave of technological advance is a supply-side shock that will shift the aggregate supply (AS) curve to the right as shown in Diagram A below.

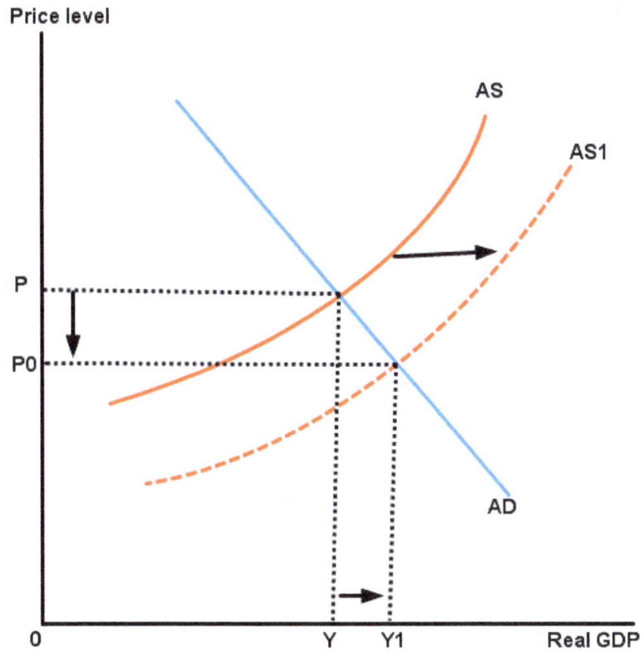

Diagram A

AD and AS are the initial aggregate demand and aggregate supply curves respectively. The equilibrium price level is P and the equilibrium level of real GDP is Y. As the AS curve shifts to the right, the price level falls from P to P0 and the real GDP rises from Y to Y1.

(b) In Diagram B below, the initial aggregate demand and aggregate supply curves are AD and AS respectively. The equilibrium price level and real GDP are P and Y respectively.

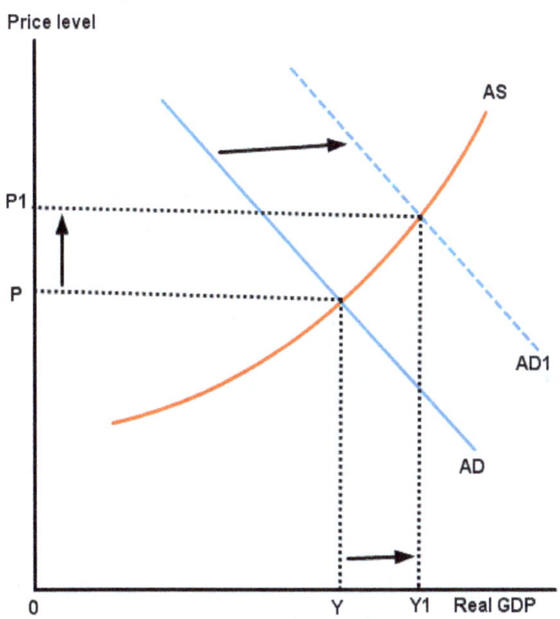

Diagram B

Investment in new machinery and buildings increases aggregate expenditure and shifts the aggregate demand curve to the right as shown. The equilibrium price level rises from P to P1, and real GDP increases from Y to Y1.

(c) Consider Diagram C below. The initial aggregate demand and aggregate supply curves are AD and AS respectively.

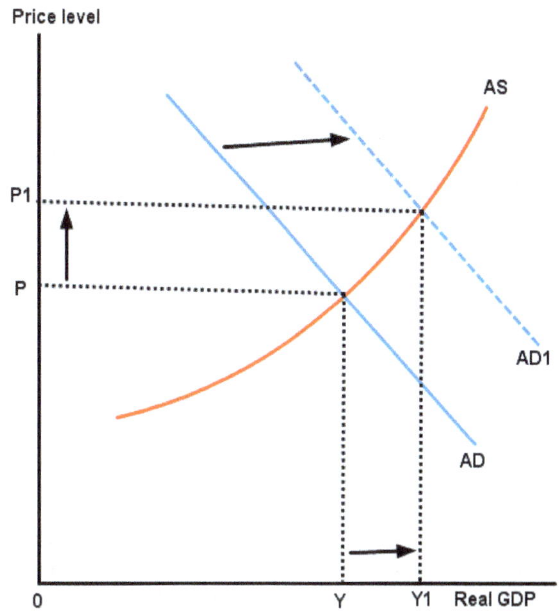

Diagram C

An increase in the money supply and a lowering of interest rates by the central bank will shift the AD curve from AD to AD_1. This results in an increase in the equilibrium price level from P to P_1, and an increase in the real GDP from Y to Y1.

(d) In Diagram D below, AD and AS are the initial aggregate demand and aggregate supply curves.

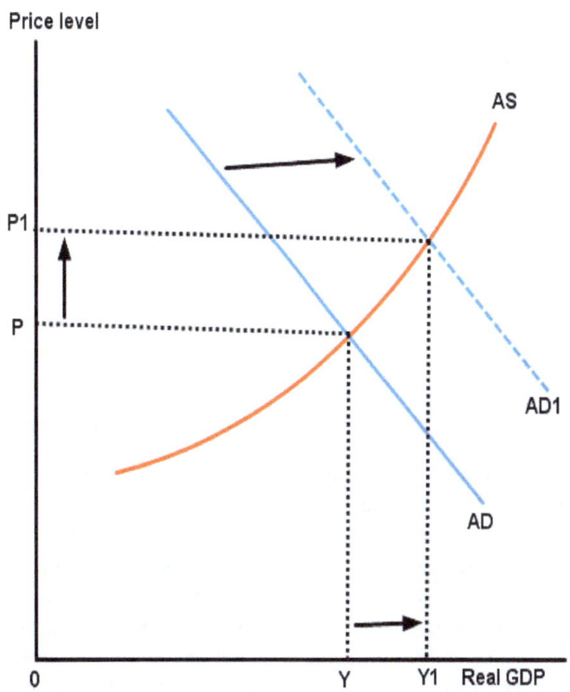

Diagram D

The equilibrium price level is initially P and the equilibrium real GDP is Y. Now, an expansionary fiscal involves an increase in government spending and a reduction in taxes that increase total spending. Thus the AD curve shifts to the right from AD to AD1. Consequently, the equilibrium price level rises from P to P1 while the equilibrium real GDP rises from Y to Y1.

Problem 7-13

Use the aggregate demand (AD)-aggregate supply (AS) model to show that fiscal and monetary policies designed to increase real output and employment need not be inflationary. Under what circumstances will such demand-side policies most likely be inflationary?

Requirement and Clue: *This is a two-part problem. Answer each partner in order. For the first part of the problem, think of the state of the economy that is suggested by the problem. For the second part, focus on the state of the economy that would cause price level increases due to increases in aggregate demand.*

Solution

The first part of the problem suggests that the economy is operating in the Keynesian (horizontal) section of the AS curve. Diagram 1 below shows that the economy is in equilibrium with real GDP at Y and the price level at P.

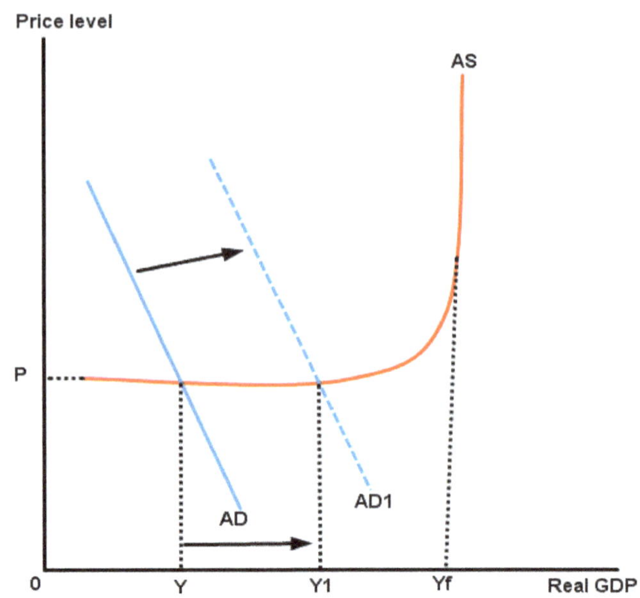

Diagram 1

The equilibrium level of real output, Y, is far below the full-employment level of Yf. Fiscal policy and monetary policy in this case would require the government to increase its spending and lower taxes, and the central bank to increase the money supply and lower interest rates. These policies would shift the aggregate demand curve to the right from AD to AD1, increasing real output and employment without putting upward pressure on the price level. The policies have increased real output from Y to Y1, which is closer to the full-employment level. The price level has remained at P.

Let us assume now that the economy was operating at or close to full employment as shown in Diagram 2 below.

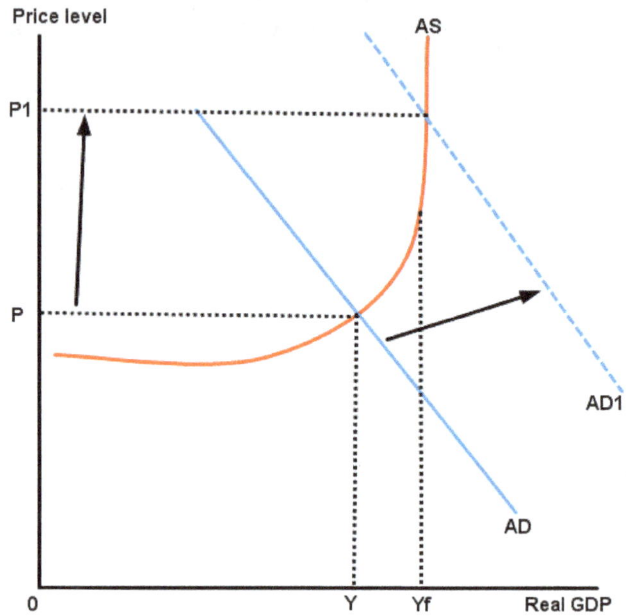

Diagram 2

AD and AS are the initial aggregate demand and aggregate supply curves respectively, and P and Y are the initial equilibrium price level and real output respectively. Notice how close the equilibrium real output is to the full-employment output of Yf. In these circumstances, the fiscal and monetary policies referred to in the problem could shift the aggregate demand curve from AD to AD1, forcing the price level up to P1, which can be considered to be inflationary. Demand-side fiscal and monetary policies designed to increase output and employment are likely to be inflationary if the economy is operating at or close to full employment.

Problem 7-14

What is the long-run aggregate supply curve and how does it differ from the short-run aggregate supply curve?

Requirement and Clue: *This is a two-part problem. Answer each part in order. The first part of the problem is definitional. Just state as clearly and as precisely as possible what the long-run aggregate supply curve is. Resist the temptation to say all you know about the long-run aggregate supply curve. It is not required. For the second part of the problem, focus on features of the long-run aggregate supply curve that the short-run aggregate supply curve does not possess.*

Solution

The long-run aggregate supply curve is a graphical representation of the amount of real GDP that will be supplied after the economy has made all necessary adjustments. It is a vertical line representing the economy's potential real GDP at full employment. Unlike the short-run aggregate supply curve that shows various quantities of real GDP that will be supplied at various price levels, and which has three sections, the long-run aggregate supply curve is defined only at full employment. Changes in the price level result in changes in the quantities of real GDP supplied in the short run; changes in the price level leave the quantity of real output supplied unchanged at the full employment level.

Problem 7-15

What are the factors that cause the long-run aggregate supply curve to shift?

Requirement and Clue: *List each important factor and comment briefly on each.*

Solution

The main factors that cause the long-run aggregate supply curve to shift are labour productivity, capital stock, natural or human resources, and technology.

Labour productivity

Even in this modern technological age, labour is still the most important economic resource. Labour productivity is measured by output per unit of labour. An increase in labour productivity will shift the long-run aggregate supply curve to the right as the economy's productive capacity increases. A reduction in labour productivity will shift it to the left.

Capital stock

An economy's stock of real capital is a major determinant of its ability to produce goods and services. Other things being equal, the greater the country's capital stock, the greater will be its capacity to produce goods and services. In fact, an economy's long-term growth depends on the extent to which it can sacrifice current consumption for future consumption by saving and building up its capital stock.

Natural and human resources

The discovery of natural resources such as coal or oil can positively affect a country's productive potential; so too can an improvement in the quality of its human resources through training and education. Such changes shift the long-run aggregate supply curve to the right. On the other hand, the loss of natural and human resources through disasters such as hurricanes, floods, and tsunamis shifts the long-run aggregate supply curve to the left.

Technology

An improvement in technology makes it possible to produce a given level of output with fewer inputs or to produce a greater level of output with given inputs. In other words, technological advances allow an economy to get more out of its resources, thus shifting the long-run aggregate supply curve to the right.

Problem 7-16

Use an appropriate diagram to show the effect of a rightward shift in the long-run aggregate supply curve on long-run macroeconomic equilibrium.

Requirement and Clue: *It is well to define long-run macroeconomic equilibrium in providing a solution to this problem. You are required to say what will happen to the equilibrium price level and potential real GDP following the rightward shift in the long-run aggregate supply curve.*

Solution

Long-run macroeconomic equilibrium exists when the long-run aggregate supply curve and the aggregate demand curve intersect. The price level and full-employment real GDP will thus be determined. The following diagram illustrates the effect of an increase in long-run aggregate supply (a rightward shift in the long-run aggregate supply curve) on the price level and potential real GDP.

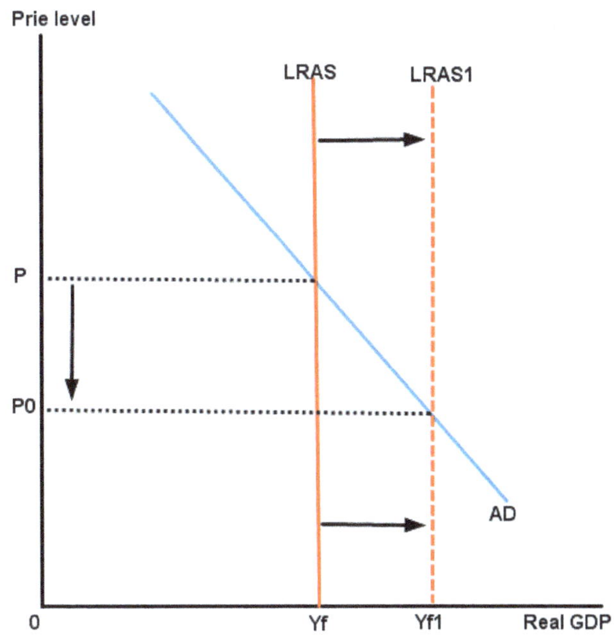

AD and LRAS are the initial aggregate demand and long-run aggregate supply curves respectively. The initial equilibrium price level is P and the equilibrium potential real GDP is Yf. An increase in the long-run aggregate supply curve from LRAS to LRAS1 results in a fall in the price level from P to P0 and in an increase in potential real GDP from Yf to Yf1.

Problem 7-17

Explain the difference between short-run macroeconomic equilibrium and long-run macroeconomic equilibrium.

Requirement and Clue: *Consider the necessary condition for short-run macroeconomic equilibrium and the condition for long-run equilibrium. This will help to bring out the difference between the two concepts.*

Solution

Short-run macroeconomic equilibrium is determined by the intersection of the short-run aggregate supply curve and the aggregate demand curve. This equilibrium condition can occur below the full-employment level of real output, at the full-employment level, or above full- employment level of real output. On the other hand, long-run macroeconomic equilibrium occurs at that price level and real GDP at which the aggregate demand curve and the long-run aggregate supply curves intersect. Unlike short-run macroeconomic equilibrium, long-run macroeconomic equilibrium can occur only at the full-employment level of real GDP.

Problem 7-18

(a) *What is economic growth?*

(b) *Define the growth rate of real GDP per capita.*

(c) *Describe how the growth rate is calculated.*

Requirement and Clue: *This is a three-part problem. Answer each part in order. For part (a), your task is to state clearly and precisely the meaning of the concept. You are not required to write an essay on it. For part (b), you should simply state clearly and precisely the meaning of the concept. For part (c), it's a good idea to show how the concept is calculated.*

Solution

(a) Economic growth is defined as a sustained increase in a country's real GDP per capita over time. If in 2014 the GDP per capita in an economy was \$5,680 and by 2016, the real GDP per capita was \$7,175, it could be said that economic growth had occurred between 2014 and 2016.

(b) The growth rate of real gross domestic product per capita is the percentage change in an economy's real gross domestic product per capita.

(c) The following formula can be used to calculate the growth rate of real GDP per capita.

Growth rate of real GDP per capita is:

$$\frac{\text{Present real GDP per capita} - \text{previous real GDP per capita}}{\text{Previous real GDP per capita}} \times 100$$

For example, if the real GDP per capita in 2015 was \$25,000, and it was \$25,500 in 2016, then the growth rate of real GDP per capita between 2015 and 2016 would be:

$$\frac{25{,}500 - 25{,}000}{25{,}000} \times 100 = \mathbf{2\%}$$

Problem 7-19

Explain why real GDP per capita might be a better measure of economic growth than real GDP.

Requirement and Clue: *Focus on what economic growth really means in terms of individuals being better off.*

Solution

Economic growth suggests that on average, people are better off. Real GDP per capita captures this idea much more accurately than does real GDP. Suppose real GDP in an economy grew by 5% in a certain period, while population grew by 7% during the same period. In this case, it can be said that the economy did not show any real growth during this period because on average, people were less well off. The per capita figure gives a much better indication of the well-being of individuals.

Problem 7-20

Briefly discuss three of the main determinants of economic growth.

Requirement and Clue: *It's a good idea to define economic growth. Focus on the main factors that affect economic growth and zoom in on three of them. Note the word "briefly" in the problem.*

Solution

The term "economic growth" often refers to a sustained increase in a country's real per capita gross domestic product over time. Three of the main determinants of economic growth are: natural resource endowment, capital formation, and technological change.

<u>Natural resource endowment</u>

Although it is possible for a country to achieve economic growth without huge amounts of natural resources, there can be little doubt that a bountiful supply of natural resources is a great contributor to economic growth. A huge amount of oil, coal, and natural gas will foster economic growth.

<u>Capital formation</u>

Capital accumulation plays an important role in economic growth. The greater the economy's stock of factories, equipment, machinery, and highways, the greater will be its capacity to produce goods and services and other resources. The rate of investment will influence the rate of economic growth.

<u>Technological change</u>

An increase in technology occurs when a given level of output can be produced with fewer inputs or when the same level of output can be produced with fewer inputs. The way in which the economy's resources combine to produce the output of goods and services obviously determines to a large extent the economy's productive capacity.

Problem 7-21

Discuss some measures that a government can take to promote economic growth.

Requirement and Clue: *Think of the factors that are likely to promote economic growth. This should enable you to come up with some measures that a government can take to promote economic growth. Three measures should be adequate.*

Solution

Among the measures that a government can take to promote economic growth are: (1) supporting investment in human capital, (2) encouraging research and development, and (3) encouraging investment. Each will be discussed.

First, a government can encourage investment in human capital by providing scholarships, educational grants, and loans to students on affordable terms. By making education more easily accessible, more people will be able to develop their human capital and thus help to propel economic growth.

Second, a government can promote technological change by

encouraging research and development. A government can provide incentives to firms to increase their research and development activities. In addition, a government can finance some research and development projects of its own.

Finally, a government can foster economic growth by encouraging investment. This can be achieved through interest rate policies (low interest rates tend to stimulate real investment), and partly through tax incentives for investment in plant and equipment.

Problem 7-22

(a) *What are some of the arguments against economic growth?*

(b) *What is sustainable development?*

Requirement and Clue: *This is a two-part problem. Answer each part in order. For part (a), you are required to focus on some of the negative effects of economic growth—the costs of economic growth. For part (b), you are expected simply to state clearly the meaning of the concept.*

Solution

(a) Those who argue against economic claim that it causes social problems such as traffic congestion, the destruction of the countryside, and overcrowding in our cities. They draw attention to the fact that economic growth creates pollution, smog, and excess waste. Critics also argue that the real problem is not insufficient real output of goods and services but rather inequity in the distribution of income and wealth.

(b) Sustainable development is development that meets the needs of the present without compromising the ability of future generations to meet their own needs. For example, widespread deforestation without any consideration of the long-term effects would be against the idea of sustainable development.

Multiple-Choice Questions

In each case, circle the letter that corresponds with the correct answer.

1. Aggregate demand is:

a. total consumer purchases at a constant price level
b. the sum of consumption and investment
c. the total output bought by domestic and foreign consumers
d. the various amounts of real GDP that will be demanded at various price levels

Answer: d

Reason: Aggregate demand is an inverse relationship between the price level and real GDP demanded.

2. The invalid assumption that what is true of the parts is also true of the whole is called:

a. the fallacy of composition
b. the invalid hypothesis
c. the parts-and whole invalidity assumption
d. none of the above

Answer: a

Reason: The fallacy of composition is an erroneous conclusion about the whole based on what is known to be true of a part of that whole.

3. An increase in the price level causes:

a. consumption to rise and investment to fall
b. both consumption and investment to rise
c. both consumption and investment to fall
d. consumption to fall and investment to rise

Answer: c

Reason: An increase in the price level leads to an increase in interest rates that decreases both consumption and investment.

4. As the price level falls, other things being equal:

a. holders of financial assets lose purchasing power
b. holders of financial assets may increases their purchases of consumer goods because of the increase in wealth
c. the aggregate demand curve shifts to the left
d. none of the above

Answer: b

Reason: This is the real wealth effect.

5. The aggregate demand curve will shift to the right if:

a. consumption increases
b. government purchases increase
c. investment increases
d. all of the above

Answer: d

Reason: Consumption, investment, and government purchases are components of aggregate expenditure that will shift the aggregate demand curve.

6. Other things being equal, an increase in imports will:

a. shift the aggregate demand curve to the right
b. shift the aggregate demand curve to the left
c. cause a movement along the aggregate demand curve
d. have no effect on the aggregate demand curve

Answer: b

Reason: Net exports are a component of aggregate expenditure. An increase in imports will reduce net exports and thus reduce aggregate expenditure, shifting the aggregate demand curve to the left.

7. The short-run aggregate supply curve assumes that:

a. the price level varies
b. at low levels of output, it is relatively difficult to increase real GDP
c. an inverse relationship exists between the price level and total output
d. as real GDP rises, it becomes relatively easy to increase real GDP even further.

Answer: a

Reason: The short-run aggregate supply curve is upward-sloping because it assumes that a direct relationship exists between the price level and the quantity of real GDP supplied.

8. The vertical section of the short-run aggregate supply curve is called:

a. the Keynesian range
b. the classical range
c. the intermediate range
d. none of the above

Answer: b

Reason: The classical economists assumed that the economy would tend to operate at full employment where the supply curve is vertical.

9. The Keynesian range of the short-run aggregate supply curve is:

a. upward sloping
b. vertical
c. horizontal
d. none of the above

Answer: c

Reason: Keynes assumed that the economy was operating at low levels of real GDP where it was easy to increase real GDP without putting upward pressure on the price level.

10. If an increase in aggregate demand occurs when the aggregate supply curve is vertical, then, other things being equal:

a. real output and the price level will both increase
b. real output and the price level will both decrease
c. real output will increase, but the price level will fall
d. real output will not change, but the price level will rise.

Answer: d

Reason: In the classical range, the economy is operating at the full-employment level of output. Any increase in aggregate demand from that position will only put upward pressure on the price level.

11. Which of the following will cause aggregate supply to decrease?

a. An increase in the price level
b. A fall in the price level
c. A disaster that disrupts production
d. A reduction in production costs.

Answer: c

Reason: A disaster would cause a fall in the quantity of goods and services that the economy could produce at any price level. This is tantamount to a decrease in supply.

12. A fall in aggregate supply, other things being equal, will result in:

a. a fall in real output and an increase in the price level
b. a fall in real output and a decrease in the price level
c. an increase in real output and a fall in the price level
d. an increase in real output and a rise in the price level.

Answer: a

Reason: The aggregate supply curve shifts to the left, raising the price level and lowering real GDP.

13. According to supply-side economists:

a. an increase in the marginal tax rate will stimulate economic activity
b. tax cuts will encourage saving and free up funds for investment
c. deregulation of industries will simply slow down the pace of economic activity
d. supply-side policies should be used only after demand-side policies have failed.

Answer: b

Reason: Supply-siders claim that tax rates are so high that they reduce economic incentives. Cutting taxes will spur economic incentives and increase savings and investment.

14. If the economy is operating on the downward-sloping section of the Laffer curve, then:

a. tax cuts will increase work incentives
b. tax increases will cause people to work harder
c. deregulation of industries is the only means of stimulating economic activity
d. none of the above

Answer: a

Reason: The downward-sloping section of the Laffer curve occurs where the tax rate is so high that it impedes the incentive to work.

15. The long-run aggregate supply is:

a. the sum of the various quantities produced in the short run
b. the real GDP that the economy can produce at full employment
c. the real GDP actually produced over a long period of time
d. none of the above.

Answer: b

Reason: Long-run aggregate supply is the economy's potential real output of goods and services.

16. The long-run aggregate supply curve is:

a. upward sloping like all other supply curves
b. horizontal because in the long run all is variable
c. downward sloping as the firms adjust to the long-run environment
d. none of the above

Answer: d

Reason: The long-run aggregate supply curve is vertical.

17. Which of the following will cause the long-run aggregate supply curve to shift to the right?

a. An increase in the average level of prices
b. A decrease in the price level
c. A sustained increase in labour productivity
d. Both b and c

Answer: c

Reason: *A sustained increase in labour productivity will increase the economy's capacity to produce goods and services and thus shift the long-run aggregate supply curve to the right.*

18. If an economy's long-run aggregate supply curve shifts to the right, then its production possibility curve will:

a. shift outward to the right
c. be convex
b. upward sloping
d. none of the above

Answer: a

Reason: *If the long-run aggregate supply curve shifts to the right, it indicates an increase in the economy's productive capacity. An outward shift of the production-possibility curve indicates the same thing.*

19. Which of the following is true?

a. An economy will be in long-run equilibrium as long as it is in short-run equilibrium
b. An economy will be in short-run equilibrium as long as it is in long-run equilibrium
c. An economy can be in long-run equilibrium and short-run equilibrium at the same time
d. An economy cannot be in long-run equilibrium and short-run equilibrium at the same time.

Answer: c

Reason: *An economy is in short-run equilibrium when the aggregate demand and short-run aggregate supply curves intersect. This can happen when at the full-employment level of real GDP.*

20. In the long run:

a. The aggregate demand curve is vertical, but the long-run aggregate supply curve is horizontal
b. The aggregate demand curve is downward sloping, but the long-run aggregate supply curve is vertical
c. The long-run aggregate supply curve is upward sloping, but the aggregate demand curve id downward sloping
d. The aggregate demand and long-run aggregate supply curves are both downward sloping.

Answer: b

Reason: *The aggregate demand curve slopes downward, but the long-run aggregate supply curve represents real output at full employment and is therefore vertical.*

21. When the aggregate demand and long-run aggregate supply curves intersect:

a. the economy is in long-run equilibrium
b. the equilibrium price level is determined but the equilibrium real GDP is indeterminate
c. the equilibrium real GDP is determined but the equilibrium price level is indeterminate
d. none of the above

Answer: a

Reason: *Choice a defines long-run equilibrium.*

22. If the long-run aggregate supply curve shifts to the left, other things being equal, we can predict that:

a. the price level will rise, but real GDP will not change
b. the price level will fall, but real GDP will not change
c. real GDP will fall, but the price level will not change
d. none of the above

Answer: d

Reason: *The price level will rise, and real GDP will fall.*

23. A secular decline in the price level can be caused by:

a. increases in long-run aggregate supply
b. a decrease in long-run aggregate supply
c. an increase in aggregate demand
d. none of the above

Answer: a

Reason: *Increases in long-run aggregate supply imply an expansion of the economy's productive capacity. This can result in a persistent reduction in the price level.*

24. If the economy is in long-run equilibrium and aggregate demand increases, other things being equal:

a. the price level will fall, but real GDP will not change
b. the price level will rise, but real GDP will not change
c. the price level and real GDP will both fall
d. the price level and real GDP will both rise

Answer: b

Reason: *With real output at the full-employment level, an increase in aggregate demand cannot increase real GDP beyond that level; but there will be upward pressure on the price level.*

25. Long-run macroeconomic equilibrium:

a. may occur above the full-employment level of real GDP
b. may occur below the full-employment level of real GDP
c. will occur at the full-employment level of real GDP
d. none of the above

Answer: c

Reason: *For long-run macroeconomic equilibrium, the aggregate demand curve crosses the long-run aggregate supply curve. This occurs at potential real GDP.*

26. The economy can be in short-run equilibrium:

a. at the full-employment level of real GDP
b. above the full-employment level of real GDP
c. below the full-employment level of real output
d. all of the above

Answer: d

Reason: *Short-run equilibrium occurs when the aggregate demand and short-run aggregate supply curves intersect. This can happen at, above, or below the full-employment level of real GDP.*

27. The economy is in long-run equilibrium if:

a. it is in short-run equilibrium above its full-employment level of real GDP
b. it is in short-run equilibrium below its potential real GDP
c. the quantity of real GDP demanded is greater or less than the economy's potential real GDP
d. none of the above

Answer: d

Reason: The economy is in long-run equilibrium if the quantity of real GDP demanded is equal to the economy's potential real GDP.

28. Short-run supply-side shocks have:

a. no effect on real GDP
b. no effect on the price level
c. no effect on long-run equilibrium
d. none of the above

Answer: c

Reason: Short-run supply shocks do not affect the long-run aggregate supply curve.

29. Economic growth refers to:

a. rapid population growth
b. an increase in political power
c. an increase in real per capita output
d. all of the above

Answer: c

Reason: An increase in real per capita output actually makes people better off.

30. All of the following are sources of economic growth except:

a. technological change
b. capital formation
c. natural resources
d. interest rates

Answer: d

Reason: The level of interest rates may influence economic growth but interest rates are not a source of economic growth.

31. If real GDP per capita in year 1 is $10,000 and real GDP per capita in year 2 is $10,500, then the rate of growth of real GDP per capita is:

a. 2.5%
b. 5%
c. 1.05%
d. cannot be determined

Answer: b

Reason: The growth rate of real GDP per capita is:

$$\frac{(10{,}500 - 10{,}000)}{10{,}000} \times 100 = 5\%$$

32. T he optimal labour force is that which:

a. results in the maximum real output per worker
b. produces the maximum GDP
c. results from the most rapid increase in population
d. has the lowest labour force participation rate

Answer: a

Reason: Any other level of labour force does not benefit the economy as much.

True-False Questions

Determine whether each of the following statements is true or false.

1. The aggregate demand curve is the sum of the market demand curves for individual goods and services.

Answer: False

Explanation: The ceteris paribus assumption which applies to individual demand curves does not apply to the aggregate demand curve. The individual demand curves cannot be added to obtain aggregate demand.

2. The aggregate demand curve slopes downward because increases in the price level cause aggregate expenditure to fall.

Answer: True

3. An increase in investment will cause the aggregate demand curve to shift outward. A fall in the price level, other things being equal, will cause more goods and services to be demanded, but the aggregate demand curve will not shift.

Answer: True

4. As the level of real output increases, the slope of the aggregate supply curve increases.

Answer: True

5. The effect of an increase in aggregate demand is unrelated to the shape of the aggregate supply curve.

Answer: False

Explanation: The slope of the aggregate supply curve when it intersects the aggregate demand curve largely determines the effect of any changes in aggregate demand.

6. Since the aggregate supply curve always has a vertical section, any increase in aggregate demand will result in an increase in the price level.

Answer: False

Explanation: The aggregate supply curve may be horizontal. In this case, an increase in aggregate demand will cause real output to rise, but the price level will not be affected.

7. The vertical section of the aggregate supply curve is called the classical range.

Answer: True

8. An increase in aggregate demand, other things being equal, will always result in an increase in real output.

Answer: False

Explanation: An increase in aggregate demand will not cause real output to rise if the aggregate supply curve is vertical.

9. Other things being equal, an increase in aggregate supply will result in an increase in real output and a fall in the price level.

Answer: True

10. Supply-side economists claim that lower marginal tax rates will provide an incentive for workers to do extra work since they will be allowed to keep a larger share of any extra income they earn.

Answer: True

11. The long-run aggregate supply curve is horizontal because in the long run, firms can make all the necessary adjustments.

Answer: False

Explanation: *The long-run aggregate supply curve is vertical because it represents the economy's potential real GDP.*

12. A rightward shift of the economy's production possibility curve is equivalent to a rightward shift of the long-run production possibility curve.

Answer: True

13. One of the main causes of shifts in the long-run aggregate supply curve is changes in labour productivity.

Answer: True

14. Factors that cause the production possibility curve to shift have absolutely no effect on the long-run aggregate supply curve.

Answer: False

Explanation: *Factors that affect the production possibility curve also affect the long-run-aggregate supply curve.*

15. An increase in labour productivity will shift the long-run aggregate supply curve to the right.

Answer: True

16. The equilibrium price level and the equilibrium long-run full-employment real GDP can be determined independently, but they cannot be determined simultaneously.

Answer: False

Explanation: *The equilibrium price level and the equilibrium long-run real GDP can be determined simultaneously. This occurs when the aggregate demand and the long-run aggregate supply curves intersect.*

17. Long-run macroeconomic equilibrium can occur below full employment, at full employment, or above full employment.

Answer: False

Explanation: *Long-run macroeconomic equilibrium occurs when the aggregate demand and long-run aggregate supply curves intersect. This can happen only at the full-employment level of real GDP.*

18. A persistent decline in the average level of prices over time is referred to as a secular decline in the price level and can be caused by an increase in long-run aggregate supply.

Answer: True

19. If the economy is in long-run equilibrium and aggregate demand increases, other things being equal, the price level will rise and so will real GDP.

Answer: False

Explanation: *The price level will rise but real GDP will remain unchanged at the full-employment level.*

20. The economy can be in short-run equilibrium at, above, or below the full-employment level of real GDP.

Answer: True

21. Long-run equilibrium can occur at, above, or below the full-employment level of real output.

Answer: False

Explanation: *Long-run equilibrium occurs when the aggregate demand curve intersects the long-run aggregate supply curve. This can occur only at the full-employment level of real output.*

22. Supply shocks can result in short-run equilibrium above or below the full-employment level of real GDP.

Answer: True

23. To account for changes in population, a concept of economic growth that is often used is an increase in real gross domestic product per capita.

Answer: True

24. In order to improve our current living standards, our productive capacity must grow as fast as the rate of increase in the population.

Answer: False

Explanation: *In order to improve our current living standards, our productive capacity must grow at a faster rate than the rate of increase in the population.*

25. A growing economy creates jobs, hence economic growth tends to reduce unemployment.

Answer: True

26. Sustainable development attempts to meet the needs of the present without compromising the ability of future generations to meet their own needs.

Answer: True

27. The optimal labour force is that which leads to the largest possible real GDP.

Answer: False

Explanation: *The optimal labour force is that which is consistent with maximum real output per worker.*

28. As far as economic growth is concerned, it is the quality and not the quantity of the labour force that is important.

Answer: False

Explanation: *The quantity and quality of the labour force are important for economic growth.*

29. Natural resources, capital accumulation, and technological change all contribute to economic growth.

Answer: True

30. Economic growth is a natural process, and governments are powerless to affect it.

Answer: False

Explanation: *Governments can take certain measures to promote economic growth. They can encourage investment in human capital, they can promote technological change, and they can create an environment in which real investment thrives.*

Completion

(Fill in the blanks)

Use each word or combination of words from the list exactly once.
*(**Hint**: Proceed by elimination)*

Word list

Aggregate x 2 — Capital — Classical — Composition — Costs — Curve — Demand x 2 — Fall — Fallacy — Human — Increase — Investment — Keynesian — Laffer — Left — Marginal — Not Change — Output — Price Level — Rate — Right x 4 — Rise — Supply-Side — Sustainable — Tax — Vertical — Will — Will Not

Questions

1. The term used for the various quantities of all goods and services demanded at various price levels is __________ __________.
2. The assumption that what is true for the parts must also be true for the whole is called the __________ of __________.
3. A fall in the price level __________ [will, will not] cause an increase in aggregate demand.
4. An increase in consumption and investment, other things being equal, __________ [will, will not] result in an increase in aggregate demand.
5. The curve relating total spending on all goods and services to the price level is called the __________ __________ curve.
6. The flat section of the aggregate supply curve is called the __________ range.
7. The vertical section of the aggregate supply curve is called the __________ range.
8. If the aggregate supply curve is horizontal, an increase in aggregate demand, other things being equal, will result in an increase in the __________ [price level, output] and no change in the __________ [price level, output].
9. If the aggregate supply curve is vertical, an increase in aggregate demand will result in an increase in (the)__________ [price level, output] and no change in (the) __________ [price level, output].
10. Policies designed to increase aggregate supply, as opposed to aggregate demand are called __________ policies.
11. The ratio of the change in taxes to the change in income is called the __________ __________ __________.
12. If the economy is experiencing severe unemployment, the government may reduce unemployment and increase real output by pursuing policies that will shift the aggregate demand to the __________ [right, left] and the aggregate supply curve to the __________ [right, left].
13. The government can reduce the price level by pursuing policies that shift the aggregate demand curve to the __________ [right, left] and the aggregate supply curve to the __________. [right, left]
14. The n-shaped curve showing the relationship between tax revenues and tax rates is called the __________ __________.
15. The long-run aggregate supply curve is __________, demonstrating the economy's potential real GDP.
16. Increases in labour productivity will shift the long-run aggregate supply curve to the to __________[right, left].
17. Other things being equal, an increase in long-run aggregate supply will result in a(n) __________ in real GDP and a(n) __________ in the price level.
18. If the economy is in long-run equilibrium and aggregate demand increases, other things being equal, the price level will __________ [rise, fall], but real GDP will __________ [change, not change].
19. Traffic congestion, general overcrowding in cities, and environmental pollution are among the __________ of economic growth.
20. Education and health, known as __________ capital, contribute to a country's economic growth.
21. Low interest rates will tend to stimulate __________. This will increase the __________ stock and promote economic growth.
22. Development that meets the needs of the present without compromising the ability of future generations to meet their own needs is called __________ development.

Solutions

1.	(aggregate demand)	12.	(right, right)
2.	(fallacy (of) composition)	13.	(left, right)
3.	(will not)	14.	(Laffer curve)
4.	(will)	15.	(vertical)
5.	(aggregate demand)	16.	(right)
6.	(Keynesian)	17.	(increase, fall)
7.	(classical)	18.	(rise, not change)
8.	(output, price level)	19.	(costs)
9.	(price level, output)	20.	(human)
10.	(supply-side)	21.	(investment, capital)
11.	(marginal tax rate)	22.	(sustainable)

8 CONSUMPTION, SAVINGS & INVESTMENT

SYNOPSIS

The **consumption function** is a relation between consumption and all its determinants, including the level of income, the availability of credit, the rate of interest, the existing stock of consumer durables, expectations, and income distribution.

Whereas the simple Keynesian consumption function states that consumption depends on disposable income, the **Permanent-Income** and **Life-Cycle** Hypotheses state that consumption depends more on permanent income (or average life-time income) and on wealth.

According to Keynes' fundamental psychological law, the value of the MPC lies between 0 and 1. A consumption curve with a declining MPC implies that high income earners have relatively low MPCs and that low income earners have high MPCs. Hence a redistribution of income from high income earners to low income earners will tend to increase overall consumption (the **Robin Hood effect).**

The major determinants of investment are the rate of interest, retained earnings, the level of profits, expectations, the rate of technological change, the level of income, and the rate of change of national income.

The **marginal efficiency of investment (MEI)** curve shows the inverse relationship between the rate of interest and the level of investment. Investment caused by changes in income is called **induced investment**.

LEARNING OBJECTIVES

In connection with this module, you should be able to:

1. describe the consumption function
2. explain the factors that influence consumption expenditure
3. distinguish between a shift of the consumption curve and a movement along the consumption curve
4. explain the Life-Cycle & Permanent Income hypotheses
5. discuss the different categories of investment
6. explain the determinants of investment spending
7. explain how interest rates affect investment
8. distinguish between a movement along the investment demand curve and a shift of the investment demand curve

DEFINITIONS & CONCEPTS

You should be able to define the following terms and concepts:

consumption function
permanent income and life-cycle hypotheses
fundamental psychological law
marginal efficiency of investment
wealth
retained earnings
Robin Hood effect
current income hypothesis
Autonomous investment
induced investment

8

CONSUMPTION, SAVINGS & INVESTMENT

Definitons, Concepts & Problems

Problem 8-1

What is the consumption function?

Requirement and Clue: *This is a definitional problem. There is a great deal that can be said about the consumption, but here you are required simply to state clearly and precisely the meaning of the concept.*

Solution

The consumption function is an equation that expresses a relationship between current consumption and all of the factors that influence consumer spending. If C represents consumption and Y represents income, and if we assume that all of the other factors that influence consumption (except income) are fixed, then the consumption function can be expressed as

$$C = C(Y)$$

The implication is that as income increases, other things being equal, consumption also increases.

Problem 8-2

List the main factors that affect the level of consumption in an economy? How will each of these factors affect the consumption curve?

Requirement and Clue: *This is a two-part problem. Answer each part in order. For the first part, focus on the main determinants of the level of consumer spending in an economy. For the second, be careful to distinguish between shifts and movements along the curve.*

Solution

Among the main factors that affect the level of consumer spending in an economy are:

1. The level of current income
2. Wealth (the dollar value of assets)
3. The availability of credit
4. The rate of interest
5. The existing stock of durable consumer goods
6. Consumers' expectations about their future economic circumstances

A change in the level of current income will cause a movement along the consumption curve but will not shift the curve. A change in any of the other factors on the list will shift the consumption curve. For example, an increase in consumers' wealth will shift the consumption curve up to the left, while an increase in interest rates will tend to shift the consumption curve down to the right.

Problem 8-3

Define each of the following concepts:

(a) *Marginal propensity to consume*

(b) *Average propensity of consume*

(c) *Consumption curve*

(d) *Saving curve*

Requirement and Clue: *This is a definitional problem. State clearly and precisely the meaning of each term with examples, if possible.*

Solution

(a) The marginal propensity to consume (MPC) is the fraction of extra income allocated to consumption. That is,

$$MPC = \frac{\Delta C}{\Delta Y}$$

where ΔC is the change in consumption and ΔY is the change in income. For example, if an increase in income of $10 million causes consumption to increase by $7 million, then

$$MPC = \frac{7}{10} = 0.7$$

(b) The average propensity to consume (APC) is the fraction of total income that is allocated to consumption. That is,

$$APC = \frac{C}{Y}$$

where C is consumption and Y is income. If out of an income of $100 million, total consumption is $80 million, then

$$APC = \frac{80}{100} = 0.8$$

(c) The consumption curve is a line showing the direct relationship between current income and current consumption. See the graph below.

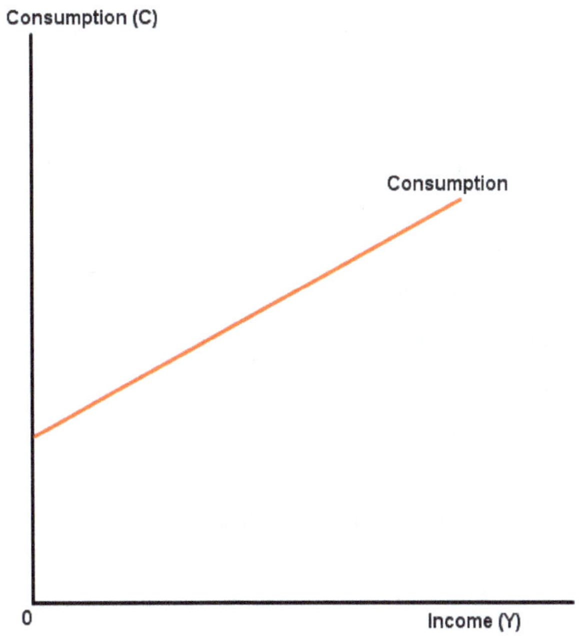

(d) A saving curve is a line that shows the relationship between saving and income. See the graph below.

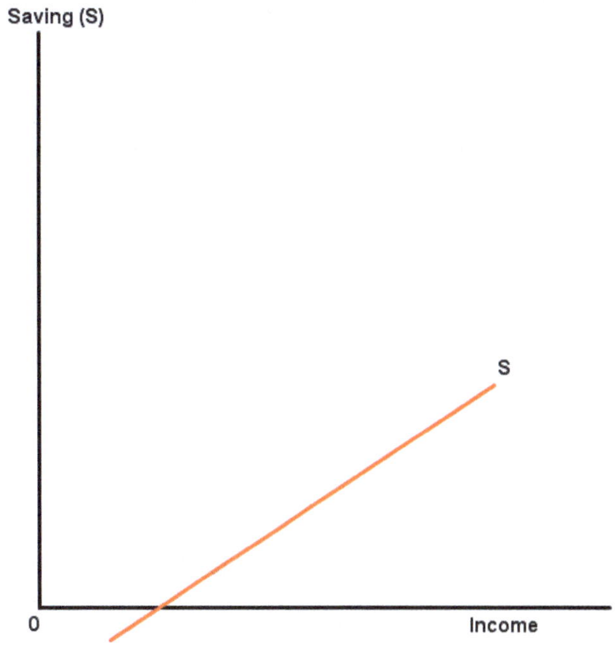

Problem 8-4

The government takes $5 billion in taxes from high- income earners and transfers it to low-income earners. What effect will this redistribution of income have on total consumption?

Requirement and Clue: *Focus on the marginal propensity to consume of each group.*

Solution

Since high-income earners have a relatively low marginal propensity to consume and low-income earners have a relatively high marginal propensity to consume, then taking $5 billion from high-income earners and giving it to low-income earners is actually taking money from where it is not likely to reduce consumption much and putting it where it is likely to increase consumption significantly. The effect is an increase in total consumption.

Problem 8-5

How might the availability of credit affect consumption?

Requirement and Clue: *The problem assumes that the availability of credit affects consumption. You task is to explain how. Focus on consumer items that are usually purchased on credit.*

Solution

Many durable consumer goods such as automobiles, furniture and appliances, and expensive musical instruments are usually purchased on credit. We can expect that if credit becomes available on good terms, expenditure on these items will increase. On the other hand, if it becomes difficult to obtain credit, or if the terms of credit become onerous, then we can expect expenditure on these items to decrease. For example, in a situation where automobiles can be purchased with low down payment and a long repayment period, consumers are likely to increase their purchases of automobiles. Moreover, easy credit terms on certain items make more funds available to consumers for the purchase of other consumer goods and services. If, for example, I can pay down 10% on a suite of furniture instead of 50%, then I am left with additional funds for other purchases.

Problem 8-6

Explain the effect of the existing stock of durable consumer goods on consumption.

Requirement and Clue: *Focus on the features of durable consumer goods and what happens to total consumer spending depending on the existing stocks of such goods.*

Solution

Durable consumer goods are goods such as automobiles, refrigerators, washing machines, and television sets that are expected to last for relatively long periods of time. Also, they tend to be relatively expensive. If the existing stock of durable consumer goods in an economy happens to fall to unusually low levels, then we can expect an increase in consumer spending on these items. Why? This is so because households will attempt to replenish their holdings of durable consumer goods. The rusted, old 2004 car will need to be replaced, and the old refrigerator, which keeps spoiling expensive cuts of meat, has seen its best days and must be put out for the garbage collectors. The drive to build up the depleted stock of durable consumer goods means that consumer spending will increase.

Problem 8-7

The following table contains data on disposable income and saving in billions of dollars.

Disposable income	Consumption	Saving
400	--------	- 5
420	--------	0
440	--------	5
460	--------	10
480	--------	15
500	--------	20
520	--------	25
540	--------	30
560	--------	35

(a) Compute consumption at each level of income and complete the consumption column.

(b) From the data, determine the break-even level of disposable income.

Requirement and Clue: *This problem requires you to know the relationship between disposable income, consumption, and saving.*

Solution

(a) Disposable income is either consumed or saved. Thus, disposable income (DI) is the sum of consumption (C) and saving (S).

$$DI = C + S$$

Therefore, $C = DI - S$

With this information, we can complete the consumption column as follows:

Disposable income	Consumption	Saving
400	405	- 5
420	420	0
440	435	5
460	450	10
480	465	15
500	480	20
520	495	25
540	510	30
560	525	35

(b) The break-even level of disposable income is that level at which disposable income and consumption are equal. It is the level of disposable income at which saving is zero. From the data, the break-even level of income is $420 billion.

Problem 8-8

If Y represents disposable income, C represents consumption, and S represents saving, and the consumption function is

$$C = 200 + 2/3Y$$

(a) *What would be the saving function?*

(b) *When would saving be zero?*

Requirement and Clue: *This is a two-part problem. Answer each part in order. For part (a), focus on the fact that Y = C + S and use this relation to find S in terms of Y. For part (b), set S = 0 and solve for Y.*

Solution

(a) $Y = C + S$

$Y = 200 + 2/3Y + S$

$S = Y - 200 - 2/3Y$

$S = 1/3Y - 200$

(b) $1/3Y - 200 = 0$

$1/3Y = 200$

$Y = 600$

When income is 600, saving will be zero.

Problem 8-9

Consider the following diagram.

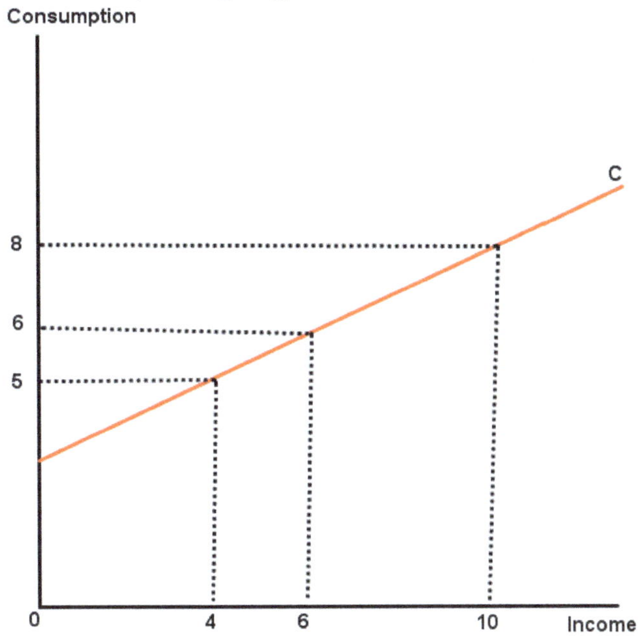

(a) *If total income is $10 million, how much will be spent on consumer goods and services?*

(b) *If income is $4, how much will have to be borrowed to finance consumption?*

(c) *At what level of income will the amount spent on consumption be exactly equal to total income?*

Requirement and Clue: *This is a three-part problem. Answer each part in order. The solution requires the ability to read graphs. Read the graph carefully and answer the questions asked.*

Solution

(a) From the graph, we see that at an income level of $10 million, consumption is $8 million.

(b) At an income level of $4 million, consumption is $5 million. This means that consumption exceeds income by $1 million. Thus $1 million will have to be borrowed to finance consumption.

(c) At an income level of $6 million, the amount spent on consumption is $6 million.

Problem 8-10

From an income of $20 billion in an economy, consumers plan to save a total of $2 billion. When total income in the economy increases to $23 billion, consumers save a total of $3 billion. What can we conclude about the marginal propensity to consume in this economy?

Requirement and Clue: *You are expected to be familiar with the concept of marginal propensity to consume. Use the data given to determine the change in income and the resulting change in consumption and use this information to calculate the marginal propensity to consume (MPC).*

Solution

Let Y = income; S = saving; and C = consumption.

According to the problem, income increased from $20 billion to $23 billion; therefore ΔY = $3 billion. From an income of $20 billion, saving is $2 billion. Thus, consumption is ($20 billion – $2 billion) = $18 billion. From an income of $23 billion, saving is $3 billion. Thus, consumption is ($23 billion – $3 billion) = $20 billion. Therefore ΔC = $2 billion.

$$MPC = \frac{\Delta C}{\Delta Y} = \frac{2}{3}$$

The MPC in this economy is 2/3.

Problem 8-11

Consider the data in the following table.

Disposable income ($million)	Savings ($million)
8,000	100
9,000	250

(a) *Calculate the marginal propensity to consume (MPC).*

(b) *Calculate the marginal propensity to save (MPS).*

Requirement and Clue: *This is a two-part problem. Answer each part in order. You must show familiarity with the MPC and the MPS.*

Solution

(a) The marginal propensity to consume is the fraction of extra income that will be consumed. Thus, MPC = ΔC/ΔY. From the available data, ΔY = $1,000 million. If income is $8,000 million and saving is $100 million, then consumption is $(8000 – 100) million = $7,900 million. If income is $9,000 million and saving is $250 million, then consumption is $(9,000 – 250) million = $8,750 million. Thus ΔC = $(8,750 – 7,900) = $850 million. Therefore,

$$MPC = \frac{\Delta C}{\Delta Y} = \frac{850}{1,000} = \mathbf{0.85}$$

(b) MPS = 1 – MPC = 1– 0.85 = **0.15**

Problem 8-12

It is given that the marginal propensity to consume is constant at 0.5 and that the break-even level of income is 8,000. How much will be consumed out of an income of 10,000 and how much will be saved. Assume that there are no taxes.

Requirement and Clue: *Focus on the information provided in the problem. What is the meaning of a constant MPC? What information is given by the notion of a break-even level of income? What is the implication of no taxes?*

Solution

A break-even level of income of 8,000 means that consumption is 8,000 when income is 8,000. If income increases to 10,000, an increase of 2,000, one-half of this (or 1,000) will be consumed. Thus, consumption will rise from 8,000 to 9,000. The remaining 1,000 will be saved since there are no taxes to consider.

Problem 8-13

What impact might a stock market crash have on consumption?

Requirement and Clue: *Focus on the effect of a stock market crash on wealth.*

Solution

A stock market crash lowers the value of assets of stock owners. Such individuals will feel a reduction in their wealth, and will tend to reduce their consumption. Some economists believe that the stock market crash of 1929 contributed to the Great Depression by causing a significant decline in consumption.

Problem 8-14

In a certain economy, average income increased over a year. During the same year, the interest rate on consumer loans rose from 12% to 15%. Since consumption is expected to rise as income rises, should furniture dealers be surprised to find their total sales down below the previous year's level?

Requirement and Clue: *Focus on the possible effect of higher interest rates on the purchases of furniture.*

Solution

Although income and consumption are directly related, it is quite possible for some non-income determinant of consumption to offset any effect of changes in income. In this case, the increase in the rate of interest may have had a greater effect in reducing expenditure on furniture than the positive effect of the increase in income. It is also possible that other determinants of consumption may have been operating.

Problem 8-15

The government decides to reduce the tax rate from 20% to 15% of taxable income. What is the likely effect of this tax change on private consumption?

Requirement and Clue: *Focus on the effect of a tax cut on disposable income.*

Solution

A reduction in the tax rate from 20% to 15% implies an increase in personal disposable income. For example, with a tax rate of 20%, an individual with a taxable income of $20,000 would pay $4,000 in taxes, keeping a disposable income of $16,000. With a tax rate of 15%, the same individual would pay $3,000 in taxes, keeping a disposable income of $17,000. So the tax reduction gives the consumer an extra $1,000, some of which will be allocated to extra consumption.

Problem 8-16

Discuss the permanent-income and the life-cycle hypotheses of consumption. How do these hypotheses differ from the current-income hypothesis?

Requirement and Clue: *This is a two-part problem. Answer each part in order. You are expected to demonstrate your knowledge of these hypotheses. Graphs will be helpful.*

Solution

The name of Milton Friedman is associated with the permanent-income hypothesis while the names of Franco Modigliani and Albert Ando are associated with the life-cycle hypothesis. These two hypotheses are quite similar and can be discussed as a single hypothesis. The central idea of these hypotheses is that a transitory increase in income will have little or no effect on households' expenditure on goods and services if it does not significantly affect households' future income expectations. Proponents of these hypotheses claim that current expenditure on consumer goods and services depends not so much on current disposable income, but more so on expected streams of future income over a considerable length of time, and on wealth.

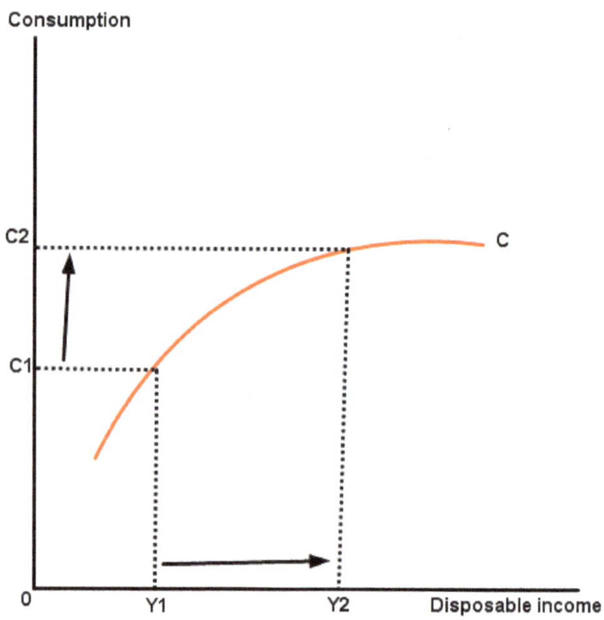

Diagram A

The following example will illustrate the idea behind the permanent-income and life-cycle hypotheses. Suppose a household wins a lottery this year. According to the current-income hypothesis, the household's consumption this year will increase dramatically to reflect the increase in current income, but will return to its normal lower level thereafter. According to the permanent-income and life-cycle hypotheses, however, since the household will not expect to win lotteries in succeeding years, it is more likely to spread the proceeds from the lottery over several years in the future and adjust its consumption pattern to this long-term income.

A graphical illustration will help to highlight the difference between these hypotheses. Diagram A above shows a current-income consumption curve relating current consumption to current disposable income.

Note that as current disposable income rises from Y1 to Y2, current consumption rises. Diagram B below illustrates the life-cycle/permanent-income consumption curve in which current consumption is related to average long-term income.

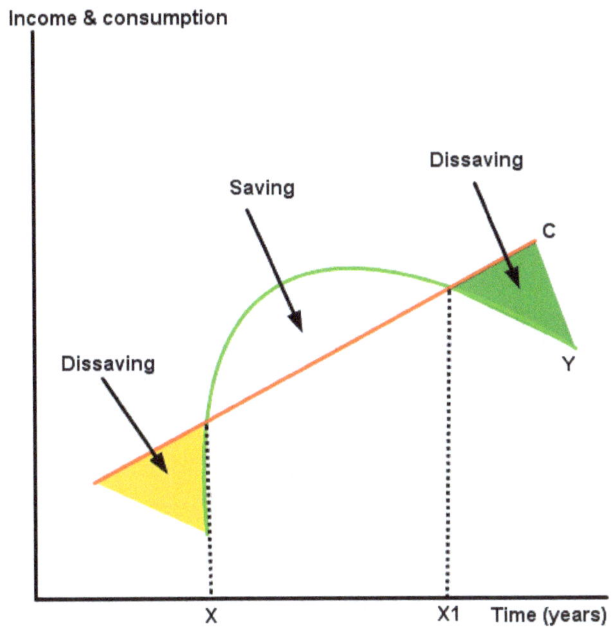

An increase in average long-term income results in an increase in current consumption. In the early years prior to X years, the consumer is dissaving since consumption exceeds income. Between years X and X1, the consumer is saving since income exceeds consumption. Beyond X1 years, the consumer is again dissaving. Finally, Diagram C below illustrates that according to the life-cycle/permanent-income consumption curve, current consumption is not affected much by current disposable income. An increase in current disposable income from Y to Y1 causes a relatively small increase in current consumption from C to C1.

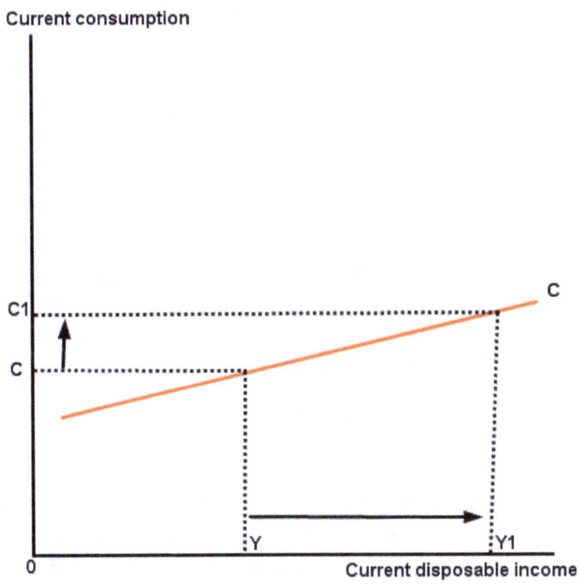

Problem 8-17

Why do people save? What determines the amount of saving that will take place in a country?

Requirement and Clue: *This is a two part problem. Answer each part in order. Since there will be some discussion on saving, it is well to define the concept. For the first part of the problem, you need to focus on the motives for saving. For the second part of the problem, discuss the main factors that influence the amount of saving that takes place.*

Solution

Saving may be defined as the difference between income and consumption expenditures. Thus, given a level of income, a reduction in consumption implies an increase in saving. People save for a variety of reasons, one of which is to provide for the future. The existence of old-age pensions and other provisions that the government makes to safeguard people after retirement have caused people to be less concerned with saving for this reason.

A second reason why people save is to be able to make some expenditure in the future. A family may save this year to be able to enjoy a vacation next year, or a young couple may save with the aim of buying a house in the future. The existence of credit and easy term payments plans will reduce the amount of saving for this purpose. For example, if the down payment on an automobile is 50 percent, a family would have to save $10,000 in order to purchase a $20,000 automobile. If the down payment were only ten percent, the family would need to save only $2,000 in order to purchase the automobile.

People also save in order to leave some form of wealth to their heirs, or they may save and accumulate wealth simply because of the prestige that the acquisition of wealth may bestow on them in their community. Finally, people may save with no particular aim in view, but just out of habit.

The reasons for saving mentioned above may have some effect on the amount of saving that actually takes place in a country. In addition, people's ability to save will be an important determinant of the volume of saving. The most important factor determining the amount of saving is the level of income. Other things being equal, the higher the level of income, the greater the amount of saving that households will be able to undertake.

The rate of interest may also exert some influence on the volume of saving. The prospects of high interest rates on savings may induce households to increase their saving. The existence of institutions such as banks, saving societies and credit unions that facilitate saving will also have some positive effects on the volume of saving that takes place in a country.

Problem 8-18

What is investment in economics?

Requirement and Clue: *This is a definitional problem. The problem suggests that investment in economics may be different from investment in general. You are expected to explain precisely the meaning of the concept as used in economics. Examples will be helpful.*

Solution

In economics, investment refers to expenditure on capital goods such as machinery, equipment, roads, residential and non-residential construction, and inventories. It is the production of new capital goods. In ordinary language, investment is the purchase of financial assets. Thus the purchase of stocks and bonds would ordinarily be considered investment, but not so in economics.

Problem 8-19

List the main determinants of investment.

Requirement and Clue: *Here you are required only to create a list of the major factors that affect investment. You should consider investment as an "economic" concept.*

Solution

The main determinants of investment are:

1. The rate of interest
2. Retained earnings
3. The level of profits
4. Expectations of business people about economic conditions
5. The rate of technological change
6. The level of national income

Problem 8-20

Discuss fully the relationship between the rate of interest and the level of investment.

Requirement and Clue: *You are to explain fully how changes in interest rates affect the investment decision.*

Solution

The rate of interest can be viewed as the cost of borrowing money. If interest rates are high, firms find it more expensive to borrow funds for investment purposes. Hence, a low level of investment is associated with a high rate of interest. On the other hand, if the rate of interest is low, firms find it more profitable to invest. An interest rate of 20% makes an investment loan much more costly than an interest rate of 10% does.

Investment decisions are often made on the basis of a comparison of the rate of interest and the expected rate of return. The expected rate of return from an investment is the expected percentage profit on the money outlay used to acquire capital goods such as new buildings and equipment. Thus, an expected rate of return of 10% means that investors expect to earn an annual profit of 10% on their investment.

The effect of the rate of interest on investment decisions can be illustrated by the following example. Suppose a firm is contemplating five investment projects with expected rates of return as shown in the following table.

Projects	Expected rate of return (%)
1	18
2	16
3	13
4	10
5	9

Let us suppose that the firm can borrow money at an interest rate of 8%. At this rate of interest, all five projects are profitable since the expected rate of return on all five exceeds the rate of interest. If the interest rate is 14%, only projects one and two are profitable; and if the interest rate is 20%, none of the projects is profitable. Clearly, high interest rates tend to reduce investment spending, while low interest rates tend to increase investment spending.

Problem 8-21

What measures can a government take to encourage private investment?

Requirement and Clue: *Consider the factors that affect investment and focus on those that can be influenced by the government (public policy).*

Solution

A government can take a number of steps to encourage private investment. First, a government may offer special financial assistance to new firms. The assistance may take the form of a loan, or a grant, or some form of subsidy. For example, a provision may be made whereby firms are permitted to deduct a certain percentages of the cost of new capital equipment for tax purposes, or a certain part of the cost of establishing a business may be refunded as soon as the business is established.

Second, a government may encourage investment in the private sector by reducing its taxes on business profits. The primary objective of a firm is to earn profits. If a huge portion of those profits is likely to be taxed away, then investment will most likely be discouraged.

A third measure that a government may take to foster private investment is to maintain low interest rates. Low interest rates imply a low cost of borrowing funds for investment purposes, hence low interest rates tend to encourage borrowing and stimulate investment.

A good portion of investment in the private sector is financed, not by borrowed funds, but by retained earnings. A fourth measure a government may take to encourage private investment is to impose a higher rate of taxation on distributed profits than on undistributed profits. There will be an incentive for profits to be re-invested in the business rather than given out to shareholders.

Finally, a government can create a climate that is conducive to investment. A favourable investment climate includes the reduction of uncertainties, the promotion of optimistic expectations, and political stability. All these measures are likely to have favourable effects on the level of investment in the private sector.

Problem 8-22

Define each of the following concepts:

(a) *Marginal efficiency of investment (MEI)curve*

(b) *Retained earnings*

Requirement and Clue: *This is a two-part problem. Answer each part in order. This problem is definitional. State clearly and precisely the meaning of each concept without getting into a lengthy discussion.*

Solution

(a) The marginal efficiency of investment curve is a graph showing the inverse relationship between the level of investment and the rate of interest. The curve is sometimes referred to as the investment demand curve. The following diagram shows the marginal efficiency of investment (MEI) curve.

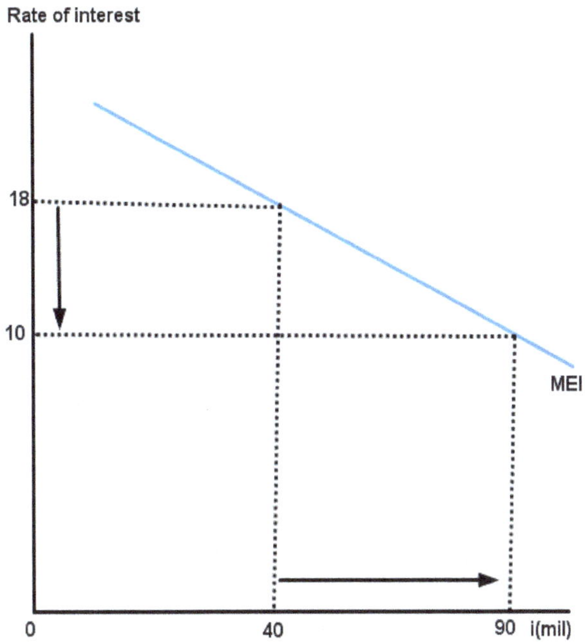

The graph shows that at a rate of interest of 18%, the level of investment is $40 million. When the rate of interest falls to 10%, the level of investment increases to $90 million.

(b) Retained earnings are a part of profits kept back by firms instead of being distributed to shareholders as dividends. That explains why they are referred to as undistributed profits. They are used largely for investment purposes.

Problem 8-23

Distinguish between autonomous investment and induced investment.

Requirement and Clue: *Your solution should be of such that the difference between the two concepts is highlighted. An example will be helpful.*

Solution

Autonomous investment is investment that does not vary with the level of income. If autonomous investment is $30 million, no matter how the level of income changes, investment will remain at $30 million. Induced investment, on the other hand, is investment that depends on the level of income. So as the level of income varies, the level of investment will change because of the changes in income.

Problem 8-24

What do economists mean by investment? What are the major categories of investment?

Requirement and Clue: *This is a two-part problem. Answer each part in order. The first part of the problem is definitional. Give a clear and precise meaning of the concept as used by economists. For the second part of the problem, focus on the different types of investment.*

Solution

Investment refers to expenditure on machinery, equipment, residential and non-residential construction, and inventories. The concept is also used in reference to the construction of new capital goods. The main categories of investment are shown in the following table:

<u>Categories of Investment</u>

Government investment
- *Fixed capital*
- *Inventories*

Business fixed capital
- *Residential structures*
- *Non-residential structures & equipment*

Business inventories

Government investment includes additions to government capital stock such as buildings, highways, motor vehicles, etc. Inventories are stocks of finished and semi-finished goods.

Business fixed capital includes residential structures such as dwellings, and non-residential structures such as offices, factories, and equipment such as machinery and tools.

Problem 8-25

Explain how each of the following events affects investment:

(a) *the discovery of a new and more efficient method of producing rubber*

(b) *a government announcement of a two-year tax concession for new firms*

(c) *a significant increase in the number of marriages*

(d) *an announcement by economists that the economy is heading for a long recessionary period.*

Requirement and Clue: *This is a multi-part problem. Answer each part in order. Focus on the determinants of investment and on the effect of each event on those determinants.*

Solution

(a) This means that more rubber can be produced with a given amount of inputs. This event will tend to motivate investors to invest not only in rubber production but also in other capital goods that are related to rubber. Investment will be positively affected.

(b) The announcement of a two-year tax concession for new firms will serve as an incentive for entrepreneurs and business people to establish new firms. This, of course, implies that investment will be positively affected.

(c) A significant increase in the number of marriages will likely increase the demand for homes. The production of new homes will increase the level of investment. Moreover, the demand for household furniture and appliances will likely increase leading to an increase in investment to produce these goods.

(d) An announcement that the economy is heading for a long recession will have an adverse effect on investment. Firms will tend to cut back their investment activities as they cancel investment projects or put them on hold.

Problem 8-26

You are given the consumption schedule shown in the following table.

Income	Consumption	MPC
80	70.00	
90	78.00	
100	85.50	
110	92.50	
120	99.00	
130	105.00	

Compute the marginal propensity to consume (MPC) and fill in the MPC column.

Requirement and Clue: You are required to show familiarity with the concept of marginal propensity to consume and the formula that describes it. Use the formula to compute the MPC.

Solution

The marginal propensity to consume (MPC) is the fraction of extra or additional income that will be devoted to consumption. The MPC can be expressed by the following formula:

$$MPC = \frac{\Delta C}{\Delta Y},$$ where C is consumption and Y is income.

Using this formula, we obtain the MPC values recorded in the MPC column in the table below.

Income	Consumption	MPC
80	70.00	0.80
90	78.00	0.75
100	85.50	0.70
110	92.50	0.65
120	99.00	0.60
130	105.00	

Problem 8-27

After completing your degree in economics, you are hired by a firm of business and economic consultants. One of your clients is asking your advice on whether or not her company should increase production of electrical home appliances. Mention two important economic variables that you would study in order to advise your client.

Requirement and Clue: *Electrical home appliances are bought by households/consumers. Basically, you should focus on two important determinants of consumer expenditure.*

Solution

In order to advise my client on whether or not her company should increase production of electrical home appliances, I would need to know the likelihood of the electrical appliances being sold. The question that I would ask is this: What are the main economic variables that would determine whether or not consumers would purchase the appliances? One economic variable that I would consider is the level of income and its trend. If the level of income is relatively high and is likely to grow, then expenditures on electrical home appliances will likely increase. If income is likely to fall in the near future, then it is probably not a good idea to produce the appliances.

Another variable that would be worth looking at is the rate of interest. Some electrical home appliances such as refrigerators and washers and dryers, are relatively expensive and are bought on credit. If the rate of interest is expected to fall, then other things being equal, electrical home appliances will be more affordable because of the lower cost of credit.

Problem 8-28

Use diagrams to show the effect of each of the following on current consumption.

(a) *An increase in income*

(b) *A rise in interest rates*

(c) *A redistribution of income from high income earners to low income earners*

(d) *An increase in personal income taxes*

Requirement and Clue: *This is a multi-part problem. Answer each part in order. Be careful not to confuse a shift in the curve with a movement along the curve.*

Solution

(a) An increase in income causes a movement along the consumption curve. As income increases from Y1 to Y2 in the following diagram, consumption increases from C1 to C2.

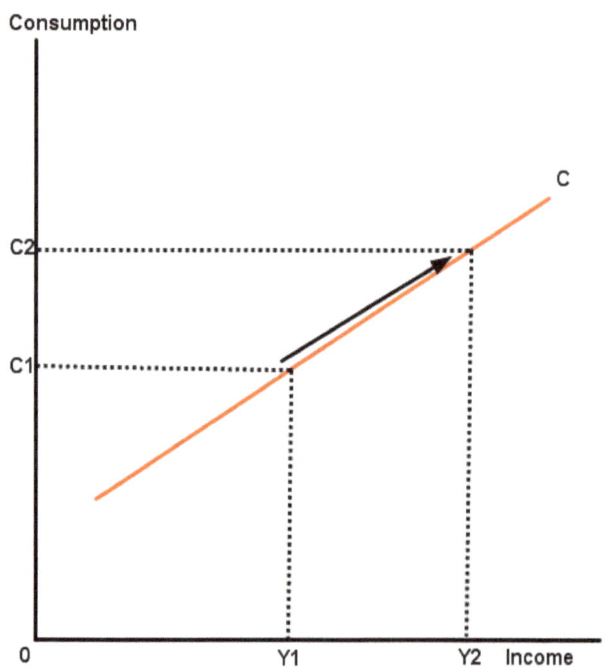

(b) A rise in interest rates causes the consumption curve to shift from C to C0 as shown in the following diagram. At any given level of income, say Y, there is a smaller level of consumption than before the rise in interest rates. Consumption falls from C to C0.

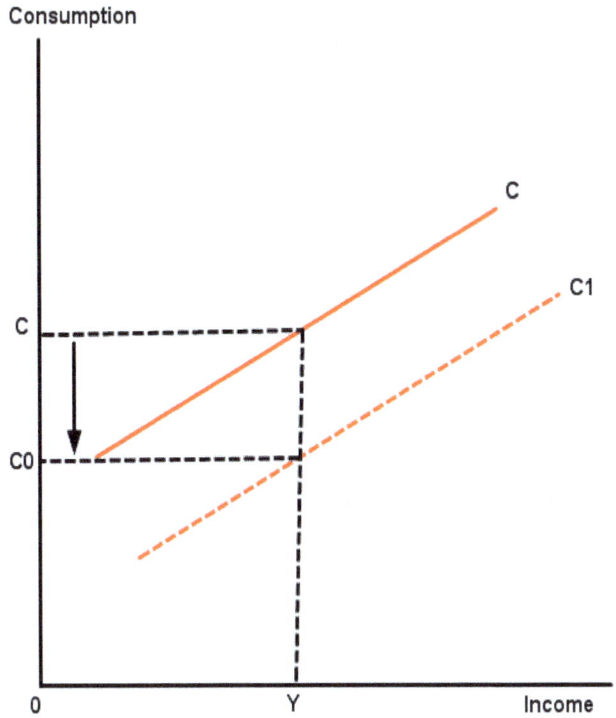

(c) A redistribution of income from high income earners to low income earners causes an upward shift of the consumption curve from C0 to C as shown in the following diagram, resulting in a greater consumption at each level of income.

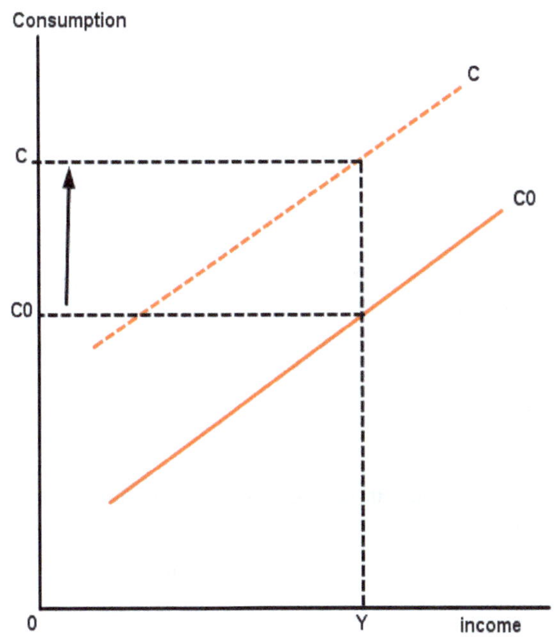

(d) An increase in personal income taxes will reduce disposable income. This reduction in income will result in a reduction in consumption as shown in the following diagram. Income falls from Y1 to Y while consumption falls from C1 to C.

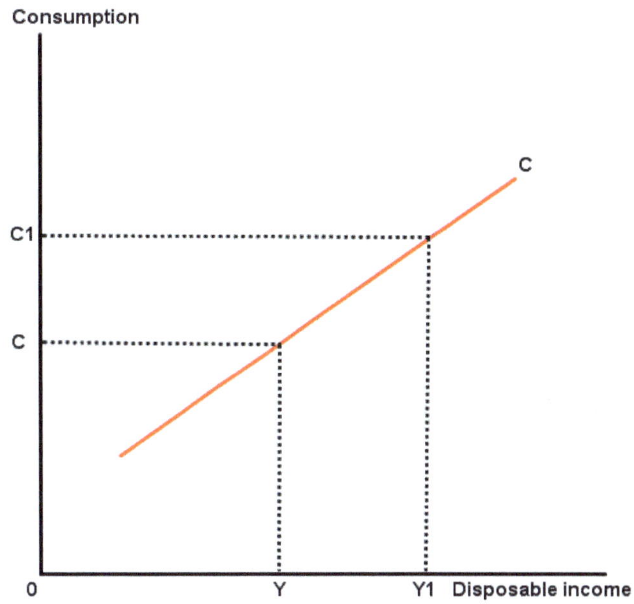

Problem 8-29

The following table shows several investment projects with their associated rates of return.

Projects	Rates of return (%)
A	20
B	19
C	17
D	16
E	14
F	10

(a) *If the rate of interest is 18%, which investment projects will be undertaken?*

(b) *If the rate of interest falls to 15%, which projects will be undertaken?*

(c) *If the rate of interest falls to 9%, which projects will be undertaken?*

Requirement and Clue: *This is a three-part problem. Answer each part in order. Focus on the investment decision rule involving the comparison of the rate of interest with the expected rate of return.*

Solution

(a) If the rate of interest is 18%, projects A and B will be undertaken because their rates of return exceed 18%.

(b) If the rate of interest falls to 15%, then projects A, B, C and D will be undertaken because their rates of return exceed the rate of interest.

(c) If the rate of interest falls to 9%, then all the projects from A to F will be undertaken because their rates of return exceed the rate of interest.

Problem 8-30

"The practice of separating consumption spending from investment spending in macroeconomic analysis is counterproductive. In macroeconomics, one is concerned with total spending and not with whether the spending is done by households or by firms."

Discuss this statement.

Requirement and Clue: *Read the statement carefully and critically. Is it partly true, entirely true, or entirely false? Try to justify studying consumption and investment separately rather than as an aggregate.*

Solution

If we are to understand the behavior of total spending, it is very important to understand the components of total spending. Households and firms may respond differently to different economic stimuli. For example, an increase in interest rates, other things being equal, will stimulate saving while it will reduce investment. If total spending falls mainly because consumer spending falls, it is important to know the factors that determine consumer spending so that action can be taken to manipulate it, if possible. Similarly, if investment is sluggish, knowing the determinants of investment will help to guide policies to encourage it. Without looking at the components of total spending, it becomes more difficult to control total spending.

Problem 8-31

Explain the paradox of saving.

Requirement and Clue: *It is a good idea to define a paradox. Then you should define the paradox of saving and explain the paradox.*

Solution

A paradox is a statement that, on the surface, seems contradictory, but turns out to be true upon closer scrutiny. The paradox of saving, also called the paradox of thrift, states that an increase in intended aggregate saving, other things being equal, will lead to a fall in total income and hence to a fall in actual saving. The paradox of saving can be defined as the apparent contradiction in the fact that an increase in intended aggregate saving results in a decrease in actual saving. Note that the statement appears to be totally contradictory if the words "intended aggregate" and "actual" are omitted. The paradox would then read: An increase in saving results in a decrease in saving. The key to explaining the paradox lies in the fact that an increase in intended aggregate saving reduces income which in turn reduces actual saving.

There is another dimension to the paradox of saving. Saving by individuals makes them better off in the future (provided that inflation does not severely reduce the value of their saving) and in therefore considered a virtue. But from an economy-wide point of view, thrift may be considered a social vice, because it makes the entire economy worse off in the future through lower income levels.

Problem 8-32

You are given the following consumption equation:

$$C = 40 + 0.5Y_d$$

where C= consumption and Y_d is disposable income.

(a) *Find the value of autonomous consumption.*

(b) *What is the numerical value of the MPC?*

(c) *If autonomous investment is 25, want is the numerical value of autonomous expenditure?*

Requirement and Clue: This is a three-part problem. Answer each part in order. If you understand the consumption equation, parts (a) and (b) will be obvious. You are expected to be familiar with the meaning of autonomous expenditure and of what it is constituted.

Solution

(a) Autonomous consumption is consumption that is independent of income. From the consumption equation given, it can be seen that autonomous consumption is **40.**

(b) From the consumption equation, it can be seen that the MPC is **0.5.**

(c) Autonomous expenditure (A) is the sum of autonomous consumption (40) and autonomous investment (given as 25), hence A = 40 + 25 = **65.**

Problem 8-33

If the consumption equation is $C = 15 + 0.6Y_d$, what is consumption when disposable income (Y_d) is:

(a) *90?*

(b) *120?*

(c) *60?*

Requirement and Clue: *This is a three-part problem. Answer each part in order. The solution is just a matter of substituting the value of disposable income into the consumption equation.*

Solution

(a) When disposable income is 90, consumption is 15 + 0.6(90) =**69**

(b) When disposable income is 120, consumption is 15 + 0.6(120) = **87**

(c) When disposable income is 60, consumption is 15 + 0.6(60) = **51**

Multiple-Choice Questions

In each case, circle the letter that corresponds with the correct answer.

1. The consumption function is an equation that expresses:

a. the relation between consumption and income

b. the relation between consumption and the rate of interest

c. the fraction of income spent on consumer goods and services

d. the relation between consumption and all the determinants of consumption.

Answer: d

Reason: The consumption function is a mathematical expression of the relationship between consumption and all its determinants.

2. Which of the following is a determinant of the level of consumption?

a. Consumer wealth

b. Interest rates

c. The level of income

d. All of the above

Answer: d

Reason: All of the choices, a, b, and c, do influence the level of consumption.

3. With income on the horizontal axis and consumption on the vertical axis, which of the following will not shift the consumption curve?

a. Changes in consumers' wealth

b. Changes in interest rates

c. Changes in the level of income

d. Changes in expectations about future economic conditions

Answer: c

Reason: Changes in the level of income will cause a movement along the consumption curve but they will not shift the curve.

4. Keynes' fundamental psychological law states that the MPC:

a. increases as income increases

b. declines as interest rates rise

c. has a value greater than 0 but less than 1

d. has a value greater than 1 but less than infinity

Answer: c

Reason: Keynes' fundamental psychological law states that people are disposed, as a rule, to increase their consumption as their income rises, but not by as much as the increase in their income. This is consistent with choice c.

5. The marginal propensity to consume is:

a. the total amount of consumption that takes place out of a given level of income

b. the relationship between the level of income and the rate of interest

c. the amount the poor people need to survive because they have marginal incomes

d. none of the above

Answer: d

Reason: The marginal propensity to consume is the fraction of extra income that is consumed.

6. If total income increases from $250 billion to $275 billion, and, as a result, total consumption increases from $200 billion to $220 billion, then the MPC is:

a. 0.80

b. 1.25

c. 0.90

d. 0.75

Answer: a

Reason: The change in income is ($275 – $250) = $25 billion. The change in consumption is ($220 – $200) = $20 billion. Therefore the MPC is 20/25 = 0.8

7. When total income rises from $500 million to $600 million, total consumption increases from $400 million to $480 million. From this we know that the MPS is:

a. 0.80

b. 1.25

c. 0.20

d. 0.75

Answer: c

Reason: The change in income is ($600 – $500) = $100 million. The change in consumption is $480 – $400) = $80 million. Therefore the MPC is 80/100 = 0.8. Since MPC + MPS = 1, then MPS = 1 – 0.8 = 0.20

8. If consumption is $8,000 when disposable income is $10,000, then the marginal propensity to consume (MPC) is:

a. 0.8

b. 1.25

c. 0.2

d. indeterminate

Answer: d

Reason: The MPC is the change in consumption divided by the change in income, and this information is not given, so we cannot determine the MPC from the information given.

9. The level of income in a society directly determines:

a. the stock of liquid assets in the society

b. how wealth is distributed in that society

c. the availability of credit in that society

d. none of the above

Answer: d

Reason: The level of income directly determines the level of consumer spending.

10. A diminishing marginal propensity to consume means that:

a. people consume a smaller fraction of any extra income received as their incomes increase

b. total consumption decreases as total income increases

c. people become less inclined to consume as they grow older

d. none of the above

Answer: a

Reason: A declining marginal propensity to consume implies that low income earners tend to high relatively high MPCs while high income earners tend to have relatively low MPCs. This is consistent with choice a.

11. The average propensity to consume (APC) is:

a. always the same as the marginal propensity to consume
b. the fraction of income that is consumed
c. the amount that is consumed by the average household
d. the extra consumption that takes place when income increases

Answer: b

Reason: The average propensity to consume is total consumption divided by total income. This is consistent with choice b.

12. The marginal propensity to consume (MPC) and the marginal propensity to save (MPS):

a. are always equal
b. must add up to more than one
c. must add up to less than one always
d. none of the above

Answer: d

Reason: The MPC + MPS = 1

13. Redistributing income from the rich to the poor will tend to:

a. reduce total consumption
b. increase total consumption
c. have no effect on total consumption
d. increase income inequality

Answer: b

Reason: Redistributing income from the rich to the poor will not significantly reduce consumption among the rich, but it will significantly increase consumption among the poor, leading to an overall increase in total consumption.

14. If consumption increases because of an increase in income:

a. the consumption curve will shift upward to the left
b. the consumption curve will shift down to the right
c. the consumption curve will become linear
d. none of the above

Answer: d

Reason: The consumption curve will not shift, but there will be a movement along the consumption curve from one point to another.

15. According to the Permanent-Income and Life-Cycle hypotheses:

a. consumption and income are inversely related
b. current income has absolutely no effect on the level of consumption
c. wealth and average life-time income are important determinants of consumption
d. transitory income exerts the greatest influence on current consumption

Answer: c

Reason: Whereas the Keynesian current income hypothesis emphasizes the role of current income in consumption, the Permanent-Income and Life-Cycle hypotheses emphasize the role of average life-time income or permanent income in consumption.

16. If a society's MPC declines as income rises, then taxing the rich and giving the proceeds to the poor will:

a. increase total consumption
b. reduce total consumption
c. reduce the level of income
d. have no effect on total income and hence no effect on consumption

Answer: a

Reason: The increase in consumption among the poor will far outweigh the decrease in consumption among the rich, leading to an increase in overall consumption.

17. The relation between consumption and current income is plotted on a graph with income on the horizontal axis and consumption on the vertical axis. An increase in income will:

a. cause the consumption line to shift upward
b. result in a greater level of consumption but the consumption line will not shift
c. result in a downward shift in the consumption line
d. none of the above.

Answer: b

Reason: Only non-income determinants of consumption will shift the consumption line.

18. The Robin Hood Effect refers to the effect of:

a. expectations on consumption
b. income redistribution on consumption
c. current income on current consumption
d. past earnings on current consumption

Answer: b

Reason: Because Robin Hood is credited with taking from the rich and giving to the poor, income redistribution is referred to as the Robin Hood Effect.

19. In economics, investment is defined as:

a. the purchase of bonds
b. the difference between income and consumption
c. consumer purchases of durable consumer goods
d. none of the above.

Answer: d

Reason: In economics, investment refers to the purchase or production of new capital goods or additions to inventories.

20. Gross fixed capital formation consists of:

a. the total profits of a firm
b. the total amount of money required to start a business
c. total inventories of goods held by firms
d. construction and machinery and equipment.

Answer: d

Reason: Gross fixed capital formation is one of the main categories of investment and includes residential and non-residential construction, plant, machinery, and equipment.

21. A curve showing the relation between the rate of interest and the level of investment is called:

a. the marginal efficiency of investment curve
b. the multiplier curve
c. the marginal propensity to invest income curve
d. none of the above

Answer: a

Reason: *The marginal efficiency of investment summarizes the inverse relationship between the rate of interest and the level of investment.*

22. Which of the following is likely to result in a fall in investment, other things being equal?

a. A fall in interest rates
b. An increase in the level of disposable income
c. An increase in interest rates
d. An increase in retained earnings.

Answer: c

Reason: *Higher interest rates make it more costly for firms to borrow funds for investment purposes. Thus, higher interest rates are a disincentive for investment.*

23. A fall in the rate of interest is likely to result in:

a. an increase in investment and a fall in consumption
b. a fall in consumption and a fall in investment
c. an increase in both consumption and investment
d. none of the above

Answer: c

Reason: *A fall in interest rates reduces the cost of borrowing funds whether for consumption or investment. Lower interest rates make investment projects more profitable.*

24. Which of the following statements is correct?

a. Autonomous investment and induced investment both depend on the level of income
b. Induced investment depends on the rate of interest while autonomous investment depends on the level of income
c. Autonomous investment and induced investment both depend on the rate of interest
d. Autonomous investment is independent of the level of income while induced investment depends on the level of income.

Answer: d

Reason: *Autonomous investment is not affected by changes in income. Induced investment is investment that results from changes in income. This is consistent with choice d.*

True-False Questions

Determine whether each of the following statements is true or false.

1. The consumption function states that increases in the rate of interest will lead to increases in consumption.

Answer: False

Explanation: *The rate of interest is one of the determinants of consumption, but increases in the rate of interest lead to decreases, not increases, in consumption.*

2. The fundamental psychological law states that the MPC declines as income increases.

Answer: False

Explanation: *The law states that the MPC lies between 0 and 1.*

3. An increase in income causes consumption to increase, other things being equal, but it will not result in any shift in the consumption curve.

Answer: True

4. If the MPC declines as income rises, then a redistribution of income from high income earners to low income earners, other things being equal, will result in an increase in total consumption.

Answer: True

5. At very low levels of income, consumption may exceed income. This means that at such low income levels, the marginal propensity to consume (MPC) is greater than 1.

Answer: False

Explanation: *The fact the consumption exceeds income tells us nothing about the fraction of extra income that will be consumed.*

6. MPC – 1 = MPS

Answer: False

Explanation: *Since MPC + MPS = 1, then 1 – MPC = MPS*

7. Once we know the marginal propensity to consume (MPC), we can compute the marginal propensity to save (MPS).

Answer: True

8. If consumers expect prices to fall in the future, the consumption curve is likely to shift downward.

Answer: True

9. It turns out that the MPC is the slope of the saving curve while the MPS is the slope of the consumption curve.

Answer: False

Explanation: *The MPC is the slope of the consumption curve while the MPS is the slope of the saving curve.*

10. The rate of interest affects spending on consumer goods but it does not affect investment spending because households and firms are motivated by different factors.

Answer: False

Explanation: The rate of interest affects both consumer spending and investment spending.

11. Consumption tends to be more stable than investment.

Answer: True

12. Investment is the purchase or construction of new capital goods or addition to inventories.

Answer: True

13. The economist would consider the purchase of bonds as an investment.

Answer: False

Explanation: The purchase of bonds does not represent the purchase or construction of new capital goods or addition to inventories.

14. The marginal efficiency of investment summarizes the relation between the rate of interest and the level of investment.

Answer: True

15. Investment that results from changes in income is called induced investment.

Answer: True

16. On a graph with the rate of interest on the vertical axis and the level of investment on the horizontal axis, a fall in the rate of interest will cause the marginal efficiency of investment (MEI) curve to shift to the right.

Answer: False

Explanation: A fall in the rate of interest will result in a movement along the MEI curve, not a shift in the curve.

17. An increase in the level of investment may be shown either by a shift in the marginal efficiency of investment (MEI) curve or by a movement along the MEI curve.

Answer: True

18. Investment cannot be autonomous. It must depend on something.

Answer: False

Explanation: Describing investment as being autonomous means that it is independent of income. It means that it will not be affected by changes in income, although it might be affected by something else.

Completion

(Fill in the blanks)

Use each word or combination of words from the list exactly once. *(**Hint**: Proceed by elimination)*

Word list

0 — 1 x 2 — Consumption x 3 — Disposable Income — Function — Higher — Increase x 4 — Induced — Inventory x 2 — Investment — Lower x 3 — Marginal Efficiency Of Investment — MPC — MPS — Net — Permanent Income/Life-Cycle — Raise — Retained — Robin Hood — Saving x 3 — Smoothing — Undistributed

Questions

1. The __________ __________ is an equation that expresses a relation between consumption and the various factors that affect consumption. (consumption function)
2. According to the fundamental psychological law, the MPC has a value between __________ and __________.
3. An increase in interest rates will tend to __________ [raise, lower] consumption, but a fall in interest rates will __________ [raise, lower] consumption.
4. If consumers expect their incomes to rise, they are likely to __________ [increase, reduce] their current consumption. If they expect prices to rise, they will likely __________ [increase, reduce] their current consumption.
5. A redistribution of income from high income earners to low income earners will tend to __________ [increase, decrease] aggregate spending on consumer goods. This effect is called the __________ __________ effect.
6. The marginal propensity to consume (MPC) plus the marginal propensity to save (MPS) equals __________.
7. The slope of the consumption curve is the __________, and the slope of the saving curve is the __________.
8. The hypothesis that consumption depends more on average life-time income than on current income is called __________ hypothesis.
9. Adjusting consumption in order to have a relatively even pattern of consumption over time is known as __________ __________.
10. __________ is the act of refraining from current consumption.
11. If consumption and disposable income are equal, __________ is zero.
12. Saving is equal to zero when consumption is equal to __________.
13. The break-even level of consumption occurs when __________ is zero, or when disposable income equals __________.

14. __________ is the purchase or construction of new capital goods or additions to inventories.

15. The difference between gross investment and depreciation is called __________ investment.

16. The curve illustrating the inverse relationship between the rate of interest and the level of investment is called the __________ curve.

17. __________ investment constitutes the smallest percentage of total investment, but it is the most volatile.

18. The most volatile component of total investment is __________ investment.

19. An increase in interest rates will tend to __________ [raise, lower] investment, but a fall in interest rates will __________ [increase, reduce] investment.

20. Earnings of firms that are not paid out as dividends to shareholders are called __________ earnings or __________ profits. The greater these are, the __________ [higher, lower] the level of investment is likely to be.

21. On the basis of investment and consumption theory, one way to increase both consumption and investment is to __________ [raise, lower] the rate of interest.

22. Investment that is caused by an increase in income is called __________ investment.

Solutions

1. (consumption function)
2. (0 and 1)
3. (lower, raise)
4. (increase, increase)
5. (increase, Robin Hood)
6. (1)
7. (MPC, MPS)
8. (Permanent income/Life-Cycle)
9. (consumption smoothing)
10. (saving)
11. (saving)
12. (disposable income)
13. (saving, consumption)
14. (Investment)
15. (net)
16. (marginal efficiency of investment)
17. (inventory)
18. (inventory)
19. (lower, increase)
20. (retained, undistributed, higher)
21. (lower)
22. (induced)

9 THE MULTIPLIER THEORY OF INCOME DETERMINATION

LEARNING OBJECTIVES

In connection with this module, you should be able to:

1. explain how households and firms interact in the product market to determine the level of income
2. describe the relation between income and consumption
3. distinguish between *ex ante* and *ex post* concepts
4. explain the saving-income relation
5. integrate the aggregate expenditure-aggregate output and the injections-withdrawals approaches
6. explain the effects of changes in investment and changes in saving
7. explain the multiplier effect
8. explain the inflationary and deflationary gaps

DEFINITIONS & CONCEPTS

You should be able to define the following terms and concepts:

autonomous investment	marginal propensity to consume (MPC)
ex ante, ex post	marginal propensity to save (MPS)
aggregate expenditure	average propensity to consume (APC)
dissaving	break-even level of income
aggregate output	average propensity to save (APS)
equilibrium income	consumption curve
Keynesian cross	consumption schedule
withdrawal	injection
paradox of thrift	marginal propensity to withdraw
multiplier effect	inflationary gap
multiplier	deflationary (recessionary) gap

SYNOPSIS

In a closed economy, aggregate expenditure (AE) is the sum of consumption and investment. Aggregate output (AO) is total production. If intended aggregate expenditure equals aggregate output, income will be at its equilibrium level.

The ratio of consumption to income is the **average propensity to consume (APC)**. The ratio of saving to income is the **average propensity to save (APS)**. The ratio of the change in consumption to the change in income is the **marginal propensity to consume (MPC)**. The ratio of the change in saving to the change in income is the **marginal propensity to save (MPS)**. APC + APS = 1. Also, MPC + MPS = 1.

An **injection** is any addition to the income-expenditure stream. A **withdrawal or leakage** is any amount withdrawn from the income-expenditure stream. Income will be at its equilibrium level when total injections equal total withdrawals.

Other things being equal, an increase in investment causes an increase in equilibrium income, whereas a fall in investment will reduce equilibrium income. An increase in saving, other things being equal, will reduce equilibrium income, whereas a fall in saving will increase equilibrium income.

The **paradox of thrift (saving)** refers to the fact an increase in aggregate saving results in a reduction in total actual saving, provided that there is no increase in any injection, such as investment, to offset the effect of the increase in saving.

The **multiplier** is the inverse of the **marginal propensity to withdraw**. Because of the **multiplier effect**, a change in income caused by a change in **autonomous** spending will be greater than the change in autonomous spending.

An **inflationary gap** exists when desired aggregate expenditure exceeds full-employment output. A **recessionary (deflationary) gap** exists when desired aggregate expenditure is less than full-employment output.

9

THE MULTIPLIER THEORY OF INCOME DETERMINATION

Concepts, Defintions & Problems

Problem 9-1

Define each of the following terms:

(a) *closed economy*

(b) *autonomous investment*

(c) *aggregate expenditure*

(d) *aggregate output*

Requirement and Clue: *This is a four-part problem. Answer each part in order. You are required to state clearly and precisely the meaning of each concept. Lengthy comments and explanations are not necessary.*

Solution

(a) A closed economy is one that does not engage in foreign trade. That the economy is closed is a simplifying assumption that economists make to enable them to ignore the complexities of exports, imports, exchange rates and other factors associated with foreign trade.

(b) Autonomous investment is investment that does not vary with the level of income. That investment is autonomous is a simplifying assumption that economists sometimes make.

(c) Aggregate expenditure is total spending in an economy and consists of consumer spending, investment spending, government spending, and spending by foreigners.

(d) Aggregate output is the total production of goods and services in an economy.

Problem 9-2

Briefly distinguish between ex ante and ex post concepts.

Requirement and Clue: *You are required to show that you clearly understand the difference between ex ante and ex post concepts. Examples will be helpful. Notice the word "briefly" in the problem.*

Solution

It is often necessary to distinguish between ex ante and ex post concepts in economics. Ex ante means *before the fact*, while ex post means *after the fact*. Ex ante concepts relate to plans or intentions; ex post concepts relate to realized or actual (historical) facts. For example, ex ante saving is the amount that consumers plan to save. Ex post saving is the amount that they actually end up saving.

Problem 9-3

Describe the equilibrium level of output or income.

Requirement and Clue: *A definition of the concept of equilibrium is in order here. Then a statement of the meaning of equilibrium income/ output could follow. Focus also on the condition that is necessary for the level of output to be in equilibrium.*

Solution:

Equilibrium is a situation in which change is unlikely to occur. It is a state of rest or balance. The equilibrium level of output or income is that level of output which, once attained, will tend to be sustained. When the economy produces a level of output that is exactly equal to the amount that the economy's customers want to buy, that output level will tend to be sustained, and that is the equilibrium level of output or income. It can be said then, that the equilibrium level of output is achieved when the desired aggregate expenditure equals aggregate output.

Problem 9-4

Define each of the following concepts:

(a) *Break-even level of income*

(b) *Dissaving*

(c) *Consumption curve*

Requirement and Clue: *This is a definitional problem with three parts. Answer each part in order. You are required only to state clearly and precise the meaning of each concept. Examples will be helpful.*

Solution

(a) The break-even level of income is that level of income at which consumption equals income, or at which saving is zero. For example, if total disposable income is \$500 and total consumption is \$500, then the break-even level of income is \$500. Note that saving will be \$500 - \$500 = 0.

(b) Dissaving is the act of spending more than current income on current consumption. This means borrowing to "finance" current consumption. If a household has disposable income of \$1,000 and spends \$1,200 on consumer goods and services, then dissaving is \$200—the amount by which consumption exceeds current disposable income.

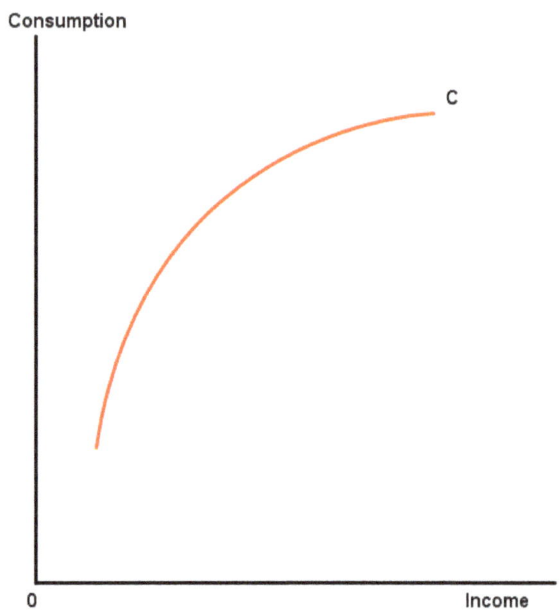

(c) The consumption curve is the curve that shows the relation between consumption and income. A consumption curve is shown in the diagram above.

Problem 9-5

(A) *Define each of the following concepts:*

(i) *Marginal propensity to consume (MPC)*

(ii) *Marginal propensity to save (MPS)*

(iii) *Average propensity to consume (APC)*

(iv) *Average propensity to save (APS)*

(B) *What is the relationship between the MPC and the MPS and between the APC and the APS?*

Requirement and Clue: *This is a multiple-part problem. Answer each part in order. Part A is purely definitional. Make sure that you state clearly and precisely the meaning of each concept, giving examples if possible. For part B, equations will suffice to show the required relationships.*

Solution

(A) (i) The marginal propensity to consume (MPC) is the fraction of extra income that is allocated to consumption. That is,

$$MPC = \frac{\Delta C}{\Delta Y}$$

where ΔC is the change in consumption and ΔY is the change in income. For example, if an increase in income of \$20 million causes consumption to increase by \$15 million, then

$$MPC = \frac{15}{20} = 0.75$$

(i) The marginal propensity to save (MPS) is the fraction of extra income allocated to saving. That is,

$$MPS = \frac{\Delta S}{\Delta Y}$$

where ΔS is the change in saving and ΔY is the change in income. For example, if an increase in income of \$20 million causes saving to increase by \$5 million, then

$$MPS = \frac{5}{20} = 0.25$$

(ii) The average propensity to consume (APC) is the fraction of total income allocated to consumption. That is,

$$APC = \frac{C}{Y}$$

where C is consumption and Y is income. For example, if income is \$200 million and consumption is \$160 million, then

$$APC = \frac{160}{200} = 0.8$$

(iii) The average propensity to save (APS) is the fraction of total income that is saved. That is,

$$APS = \frac{S}{Y}$$

where S is saving and Y is income. For example, if total income is $200 million and saving is $40 million, then

$$APS = \frac{40}{200} = 0.2$$

(B) The relationship between the MPC and the MPS can be expressed by the following equation:

MPS + MPC = 1

The relationship between the APC and the APS can be summarized by the following equation:

APC + APS = 1

Problem 9-6

The following table shows income and saving data for a simple economy. There is no government spending and there are no taxes.

Disposable Income ($ million)	Saving ($ million)	Consumption ($ million)
350	- 4	------
360	0	------
370	4	------
380	8	------
390	12	------
400	16	------
410	20	------

(a) *Complete the consumption column.*

(b) *What is the break-even level of income?*

Requirement and Clue: *This is a two-part problem. Answer each part in order. For part (a) if disposable income and saving are known, then consumption can be determined because disposable income minus saving equals consumption. For part (b), you are required to know the meaning of the break-even level of income.*

Solution

(a) Disposable income is distributed between consumption and saving. Thus, consumption equals disposable income minus saving. See table below.

Disposable Income ($ million)	Saving ($ million)	Consumption ($ million)
350	- 4	354
360	0	360
370	4	366
380	8	372
390	12	378
400	16	384
410	20	390

(b) The break-even level of income is that level at which income and consumption are equal or at which saving is zero. From the table, income and consumption are equal at a level of income of $360 million. Here also, saving is zero. Therefore the break-even level of income is $360 million.

Problem 9-7

What is the difference between aggregate expenditure and aggregate demand?

Requirement and Clue: *Some authors use the two terms interchangeably but in fact, there is a difference between them and the problem suggests as much. You are required to describe the concepts in a way that emphases the difference between them.*

Solution

Although the two terms are often treated as if they are synonymous, a difference does exist between them. Aggregate expenditure is total spending and is the sum of consumer spending, investment spending, government spending, and spending by foreigners. Aggregate demand, on the other hand, is the total quantity of all goods and services that will be demanded at various price levels. Thus, aggregate demand is a relationship between the price level and the various quantities of goods and services that the economy's customers will buy.

Problem 9-8

Define each of the following concepts:

(a) *Autonomous consumption*

(b) *Induced consumption*

(c) *Consumption curve*

Requirement and Clue: *This is a definitional problem consisting of three parts. Answer each part in order. You are required merely to state the meaning of each concept clearly and precisely. A lengthy discussion is not required. Of course, examples will be helpful.*

Solution

(a) Autonomous consumption is consumption that that does not depend on income. Even if the level of income is zero, there will be some level of consumption. That level of consumption when income is zero is autonomous consumption.

(b) Induced consumption is the part of consumption that depends on the level of income. As income rises, consumption tends to increase as a result. Consumption that is influenced by income is said to be induced consumption. For example, if income rises by $100 million and consumption increases by $75 million as a consequence, then that consumption is induced consumption.

(c) The consumption curve is a curve that shows the relation between consumption and income. The following diagram shows a consumption curve.

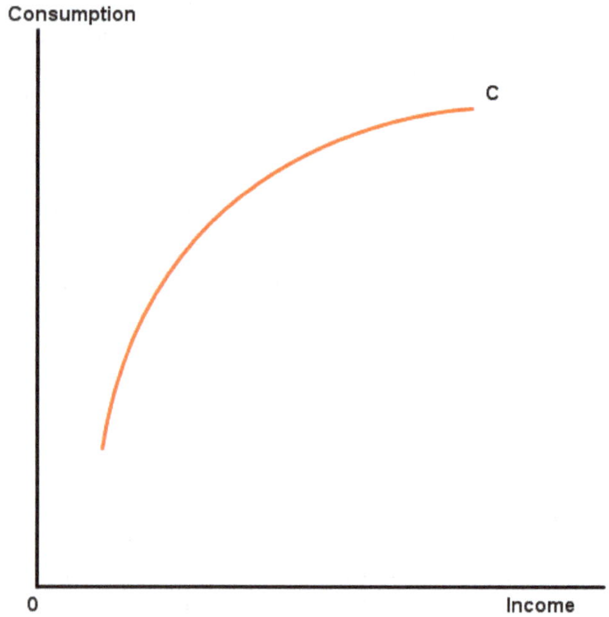

Problem 9-9

Define each of the following concepts:

(a) *Closed economy*

(b) *Aggregate output*

(c) *Keynesian expenditure model*

Requirement and Clue: *This is a definitional problem with three parts. Answer each part in order. You are expected to state clearly and precisely the meaning of each concept without entering into a lengthy discussion of the concepts.*

Solution

(a) A closed economy is one that does not engage in foreign trade. To avoid the complications of having to deal with imports, exports, and foreign exchange, economists may assume that they are dealing with a closed economy.

(b) Aggregate output is the total amount of goods and services produced in an economy. It is what is often referred to as gross domestic product (GDP).

(c) The Keynesian expenditure model is a macroeconomic model that emphasizes aggregate expenditure, with the assumption of a constant price level and unemployed resources. The model explains that total production is determined by aggregate expenditure.

Problem 9-10

How do unintended changes in inventories signal producers to vary their output?

Requirement and Clue: *Focus on how firms react in order to maintain their inventories at the desired level.*

Solution

Firms keep a certain amount of inventory to meet unanticipated changes in demand for their products. If inventories rise above their intended or planned levels, then the firm's production levels are too high for the current level of demand. An unplanned accumulation of inventories is therefore a signal to producers to reduce their volume of output. On the other hand, if inventories fall below their intended levels, then the firms' production levels are too low for the current level of expenditures. This situation would be a signal to the firms to increase their volume of output. Unintended changes in inventories thus serve as a barometer that firms may use to adjust their output to the desired level.

Problem 9-11

The following diagram is for a hypothetical economy.

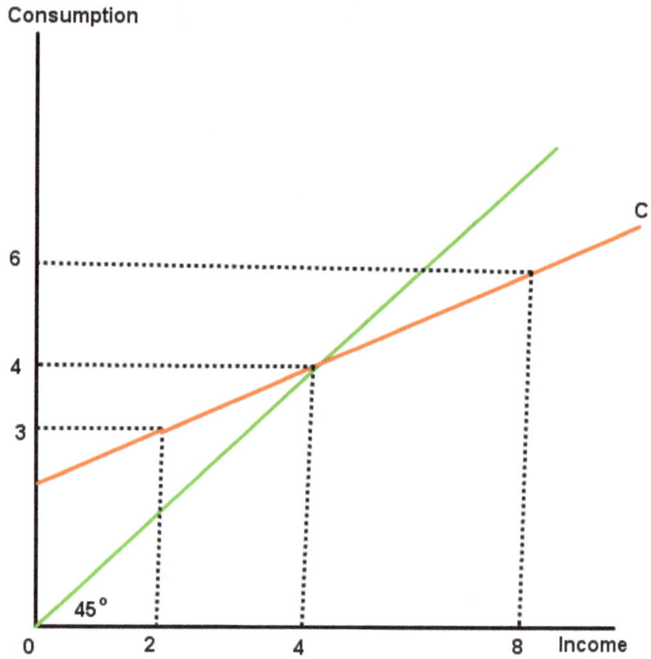

(a) *If income is $8 billion, what is the level of consumption?*

(b) *What is the level of consumption when income is $2 billion?*

(c) *How much will have to be borrowed if income is $2 billion?*

(d) *What is the break-even level of income?*

Requirement and Clue: *This is a multiple-part problem. Answer each part in order. This problem is a test of your ability to read graphs. Read the graph carefully and answer the questions accordingly.*

Solution

(a) At an income level of $8 billion, we read vertically up to the consumption curve; at that point, we note that the level of consumption is **$6 billion.**

(b) When income is $2 billion, as we read vertically up to the consumption curve, we note that consumption is **$3 billion.**

(c) If income is $2 billion and consumption is $3 billion, then **$1 billion** would have to be borrowed to finance consumption.

(d) The break-even level of income is that level at which income and consumption are equal. This occurs at **$4 billion** where the consumption line crosses the 45-degree line.

Problem 9-12

The economy will be in equilibrium as long as saving equals investment. Is this true or false? Explain.

Requirement and Clue: *Consider the statement carefully. Can saving and investment be equal and yet the economy not be in equilibrium. A true or false answer is not sufficient. You are required to offer an explanation.*

Solution

The statement is correct under certain simplifying assumptions, and only if it refers to ex ante saving and investment. In an ex post sense, saving and investment must always be equal. Saving, by definition, is that part of income that is not spent on current consumption. Investment is the unconsumed part of current output. In this sense, saving and investment are one and the same thing. Their equality does not define equilibrium income. If we are dealing with an economy where government neither spends nor taxes, and which does not engage in foreign trade, then the statement is true, ex ante. If, however, we are dealing with an open economy with government spending and taxing, then the statement is incorrect. In such an economy, total injections and total withdrawals may not be equal even if saving and investment are equal. The economy may not be in equilibrium.

Problem 9-13

What are the limitations of the simple Keynesian model of income determination?

Requirement and Clue: *There may be many limitations that you can think of. Perhaps three will suffice.*

Solution

The simple Keynesian model has certain limitations, three of which will be presented in this solution. First, the simple Keynesian model is not a complete model of the macroeconomy. The model does not analyze what is happening in the money market and in the labour market. It deals exclusively with the product market.

Second, the model is a demand-side model in the sense that the level of output or income is determined exclusively by aggregate expenditure. If aggregate expenditure increases, aggregate output will increase. If aggregate expenditure falls, aggregate output will fall. In this model then, expenditure creates output.

Third, this simple model assumes that the price level is fixed, and that the economy is operating with idle human and non-human resources that can be employed as long as there is enough expenditure to purchase the goods and services produced. In other words, the economy is assumed to be operating along the horizontal portion of the aggregate supply curve, where it is possible to increase production without any increase in prices.

Problem 9-14

The following diagram is for a closed economy without government. Investment is autonomous and is 40.

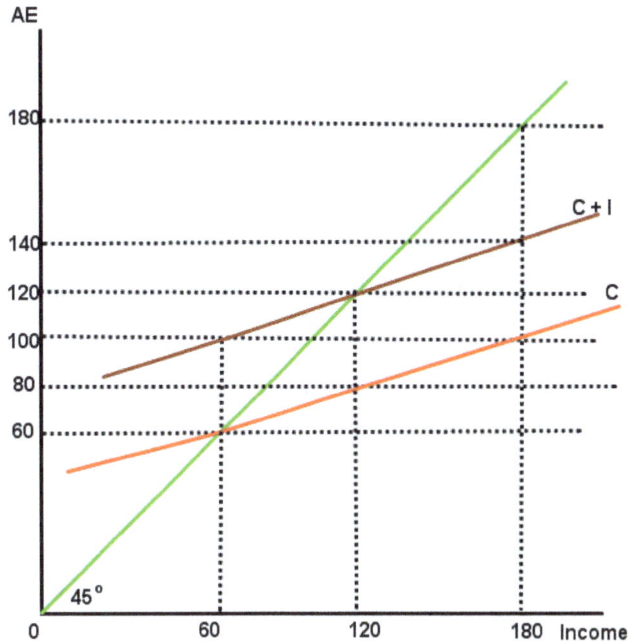

(a) *What is the break-even level of income?*

(b) *At a level of income of 60, what is aggregate expenditure?*

(c) *At a level of income of 120, what is consumption?*

(d) *At a level of income of 180, by how much does aggregate output exceed aggregate expenditure?*

(e) *Indicate the equilibrium level of income.*

Requirement and Clue: *This is a multiple-part problem. Answer each part in order. The problem tests your ability to read graphs. Remember that in this case, aggregate expenditure is consumption plus investment (C + I) and that aggregate output is read from the 45-degree line.*

Solution

(a) The break-even level of income occurs where income and consumption are equal. That is where the consumption line crosses the 45-degree line. This occurs at a level of income of 60.

(b) At a level of income of 60, aggregate expenditure is 100.

(c) At a level of income of 120, consumption is 80.

(d) At a level of income of 180, aggregate output 180 and aggregate expenditure is 140. Therefore, aggregate output exceeds aggregate expenditure by 180 – 140 = 40.

(e) The equilibrium level of income occurs where aggregate expenditure and aggregate output are equal. That is where the aggregate expenditure line crosses the 45-degree line. This occurs at a level of income of 120.

Problem 9-15

(i) *Define each of the following terms:*

(a) *Injection*

(b) *Withdrawal*

(ii) *What is the relationship between these concepts and the equilibrium level of income?*

Requirement and Clue: *This is a two-part problem. Answer each part in order. The first part is definition. Give the meaning of each concept clearly and precisely. For the second part, consider that equilibrium can be described in terms of injections and withdrawals.*

Solution

(i) (a) An injection is any income or expenditure that is injected into the income-expenditure stream. Examples are investment, exports, and government spending. An injection tends to increase the level of income.

(b) A withdrawal is any income or expenditure that is withdrawn from the income-expenditure stream. Examples of withdrawals are saving, imports, and taxes. A withdrawal tends to reduce the level of income.

(ii) The equilibrium level of income occurs when total injections equal total withdrawals. If injections exceed withdrawals, the level of income will tend to rise. If injections are less than withdrawals, then the level of income will tend to fall. When balance exits between injections and withdrawals, the level of income will tend not to rise or fall, but remain stable. This is the condition described as equilibrium.

Problem 9-16

In the following diagram, the equilibrium level of income is Y. Explain the process by which income will gravitate to the equilibrium level if income is above or below Y.

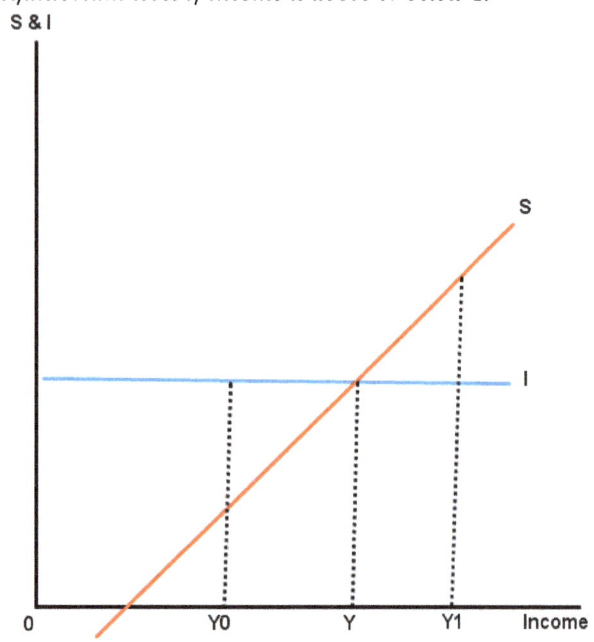

Requirement and Clue: *In order to solve this problem, you must be able to interpret the graph. Focus on the forces that will operate to restore equilibrium.*

Solution

If income is above the equilibrium level, at Y1, say, then saving exceeds investment. Households want to save more than firms are willing to invest. This will lead to an accumulation of inventories above the desired level. Firms will reduce their production levels, thus using fewer resources. This will cause income to fall from Y1 towards Y.

On the other hand, if income is below the equilibrium level, at Y0, say, then households' planned saving is less than firms' intended investment. This means that households want to buy more than what the firms are currently producing. Inventories will fall below desired levels. This will serve as a signal to increase production, thus using more resources. This will cause income to rise from Y0 towards Y.

Problem 9-17

Demonstrate algebraically that the equilibrium condition Y = C + I is identical to the equilibrium condition S = I. (Y = income, C = consumption, I = investment, and S = saving).

Requirement and Clue: *The solution involves manipulating either the Y = C + I equation or the S = I equation to show that they are identical.*

Solution

Assuming a closed economy with neither government spending nor taxes, and using the injections-withdrawals approach, equilibrium occurs when S = I. Using the aggregate expenditure/aggregate output approach, equilibrium occurs when Y = C + I. Since each approach expresses equilibrium under the same circumstances, both approaches are equivalent.

Algebraically,

	$Y = C + I$
By transposing C, we obtain	$Y - C = I$
But Y – C = S, therefore	$S = I$
Alternatively, we can begin with	$S = I$
But S = Y – C , so	$Y - C = 1,$

which means Y = C + I

Thus we see that Y = C + I is identical to S = I.

Problem 9-18

The consumption function is given by the following equation:

$C = 20 + 0.8Y_d$ where C is consumption and Y_d is disposable income.

Autonomous investment is 40.

(a) *What is the equilibrium level of income?*

(b) *What is the break-even level of disposable income?*

Requirement and Clue: *This is a two-part problem. Answer each* *part in order. For part (a), use the formula for equilibrium income and the given consumption equation to find the equilibrium level of income. For part (b), use the definition of break-even income along with the given consumption equation to find the break-even level of disposable income.*

Solution

(a) The formula for the equilibrium level of disposable income is,

$$Yd = \frac{A}{1 - b}$$

where A is autonomous spending; b is the MPC.

Here, autonomous consumption is 20 and autonomous investment is 40, therefore A = 60.

The MPC is 0.8; hence the equilibrium level of disposable is:

$$Yd = \frac{60}{(1 - 0.8)} = \frac{60}{0.2} = \mathbf{300}$$

(b) The break-even level of disposable income is that level of disposable income that is equal to consumption. Thus at break-even, $C = Y_d$

$$Yd = 20 + 0.8Y_d$$

$$0.2Y_d = 20$$

$$Y_d = 100$$

The break-even level of disposable income is **100.**

Problem 9-19

"The basic model of equilibrium in the product market contains a fundamental flaw. One of the crucial assumptions of the model is that as income rises, consumption also rises. This is plausible. However, the model also assumes that as income increases, saving also increases. This is an obvious contradiction. If consumption increases, saving must decrease. One cannot consume more and save more at the same time."

Are there any errors in the above statement?

Requirement and Clue: *You are required to read the statement carefully and see if you detect any errors. If you detect any errors, you should indicate them and offer a correction.*

Solution

It is inaccurate to say that if consumption increases, saving must decrease without stating what is assumed about income. If income is given, then an increase in consumption implies a decrease in saving. It is impossible to consumer more and save more out of a given level of income. But if income increases, a part of the increase can be allocated to consumption and a part to saving. Thus, there is nothing contradictory in assuming that both consumption and saving increase when income increases.

Problem 9-20

Explain why an increase in saving may be good or bad for the economy.

Requirement and Clue: *Focus on the effects of saving on the economy under certain conditions. Consider the conditions under which saving will have a negative impact on income and the conditions under which it will have a positive impact.*

Solution

Given the level of income, an increase in saving by households implies that they are reducing their spending on consumer goods and services. Firms may then notice a reduction in sales, or an unplanned increase in inventories, and consequently reduce production, thereby spending less on the factors of production. Thus, income will fall. In this sense, an increase in saving is bad for the economy because it reduces income. If however, households increase their saving and at the same time firms, through borrowing, channel those savings into investment, then the economy's capital stock will increase, and the economy's capital stock will increase, and the economy's productive capacity will thus increase. In this case, an increase in saving is good for the economy.

Problem 9-21

What is the multiplier effect? On what does the value of the multiplier depend?

Requirement and Clue: *This is a two-part problem. Answer each part in order. For the first part of the problem, explain clearly how income gets "multiplied up." For the second part of the problem, focus on the factors that affect the amount of income that gets passed on into the income-expenditure stream.*

Solution

Investment expenditures accrue to the recipients of these expenditures as income. Some of this income will be spent. This additional expenditure will become income to those who receive it. They, in turn, will spend a part of it, thus creating additional income. The process continues until the effect eventually peters out. This process whereby income is multiplied up is called the multiplier effect, and the ratio of the change in income to the change in investment that generates it is called the multiplier.

The value of the multiplier depends on how much of their extra income people will devote to consumption. This is referred to as the marginal propensity to consume or MPC. Obviously, the greater the MPC, the greater will be the multiplier effect. In fact, if we assume a closed economy with no government spending or taxes, the value of the multiplier can be calculated by using the formula:

$$k = \frac{1}{1 - MPC}$$

where k in the multiplier. Thus given an NPC of 0.8, the value of the multiplier will be

$$k = \frac{1}{1 - 0.8} = \frac{1}{0.2} = 5$$

Of course, the multiplier can be expressed in terms of the marginal propensity to save (MPS). Since MPC + MPS = 1, then the multiplier, given as

$$k = \frac{1}{1 - MPC}$$

which can be expressed as

$$k = \frac{1}{MPS}$$

The MPC is not the only factor that affects the value of the multiplier. Let us suppose that a certain portion of income is used for purchasing imports. The expenditure on imports generates income abroad rather than in the domestic economy. Thus the fraction of extra income that is devoted to imports (that is, the marginal propensity to import) is another factor that will determine the value of the multiplier. Taxes also can be included as a factor that affects the value of the multiplier.

Problem 9-22

If the multiplier is 1, what is the slope of the saving line?

Requirement and Clue: *Using the formula for the multiplier will help you to solve this problem.*

Solution

The multiplier (k) is given by the formula 1/MPS. MPS is the marginal propensity to save which is the slope of the saving curve.

$$k = \frac{1}{MPS}$$

If k = 1, then,

$$1 = \frac{1}{MPS}$$

Therefore, MPS = 1, the slope of the saving line.

Problem 9-23

In a closed economy without government spending or taxes, the MPC is 0.8. What effect will an investment of $40 million have on the level of income?

Requirement and Clue: *This problem is related to the multiplier. The clue here is to use the multiplier formula to derive the change in income resulting from the investment.*

Solution

We know that the multiplier, k, is the ratio of the change in income to the change in investment that generates the change in income. That is,

$$k = \frac{\Delta Y}{\Delta I}$$

where ΔY is the change in income and ΔI is the change in investment.

From this we obtain

$$\Delta Y = k\Delta I$$

Since the MPC is 0.8, the MPS is 0.2, which means that the multiplier is 1/0.2 = 5, and ΔI is $40 million.

Therefore, ΔY = 5 × 40 = $200 million.

The investment of $40 million will increase income by **$200 million.**

Problem 9-24

If an investment of $100 million causes income to increase by $300 million, calculate the MPC.

Requirement and Clue: *From the information given, you should be able to figure out the multiplier. Once the multiplier is known, it should be easy to figure out the MPC.*

Solution

If an investment of $100 million causes income to rise by $300 million, then the multiplier is 3. But the multiplier is the reciprocal of the marginal propensity to save (MPS); hence the MPS = 1/3. MPS + MPC = 1. If the MPS = 1/3, then MPC = 1 – 1/3 = **2/3**.

Problem 9-25

Consider the following argument:

"Simple arithmetic can help us to figure out the effect of an increase in investment (I) on income (Y) in a closed economy without government. In such an economy, equilibrium in the product market is given by

$$Y = C + I \quad (C = \text{consumption})$$

If C = 500 and I = 120, then Y = 500 + 120 = 620

Now, if investment increases to 150 (an increase of 30), then the new level of equilibrium income will be:

$$Y = C + I + \text{change in } I$$
$$= 500 + 120 + 30 = 650$$

Thus, if investment increases by 30, income will eventually rise by 30."

Is the statement correct?

Requirement and Clue: *You are required to read the statement carefully and see if it contains any errors. If you detect any errors, identify them and offer possible corrections.*

Solution

The argument presented ignores what economists refer to as the multiplier effect. When investment increases, income will increase initially by 30. But this is only the beginning. As income increases, additional spending on consumer goods will occur so that consumption does not remain at 500 as the argument suggests.

Successive rounds of spending will result in an increase in income that exceeds the increase in investment that started the process.

Problem 9-26

What are the limitations of the Keynesian expenditure model of income determination?

Requirement and Clue: *Focus on what the model does not or cannot do as a macroeconomic model.*

Solution

All economic models have limitations in the sense that the assumptions of the models place limitations on them. We can identify three specific limitations of the simple Keynesian expenditure model. First, it is not a complete model of the macroeconomy. The model does not analyze what is happening in the money market and the labour market. It deals exclusively with the product market—the market for goods and services.

Second, the model is a demand-side model in the sense that the level of output (income) is determined exclusively by aggregate expenditure. If aggregate expenditure increases, aggregate output will increase. If aggregate expenditure falls, aggregate output will fall. In this model, expenditure creates output. Alternatively, it can be said that in this model, demand creates its own supply.

Third, this simple model assumes that the price level is fixed and that the economy is operating with idle human and non-human resources that can be employed as long as there is enough expenditure to purchase the goods and services produced. In other words, the economy is assumed to be operating along the horizontal portion of the aggregate supply curve, where it is possible to increase production without increasing prices.

Problem 9-27

By how much must investment rise to bring about a $400 million change in income if the MPC is 0.75?

Requirement and Clue: *You can use the multiplier formula to arrive at the solution.*

Solution

We know that the multiplier (k) is $\Delta Y/\Delta I$, where ΔY is the change in income and ΔI is the change in investment. From this, we obtain,

$$k\Delta I = \Delta Y$$

which means that $\Delta I = \Delta Y/k$

If the MPC is 0.75, then the multiplier (k) is

$$k = \frac{1}{1 - MPC} = \frac{1}{1 - 0.75} = \frac{1}{0.25} = 4$$

Therefore, $\Delta I = 400 \div 4 = 100$

Investment must rise by **$100 million** to bring about a $400 million change in income.

Problem 9-28

Explain how an excess of aggregate expenditure over aggregate output can lead to an increase in employment.

Requirement and Clue: *Focus on what happens when aggregate expenditure exceeds aggregate output and how firms will respond.*

Solution

If aggregate expenditure exceeds aggregate output, firms will notice that their inventories are falling below their desired levels. In response to this situation, they will increase production to restore inventories to their desired levels. In order to increase production, firms will use more resources, including human resources. Hiring more workers means an increase in employment.

Problem 9-29

Define each of the following terms:

(a) Inflationary gap

(b) Income gap

(c) Recessionary gap

Requirement and Clue: *This is a three-part problem. Answer each part in order. The problem is definitional. You are expected to state clearly and precisely the meaning of each concept.*

Solution

(a) The inflationary gap is the amount by which desired aggregate expenditure exceeds aggregate output at full employment. In this situation, prices will tend to rise.

(b) The income gap is the difference between the equilibrium level of income and the full-employment level of income. It is also called the *output gap*.

(c) The recessionary gap is the amount by which aggregate expenditure falls short of aggregate output at full employment. It is also called the *deflationary gap*.

Problem 9-30

How can a recessionary gap be closed or narrowed?

Requirement and Clue: *You should demonstrate your familiarity with the concept of the recessionary gap. Focus on the change that is required. A diagram would be helpful.*

Solution

A recessionary gap, also called a deflationary gap, exists when aggregate output (AO) at full-employment exceeds aggregate expenditure. The following diagram will help to explain how a recessionary gap can be closed or narrowed.

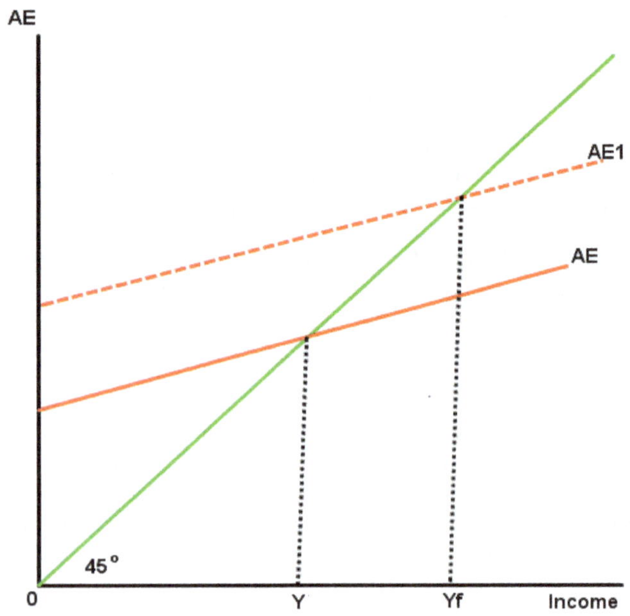

The economy is in equilibrium at a level of income of Y, which is below the full-employment level of Yf. What is required is to have equilibrium at full-employment and thus eliminate the gap. As can be seen from the diagram, the aggregate expenditure (AE) curve needs to be shifted up from AE to AE1. Equilibrium will then occur at the full-employment level. Any policy that increases aggregate expenditure will be appropriate. Increases in government spending, tax cuts, and reductions in interest rates are examples of policies that will stimulate aggregate expenditure and reduce or eliminate a recessionary gap.

Multiple-Choice Questions

In each case, circle the letter that corresponds with the correct answer.

1. In an *ex ante* sense:

a. total expenditure must equal the value of total output
b. total expenditure and the value of total output have no significance
c. total expenditure and the value of total output may diverge
d. none of the above

Answer: c

Reason: *The spending plans of households need not coincide with the production plans of firms.*

2. The decision-making process is such that:

a. the plans of households and firms are always realized
b. the plans of households and firms are based on identical objectives
c. the realization of the plans of firms depends, in part, on decisions made by households
d. households and firms must have frequent meetings to ensure that their plans will be realized

Answer: c

Reason: *The realization of the investment plans of firms will depend, for example, on the saving decisions of households.*

3. Which of the following is correct?

a. Aggregate expenditure and aggregate demand are synonymous
b. Aggregate expenditure and aggregate demand are different but related concepts
c. Aggregate expenditure relates spending to the price level
d. None of the above

Answer: b

Reason: *Aggregate expenditure is total spending by households, firms, government and foreigners. Aggregate demand is a relationship between total spending and the price level.*

4. In a closed economy without government:

a. planned aggregate expenditure and aggregate output must be equal
b. planned aggregate expenditure must exceed aggregate output
c. planned aggregate output must exceed aggregate expenditure
d. none of the above

Answer: d

Reason: *Planned aggregate expenditure may be equal to, less than, or greater than aggregate output.*

5. In a closed economy without government, aggregate expenditure is:

a. income plus consumption
b. consumption plus investment
c. income plus investment
d. saving plus investment

Answer: b

Reason: In such an economy, the economy's customers are households and firms. So total expenditure consists of expenditure by households, which is consumption, plus expenditure by firms, which is investment.

6. Aggregate expenditure is:

a. total injections plus total withdrawals
b. total spending on the economy's output of goods and services
c. the sum of the expenditures of all households
d. all of the above

Answer: b

Reason: Aggregate expenditure is the sum of consumer spending, spending by firms, government purchases, and spending by foreigners. This is consistent with choice b.

7. If desired aggregate expenditure exceeds current output, we expect:

a. inventories of finished goods to increase
b. inventories to fall below desired levels, causing firms to increase production
c. prices to fall to encourage more sales
d. firms to reduce their production levels and lay off workers.

Answer: b

Reason: As firms serve their customers from current stocks, those stocks will tend to fall below desired levels. To restore inventories to desired levels, firms increase their production.

8. Aggregate output is:

a. always identical to aggregate expenditure
b. identical to aggregate supply
c. the total output of goods and services produced
d. none of the above

Answer: c

Reason: Aggregate output is GDP which choice c defines.

9. In a closed economy without government, equilibrium occurs when:

a. consumption and income are equal
b. the sum of planned consumption and investment equals total output
c. investment and income are equal
d. consumption and investment are equal

Answer: b

Reason: Inventories would neither rise above nor fall below desired levels so output would remain stable.

10. If income is below the break-even level, then:

a. the average propensity to consume (APC) is greater than 1
b. the average propensity to consume equals the marginal propensity to consume (MPC)
c. the average propensity to consume is less than 1
d. the average propensity to consume equals zero

Answer: a

Reason: If income is below the break-even level, it means that consumption (C) is greater than income (Y). Therefore, the APC, which is C/Y, must be greater than 1.

11. If total income increases from \$275 billion to \$300 billion, and total consumption increases from \$230 billion to \$250 billion, then the MPC is:

a. 0.80
b. 1.25
c. 0.90
d. 1.10

Answer: a

Reason: The MPC = $\Delta C/\Delta Y$. $\Delta C = 250 - 230 = 20$ billion. $\Delta Y = 300 - 275 = 25$ billion. $\Delta C/\Delta Y = 20/25 = 0.8$

12. When total income rises from \$600 million to \$700 million, total consumption increases from \$500 to \$580. From this we know that the MPS is:

a. 0.80
b. 1.25
c. 0.20
d. 0.75

Answer: c

Reason: MPC = $\Delta C/\Delta Y$. $\Delta C = 580 - 500 = 80$ million. $\Delta Y = 700 - 600 = 100$ million.

$\Delta C/\Delta Y = 80/100 = 0.80$. Since the MPC = 0.80, then the MPS = 1 – 0.80 = 0.20

13. The equilibrium level of income is that level which:

a. produces the maximum output
b. indicates stagnation in the economy
c. will be maintained unless it is disturbed
d. occurs when consumption is at its highest level.

Answer: c

Reason: Equilibrium is a state of rest; a situation in which change is unlikely to occur.

14. The break-even level of income occurs where:

a. the average propensity to consume (APC) is 1
b. saving is zero
c. the saving line cuts the horizontal (income) axis
d. all of the above

Answer: d

Reason: Choices a, b, and c each defines the break-even level of income where income and consumption are equal.

15. Any amount of money released into the income-expenditure stream is called:

a. income release
b. injection
c. income-expenditure input
d. income addition

Answer: b

Reason: An injection is any income or expenditure injected into the income-expenditure flow. This is consistent with choice b.

16. The break-even level of income occurs where:

a. total income and total consumption are equal
b. saving is zero
c. the saving schedule cuts the horizontal income axis
d. all of the above

Answer: d

Reason: Each of the choices defines the break-even level of income where there is neither saving nor dissaving.

17. In a closed economy without government, equilibrium income occurs where:

a. the sum of saving and investment equals output
b. the sum of saving and investment equals consumption
c. saving equals investment
d. all of the above

Answer: c

Reason: If the amount that households want to save just coincides with the amount that firms want to invest, then there will be no tendency for the level of income to change.

18. Which of the following are all withdrawals from the income-expenditure stream?

a. Taxes, imports, and saving
b. Saving, investment, and imports
c. Government purchases, exports, and saving
d. Taxes, imports, and government purchases

Answer: a

Reason: Withdrawals represent leakages from the income-expenditure stream. They tend to reduce the level of income. Choice *a* fits the bill.

19. Which of the following is a limitation of the simple Keynesian expenditure model?

a. It is a demand-side only model
b. It deals only with the product market
c. It assumes that the price level is fixed and that the economy is operating with significant unemployed resources
d. All of the above

Answer: d

Reason: The simplicity of the simple Keynesian model turns out to be its limitation. Choices a, b, and c all limit the applicability of the model.

20. An increase in investment:

a. causes spending to rise and income to fall
b. causes total spending and income to rise
c. causes total spending to fall and income to rise
d. causes total spending and income to fall

Answer: b

Reason: Investment is an addition to the income-expenditure stream.

21. Investment can be viewed as:

a. an injection
b. a withdrawal
c. neither an injection nor a withdrawal
d. both an injection and a withdrawal

Answer: a

Reason: Investment increases the level of income and that's what injections do.

22. An increase in investment, other things being equal, results in:

a. a fall in income as resources are diverted away from consumption
b. an increase in income as aggregate expenditure rises
c. a depletion of savings and hence a fall in income
d. none of the above

Answer: b

Reason: Investment is an expenditure item. As expenditures increase, resources are used to produce the extra goods and services demanded. This increases income.

23. Saving is regarded as:

a. an injection
b. a withdrawal
c. neither an injection nor a withdrawal
d. both an injection and a withdrawal

Answer: b

Reason: Saving reduces the level of income and that's what withdrawals do.

24. Other things being equal, an increase in saving implies:

a. a fall in consumption
b. an increase in consumption
c. a reduction in withdrawals
d. none of the above

Answer: a

Reason: Out of a given level of income, one can save more only by consuming less.

25. Other things being equal, an increase in total desired saving will result in:

a. an increase in income
b. a fall in income
c. an increase in actual saving
d. no change in income

Answer: b

Reason: Inventories will pile up and firms will reduce their production, thus causing income to fall.

26. The paradox of thrift refers to the effect of:

a. an increase in actual saving
b. an increase in investment
c. a fall in total planned consumption
d. inflation on consumption and investment

Answer: c

Reason: The paradox of thrift or saving refers to the effect of an increase in planned saving, which is the same as a fall in total planned consumption.

27. In a closed economy without government, the formula for the multiplier is:

a. 1 – MPC
b. MPC + MPS
c. 1/MPS
d. 1 – MPS

Answer: c

Reason: The multiplier is the reciprocal of the MPS.

28. Induced investment is investment that:

a. depends on the price level
b. is independent of income
c. changes as income changes
d. none of the above

Answer: c

Reason: Induced investment is investment that results from a change in income. This is consistent with choice c.

29. Other things being equal, an increase in investment of $30 million will cause equilibrium income to:

a. increase by $30 million
b. increase by more than $30 million
c. increase by less than $30 million
d. fall by $30 million

Answer: b

Reason: *That is because of the multiplier effect.*

30. In a closed economy without government, if the MPC is 7/9, then the multiplier is:

a. 2/9   c. 7/9
b. 9/7   d. 9/2

Answer: d

Reason: *If the MPC is 7/9, the MPS is 2/9. The multiplier is the reciprocal of the MPS and is 9/2.*

31. In a closed economy without government, the MPS is 0.25. If investment increases from $20 million to $30 million, income will increase by:

a. $40 million   c. $30 million
b. $10 million   d. $50 million

Answer: a

Reason: *If the MPS is 0.25, the multiplier is 4. The change in investment is $30 - $20 = 10 million. The change in income will be 4 × 10 = $40 million.*

32. An inflationary gap exists when:

a. output is far below the equilibrium level
b. aggregate expenditure is far below the equilibrium level of income
c. aggregate expenditure exceeds aggregate output at full employment
d. none of the above

Answer: c

Reason: *If the economy's customers want to spend more than what the economy can produce at full employment, there will be upward pressure on the price level. This is the situation described as an inflationary gap. This is the concept that is reflected in choice c.*

Questions 33, 34, and 35 refer to the following diagram.

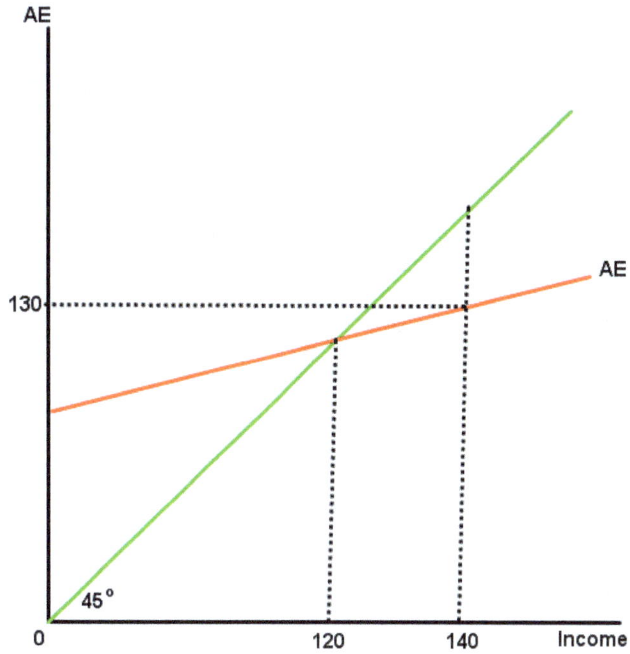

33. If the full-employment output is $140, there is:

a. an inflationary gap of $20
b. an inflationary gap of $10
c. a recessionary gap of $10
d. a recessionary gap of $20

Answer: c

Reason: *A recessionary gap is the amount by which aggregate output exceeds aggregate expenditure at full employment. At full employment of $140, aggregate output is 140 and aggregate expenditure is 130. Therefore there is a recessionary gap of $10.*

34. To eliminate this gap, aggregate expenditure must:

a. fall by $10   c. rise by $20
b. fall by $40   d. rise by $10

Answer: d.

Reason: *Aggregate expenditure is $10 below the full-employment level ($140 - $130).*

35. In this case, the multiplier is:

a. 4   c. 10
b. 2   d. 5

Answer: b

Reason: *A $10 increase in spending results in a $20 increase in income. This means that the multiplier is 2.*

36. The greater the slope of the saving line is:

a. the greater the multiplier
b. the smaller the multiplier
c. the greater the slope of the consumption line
d. the flatter will be the saving line

Answer: b

Reason: *the multiplier is the reciprocal of the slope of the saving line.*

True-False Questions

Determine whether each of the following statements is true or false.

1. Aggregate expenditure and aggregate demand are identical concepts.

Answer: False

Explanation: Aggregate expenditure and aggregate demand are closely related concepts, but they are not identical. Aggregate expenditure is simply total spending whereas aggregate demand relates total spending to the price level.

2. Aggregate output, gross domestic product (GDP) and aggregate supply are just different terms used for the same concept.

Answer: False

Explanation: Aggregate output and GDP are identical concepts, but aggregate supply relates aggregate output to the price level.

3. A closed economy is one in which people are prevented from entering or leaving. Freedom of movement is severely limited.

Answer: False

Explanation: A closed economy is one that does not engage in international trade. It has neither imports nor exports.

4. Autonomous investment is investment that is independent of income while induced investment depends on income.

Answer: True

5. In the simple Keynesian model of equilibrium in the product market, we assume that intended saving and investment are always equal.

Answer: False

Explanation: Households and firms are assumed to act independently of each other so that planned or intended saving and investment may or may not be equal.

6. Ex ante means before the fact or planned or intended; ex post means after the fact or actual or realized.

Answer: True

7. In discussing the process of equilibrium, the focus is on planned spending rather than on actual spending.

Answer: True

8. If desired aggregate expenditure exceeds aggregate output, inventories will fall below desired levels. Firms will then tend to increase their production levels, and the level of income will tend to rise.

Answer: True

9. If desired aggregate expenditure falls short of aggregate output, there will be an unplanned fall in inventories; firms will tend to reduce their production levels, and income will tend to fall.

Answer: False

Explanation: In this scenario, there will be an unplanned rise in inventories.

10. In a closed economy without government, the product market is always in equilibrium because saving always equals investment.

Answer: False

Explanation: Saving and investment are always equal ex post, but not ax ante. For equilibrium to occur in a closed economy without government, ex ante saving must be equal to ex ante investment.

11. A closed economy without government will be at its equilibrium level of income when the sum of planned consumption and investment equals aggregate output.

Answer: True

12. The consumption schedule is a table showing the relationship between total spending and total income.

Answer: False

Explanation: It shows the relationship between total consumer spending and total income.

13. At the break-even level of income, consumers are dissaving.

Answer: False

Explanation: Dissaving implies negative saving. At break-even, saving is zero, not negative.

14. If an increase in income of $500 causes an increase of $400 in consumption, then the MPC is 0.8.

Answer: True

15. Autonomous consumption is consumption that can never be influenced by any factor.

Answer: False

Explanation: Autonomous consumption is consumption that is not affected by income.

16. If people save 30 cents out of every extra dollar of income they receive, then their MPC is 0.3.

Answer: False

Explanation: Their MPS is 0.3, but their MPC is 0.7.

17. The MPC + MPS = APC + APS

Answer: True

18. Induced consumption is consumption that is affected mainly by changes in interest rates.

Answer: False

Explanation: Induced consumption is consumption that is affected by changes in income.

19. On a graph with aggregate expenditure on the vertical axis and income (output) on the horizontal axis, points along the 45-degree line shows the equality of aggregate expenditure and aggregate output.

Answer: True

20. An injection will increase the level of the flow of income and expenditure. A withdrawal will reduce it.

Answer: True

21. Saying that saving and investment are equal is equivalent to saying that income equals the sum of consumption and investment.

Answer: True

22. The simple Keynesian expenditure model is a demand-side and supply-side model. Thus it is a complete model of the economy.

Answer: False

Explanation: *It is a demand-side only model.*

23. Other things being equal, an increase in investment will cause the aggregate expenditure curve to shift to the right, resulting in an increase in income.

Answer: True

24. If the investment line is horizontal, an increase in investment will have no multiplier effect.

Answer: False

Explanation: *The multiplier effect will be present regardless of the shape of the investment line. It is the slope of the saving line that affects the multiplier.*

25. The multiplier effect refers to changes in investment, but not to changes in government spending, because the latter is offset by taxes.

Answer: False

Explanation: *The multiplier effect refers to any expenditure; not just investment.*

26. An increase in intended aggregate saving, other things being equal, will result in a fall in the total amount of actual saving.

Answer: True

27. The paradox of thrift applies only to situations where investment increases in proportion to the increase in saving.

Answer: False

Explanation: *If investment rises, the paradox of thrift will be invalid. The paradox assumes that other things remain equal.*

28. If 20% of extra income is saved, 10% is paid in taxes, and 10% is used to buy foreign goods and services, then the marginal propensity to withdraw is 40%.

Answer: True

29. In a closed economy without government, if equilibrium income increases from $300 million to $380 million as a result of an increase in investment of $30 million, then the MPC must be 5/8.

Answer: True

30. If firms produce $50 billion worth of goods and services, and desired aggregate expenditure is $45 billion, there is a deflationary gap of $5 billion.

Answer: False

Explanation: *It is not known whether or not the full-employment level of output is $50 billion.*

31. If the full-employment output in an economy is $80 billion, and desired aggregate expenditure is $87 billion, there is an inflationary gap of $7 billion.

Answer: True

32. Desired aggregate expenditure and aggregate output are equal at an income level of $120 million. At a full-employment income of $140 million, desired aggregate expenditure is $130 million. In this case, an expenditure of $10 million is required to move the economy to full employment.

Answer: True

Completion

(Fill in the blanks)

Use each word or combination of words from the list exactly once.
*(**Hint**: Proceed by elimination)*

Word list

$220 — 1 — 1/3 — 11/3 — 3/11 — 30 x 2 — 33 — Ante — APC — APS — Consumption — Deflationary/recessionary — Equilibrium — Exceed — Excess — Fall — Increase x 4 — Inflationary — Injection — Inventories — Investment x 3 — Less than — Multiplier — Paradox — Post x 2 — Rise x 3 — Saving x 2 — Saving or thrift — Smaller — Withdraw — Withdrawal or leakage

Questions

1. In an ex __________ sense, total expenditure on an economy's output of goods and services must be equal to the total value of the economy's output.
2. Ex __________ concepts refer to plans or intentions, whereas ex __________ concepts refer to historical or realized facts.
3. If desired aggregate expenditure exceeds current output, __________ will tend to fall below desired levels. This will be a sign for firms to __________ their production levels.
4. In a closed economy without government, aggregate expenditure equals the sum of __________ and __________.

5. If the MPC is 2/3, then the MPS is ________. This means that out of every extra dollar of income, ________ cents will be saved.

6. The ________ is the fraction of income that is consumed. The ________ is the fraction of income that is saved. The sum of these two fractions equals ________.

7. In a closed economy without government, ________ is a withdrawal, while ________ is an injection.

8. Any amount released into the income-expenditure flow is called a(n) ________. Any amount taken out of that flow is called a(n) ________.

9. In a closed economy without government, income will be at its equilibrium level when ex ________ equals ________.

10. In a closed economy without government, if investment exceeds saving, then the level of income will tend to ________. If investment is less than saving, then the level of income will tend to ________. If investment is equal to saving, then income will be at its ________ level.

11. An increase in investment, other things being equal, will result in a(n) ________ [increase, decrease] in the equilibrium level of income. This ________ [increase, decrease] in income will ________ [equal, exceed] the increase in investment that caused it.

12. The conclusion that an increase in aggregate desired saving will result in a decrease in total actual saving is called the ________ of ________.

13. The ________ is the number by which a change in an injection must be multiplied to arrive at the resulting change in equilibrium income.

14. In a closed economy without government spending or taxes, if the MPC is 8/11, then the MPS is ________ and the multiplier is ________. An increase in investment of $60 will result in a(n) ________ [increase, decrease] in the equilibrium level of income of ________.

15. The greater the slope of the saving line, other things being equal, the ________ [greater, smaller] the value of the multiplier.

16. The generalized multiplier is the reciprocal of the marginal propensity to ________.

17. An economy will be in a(n) ________ situation if all its resources are fully employed and there is excess aggregate expenditure.

18. If full-employment output/income is $120 billion and desired aggregate expenditure at that level of output is $90 billion, there is a(n) ________ gap of $________ billion. To eliminate this gap, aggregate expenditure will have to ________ [rise, fall] by $ ________ billion.

19. If the full-employment level of income exceeds the equilibrium level of income by $60 million, an expenditure ________ [less than, equal to, greater than] $60 million will be required to bring the equilibrium level of income up to the full-employment level.

20. If the aggregate expenditure line crosses the 45-degree line at an income level to the right of the full-employment level of income, then there is a(n) ________ of aggregate expenditure, and the price level will tend to ________ [rise, fall].

Solutions

1. (post)
2. (ante, post)
3. (inventories, increase)
4. (consumption, investment)
5. (1/3, 33)
6. (APC, APS, 1)
7. (saving, investment)
8. (injection, withdrawal or leakage)
9. (saving, investment [in any order])
10. (rise, fall, equilibrium)
11. (increase, increase, exceed)
12. (paradox, saving or thrift)
13. (multiplier)
14. (3/11, 11/3, increase, $220)
15. (smaller)
16. (withdraw)
17. (inflationary)
18. (deflationary/recessionary, 30, rise, 30)
19. (less than)
20. (excess, rise)

10 UNEMPLOYMENT INFLATION

SYNOPSIS

Frictional unemployment, seasonal unemployment, structural unemployment, and seasonal unemployment are different types of unemployment.

The **unemployment rate** is the percentage of the labour force that is unemployed, while the **labour force participation rate** is the percentage of the adult population in the labour force.

The economic cost of unemployment may be measured in terms of lost income or lost output. The noneconomic costs of unemployment include the suffering, frustration, and misery of the unemployed. These hardships may find expression in violence, damage to property, and social unrest.

According to **classical economists**, flexible wages and prices would ensure full employment. Any lapses from full employment would be only temporary. The Keynesian theory of unemployment suggests that insufficient spending could result in unemployment.

Inflation is a persistent rise in the average level of prices, and is measured by changes in prices indexes. The *rule of 70* allows us to calculate quickly the number of years required for the price level to double.

Inflation benefits debtors, sellers of goods whose prices are rising, and owners of real assets. It hurts people on fixed incomes, creditors, and holders of financial assets. It also affects the performance of the entire economy.

An inverse relationship exists between inflation and unemployment. Whether this relationship exists in the long run or only in the short run is a matter of some controversy.

LEARNING OBJECTIVES

In connection with this module, you should be able to:

1. discuss unemployment
2. explain the various types of unemployment
3. explain how unemployment is measured
4. explain the incidence of unemployment
5. discuss the costs of unemployment
6. explain the classical and Keynesian theories of unemployment
7. explain how inflation is measured
8. discuss the effects of inflation
9. explain the relationship between inflation and unemployment

DEFINITIONS & CONCEPTS

You should be able to define the following terms and concepts:

frictional unemployment
full employment
seasonal unemployment
structural unemployment
technological unemployment
cyclical unemployment
labour force
labour force participation rate
discouraged workers
potential GDP
actual output
hyperinflation
output (income) gap
Okun's law/ratio
classical economists
Say's law
inflation
consumer price index
wholesale price index
implicit price deflator
rule of 70
creeping inflation
galloping inflation

10

UNEMPLOYMENT & INFLATION

Concepts, Definitions & Problems

Problem 10-1

Define unemployment. How is unemployment measured?

Requirement and Clue: *This is a two-part problem. Answer each part in order. The first part is definitional. You are required to state clearly and precisely the meaning of the concept of unemployment. For the second part of the problem, focus on a measure that gives information about the state of unemployment.*

Solution

Unemployment is a condition that exists when workers are without jobs even though they are willing and able to work at the prevailing wage rate. The condition of unemployment refers to people who want to work; not to people who are not working because they are not interested in work.

Unemployment is typically measured by the rate of unemployment or the un employment rate, which is the number of people who are unemployed expressed as a percentage of the labour force. The labour force consists of the employed and the unemployed. For example, in an economy with a labour force of 500,000, if 50,000 of those people are unemployed, then the unemployment rate is

$$\frac{50{,}000}{500{,}000} \times 100 = 10\%$$

Problem 10-2

List the major types of unemployment and describe any two of them.

Requirement and Clue: *This is a two-part problem. Answer each part in order. The first part is straightforward. You just need to show that you know the different types of unemployment. For the second part of the problem, you are required to demonstrate some measure of familiarity with at least two of them.*

Solution

The major types of unemployment are:

- Frictional unemployment
- Seasonal unemployment
- Structural unemployment
- Cyclical unemployment

<u>Structural unemployment</u>
Structural unemployment is unemployment that is caused a mismatch between the types of skills that unemployed workers possess and the types of workers that employers would like to hire. Consequently, workers remain unemployed. Techniques of

production also change, resulting in structural unemployment. For example, if there is a permanent decline in the demand for textiles, then the industry will demand fewer workers and unemployment will result. Another example is the number of people whose jobs have become obsolete because of the introduction of computers into various aspects of business.

Cyclical unemployment

Cyclical unemployment is unemployment that arises because of a decline in aggregate expenditure and aggregate output. A reduction in total spending may cause firms not to be able to sell their output of goods and services. This deficiency of aggregate expenditure results in a decrease in production and a concomitant increase in unemployment. This type of unemployment is associated with the downswing of the economy.

Problem 10-3

What is the difference between unemployment and underemployment?

Requirement and Clue: *You are required to demonstrate familiarity with both concepts. Your solution should emphasize the difference between them.*

Solution

The concept of unemployment defines the condition that exists when people are without jobs even though they are willing and able to work at the prevailing wage rate. The concept refers to a situation where people are involuntarily out of work. Underemployment, on the other hand, refers to a situation where people have jobs but their skills are being underutilized. For example, a law school graduate who is working as a legal secretary can be considered to be underemployed if his or her legal skills are not utilized in his or her duties as a secretary. A worker who is underemployed has a job, but he or she is not being efficiently employed.

Problem 10-4

Write a paragraph or two on seasonal unemployment.

Requirement and Clue: *Evidently, the solution requires knowledge of the concept of seasonal unemployment. Since your solution is limited to only one or two paragraphs, you must decide on the content to be included.*

Solution

Seasonal unemployment is unemployment that is caused by seasonal variations. Its effects are most visible where seasonal variations are pronounced. In cold climates, such as in much of North America and Europe, agricultural activities slow down during the winter months, and as a result, unemployment in the agricultural sector increases. Similarly, outdoor economic activities such as roofing, road repair, and paving and landscaping tend to be almost non-existent during the winter season, resulting in unemployment. During the summer months, unemployment increases among workers whose jobs are related to winter activities such as ice skating and skiing.

Workers may experience seasonal unemployment even in economies in which seasonal variations are slight. For example, in the winter season, many countries in the Caribbean depend heavily on tourism from North America and Western Europe. Such countries often experience in their rate of unemployment during the summer months when the flow of tourists from North America and Western Europe declines. Obviously, the scope of policies to reduce seasonal unemployment in these countries is limited.

Problem 10-5

What is frictional unemployment? Why might frictional unemployment be desirable?

Requirement and Clue: *This is a two-part problem. Answer each part in order. The first part requires a clear and precise statement of the meaning of the concept. For the second part of the problem, focus on any advantages that you can think of that may result from frictional unemployment.*

Solution

Frictional unemployment is unemployment that results from people moving between jobs or entering or re-entering the labour force. People have freedom of occupational choice, and exercising that choice can cause unemployment. For example, a new college graduate may take some time before landing that new job. Until he or she finds a job, he or will experience frictional unemployment.

Frictional unemployment may be desirable because a worker does not have to be stuck with any particular job. If he or she does not like a particular job, he or she has the freedom to find another one. Furthermore, workers tend to leave lower-paying jobs for higher-paying ones, thus increasing their incomes. The low-paying jobs tend to have low productivity while the higher-paying ones tend to have higher productivity. Therefore, the movement from low-paying jobs to higher-paying jobs tends to increase overall productivity; hence the entire economy benefits.

Problem 10-6

Define each of the following labour market statistics:

(a) *Full employment*
(b) *Labour force participation rate*
(c) *Unemployment rate*

Requirement and Clue: *This is a definitional problem with three parts. Answer each part in order. State the meaning of each concept clearly and precisely.*

Solution

(a) Full employment is the condition that prevails when only fractional and structural unemployment exist. Full employment does not mean that 100% of the labour force is employed. For example, if frictional and structural unemployment is 4%, then full employment is defined as the employment of 96% of the labour force.

(b) The labour force participation rate is the labour force expressed as a percentage of the adult population. If the adult population is 800,000 and the labour force is 500,000, then the labour force participation rate is:

$$\frac{500,000}{800,000} \times 100 = 62.5\%$$

The labour force participation rate measures the size of the pool from which workers can be drawn.

(c) The unemployment rate is the number of people who are unemployed expressed as a percentage of the labour force. If the labour force consists of 500,000 people and 27,500 of them are unemployed, then the unemployment rate is:

$$\frac{27,500}{500,000} \times 100 = 5.5\%$$

The unemployment rate is a measure of the extent to which an economy is using its human resources.

Problem 10-7

How does underemployment affect the reported official rate of unemployment?

Requirement and Clue: *Focus on what the official rate of unemployment does or does not measure.*

Solution

Underemployment is a situation in which workers accept low-paying jobs or part-time jobs because they cannot find full-time jobs consistent with their qualifications. Surveys of the employment status of households do not account for underemployment and classify underemployed people simply as employed. In such cases, the unemployment statistics do not adequately reflect the extent of unemployment. If underemployed workers were counted as unemployed, the unemployment rate would be higher than the officially reported figure.

Problem 10-8

Discuss the economic costs of unemployment. How can the economic cost of unemployment be measured?

Requirement and Clue: *This is a two-part problem. Answer each part in order. For the first part, focus on the negative effects of unemployment. For the second part of the problem, consider the loss of output/income caused by unemployment.*

Solution

Unemployment affects not only the unemployed but also the economy and society as a whole. Unemployment hurts individuals economically because it reduces their incomes. Individuals and their families may be forced to drastically curtail their consumption. This loss of income may also force individuals to liquidate some of their assets at a loss in order to meet their financial obligations.

Unemployment results in a loss of output of goods and services that could have been produced by the unemployed. An economy with a high unemployment rate is producing a level of output that is substantially below its potential. The total production of goods and services is less than it could have been at full employment.

Unemployment imposes a financial cost on society as well. Many governments provide employment insurance benefits to unemployed individuals, amounting to billions of dollars each year. If these individuals had been employed, governments could have spent this money on providing better health care services or education, on improving the economy's infrastructure, or on other services. Because of unemployment, everyone loses.

The economic cost of unemployment can be measured by estimating how much the economy could produce with full employment and then subtracting the amount that the economy actually produces. The difference would be an estimate of the economic cost of unemployment.

Problem 10-9

Explain the classical theory of unemployment.

Requirement and Clue: *Recall that the classical economists supported the idea of rapid adjustments in markets. A graph would be helpful.*

Solution

The classical economists claimed that if there is unemployment for any reason, competition among workers for the available jobs will cause wages to fall. Lower wages will act as an incentive for firms to hire more workers and thus restore full employment. Thus, as far as the classical economists were concerned, deviations from full employment last only for a short time, since market forces will automatically eliminate them; unemployment was only a temporary phenomenon.

Classical theory suggests that, when the wage rate is set above the market equilibrium wage rate, the high wage rate creates unemployment. The position of the classical economists is illustrated by the following diagram.

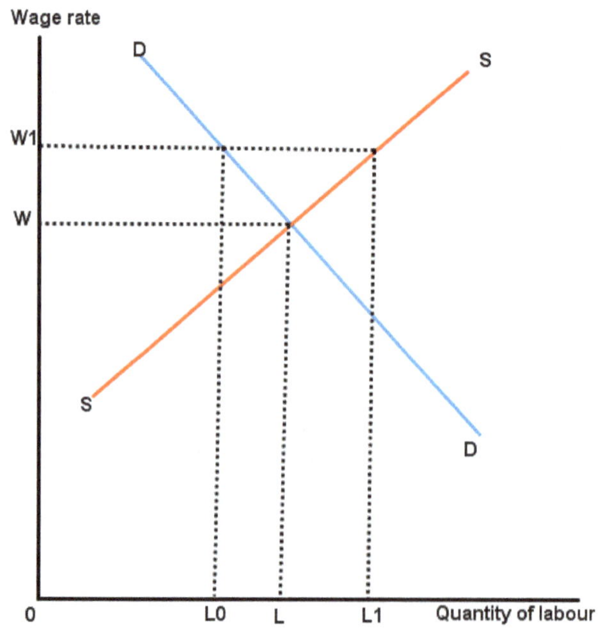

Classical theory of unemployment

The diagram represents the labour market. The demand for labour is DD and the supply is SS. The demand curve is downward sloping because smaller quantities of labour services will be demanded at higher wage rates; and the supply curve is upward sloping because more labour services will be supplied (offered) at higher wage rates. The equilibrium wage rate is W, where the demand and supply curves intersect, and the equilibrium quantity of labour is L. If the wage rate happens to be W1, then the quantity of labour supplied at that wage rate will be L1, and the quantity demanded will be L0. The quantity of labour supplied will be greater than the quantity demanded. This excess of labour in the labour market, represented by L1 – L0, is unemployment. This surplus of labour would force the wage rate to decrease until the market clears. In summary, the classical economists maintained that the economy operates at full employment provided that output prices and wages are flexible. Lapses from full employment would be only temporary.

Problem 10-10

Explain Say's Law.

Requirement and Clue: *For a solution to this problem, it is a good idea to state Say's Law. Then you are required to say what the law means and entails.*

Solution

Say's law is names after a French economist, Jean Baptiste Say. The law is usually summarized by the phrase, "Supply creates its own demand." The law can be explained as follows: People engage in the production of goods and services not so much for the sake of work, but in order to be able to buy goods and services to satisfy their wants. This implies that production in itself constitutes the demand for goods and services. That being the case, then a situation in which total output of goods and services exceeded the total amount that the economy's customers would want to buy is impossible. The mere existence of production represents a corresponding demand for the output which results from that production.

Problem 10-11

Briefly explain the Keynesian theory of unemployment.

Requirement and Clue: *Focus on what Keynes claimed to be the cause of unemployment. Do not ignore the word "briefly" in the problem.*

Solution

Keynes argued that unemployment could result from a deficiency of aggregate expenditure. Simply stated, Keynes' theory of unemployment says that if total spending in an economy was insufficient to enable firms to sell off what they produced, they would reduce their production levels, lay off workers, and thus cause the economy to settle down to a less-than-full employment equilibrium. Such a case would necessitate direct intervention in the form of changes in government spending and taxes to move the economy to full-employment equilibrium.

Problem 10-12

A labour force survey contains the following data for a hypothetical economy. Fill in the blank spaces.

	Jan.	Feb.	Mar.	Apr.
Adult population	200	200	220	220
Not in labour force	80	---	90	90
Labour force	---	110	---	---
Employed	100	---	---	---
Unemployed	---	10	30	20
Unemployment rate (%)	---	---	---	---
Participation rate (%)	---	---	---	---

Requirement and Clue: *The solution to this problem requires familiarity with labour force statistics and relationships among them.*

Solution

Not in labour force in February: The adult population consists of the labour force plus those who are not in the labour force. The adult population is 200 and the labour force is 110. Therefore, 200 – 110 = **90** were not in the labour force.

Labour force in January, March, and April: The labour force is the adult population minus those not in the labour force. For January, this was 200 – 80 = **120**; for March, this was 220 – 90 = **130**; and for April, this was 220 – 90 = **130**.

Employed in February, March, and April: The employed is the labour force minus the unemployed. Thus for February, the employed was 110 – 10 = **100**; for March it was 130 – 30 = **100**; and for April it was 130 – 20 = **110**.

Unemployed in January: Unemployed is labour force minus the employed. Thus in January, the unemployed was 120 – 100 = **20**.

Unemployment rate for January, February, March, and April: The unemployment rate is the percentage of the labour force that is unemployed. It is calculated by:

$$\frac{\text{Number unemployed}}{\text{Labour force}} \times 100$$

For January it was 20/120 × 100 = **16.67%**

For February it was 10/110 × 100 = **9.09%**

For March it was 30/130 × 100 = **23.1%**

For April it was 20/130 × 100 = **15.4%**

The participation rate is:

$$\frac{\text{Labour force}}{\text{Adult population}} \times 100$$

For January it was 120/200 × 100 = **60%**

For February it was 110/200 × 100 = **55%**

For March it was 130/220 × 100 = **59.1%**

For April it was 130/220 × 100 = **59.1%**

The information is contained in the table below.

	Jan	Feb.	Mar.	Apr.
Adult population	200	200	220	220
Not in labour force	80	**90**	90	90
Labour force	**120**	110	**130**	**130**
Employed	100	**100**	**100**	**110**
Unemployed	**20**	10	30	20
Unemployment rate (%)	**16.67**	**9.1**	**23.1**	**15.4**
Participation rate (%)	**60**	**55**	**59.1**	**59.1**

Problem 10-13

You are given the following data for a hypothetical economy.

Item	Number
Adult population	25,000,000
Labour force	15,000,000
Employed	12,000,000

Calculate:

(a) *The participation rate*

(b) *The unemployment rate*

Requirement and Clue: *This is a two-part problem. Answer each part in order. Use the formula to do the calculations.*

Solution

(a) The participation rate is given by the following formula:

$$\text{Participation rate} = \frac{\text{Labour force}}{\text{Adult population}} \times 100 = \frac{15{,}000{,}000}{25{,}000{,}000} \times 100 = \mathbf{60\%}$$

(b) The unemployment rate is given by the following formula:

$$\text{Unemployment rate} = \frac{\text{Unemployed}}{\text{Labour force}} \times 100$$

Since the labour force is 15,000,000 and 12,000,000 are employed, it follows that 3,000,000 are unemployed. Using the formula we obtain:

$$\text{Unemployment rate} = \frac{\text{Unemployed}}{\text{Labour force}} \times 100 = \frac{3{,}000{,}000}{15{,}000{,}000} \times 100 = \mathbf{20\%}$$

Problem 10-14

What do economists mean by inflation? What is the difference between inflation and an increase in the prices of certain items?

Requirement and Clue: *This is a two part problem. Answer each part in order. The first part of the problem is definitional. You are required to state clearly and precisely the economic meaning of inflation. For the second part of the problem, your definition of inflation should help to distinguish the concept from an increase in certain prices.*

Solution

Inflation refers to a sustained or persistent increase in the average level of prices over time. Inflation means that a given amount of money buys less today than it did last year and more today that it will next year.

If the demand for certain items increases, other things being equal, the prices of those items will rise. The increase in the prices of these items, however, is a change in relative prices and may not reflect the presence of inflation at all; other prices may be falling due to changes in demand and supply in other markets.

Problem 10-15

(a) *Define the rate of inflation.*

(b) *How is inflation measured?*

(c) *How is the rate of inflation calculated?*

Requirement and Clue: *This is a three-part problem. Answer each part in order. Part (a) is definitional. You are required to state the meaning of the concept clearly and precisely. For part (b), think of price indexes. For Part (c), focus on the general formula used to calculate the percentage change.*

Solution:

(a) The rate of inflation is the rate of change in the average level of prices. It tells us how fast inflation is increasing. If the rate of inflation is 5% per year, then a basket of goods that cost \$100 now will be expected to cost \$105 a year later.

(b) Inflation is measured by using price indexes. The three popular price indexes are the consumer price index (CPI), the producer price index (PPI) or the wholesale price index, and the GDP deflator or the implicit GDP price index. The CPI is the index that is most often used. The consumer price index measures changes in the prices of consumer goods and services. The producer price index measures changes in the prices of producer goods (goods bought by manufacturers). The implicit price deflator (also called the GDP deflator) measures changes in the average level of prices of all final goods and services.

(c) The rate of inflation from one period to another is calculated by taking the percentage change in the price index between the two periods. The rate of inflation can be measured by the following formula.

$$\text{Rate of inflation} = \frac{PI_c - PI_p}{PI_p} \times 100$$

where PI_c is price index in the current year and PI_p is price index in the previous year. For example, suppose the price index in 2011 was 105 and the price index in 2012 was 111, then the rate of inflation between 2011 and 2012 was:

$$\text{Rate of inflation} = \frac{111 - 105}{105} \times 100 = 5.7\%$$

Problem 10-16

What is the "rule of 70"?

Requirement and Clue: *You are required to state clearly and precisely the meaning of the rule of 70. An example of its use will be helpful.*

Solution

The "rule of 70" provides a quick method for calculating the number of years required for the price level to double, given the rate of inflation. According to this rule, the number of years required for a doubling of the price level is determined by dividing 70 by the annual rate of inflation. That is,

$$N = \frac{70}{\text{Rate of inflation}}$$

where N is the number of years required for the price level to double. For example, if the rate of inflation is 5% per year, then the price level will double in (70 ÷ 5) = 14 years.

Problem 10-17

Can inflation occur in a barter economy?

Requirement and Clue: *It is a good idea to define a barter economy. A "yes" or "no" answer is not sufficient as a solution to this problem. You are expected to explain your position.*

Solution

A barter economy is one in which goods and services exchange directly for other goods and services without the use of money. Inflation is a sustained increase in the general level of prices. In a barter economy, the price of one good or service is expressed in terms of another good or service. Thus, if the price of one good, say A, doubles in terms of good B, then it means that the price of B is halved in terms of good A. Hence in a barter economy, there cannot be an increase in the general level of prices—inflation cannot occur. In that sense then, inflation is a purely monetary phenomenon.

Problem 10-18

How does inflation affect the macroeconomy?

Requirement and Clue: *Focus on the various ways whereby inflation may influence the operation of the entire economy.*

Solution

Inflation may affect the economy through its effects on the allocation of resources. In an inflationary situation, people will try to protect their savings by reducing their savings accounts at financial institutions and purchasing real assets, many of which may be non-productive, like antique furniture and old coins. These savings will not then be available to firms for productive investments. As a consequence, the economy's productive capacity may decline.

Inflation may also destroy the incentive to work. Since real income or purchasing power declines in a period of inflation, people may consider it pointless to work harder. They may even be discouraged and work less. Total production may therefore decline. Inflation tends to push people into higher income brackets. If the tax structure is progressive, the proportion of income spent in taxes will increase. To avoid the higher tax burden occasioned by the higher income bracket, people may reduce their work effort by refusing to accept over-time work, and taking time off from work without pay.

Because money loses its value quickly during periods of high inflation, people tend to spent it as fast as they can in order to avoid the loss. At the extreme, people could refuse to accept it as payment for goods and services, and revert to an inefficient barter system where goods and services are exchanged without the use of money. Such a situation would result in a drastic reduction in total output.

Problem 10-19

Identify the winners and losers from inflation. Explain why there are winners and losers from inflation.

Requirement and Clue: *This is a two-part problem. Make sure you address both parts. Focus on who is affected positively by inflation and who is affected negatively. Explain why the winners win and why the losers lose.*

Solution

The winners from inflation include debtors, producers (sellers), and owners of real assets. The losers from inflation include creditors, people on fixed incomes or people whose incomes lag behind inflation, and owners of financial assets.

Debtors gain from inflation because they repay their debts with money whose value has fallen. Producers of goods and services benefit from inflation for two main reasons. First, during a period of inflation, the prices of goods and services tend to rise at a faster rate than the rate of increase in the prices inputs. This implies that profits increase during inflationary periods. Second, the firms buy their inputs at current prices but their output is sold at future higher prices, thus profits increase. Owners of real assets benefit from inflation because during an inflation, the value of real assets such as real estate increases.

Creditors lose because, when they are repaid, the money they receive will have lost some purchasing power. People on fixed incomes lose because, as inflation proceeds, they have to put out a larger sum of money for a given quantity of goods and services while their incomes remain unchanged. To see how inflation harms owners of financial assets, consider an individual with savings of $5,000. If the price level increases annually by 10%, that individual's $5,000 will be able to buy 10% fewer goods and services after one year. In other words, the original $5,000 will be worth $4,500 in real terms—a loss of $500.

Problem 10-20

What is the relationship between unemployment and inflation?

Requirement and Clue: *Focus on how changes in total spending affect employment and the price level.*

Solution

The level of total spending in an economy affects both the rate of inflation and the rate of unemployment. If total spending falls to very low levels, firms will find themselves with a large volume of goods and services that are unsold (an accumulation of inventories). They will lay off workers and will most likely not raise prices. The economy will be operating in section A in the following diagram, where output and employment are well below their full-employment levels. The unemployment rate will be high.

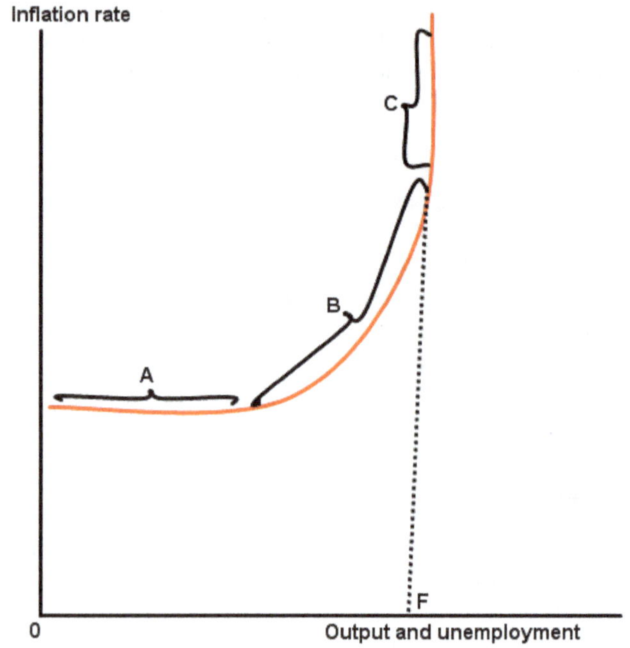

If total spending rises, firms will notice an increase in demand for their goods and services. Their inventories may even fall below desired levels, so they hire more workers in order to increase their production, and the unemployment rate falls. As this continues, resources become relatively scarcer, and resource prices rise. Labour also demands wage increases, and firms are less reluctant to grant such increases. For these reasons, the price level begins to rise. The economy will be operating in Section B of the diagram, which shows the price level rising and employment rising (the unemployment rate falling).

If total spending continues to rise, the economy will eventually reach the full-employment level (point F in the diagram). Output and employment cannot rise beyond this level, that is, the unemployment rate cannot fall any further. The pressure of spending on the fixed total output results in a high rate of inflation as shown by Section C of the diagram.

Problem 10-21

What is the difference between demand-pull inflation and cost-push inflation?

Requirement and Clue: *Your solution should really highlight and emphasize the difference between these two concepts.*

Solution

Demand-pull inflation emphasizes demand forces such as excess spending caused by monetary expansion or government deficit spending. Demand-pull inflation occurs when aggregate expenditure is so high that it exerts an upward pressure on the price level. This phenomenon finds expression in the phrase. "too much money chasing too few goods."

Demand-pull inflation is illustrated in the diagram below.

Suppose that the economy is in equilibrium at the full-employment level of real output, Yf, with the price level at P. An increase in aggregate expenditure will cause the aggregate demand curve AD to shift to the right to AD1 as shown in the diagram. The price level rises from P to P1. The process of demand-pull inflation has been set in motion.

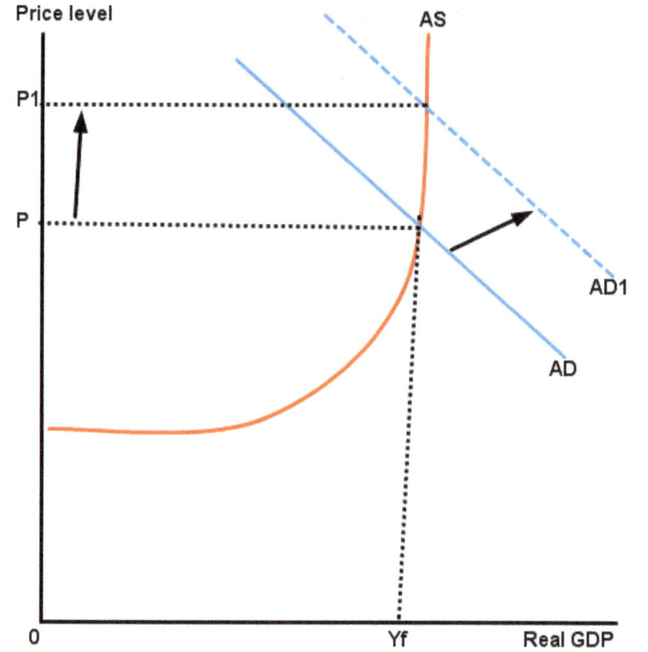

Cost-push inflation, on the other hand, emphasizes supply or cost factors as the dominant cause. According to this theory, inflation is caused by powerful labour unions or by powerful firms. The process is explained as follows: Unions demand higher wages for their members. Because unions are so powerful, employers accede to their demands even if there are no increases in productivity to justify the increase in wages. But higher wages mean higher costs for the firms. So in order to protect their profits, the firms raise their prices. These higher prices lead the unions to demand even higher wages. The firms then raise their prices even higher. This wage-price spiral continues, and the process becomes a vicious cycle.

The following diagram illustrates cost-push inflation.

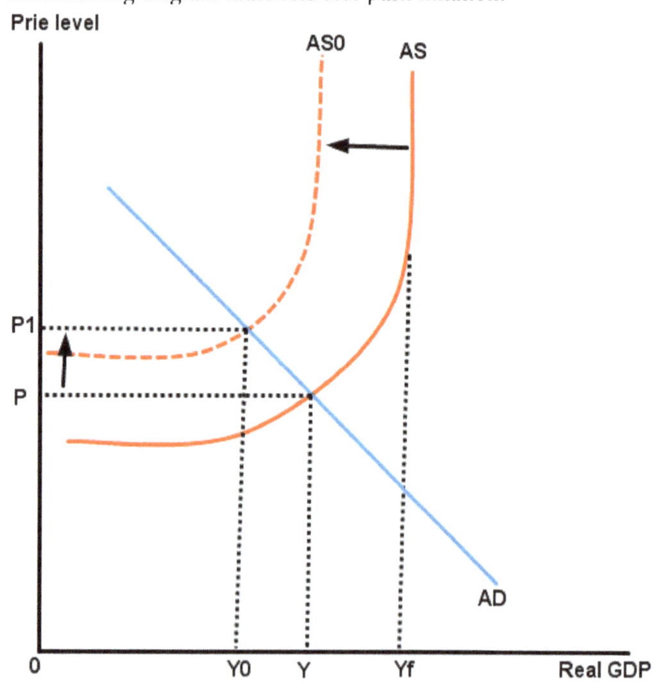

Suppose the economy is operating at a level of real output of Y with the price level at P. An increase in the firms' costs will cause the aggregate supply curve to shift from AS to AS0. Cost-push inflation is initiated with the increase in the price level from P to P1.

Problem 10-22

Explain the monetary theory of inflation.

Requirement and Clue: *You are expected to point out the crucial elements of this theory.*

Solution

According to the monetary theory of inflation, inflation is caused by increases in the quantity of money that occur at a faster rate than the increase in real output in the economy. The theory states that people wish to hold a certain amount of cash balances. An increase in the quantity of money will cause people to have larger cash balances than they wish to hold. They will therefore spend the excess money balances on goods and services. If the real output of the economy increases more quickly than the quantity of money does, then inflation will not result. It is when the quantity of money increases more quickly than the real output does that the average level of prices rises.

Problem 10-23

"After the rapid increase in the price of OPEC oil in the 1970s, the rate of inflation in North America rose dramatically. We can therefore conclude that the inflation of the 1970s was due to the increase in the price of oil."

Discuss this statement.

Requirement and Clue: *Look for any possible flaw in the logic.*

Solution

This is a classic example of what is called the *post hoc* fallacy. The fallacy lies in the argument that because one event follows another event, it is caused by the other event—an argument that is not necessarily valid. In this problem, the inflation of the 197s has been attributed to the increase in the price of OPEC oil because it followed the increase in the price of OPEC oil. It is quite possible, however, that the inflation could have been caused by other factors and not solely to the OPEC oil increase.

Problem 10-24

What is expectational inflation?

Requirement and Clue: *This problem is mainly definitional. Besides defining the concept, you should also explain the role of expectations in inflation.*

Solution

Expectational inflation is inflation that is sustained by expectations. It contains elements of both demand-pull and cost-push inflation. The expectational theory of inflation, also called inertial inflation, states that inflation is caused by inflationary expectations. If people expect inflation, they will tend to increase their current spending in order to avoid paying higher prices in the future. This is the demand element of expectational inflation. There is also a supply (cost) element. If unions expect inflation, they will ask for wage increases that incorporate the expected rate of inflation. The increase in wage cost will cause firms to respond by raising the prices of their products, thus setting the wage-price spiral in motion.

Problem 10-25

(a) *Define the natural rate of unemployment.*

(b) *List the main factors that determine the natural rate of unemployment.*

Requirement and Clue: This is a two-part problem. Answer each part in order. Part (a) is definitional. You are to state clearly and precisely the meaning of the concept. For part (b), you are asked merely to list. Focus on factors that affect the job-finding rate and the rate of job loss.

Solution

(a) The natural rate of unemployment is the unemployment rate that is unavoidable in order to achieve price stability. This rate of unemployment is consistent with the non-accelerating rate of inflation.

(b) The main factors that determine the natural rate of unemployment are:

1. The effort exerted in searching for jobs
2. Information about job vacancies
3. The rate of growth of the labour force
4. The existence of employment insurance.

Problem 10-26

What is the relationship between inflation and unemployment?

Requirement and Clue: *You should recognize this as a reference to the Phillips Curve. A diagram would be helpful.*

Solution

The Phillips curve specifies a relationship between the rate of change in wages and the rate of unemployment. From this relationship, we can obtain a relationship between inflation and unemployment. By hypothesizing a direct relationship between the rate of change in wages and the rate of inflation, we arrive at the conclusion that the higher the rate of unemployment, the lower the rate of inflation will be; and the lower the rate of unemployment, the higher the rate of inflation.

This inverse relationship between inflation and unemployment is illustrated in the following diagram.

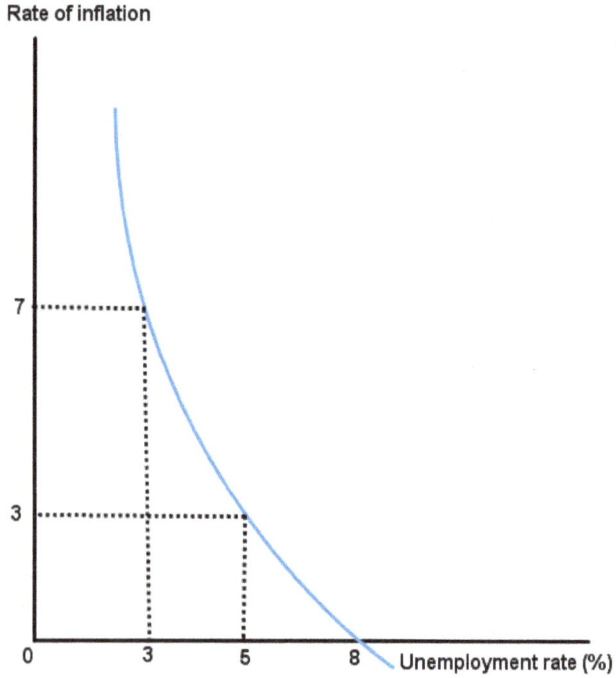

The curve shows various combinations of unemployment rates and inflation rates that the economy can attain. It shows, for example, that in order to attain an unemployment rate of 5%, the economy must accept an inflation rate of 3%. To reduce the unemployment rate from 5% to 3%, for example, the economy must accept the inflation rate to rise from 3% to 7%. A zero inflation rate requires an unemployment rate of 8%.

Problem 10-27

What is the accelerationists' view of the trade-off between inflation and unemployment?

Requirement and Clue: *It is well to define accelerationists and then explain their view of the trade-off, pointing out how they arrive at their position.*

Solution

Accelerationists are economists who argue that there is no long-run trade-off between inflation and unemployment. For them, the long-run Phillips curve is vertical. The diagram below will help to explain the accelerationists' point of view.

Let us suppose that the natural rate of unemployment is 7% as shown in the diagram, but policy-makers attempt to reduce it to 4%, believing that 4% constitutes full employment. The policy-makers will use monetary and fiscal policies to increase aggregate demand. Because the economy is already at its natural rate of unemployment, the increase in aggregate demand will cause the price level to rise. If nominal wages remain constant, then the increase in prices raises the profit margins of firms. Higher profits cause businesses to expand, hire more workers, and thus reduce the rate of unemployment from 7% to 4%. The economy thus moves from A to B along the short-run Phillips curve PC1. The rate of inflation has risen from 0% to 3% at B. Policy-makers have chosen to live with a 3% inflation rate in order to achieve a 4% unemployment rate.

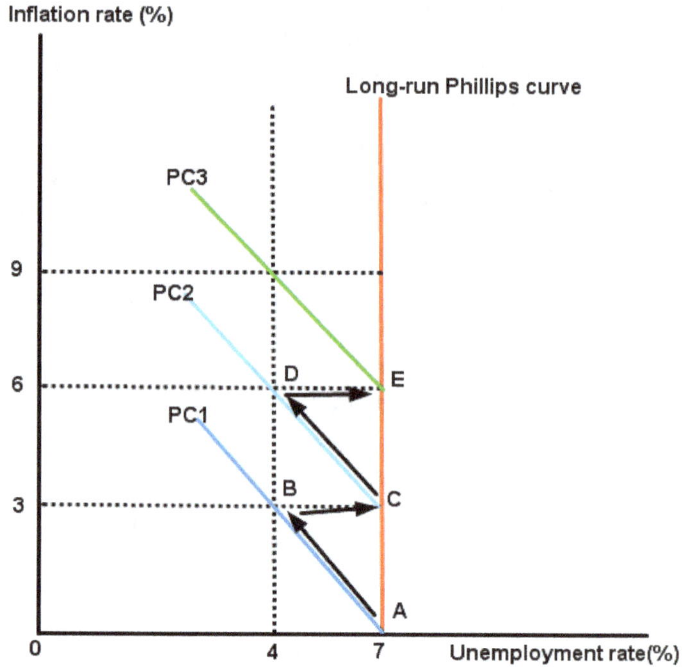

According to the accelerationists, however, the economy will not remain at B for long. That position is only transitory. Now that the rate of inflation has risen to 3%, workers adjust their expectations of inflation and demand higher wages to compensate for the loss in real wages caused by the increase in the price level. The higher wages reduce the firms' profits and cause them to reduce employment and output. The rate of unemployment therefore returns to its natural rate of 7%, but the inflation rate is still 3%. The economy is now at C. The short-run supply curve has shifted from PC1 to PC2.

With the unemployment rate back at 7%, the government once again tries to reduce it to 4% by using expansionary monetary and fiscal policies. The unemployment rate falls temporarily to 4%, but the increase in aggregate demand causes the rate of inflation to rise from 3% to 6%. The economy moves along the short-run Phillips curve PC2 from C to D, as shown in the diagram. But the economy does not remain at D. As before, workers revise their inflationary expectations, and, as before, firms react by reducing employment and output. The unemployment rate returns to its natural rate of 7%, while the inflation rate remains at 6%, as shown by point E in the diagram. The short-run Phillips curve shifts from PC2 to PC3.

Thus, the policy-makers' attempts to force unemployment below its natural rate have resulted only in raising the rate of inflation from 0% to 6%. The accelerationists claim that further attempts will just continue the spiral. They therefore conclude that there is no long-run trade-off between inflation and unemployment.

Problem 10-28

(a) *What is stagflation?*

(b) *How can it be remedied?*

Requirement and Clue: *This is a two-part problem. Answer each part in order. For Part (a), you are expected to state clearly and precisely the meaning of the concept. For Part (b), focus on policies to deal with stagflation.*

Solution

(a) Stagflation describes the economic condition that occurs when high inflation and high unemployment exist simultaneously.

(b) Remedies for stagflation involve policies that will shift the Philips curve to the left. Among the factors that will achieve this are greater labour mobility, the development of relevant skills through education, training and retraining, better information about available jobs, and a reduction in inflationary expectations. All these factors will tend to reduce unemployment without putting undue upward pressure on prices. Hence, the Phillips curve will shift toward the origin. Direct intervention by government to limit increases in wages and prices, referred to as incomes policies, may also be used as a measure against stagflation.

Problem 10-29

(a) *Explain the rational expectations hypothesis.*

(b) *What is the implication of this hypothesis for economic stabilization policies?*

Requirement and Clue: *This is a two-part problem. Answer each part in order. For Part (a), you are expected to point out the main elements of the hypothesis. For Part (b), focus on the success of monetary and fiscal policies if peoples' expectations are rational.*

Solution

(a) The theory of rational expectations assumes that, on average, people base their inflation expectations on their knowledge of the economy and the effects of government policies. People generally understand the variables that affect inflation and use this information in forming their inflationary expectations. The rational expectations hypothesis predicts that, on average, people's inflationary expectations and their subsequent decisions on wages and prices are correct. The theory suggests that people's decisions take into account the effects of government policies, which are known in advance. Rational expectations theorists contend that markets are efficient and firms and households use their resources to achieve their objectives. They conclude that the economy will achieve equilibrium at full employment, that is, at the natural rate of unemployment.

(b) If policy-makers decide to reduce unemployment with expansionary monetary and fiscal policies, firms and workers know the effects of such policies in advance. As a result of the policies, they expect the rate of inflation to increase. They also expect interest rates to rise. Workers will demand wage increases to protect their real wage. With expectations of higher interest rates and higher wages, firms will raise prices and will not find it profitable to undertake new investment projects. Expansionary monetary and fiscal policies will thus be in effective.

Problem 10-30

Explain the concept of imported inflation.

Requirement and Clue: *This problem is not just definitional. It requires a discussion of the concept.*

Solution

Imported inflation is an example of cost-push inflation. This theory of inflation states that inflation can be caused by an increase in the prices of imported consumer goods. If the prices of imported inputs rise, domestic manufacturers using the imported inputs will raise the prices of their products. Also, if there is inflation abroad, the prices of imported consumer goods will rise, which could cause the prices of domestic consumer goods to increase, resulting ultimately in domestic inflation.

Problem 10-31

Define each of the following terms:

(a) *wage-price spiral*

(b) *technological unemployment*

(c) *discomfort index*

Requirement and Clue: *This is a definitional problem with three parts. Answer each part in order. You are expected to give a clear and precise meaning of each concept.*

Solution

(a) The wage-price spiral is a process whereby wage and price interact to push up the price level. It may start with labour demanding higher wages. Firms then respond by raising prices which in turn cause labour to demand higher wages, which causes firms to raise prices, and the spiral continues.

(b) Technological unemployment is a form of structural unemployment that is caused by technological advance. Improvements in technology may result in machines replacing labour in certain production processes. For example, a machine that mixes concrete may replace a number of men with shovels. These displaced workers will join the ranks of the unemployed.

(c) The discomfort index is the sum of the rate of inflation and the rate of unemployment. Thus an inflation rate of 6% coupled with an unemployment rate of 8% gives a discomfort index of 14%. The discomfort index is also referred to as the misery index.

Problem 10-32

Consider the following statement:

> *"It should be obvious to anyone who has taken even a cursory look at the inflationary process, that inflation is truly the effect of increases in wages. It does not take a genius to figure out that if labour is paid more, firms will raise the prices of their products. This increase in prices simply pushes up the cost*

of living which incites workers to seek higher wages, and so it goes on. The only way to get inflation under control is to control wages. It is that simple."

Comment on the statement.

Requirement and Clue: *You should study the statement carefully and critically. Look for erroneous conclusions and point them out and suggest a possible correction.*

Solution

The simplistic view of inflation presented in the passage is misleading. Inflation is such a complicated process that a cursory look is unlikely to reveal much. Wage inflation is only one of several theories of inflation, and most economists probably agree that wage inflation is unlikely tp persist unless it is fueled by monetary expansion. The success of central banks in maintaining inflation at relatively low levels is a testimony to the effectiveness of monetary policy in controlling inflation. Cont rolling inflation is not a simple matter.

Multiple-Choice Questions

In each case, circle the letter that corresponds with the correct answer.

1. People are unemployed:

a. as long as they are not working
b. if they are without jobs and are actively looking and available for work
c. if they are on a two-week sick leave
d. all of the above

Answer: b

Reason: *That is the official definition of what it means to be unemployed.*

2. Which of the following is a type of unemployment?

a. Seasonal c. Cyclical
b. Frictional d. All of the above

Answer: d

Reason: *Choices a, b, and c list types of unemployment.*

3. Unemployment resulting from a deficiency of aggregate spending is called:

a. deficiency unemployment c. frictional unemployment
b. aggregate unemployment d. cyclical unemployment

Answer: d

Reason: *Choices a and b are not types of unemployment. Cyclical unemployment is due to cyclical changes in economic activity. This is consistent with the statement.*

4. Unemployment that results from changes in demand patterns is called:

a. frictional unemployment c. structural unemployment
b. cyclical unemployment d. none of the above

Answer: c

Reason: *Structural unemployment is unemployment that is caused by changes in the overall economy such as changes in government policies, technology, consumer tastes, etc. This is consistent with choice c.*

5. Full employment exists when:

a. the unemployment rate is zero
b. 100% of the labour force is employed
c. only frictional and structural unemployment exist
d. the unemployed consists only of discouraged workers

Answer: c

Reason: Choice c is the official definition of full employment.

6. The labour force participation rate is:

a. the percentage of the labour force actually employed
b. the percentage of the population actually looking for work
c. the labour force expressed as a percentage of the adult population
d. none of the above

Answer: c

Reason: *The labour force participation rate is the percentage of the adult population in the labour force. This is consistent with choice c.*

7. Which of the following statements is true of seasonal unemployment?

a. It affects only countries with marked seasonal variations
b. It results in unemployment only during one season of the year
c. It affects only young workers who are not yet seasoned in their jobs
d. It affects even countries where seasonal variations are slight

Answer: d

Reason: *Because of international economic interactions, seasonal economic activity is transferred internationally and may affect countries with limited seasonal variations.*

8. Which of the following groups is most likely to be unemployed?

a. Children under the age of 12
b. People between the ages of 15 and 24
c. Men over the age of 25
d. None of the above

Answer: b

Reason: Young workers, between the ages of 15 and 24 have a high incidence of unemployment because they often lack education and experience.

9. Which of the following groups is most likely to be underemployed?

a. Educated workers for whose qualifications there is little demand
b. Skilled and highly educated workers
c. Workers who are close to retirement
d. All of the above

Answer: a

Reason: Such workers will tend to accept jobs for which they are overqualified until they find something more suitable.

10. The total economic cost of unemployment is measured by:

a. the amount paid out in employment insurance
b. the loss in income tax caused by unemployment
c. the difference between potential output and actual output
d. all of the above

Answer: c

Reason: The economic cost of unemployment is the loss of output that is due to unemployment. This is consistent with choice c.

11. According to Keynesian theory, unemployment results from:

a. wage and price flexibility
b. the unwillingness of people to work
c. a deficiency in total spending
d. all of the above

Answer: c

Reason: A deficiency in total spending results in unsold output, which causes firms to lay off workers.

12. Inflation is:

a. any increase in the price level
b. a sustained increase in the money supply
c. a sustained increase in the average level of prices
d. all of the above

Answer: c

Reason: The increase in the price level must be persistent to qualify as inflation.

13. The "rule of 70" states that:

a. the price level will double every 70 years
b. it takes about 70 years for an economy to recover completely from hyperinflation
c. the number of years required for a doubling of the price level can be determined by dividing 70 by the annual rate of inflation
d. none of the above

Answer: c

Reason: 70/rate of inflation = number of years for price level to double. This is consistent with choice c.

14. Unanticipated inflation benefits:

a. lenders
b. borrowers
c. holders of financial assets
d. no one

Answer: b

Reason: Borrowers benefit because they repay their debts with money that has lost its purchasing power.

15. Inflation may cause:

a. a misallocation of resources
b. a redistribution of income
c. a reduction in work effort
d. all of the above

Answer: d

Reason: Choices a, b, and c are all consequences of inflation.

16. The short-run relationship between inflation and unemployment is expected to be:

a. inverse
b. direct
c. none existent
d. uncertain

Answer: a

Reason: In the short run, there is a trade-off between inflation and unemployment. This is consistent with choice a.

17. Inflation caused by too much aggregate expenditure is called:

a. excessive inflation
b. demand-pull inflation
c. cost-push inflation
d. deficiency inflation

Answer: b

Reason: Demand-pull inflation is inflation that results from aggregate quantity demanded exceeding aggregate quantity supplied, thus putting upward pressure on the price level.

18. Demand-pull inflation may be caused by:

a. excessive wage demands
b. price hikes by monopolies
c. rapid increases in the price of oil
d. rapid increases in the money supply

Answer: d

Reason: Rapid increases in the quantity of money will lead to increased spending that exerts upward pressure on the price level.

19. Inflation defined as "too much money chasing too few goods" is:

a. demand-pull inflation
b. cost-inflation
c. sellers' inflation
d. none of the above

Answer: a

Reason: "Too much money chasing too few goods" suggests a general shortage of goods and services that tends to bid up the price kevel.

20. Theories of inflation that emphasize increases in aggregate demand are called:

a. price-push inflation
b. excess demand inflation
c. wage inflation
d. none of the above

Answer: b

Reason: Excess demand inflation is inflation that results from spending in excess of the value of total output.

21. According to the monetary theory of inflation, the prime cause of inflation is:

a. reductions in the money supply which force interest rates up
b. reductions in government spending which reduce taxes and increase overall spending
c. increases in the quantity of money which lead to an increase in aggregate expenditure
d. increases in government spending which reduce private-sector spending

Answer: c

Reason: The theory states that when the quantity of money increases people will have more money than they want to hold, so they spend the excess money, thus putting upward pressure on the price level.

22. Which of the following is an example of cost-push inflation?

a. Sellers' inflation
b. Wage inflation
c. Neither a nor b
d. both a and b

Answer: d

Reason: Cost-push inflation is inflation that originates from the supply or cost side. Therefore, a and b both qualify.

23. Cost-push inflation may be initiated by:

a. an upward shift in the aggregate supply curve
b. a downward shift in the aggregate supply curve
c. severe reductions in the money supply
d. none of the above

Answer: a

Reason: Cost-push inflation originate from the supply or cost side. An upward shift in the aggregate supply curve, other things being equal, exerts an upward pressure on the price level.

24. Government deficit spending can result in:

a. cost-push inflation
b. demand-pull inflation
c. deficiency in aggregate expenditure
d. none of the above

Answer: b

Reason: Government deficit spending can result in an increase in overall spending which exerts upward pressure of prices. Since this is from the demand side, it would be demand-pull inflation.

25. If there is significant unemployment and inflation at the same time, the inflation is likely to be of the:

a. demand-pull variety
b. cost-push variety
c. seasonal variety
d. none of the above

Answer: b

Reason: Supply-side shocks can force the price level up and initiate an inflation even before the economy has reached full employment.

26. The simultaneous existence of inflation and unemployment is known as:

a. the business cycle
b. the Phillips curve
c. stagflation
d. none of the above

Answer: c

Reason: Stagflation consists of stagnation and inflation. This is consistent with choice c.

27. If the aggregate supply curve shifts to the left, other things being equal:

a. the price level will fall and real output will rise
b. the price level will rise and real output will fall
c. the price level and real output will both fall
d. the price level and real output will both rise

Answer: b

Reason: The leftward shift of the aggregate supply curve will create an overall shortage at the initial price level. This shortage will exert an upward pressure on the price level. A decrease in aggregate supply means a fall in real output.

28. According to accelerationists:

a. there is a stable long-run trade-off between inflation and unemployment
b. the short-run Phillips curve is vertical
c. the long-run Phillips curve is vertical
d. none of the above

Answer: c

Reason: The accelerationists claim that there is no long-run trade-off between inflation and unemployment. That is, the long-run Phillips curve is vertical.

29. The imposition of wage and price controls is designed to:

a. shift the Phillips curve to the left
b. deal with the problem of stagflation
c. reduce inflation without increasing unemployment
d. all of the above

Answer: d

Reason: Choices a, b, and c will be the result of wage and price controls.

30. Rational expectations theorists conclude that:

a. stabilization policies will be extremely effective
b. stabilization policies will be ineffective
c. only fiscal policy will have any effect on economic activity
d. none of the above

Answer: b

Reason: People's rational expectations will thwart attempts by policy-makers to promote economic stability.

True-False Questions

Determine whether each of the following statements is true or false.

1. Frictional unemployment cannot occur in a market oriented economy.

Answer: False

Explanation: *Frictional unemployment is unavoidable in a market oriented economy where people are free to move from job to job.*

2. Unemployment may result from cyclical fluctuations in aggregate expenditure.

Answer: True

3. Technological unemployment will be found only among people with little or no technical training.

Answer: False

Explanation: *Even very highly skilled workers can experience technological unemployment. Technological changes may significantly reduce the demand for their particular skills.*

4. The unemployment rate is calculated by dividing the number of unemployed people by the labour force and then multiplying the result by 100.

Answer: True

5. The labour force participation rate is defined as the labour force expressed as a percentage of the adult population.

Answer: True

6. Discouraged workers who are not actively seeking employment are not counted as officially unemployed.

Answer: True

7. The total cost of unemployment may be measured by the amount of unemployment insurance payments.

Answer: False

Explanation: *The total cost of unemployment is the loss of out (income) cause by unemployment (i.e., the economic cost) and the noneconomic costs such as the suffering and frustration that the unemployed experience.*

8. Inflation refers to a situation of high prices.

Answer: False

Explanation: *Inflation refers to a situation of persistently rising prices. If prices are high but not rising, inflation does not exist.*

9. According to the "rule of 70", the price level will double in 7 years if the annual rate of inflation is 10%.

Answer: True

10. Inflation always benefits holders of financial assets.

Answer: False

Explanation: *Holders of financial assets lose during an inflation because the real value of financial assets will fall.*

11. Even a very mild inflation hurts everyone and benefits no one.

Answer: False

Explanation: *Inflation does benefit certain groups such as debtors and owners of real assets.*

12. There is likely to be an inverse relationship between inflation and unemployment in the short run.

Answer: True

13. Demand-pull inflation results from under-consumption.

Answer: False

Explanation: *Under-consumption will tend to be deflationary rather than inflationary.*

14. Inflation resulting from excessive wage settlements is of the cost-push variety.

Answer: True

15. The monetary theory of inflation states that any increase in the quantity of money will cause inflation.

Answer: False

Explanation: *The theory says that inflation will result if the rate of increase in the quantity of money is greater than the rate of growth of output.*

16. Government spending in excess of tax revenues may result in in increase in the price level.

Answer: True

17. Proponents of the monetary theory of inflation claim that government deficits are inflationary only if they cause the quantity of money to increase.

Answer: True

18. Cost-push inflation results from supply factors such as increases in production costs.

Answer: True

19. A downward shift in the aggregate supply curve will initiate cost-push inflation.

Answer: False

Explanation: *A downward shift in the aggregate supply curve will result in a lower, not higher, price level.*

20. Inertial inflation theory suggests that inflationary expectations play no role in the inflationary process.

Answer: False

Explanation: *Inertial inflation theory states that inflationary expectations may sustain inflation.*

21. According to the Phillips curve, there is a trade-off, at least in the short run, between inflation and unemployment.

Answer: True

22. Excess demand inflation may be reduced by reducing the quantity of money.

Answer: True

23. One way of dealing effectively with cost-push inflation is to increase the money supply.

Answer: False

Explanation: An increase in the money supply will tend to aggravate inflation. Moreover, the money supply is associated with demand-pull, not cost-push, inflation.

24. Stagflation is a situation of economic stagnation accompanied by inflation.

Answer: True

25. Accelerationists claim that the long-run Phillips curve is vertical.

Answer: True

26. Tax-based incomes policies provide an incentive for firms to accede to excessive wage demands.

Answer: False

Explanation: On the contrary, they encourage firms to limit wage increases.

27. In the new classical macroeconomic model, wages and prices adjust very quickly so activist macroeconomic policies are not necessary to move the economy towards its natural level of employment.

Answer: True

28. The theory of rational expectations leads to the conclusion that stabilization policies will be generally ineffective.

Answer: True

29. There is little or no difference between the new classical macroeconomic model and the new Keynesian macroeconomic model.

Answer: False

Explanation: The new classical macroeconomic model claims that flexible wages and prices help the economy to move quickly to the natural level of unemployment. On the other hand, the new Keynesian macroeconomic model claims that sticky wages and prices prevent the economy from moving quickly towards its natural level of unemployment and that activist policies are necessary.

30. The policy irrelevance hypothesis states that monetary policy and fiscal policy will be ineffective if people have rational expectations.

Answer: True

Completion

(Fill in the blanks)

Use each word or combination of words from the list exactly once.
***(Hint:** Proceed by elimination)*

Word list

Classical — Consumer — Cost-push x 2 — Creeping — Cyclical — Demand-pull x 3 — Downward — Economic — Force — Hyperinflation — Ineffective — Inertial or expectational — Inverse — Keynesian — Labour — Lose — Monetary — Okun's — Phillips — Price — Rise — Say's — Stagflation — Structural — Supply — Unemployment — Vertical — Win

Questions

1. Unemployment resulting from changes in demand patterns and changes in techniques of production is called ____________ unemployment.
2. ____________ unemployment is caused by a deficiency of aggregate expenditure.
3. The ____________ ____________ comprises all unemployed and employed persons. (labour force)
4. The difference between potential GDP and actual GDP is a measure of the ____________ cost of ____________.
5. ____________ law states that for every 1% rise in the unemployment rate above full employment, output falls by 3%.
6. ____________ law states that supply creates its own demand.
7. The ____________ ____________ index measures changes in the prices of consumer goods and services.
8. Moderate increases in the average level of prices is called ____________ inflation. A rapid rate of inflation such as 1000% is called ____________.
9. Debtors and owners of real assets will tend to ____________ [win, lose] during an inflation. Creditors and owners of final assets will tend to ____________ [win, lose].
10. There is a(n) ____________ [direct, inverse] relationship between inflation and unemployment.
11. ____________ inflation results from too much aggregate expenditure, while ____________ inflation results from increases in cost.
12. If the aggregate demand curve shifts to the right, other things being equal, the price level will ____________ [rise, fall].
13. Increases in the quantity of money at a rate faster than the increase in real output results in ____________ [demand-pull, cost-push] inflation.

14. The budget-deficit theory of inflation is an example of ____________ [demand-pull, cost-push] inflation.

15. Inflation resulting from excessive wage settlements is an example of ____________ inflation.

16. According to the ____________ theory of inflation, the prime cause of inflation is monetary expansion. (monetary)

17. ____________ inflation theory states that inflation may be sustained by inflationary expectation.

18. The ____________ curve expresses a trade-off between the rate of inflation and the rate of unemployment.

19. Upward shifts of the aggregate ____________ curve explains stagflation.

20. Accelerationists claim that the long-run Phillips curve is ____________.

21. A(n) ____________ [upward, downward] shift of the Phillips curve reduces unemployment without raising inflation.

22. Income policies are designed to solve the problem of ____________.

23. The policy irrelevance hypothesis says that monetary and fiscal policies will be ____________ [effective, ineffective] if people have rational expectations.

24. The new ____________ macroeconomic model assumes that wages and prices are sticky and that economic adjustment will be slow.

25. The new ____________ macroeconomic model assumes that sages and prices are flexible and that economic adjustment will be swift.

Solutions

1. (structural)
2. (cyclical)
3. (labour force)
4. (economic, unemployment)
5. (Okun's)
6. (Say's)
7. (consumer price)
8. (creeping, hyperinflation)
9. (win, lose)
10. (inverse)
11. (demand-pull, cost-push)
12. (rise)
13. (demand-pull)
14. (demand-pull)
15. (cost-push)
16. (monetary)
17. (inertial or expectational)
18. (Phillips)
19. (supply)
20. (vertical)
21. (downward)
22. (stagflation)
23. (ineffective)
24. (Keynesian)
25. (classical)

11 BUSINESS CYCLES

LEARNING OBJECTIVES

In connection with this module, you should be able to:

1. explain the meaning of business cycles
2. describe the phases of the business cycle
3. discuss the causes of economic fluctuations
4. discuss the role of politics in the business cycle
5. explain the real business cycle
6. explain how to forecast business cycles

DEFINITIONS & CONCEPTS

You should be able to define the following terms and concepts:

business cycles	acceleration principle
trough	capital-output ratio
depression	political business cycle
expansion (recovery)	the real business cycle
peak	leading indicators
recession	coincidental indicators
inventory cycles	lagging indicators

SYNOPSIS

Business cycles are the cyclical swings in economic activity. Each business cycle has the following four phases:

- trough
- expansion or recovery
- peak
- recession

Business cycles may be caused by fluctuations in consumer spending, changes in inventory investment, changes in government spending, changes in the expectations of business people, periodic bouts of innovation, changes in the money supply, and by the interaction of the multiplier and the accelerator.

The theory of the political business cycle states that attempts by the government to use its spending and taxing powers to retain power contribute to business cycles.

Business cycles initiated by supply-side shocks such as technological changes and severe and prolonged shortages of important inputs are called **real business cycles**.

Leading indicators help in forecasting business cycles.

11 BUSINESS CYCLES

Concepts, Definitions & Problems

Problem 11-1

(a) *What are business cycles?*

(b) *List the phases of a business cycle.*

Requirement and Clue: *This is a two-part problem. Answer each part in order. For Part (a), state clearly and precisely the meaning of the concept. For Part (b), you are required only to list (without discussion or amplification) the phases.*

Solution:

(a) Business cycles are alternating periods of economic expansions and contractions. They are ups and downs in economic activity that seem to occur in most sectors of the economy at the same time. Business cycles are also referred to as economic fluctuations or business fluctuations.

(b) The phases of a business cycle are:

- Trough
- Expansion
- Peak
- Recovery

Problem 11-2

During the Christmas season, spending usually increases. In January and February, spending usually declines. Is this an example of a business cycle?

Requirement and Clue: *Focus on the difference between predictable short-term variations in spending and business cycles.*

Solution

Seasonal variations in spending such as those occurring during Christmas holiday season and the spike in spending occasioned by a week-end of Grand Prix racing in a city, should not be confused with cyclical fluctuations. Seasonal fluctuations occur at specific times, are of relatively short duration, and are quite predictable. Business cycles, on the other hand, exhibit four distinct phases (peak, recession, trough, and recovery). The times of their occurrence and their duration are not easily predictable.

Problem 11-3

Describe the expansion phase of a business cycle.

Requirement and Clue: *You are required not only to define the expansion phase but also to give details of its basic elements.*

Solution

The expansion phase of a business cycle is the phase that follows the trough and is characterized by an increase in employment, income, and economic activity in general. In this phase of the cycle, output begins to expand, and income increases. Consumption expenditures and employment also increase. Businesspeople become optimistic about the future and increase their investment spending. People are confident and feel quite good about the economy. In this phase, because the economy appears to be recovering from a state of low growth or stagnation, we say that it has entered a period of recovery.

Problem 11-4

Draw a diagram showing the four phases of a business cycle.

Requirement and Clue: *Your diagram should show the order in which the phases occur.*

Solution

The following diagram shows the phases of a business cycle.

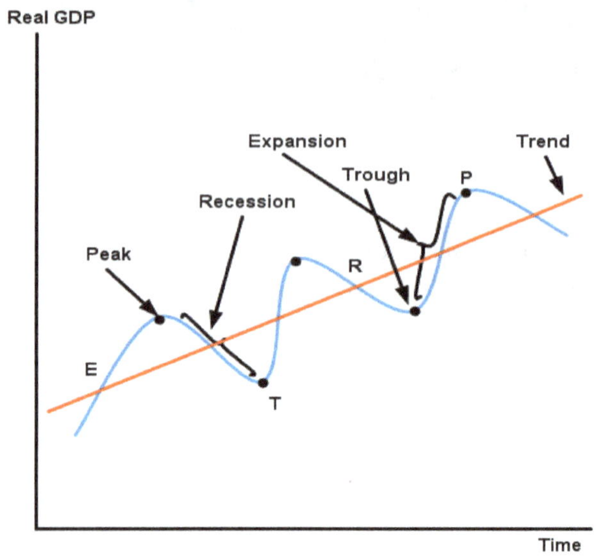

We can begin the cycle at any phase. Let us begin with the expansion, denoted by E. The phase following the expansion is the peak, denoted by P in the diagram. After the peak comes the recession, denoted by R, after which follows the trough, denoted by T and the process is repeated.

Problem 11-5

How do business cycles affect different sectors of the economy?

Requirement and Clue: *Focus on how business cycles affect different industries such as durable consumer goods, capital goods, and non-durable consumer goods.*

Solution

Business cycles do not affect all sectors of the economy equally. Durable consumer goods industries, such as those producing automobiles and appliances such as washing machines, refrigerators, and stoves and capital goods industries, such as those producing tractors, heavy equipment, residential and non-residential structures, trucks, and business machinery, feel the impact of a business cycle the most. During an economic slowdown, businesses postpone expenditures on capital goods. Producers are reluctant to increase their stock of capital goods during such times. Instead, they repair broken machines to try to keep them running. During vibrant economic times, businesses view the economic outlook with optimism and are willing to invest in new capital.

Expenditures on durable consumer goods follow a pattern similar to that of the capital goods industries. In an economic downturn, consumers are reluctant to replace automobiles and appliances with new ones, preferring instead to call in the repair person and to pay the mechanic to repair the old car. They may defer plans to purchase new furniture for a year or more. These decisions have negative impacts on the manufacturers of these consumer durables. During periods of economic expansion, manufacturers of capital goods and durable consumer goods receive the greatest benefits.

It is not so easy to postpone the purchase of food, school supplies, and medical and dental services. These service industries and producers of non-durable consumer goods are somewhat shielded from an economic downturn. In fact, some services businesses such as repair technicians, auto mechanics, and upholsterers may even prosper during a recession.

Problem 11-6

List the various theories of business fluctuations.

Requirement and Clue: *This problem requires only a listing of the theories of business fluctuations. It does not require any explanations or discussions.*

Solution

The following theories of business fluctuations have been propounded.

1. The under-consumption theory
2. The volatile investment theory
3. The government spending theory
4. The expectations theory
5. The innovations theory
6. The monetary theory
7. The multiplier-accelerator theory.

Problem 11-7

Explain the "volatile investment theory" of business cycles.

Requirement and Clue: *Focus on the instability of inventory investment.*

Solution

The volatile investment theory of business cycles claims that increases and decreases in inventory investment cause economic fluctuations. Of all the components of aggregate expenditure, investment is the most volatile. Because investment fluctuates substantially from one period to the next, many economists consider it to be the prime cause of fluctuations in economic activity. Inventory investment is relatively small but highly unstable. Its instability is the major cause of fluctuations in total investment. Proponents of the volatile investment theory of business cycles use the term *inventory cycles* to refer to the volatile investment theory. Inventory cycles are economic fluctuations caused by changes in inventory investment. During a period of low economic activity, businesspeople run down their production levels in response to reductions in their orders, and unemployment results. When the economy recovers, they restore their inventory levels. This investment in inventories increases employment and income.

Problem 11-8

What is the acceleration principle? Explain the multiplier-accelerator theory of business cycles.

Requirement and Clue: *This is a two-part problem. Answer each part in order. For the first part of the problem, you are required only to state clearly and precise the meaning of the concept. For the second part of the problem, you are required to explain how interactions between the multiplier and the accelerator can intensify economic fluctuations.*

Solution

An increase in income will cause an increase in demand for consumer goods and services. This increase in demand will give rise to a demand for capital goods to produce the larger volume of consumer goods now being demanded. The capital goods industries will meet this demand for capital goods by increasing their production. This investment induced by the increase in income, will be proportionately larger than the increase in demand for consumer goods and services. This principle is referred to as the acceleration principle.

The interaction of the multiplier and the accelerator can produce wide fluctuations in economic activity. If the economy is expanding, the increase in income accelerates investment. The increased investment generates an even greater increase in income. But as the economy's resources become fully employed, the acceleration of output shows down. This slowing down hinders investment. The decreased investment, other things being equal, causes an even greater reduction in output via the multiplier. Hence, the interaction of the multiplier and the accelerator acts to intensify fluctuations in economic activity.

Problem 11-9

Does it make good economic sense for the business sector to undertake new investment as soon as there is an increase in demand for goods and services?

Requirement and Clue: *Consider whether the goods producing industries have idle capacity and whether the increase in demand is expected to be long-term or just temporary.*

Solution

An increase in demand for goods and services will be an incentive for the business sector to increase production. This can be done by new investment, by utilizing idle capacity, or by working existing plants harder (for example, operating beyond normal capacity, and working overtime). When an increase in production is warranted by an increase in demand for goods and services, it makes good economic sense for firms to use any excess capacity that might be available and to run their plants harder until it is ascertained whether the increase in demand is permanent or just transitory. Once it is determined that the increase in demand is permanent, then investment can be justified, because it is costly to run plants beyond their normal capacity for a long period of time.

Problem 11-10

Discuss three objections that have been raised with regard to the acceleration principle.

Requirement and Clue: *Focus on capacity within the consumer goods industries and the capital goods industries. Consider also incentives to invest.*

Solution

First, the acceleration principle implies that there is no excess capacity in the industries producing consumer goods, so that any increase in demand for consumer goods and services will give rise to an increased demand for equipment used to produce these goods. In fact, however, firms are unlikely to purchase new equipment as soon as there is a demand for their products. Instead, they may use excess capacity which may exist, or they may decide to run existing plant and equipment a little harder, such as going into over-time production.

Second, the accelerator theory also implies that the supply of capital goods is elastic. In fact, however, the industries producing capital goods may not be able to respond immediately to increases in demand. The implication that there is always excess capacity in the industries producing capital goods is a gross over-simplification of reality.

Third, it should be noted that an increase in demand is only one possible explanation of investment behaviour. Factors such as the rate of interest, expectations, and the amount of retained earnings are likely to exert some influence on investment decisions.

Problem 11-11

Define each of the following concepts that are related to business cycles:

(a) *Boom*
(b) *Capital-output ratio*
(c) *Real business cycle*
(d) *Leading indicators*

Requirement and Clue: *This problem is definitional and has four parts. Answer each part in order. Lengthy discussions and explanations are not required. Just state clearly and precisely the meaning of each concept. Examples will be helpful.*

Solution

(a) A boom is a period of economic expansion. In this period, income increases and consequently, spending also increases. This increase in spending reduces inventories below their desired levels and triggers production which increases GDP.

(b) The capital-output ratio is the value of capital stock to the value of annual output. If it takes $3 worth of capital to produce $1 of output per year, then the capital-output ration is 3/1 = 3. The capital-output ratio is the same as the accelerator.

(c) The real business cycle is a business cycle that owes its origin to shifts in aggregate supply.

(d) Leading indicators are economic variables that turn downward before the cycle peak and upward before the trough. Examples are stock prices, orders for durable goods, and net business formation.

Problem 11-12

What effect can the maturation of industries be expected to have on economic fluctuations?

Requirement and Clue: *Consider the relationship between mature industries and new investment.*

Solution

A major explanation of economic fluctuations is changes in investment. Mature industries are industries that have reached their full growth. They will likely not engage in much net (new) investment. Gross investment is likely to consist mainly of replacement investment rather than addition to the capital stock. Fluctuations, therefore, are likely to be less than in the case of expanding or contracting industries.

Problem 11-13

Explain the expectations theory of economic fluctuations.

Requirement and Clue: Focus on the effects of expectations on investment.

Solution

The expectations theory of the business cycle states that business people's expectations play a key role in business fluctuations. In a recession, businesspeople become pessimistic about the future economic outlook. This pessimism results in postponement of investment spending and possibly leads to cutbacks in certain business ventures. Certain investment projects remain on the drawing board, and others are shelved. Output and employment decrease as a result. When economic activity revives, businesspeople become optimistic about the future. Projects that were shelved are now reactivated and investment spending increases. Consequently, employment, income, and output also increase.

Problem 11-14

Can business cycles be controlled?

Requirement and Clue: *Focus on progress made in understanding business cycles and the success achieved in managing them.*

Solution

There can be little doubt that the ability to predict business fluctuations and to use macroeconomic policy tools have resulted in policymakers being able to reduce the frequency and the intensity of business cycles. Economic policy has been successful in averting major economic depressions of the magnitude of the Great Depression of the 1930s.

Economists have learnt much about how the economy operates, but their knowledge is still imperfect. Mild ups and downs in economic activity, resulting from a variety of causes can be expected. There will be fluctuations in private-sector investment, including inventories, and government spending, and changes in taxes—all of which are potentially destabilizing. Economists are not yet at the stage where they can fine-tune the economy to the point where they can iron out all of the wrinkles and smooth all the ripples. But significant progress has been made in controlling business cycles.

Problem 11-15

Discuss the relationship between politics and the business cycle.

Requirement and Clue: *Focus on how political choices might affect economic activity.*

Solution

It has been suggested that elected government officials may use certain tools of economic policy, not to achieve economic stability, but to advance their own political objectives. Fluctuations in economic activity caused by the use of economic policy tools to further political ends are referred to as political business cycles. The main objective of elected government officials is to be re-elected. Prior to an election, the government in office pursues expansionary economic policies—introducing a variety of spending programs and tax cuts—whether or not the economic situation warrants such policies. These expansionary policies increase income and employment. Voters are pleased with the present state of the economy, so they return the government to power.

Once the election has been won, however, the longer-term impact of the expansionary economic policies begins to be felt. If the economic stimulus occurred when the economy was operating close to full employment, the increase in aggregate expenditure is likely to result in inflation some time after the election. The electorate begins to complain and the opposition parties begin to scream for anti-inflationary action. The government then reduces its spending and may also raise taxes to eliminate the inflationary y pressures and appease those crying for policies to combat inflation. These contractionary policies plunge the economy into a recession. The recession succeeds in eliminating the inflationary pressures. By the time the process is completed, it is again close to another election, and the government is again ready to engage in another round of pre-election spending that will simply start the entire process again.

Problem 11-16

Define each of the following concepts and give examples of each.

(a) *Leading indicators*

(b) *Coincidental indicators*

(c) *Lagging indicators*

Requirement and Clue: *This is a two-part problem. Make sure you answer each part. You are expected to state clearly and precisely the meaning of each concept. Examples are mandatory.*

Solution

(a) Leading indicators are economic variables that turn downward before the peak of the cycle and upward before the trough of the cycle. Examples of leading indicators are orders for durable consumer goods, growth of the money supply, and new business formation.

(b) Coincidental indicators are economic variables that coincide exactly with the business cycle. Examples of coincidental indicators are gross domestic product, employment, and business profits.

(c) Lagging indicators are variables that turn downward after the peak of the business cycle and upward after the trough of the cycle. Examples of lagging indicators are inventories, personal income, and labour costs.

Problem 11-17

The total demand for goods and services in an economy increases from \$205 billion to \$215 billion. Given a capital-output ratio of 3, compute the amount of investment required to meet this increase in total demand.

Requirement and Clue: *Use the formula involving the accelerator to determine the required investment.*

Solution

The formula for the required investment is:

$I = v\Delta Y$ where I = investment, v = accelerator, and Y = aggregate demand.

In the problem, the capital-output ration (the accelerator) is given as 3, and the change in aggregate demand is (\$215 billion – 205 billion) = \$10 billion.

I = 3 × \$10 billion = **\$30 billion.**

Problem 11-18

In the left column of the following table are items pertaining to a particular theory of business cycles. In the right-hand column, identify the relevant theory.

	Item	Theory identification
a.	*Fluctuations in the relation between saving and investment cause economic cycles.*	
b.	*Fluctuating interest rates and credit conditions result in business fluctuations.*	
c.	*Inventory volatility causes fluctuations in economic activity.*	
d.	*Alternating pessimistic and optimistic economic outlooks result in ups and downs in output and employment.*	
e.	*Fluctuations in government spending cause changes in output and employment.*	
f.	*Research and development lead to new ways of doing things that produce temporary upswings in economic activity.*	
g.	*A change in income causes a change in investment, which causes a change in income, and so on.*	

Requirement and Clue: *The solution to this problem requires a good understanding of the various theories of the business cycle.*

Solution:

See completed table below.

	Item	Theory identification
a.	Fluctuations in the relation between saving and investment cause economic cycles.	The under-consumption theory.
b.	Fluctuating interest rates and credit conditions result in business fluctuations.	The monetary theory.
c.	Inventory volatility causes fluctuations in economic activity.	The volatile investment theory (inventory cycles).
d.	Alternating pessimistic and optimistic economic outlooks result in ups and downs in output and employment.	The expectations theory.
e.	Fluctuations in government spending cause changes in output and employment.	The government spending theory.
f.	Research and development lead to new ways of doing things that produce temporary upswings in economic activity.	The innovations theory.
g.	A change in income causes a change in investment, which causes a change in income, and so on.	The multiplier-accelerator theory.

Multiple-Choice Questions

In each case, circle the letter that corresponds with the correct answer.

1. Business cycles refer to:
   a. periods of rapid inflation
   b. situations of severe unemployment such as that experienced in the 1930s
   c. fluctuations in economic activity
   d. none of the above

Answer: c

Reason: Business cycles are ups and downs in economic activity as defined in choice c.

2. Which of the following is not a phase of the business cycle?
   a. Recession c. Inflation
   b. Recovery d. Trough

Answer: c

Reason: The phases of a business cycle are trough, recovery, teak, and recession.

3. The phase of the business cycle which follows the peak is the:
   a. trough c. recession
   b. recovery d. inflation

Answer: c

Reason: The phases of the business cycle in order, beginning at the peak, are peak, recession, trough, and recovery.

4. The phase of the business cycle which precedes the peak is:
   a. expansion c. trough
   b. recession d. depression

Answer: a

Reason: The phases of the business cycle in order, beginning at the peak, are peak, recession, trough, expansion or recovery.

5. If investment, consumption, real output, and employment are increasing, the economy is most likely:
   a. in its recessionary phase c. at its peak
   b. in a depression d. in the expansion phase

Answer: d

Reason: These are the characteristics of an expanding economy.

6. A trough is characterized by:
   a. rapid inflation and expanding real output
   b. high unemployment and no economic growth
   c. a rapid increase in employment and investment
   d. none of the above

Answer: b

Reason: A trough is the lowest phase of the cycle where economic activity is at its lowest. This is consistent with choice c.

7. Which of the following is not a theory of business cycles?
   a. The cyclical theory c. The inventory cycles theory
   b. The innovations theory d. The monetary theory

Answer: a

Reason: There is no cyclical theory of business cycles.

8. If the capital-output ratio is 2.4, and there is no excess capacity in consumer goods industries, then to increase output by $24 million requires an increase in investment of:
   a. $10 million c. $26.4 million
   b. $21.6 million d. $57.6 million

Answer: d

Reason: The formula $I = v\Delta Y$ where I = investment, v is the capital-output ratio and Y = output, gives the required investment. $I = 2.4 \times 24 = 57.6$.

9. The notion that business cycles may be caused by government manipulation of spending and taxes is called:
   a. political business cycle
   b. electioneering business cycle
   c. government induced business cycle
   d. none of the above

Answer: a

Reason: The political business cycle has as its premise that government uses its spending and taxing powers to try to win the next election. This causes economic fluctuations.

10. The real business cycle theory states that business cycles are caused by:
   a. changes in real spending c. changes in aggregate supply
   b. demand-side changes d. none of the above

Answer: c

Reason: Real business cycles are due to supply-side shocks.

11. Business cycles that originate from the supply side of the economy are called:
   a. economy-wide cycles c. real business cycles
   b. secular cycles d. real inventory cycles

Answer: c

Reason: Shocks such as technological changes and severe and prolonged shortages of important inputs may cause economic fluctuations called real business cycles. This is consistent with choice c.

12. Which of the following is an example of a leading indicator?
   a. Orders for durable goods c. Inventories
   b. Gross domestic product d. None of the above

Answer: a

Reason: Leading indicators turn downward before the peak of the cycle and upward before the trough. Orders for durable goods tend to do this.

13. Which of the following would be considered favourable factors in terms of business cycles?

a. Falling interest rates
b. An increase in purchasing intensions
c. An increase in construction activities
d. All of the above

Answer: d

Reason: *Choices a, b, and c contribute to economic expansion and are therefore considered to be favourable factors.*

14. Which of the following would be considered unfavourable factors in terms of business cycles?

a. A fall in the unemployment rate
b. A fall in the savings rate
c. An increase in marriages and new family formation
d. Contractionary monetary and fiscal policies

Answer: d

Reason: *Choice d can contribute to a recession and is therefore an unfavourable factor.*

True-False Questions

Determine whether each of the following statements is true or false.

1. Developed economies have not experienced any cyclical fluctuations since the governments began to use fiscal policy.

Answer: False

Explanation: *Economic fluctuations still occur in developed countries but with a decreased degree of frequency and severity.*

2. All business cycles have peaks and troughs.

Answer: True

3. Some business cycles do not have an expansion phase.

Answer: False

Explanation: *All business cycles have a peak, a recession, a trough, and an expansion or recovery.*

4. After the business cycle has reached its peak and there is a reduction in consumption and investment, it is said to be in a trough.

Answer: False

Explanation: *The phase that follows the peak is the recession, nit the trough.*

5. In business cycle terminology, an expansion is also called a recovery.

Answer: True

6. Inventory investment fluctuates substantially and may contribute to fluctuations in economic activity.

Answer: True

7. The innovations theory of the business cycle owes its origin to Joseph Schumpeter.

Answer: True

8. The principle of acceleration states that an increase in investment will cause an eben greater increase in income.

Answer: False

Explanation: *The principle of acceleration states that an increase in income will cause an even greater increase in investment.*

9. The capital-output ratio and the accelerator are identical.

Answer: True

10. The amount of investment required to increase output by a certain amount can never be as large as the required increase in income.

Answer: False

Explanation: *The effect of the accelerator makes the required amount of investment greater than the required increase in income.*

11. All business cycles are due to fluctuations in aggregate demand.

Answer: False

Explanation: *Fluctuations in aggregate supply may cause business cycles. That is the claim of the real business cycle theory.*

12. The theory of the real business cycle claims that economic fluctuations are caused by changes in aggregate supply.

Answer: True

13. Through the judicious use of monetary and fiscal policies, policymakers have been able to totally eliminate business cycles.

Answer: False

Explanation: *Through the use of monetary and fiscal policies, policymakers have been able to reduce the frequency and severity of business cycles. They have not been eliminated.*

14. Economists have made no progress in terms of forecasting business cycles.

Answer: False

Explanation: *Economists have had some success in forecasting business cycles by using leading, coincidental, and lagging indicators as well as looking at favourable and unfavourable factors.*

Completion

(Fill in the blanks)

Use each word or combination of words from the list exactly once.
*(**Hint**: Proceed by elimination)*

Word list

Capital-output — Cycles — Expectations — Income — Innovations — Inventory — Investment — Leading — Peak — Political — Ratio — Recession x 2 — Recovery or expansion — Supply — Supply-side — Trough x 2

Questions

1. The phases of the business cycle are: ________, ________, ________, and ________.
2. According to the ________ theory of the business cycle, economic fluctuations are caused by alternative periods of pessimism and optimism on the part of investors.
3. Expansion is the phase that follows the ________.
4. If real output is decreasing and unemployment is increasing, then the economy is in the phase called ________.
5. Economic fluctuations caused by changes in inventory investment are called ________ ________.
6. The name of Joseph Schumpeter is associated with the theory of the business cycle known as the ________ theory.
7. The ________________ ________ measures the amount of capital required to increase output by one dollar.
8. The principle of acceleration states that an increase in ________ leads to an even greater increase in ________.
9. The ________ business cycle is caused by the government's use of its spending and taxing powers to secure its position.
10. Supporters of the real business cycle theory believe that severe movements in aggregate ________ are the primary cause of business cycles.
11. Changes in technology, the supply of labour, and weather conditions that affect production are ________ shocks.
12. Economic variables that typically turn downward before the cycle has reached its peak, and turn upward before the trough are called ________ indicators.

Solutions

1. (peak, recession, trough, recovery or expansion (any consecutive order)
2. (expectations)
3. (trough)
4. (recession)
5. (inventory cycles)
6. (innovations)
7. (capital-output ratio)
8. (income, investment)
9. (political)
10. (supply)
11. (supply-side)
12. (leading)

12 FISCAL POLICY

SYNOPSIS

An increase in government spending will tend to increase national income while a decrease in government spending will ten to reduce national income. An increase in taxes will tend to reduce national income, while a decrease in taxes will tend to increase national income.

A **budget deficit** exists when government spending exceeds its tax revenues. A **budget surplus** exists when government spending is less than its tax revenues, and a **balanced budget** exists when government spending is equal to its tax revenues.

A **balanced budget change in spending** will cause national income to increase by the increase in government spending. This concept is known as the **balanced budget theorem.**

Automatic stabilizers include progressive taxes, government assistance to agriculture, and employment insurance payments. These built-in fiscal policy measures help to stabilize the economy. The **fiscal drag** is an economic stabilizer that prevents the economy from recovering from a recession.

Limitations of fiscal policy include time lags, the difficulty of changing government and taxes in response to changing economic conditions, and the actions of other levels of government.

LEARNING OBJECTIVES

In connection with this module, you should be able to:

1. explain how government spending and taxes affect the equilibrium level of income
2. identify a budget deficit, a budget surplus, and a balanced budget
3. explain the effects of a balanced budget change in spending
4. describe automatic stabilizers and how they work
5. explain how discretionary fiscal policy can be used to close full employment gaps
6. state the significance of the full employment budget
7. discuss the limitations of fiscal policy

DEFINITIONS & CONCEPTS

You should be able to define the following terms and concepts:

government spending multiplier	discretionary fiscal policy
lump-sum tax	progressive taxes
budget deficit	fiscal drag
balanced budget	contractionary fiscal policy
functional finance	expansionary fiscal policy
balanced budget theorem	recognition lag
balanced budget change in spending	decision lag
	implementation lag
automatic stabilizers	impact lag

12

FISCAL POLICY

Concepts, Definitions & Problems

Problem 12-1

Define each of the following concepts:

(a) *Fiscal policy*

(b) *Government spending multiplier*

(c) *Balanced budget change in spending*

(d) *Automatic stabilizers*

Requirement and Clue: *This is a multiple-part problem. Make sure you answer each part in order. The entire problem is definitional. You are to state clearly and precisely the meaning of each concept. Where possible, give examples.*

Solution

(a) Fiscal policy is the use of government spending and taxes to regulate economic activity. For example, the government can increase its spending in an attempt to create employment.

(b) The government spending multiplier is the number by which a change in government spending is multiplied to arrive at the change in equilibrium income. It is the reciprocal of the marginal propensity to save (MPS). For example, if the MPS is 1/3, and the government increases its spending by \$50 billion, then equilibrium income will increase by (3 × 50) = \$150 billion.

(c) A balanced budget change in spending is the condition in which a change in government spending equals the change in taxes. Thus, if the government increased its spending by \$100 billion and at the same time it raised taxes by \$100 billion, then it would have undertaken a balanced budget change in spending.

(d) Automatic stabilizers or automatic fiscal policy are fiscal policy measures that are built into the economic system. They automatically increase the budget surplus in inflationary periods and increase the budget deficit in periods of recession. In this way, they stabilize the economy. Examples of automatic stabilizers are progressive taxes, government assistance to agriculture, and employment insurance benefits.

Problem 12-2

What effect does an increase in government spending have on the equilibrium level of income? Illustrate graphically.

Requirement and Clue: *This is a two-part problem. Answer each part in order. You can use either the aggregate demand-aggregate supply model or the Keynesian cross diagram.*

Solution (AD/AS model):

In the following diagram, the economy is in equilibrium at a level of income (output) of y, where the AD and AS curves intersect.

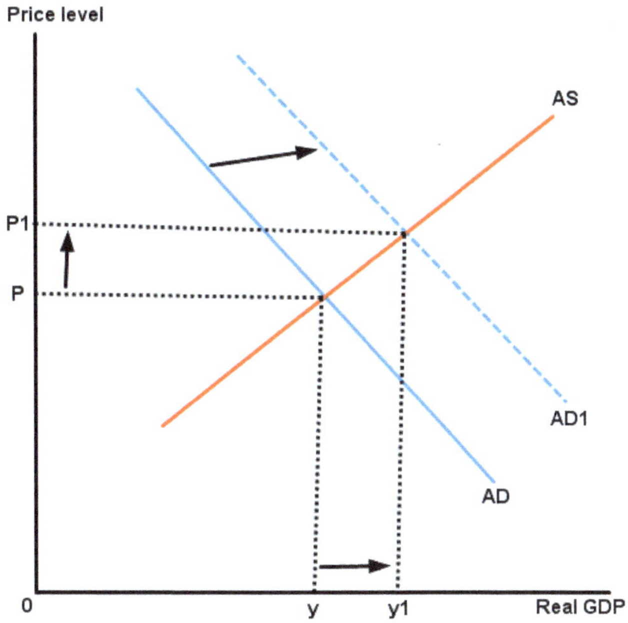

An increase in government spending, other things being equal, will shift the AD curve from AD to AD1 as shown in the diagram. As a result, the equilibrium level of income increases from y to y1 as shown in the diagram. (Incidentally, the price level rises from P to P1).

(Keynesian Cross Diagram)

For simplicity, let's assume that the economy is closed. The equilibrium level of income occurs where Y = C + I + G, where C = consumption, I = investment, and G = government spending. In the following diagram, the economy is initially in equilibrium at Y where the C + I + G line crosses the 45-degree line.

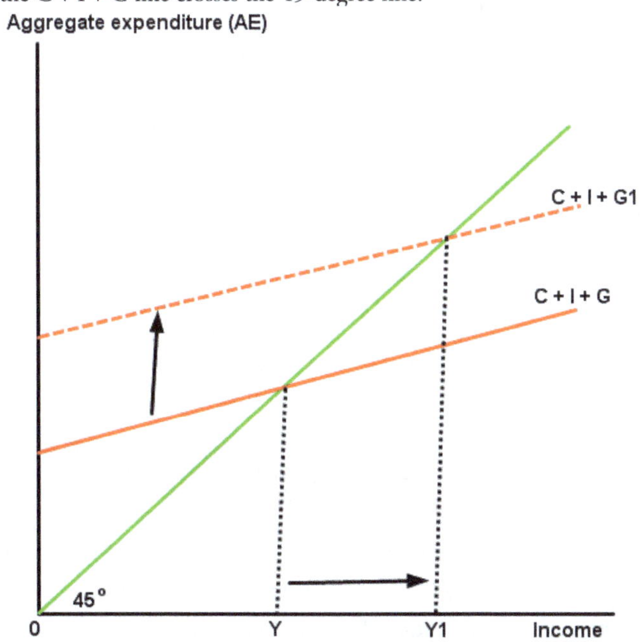

An increase in government spending from G to G1 will shift the C + I + G line up to C + I + G1 as shown in the diagram. The equilibrium level of income rises from Y to Y1. Thus, we can conclude that the effect of an increase in government spending, other things being equal is to increase the equilibrium level of income.

Problem 12-3

Tax cuts are expansionary. Discuss.

Requirement and Clue: *You are required to examine the statement carefully and decide whether it is true. The discussion would involve an explanation as to why you agree or disagree with the statement.*

Solution

To say that an action is expansionary in an economic sense means that it increases aggregate expenditure, thus causing the economy to expand.

Tax cuts leave more money in people's hands so they can spend more. Thus tax cuts enable consumers to buy more consumer goods and services and enable firms to spend more on investment. Tax cuts therefore increase private-sector spending. We can see the effect of this increase in private-sector spending on the economy with the help of the following diagram.

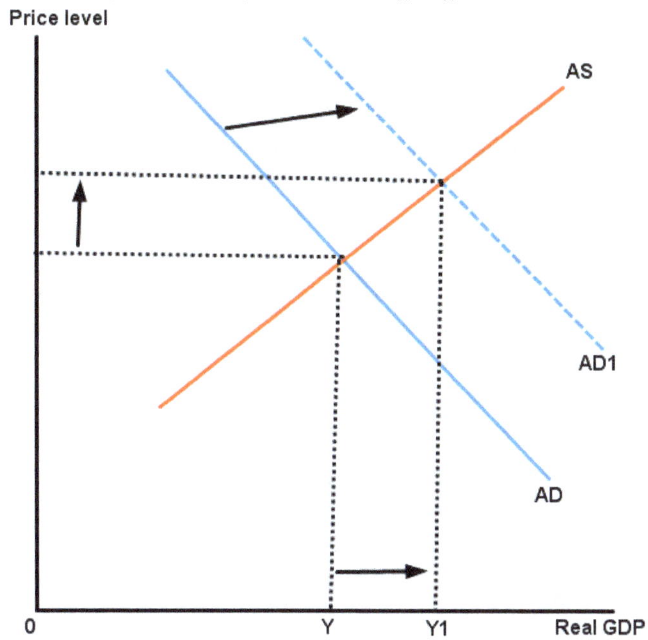

The diagram shows the economy in equilibrium initially at Y where the aggregate demand and aggregate supply curves intersect. A tax cut will increase consumption and investment and shift the aggregate demand (AD) curve to the right from AD to AD1 as shown in the diagram. As a result, real GDP rises from Y to Y1 as shown. It can be concluded then that tax cuts are expansionary.

Problem 12-4

Define each of the following concepts with respect to the government's budget:

(a) Budget deficit

(b) Balanced budget

(c) Functional finance

(d) Budget surplus

Requirement and Clue: This is a definitional problem. State exactly and precisely the meaning of the concepts without entering into any lengthy discussion.

Solution

(a) A budget deficit is the condition that exists when government spending exceeds tax revenues. For example, if government spending in a year is $750 billion while its tax revenues in the same year amount to $700 billion, then there is a budget deficit of $50 billion. It means that the government is borrowing money.

(b) A balanced budget is a condition in which government spending equals its tax revenues. For example, if the government spends $700 billion in one year and collects $700 billion in the same year, then it has a balanced budget.

(c) Functional finance is the intentional use of deficits and surpluses to achieve desired economic objectives. For example, a government may deliberately run a deficit in order to increase total spending to stimulate economic activity.

(d) A budget surplus is the condition in which government spending is less than its tax revenues. For example, if the government spends $700 billion in a year and collects $730 billion in the same year, then it has a budget surplus of $30 billion. This means that the government is saving.

Problem 12-5

Use an appropriate diagram to show the effect of an increase in government spending on the equilibrium level of income, other things being equal.

Requirement and Clue: *This problem is a test of your ability to use graphs. Either the Keynesian cross diagram, the injections-withdrawals diagram, or the AD/AS model would be appropriate.*

Solution

An increase in government spending is an injection into the circular flow of income and expenditure. Other things being equal, the effect of such an injection is to raise the equilibrium level of income. Consider the diagram below.

In the diagram, the I + G line represents the sum of investment and government spending. The economy is assumed to be closed. The S + T line represents the sum of saving and taxes. The economy is in equilibrium initially at a level of income of Y where the I + G line and the S + T line intersect.

An increase in government spending from G to G1 shifts the I + G line up from I + G to I + G1. The equilibrium level of income increases from Y to Y1 as shown in the diagram. It is shown that an increase in government spending, other things being equal, will increase the equilibrium level of income.

Note: See also Problem 12-2 and the solution provided.

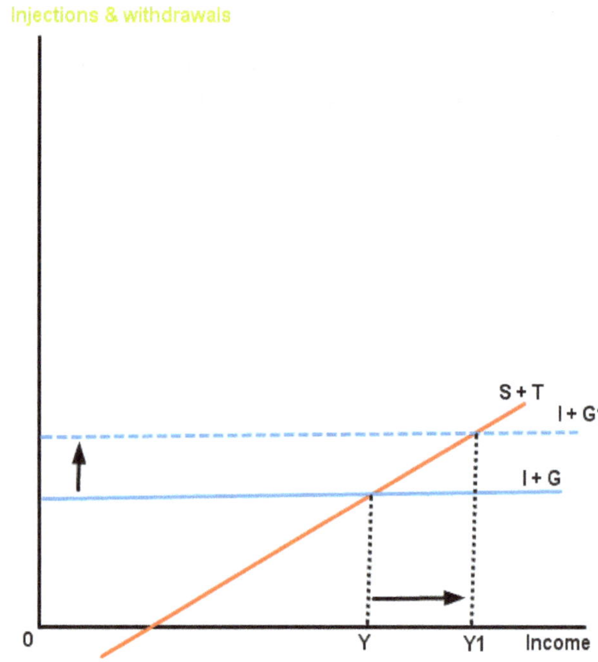

Problem 12-6

Explain the balanced budget theorem.

Requirement and Clue: *It is a good idea to state the balanced budget theorem and then explain, with an example, why a change in government spending exerts a more powerful influence on the equilibrium level of income than does an equivalent change in taxes.*

Solution

The balanced budget theorem states that if government spending and taxes increase by the same amount, the resulting increase in income will equal the increase in government spending. In other words, the balanced budget multiplier is 1.

Suppose that the spending multiplier is 2 throughout the economy. An increase in government spending of $20 million will generate an increase in income of $40 million. A government spending multiplier of 2 implies a marginal propensity to save (MPS) of 0.5 and a marginal propensity to consume (MPC) of 0.5. An increase in taxes of $20 million will therefore cause domestic spending to fall initially not by $20 million, but by $10 million (one half of $20 million). With a multiplier of 2, the total decrease in income will be $20 million. Thus, a balanced budget change in spending is not neutral. A balanced budget change in spending is actually expansionary.

Problem 12-7

What is the difference between automatic fiscal policy and discretionary fiscal policy? Give an example of each.

Requirement and Clue: *This is a two-part problem. Answer each part in order. For the first part of the problem, you are required to emphasize the difference between both types of fiscal policy. One example of automatic fiscal policy and one of discretionary fiscal policy is required.*

Solution

Automatic fiscal policy is fiscal policy that is built into the economic system and works automatically. These automatic fiscal policy measures are also called built-in stabilizers because they tend to stabilize the economy. Discretionary fiscal policy, on the other hand, is deliberate changes in government spending and taxes aimed at achieving desired economic objectives. Automatic fiscal policy does not require deliberate intervention. Discretionary fiscal policy does require government intervention.

An example of an automatic (built-in) stabilizer is the progressive tax system. In a progressive tax system, as income increases, the proportion of income paid in taxes increases. The more income one earns, the greater the percentage of that income one must pay in taxes. Because taxes are withdrawals from the income-expenditure stream, they tend to have a contractionary effect on income. Progressive taxes prevent the economy from expanding as fast as it would in the absence of progressive taxes. Conversely, when the economy is in a recession, income tends to fall; and in a progressive tax system, taxes fall even faster. This decrease in taxes prevents the economy from falling as deeply into the recession as would be the case in the absence of progressive taxes.

An example of discretionary fiscal policy is deliberate increase in government spending designed to stimulate economic activity. Suppose that the economy is experiencing unemployment and that the government wants to reduce the unemployment rate. One fiscal policy action it can take is to increase its spending. This deliberate increase in government spending will tend to increase income and consumption. Firms noticing that the demand for their products is increasing, will want to produce more goods and services and will tend to hire more workers, thus reducing the unemployment rate.

Problem 12-8

Explain the fiscal drag.

Requirement and Clue: *You are required not only to define the fiscal drag but also to explain it.*

Solution

Built-in stabilizers help to prevent the economy from accelerating into inflation and decelerating into a recession. However, but-in stability is not always desirable. Suppose the economy is recovering from a state of severe unemployment and low level of economic activity. As income increases, under a progressive tax system, t axes increase at a faster rate. The increase in taxes will exert a downward pressure on the economy and will this hamper economic recovery. Known as the fiscal drag, this automatic stabilizer prevents the economy from recovering from a recession.

Problem 12-9

Define each of the following concepts:

(a) *Inflationary gap*
(b) *Recessionary gap*
(c) *Contractionary fiscal policy*
(d) *Expansionary fiscal policy*

Requirement and Clue: *This is a definitional problem. You are to state clearly and precisely the meaning of each concept. Lengthy discussions are not expected.*

Solution

(a) The inflationary gap is the amount by which desired aggregate expenditure exceeds aggregate output at full employment. If the full employment level of output is $50 billion and total desired spending is $56 billion, then the inflationary gap is $6 billion.

(b) The recessionary gap, also called the deflationary gap, is the amount by which aggregate expenditure falls short of aggregate output at full employment. For example, if aggregate expenditure at full employment is $60 billion and the full-employment output is $53 billion, then the recessionary gap is $7 billion.

(c) Contractionary fiscal policy is any fiscal policy measure that results in a decrease in aggregate expenditure. Thus, decreases in government spending and/or increases in taxes are examples of contractionary fiscal policy.

(d) Expansionary fiscal policy is any fiscal policy measure that results in an increase in aggregate expenditure. Thus, increases in government spending and/or reductions in taxes are examples of expansionary fiscal policy.

Problem 12-10

With the help of an appropriate diagram, explain how fiscal policy can be used to lessen an inflationary gap.

Requirement and Clue: *When an inflationary gap exists, there is upward pressure on the price level. Focus on fiscal policy measures that can be used to reduce the pressure on the price level.*

Solution

An inflationary gap is the amount by which aggregate expenditure exceeds aggregate output at full employment. In terms of the aggregate demand-aggregate supply model, aggregate demand is too high and needs to be reduced. The following diagram will help to illustrate how fiscal policy can be used to reduce an inflationary gap.

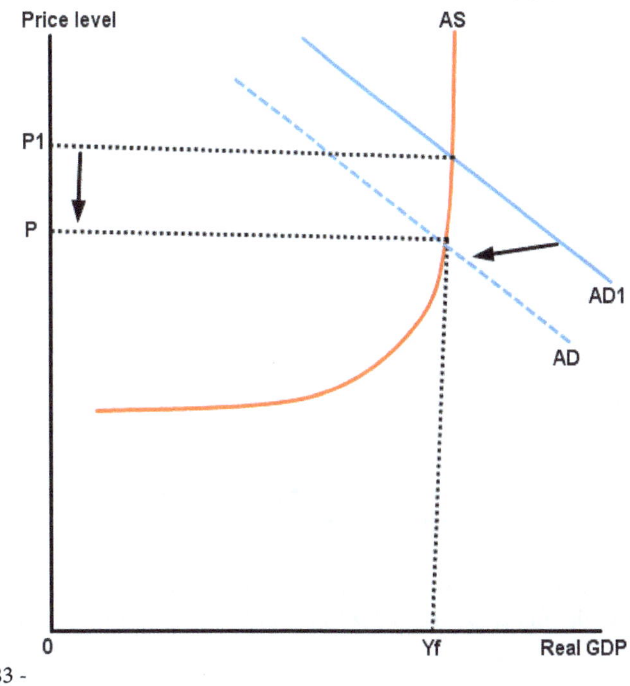

The diagram illustrates an inflationary situation. Aggregate demand is currently represented by AD1. It intersects the aggregate supply (AS) curve at a price level of P1 instead of the desired full-employment price level of P. The problem here is that aggregate demand is too high and must be reduced from AD1 to AD to eliminate the inflationary gap.

A reduction in government spending reduces desired aggregate expenditure and hence income. The fall in income results in a reduction in planned consumption and investment. In the diagram, the reduction in planned aggregate expenditure shifts the aggregate demand curve from AD1 to AD. This eliminates the inflationary gap, and equilibrium occurs at the full-employment level of output with a price level of P.

An increase in taxes will produce a similar result. An increase in taxes reduces disposable income, which in turn decreases planned consumption and investment spending. As before, the aggregate demand curve shifts downward from AD1 to AD, reducing or eliminating the inflationary pressure.

Problem 12-11

Explain how fiscal policy may be used to reduce unemployment. What difficulties are associated with the use of fiscal policy?

Requirement and Clue: *This is a two-part problem. Answer each part in order. A diagram will be helpful in solving the first part of the problem. For the second part of the problem, focus on the accuracy of the available information and the problems caused by time lags.*

Solution

Fiscal policy refers to the government's spending and tax policies aimed at affecting changes in income and employment. Since the budget is the instrument of fiscal policy, the term "budgetary policy" is sometimes used. Unemployment may be caused by a deficiency of aggregate demand. The situation is illustrated in the following diagram.

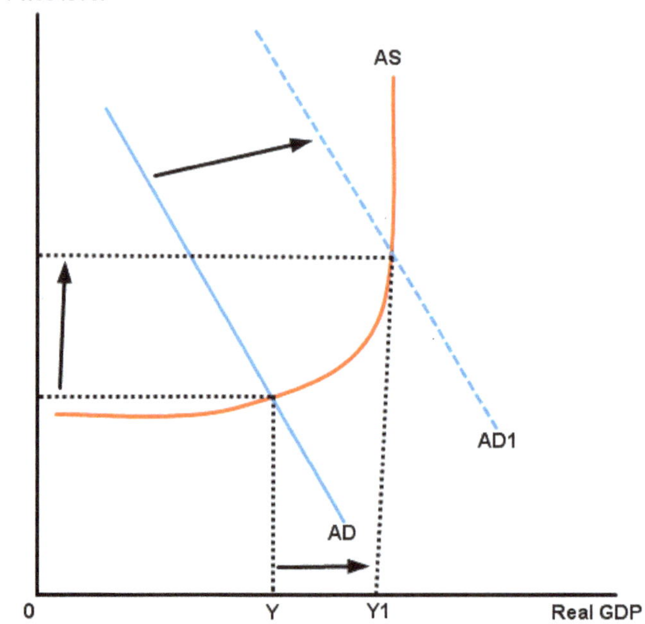

The economy is at an equilibrium level of income of Y, which is below the full-employment level of Yf. In order to achieve full employment, aggregate demand (AD) will have to increase from AD to AD1. This increase in aggregate demand can be achieved by increasing government spending or by reducing taxes. If the government increases its spending, income will rise. As income increases, consumption and investment will likely increase. Thus, aggregate demand and employment will increase. If the government reduces taxes, disposable income will increase. This increase in disposable income will likely generate additional consumption and investment, causing an increase in real GDP and employment.

However, the situation is unlikely to be so easy in the real world. There are two main difficulties associated with the use of fiscal policy. First, it is often difficult to obtain precise estimates of the magnitude of expenditure that would be required to eliminate the unemployment. Because of the pressing need to counteract a situation of unemployment, there is a tendency to apply an overdose of medicine. The expenditure that is undertaken may be so large that after the multiplier has had its effect, the economy plunges into a situation of excess demand inflation.

The second difficulty associated with the use of fiscal policy is the time lag. The time that it takes for the effects of fiscal policy to be felt in the economy is very uncertain. It could very well turn out that by the time fiscal policy takes effect, other factors may have ca used certain changes in the economic situation so that the effects of fiscal policy may do more harm than good.

Problem 12-12

What tax policy would you suggest to offset the fiscal drag?

Requirement and Clue: *To begin with, a definition of fiscal drag is in order. Focus on how to increase spending without increasing taxes.*

Solution

The fiscal drag is an undesirable built-in stabilizer that prevents the economy from recovering from a state of high unemployment and low economic activity. The solution to the fiscal drag is to increase spending without at the same time increasing taxes. Thus, the granting of tax rebates will help to offset the fiscal drag.

Problem 12-13

Discuss the advantages and disadvantages of government spending over taxes as a tool of fiscal policy.

Requirement and Clue: *Changes in government spending and taxes can help to bring about desired economic conditions. You are to focus on ways by which changes in government spending are superior to tax changes and ways in which they are inferior.*

Solution

One of the advantages of using government spending to control macroeconomic activity is that it is a more powerful tool than tax changes. A $20 billion increase in government spending will have a greater impact on the economy than a tax cut of the same magnitude. Another advantage of government spending over tax changes is that changes in government spending can be focussed specific areas or regions. For example, if there is widespread unemployment in certain regions but not in others, a tax cut designed to reduce unemployment in those regions may cause inflation in other regions. In such a case, government spending programs can be targeted to increase expenditure in regions suffering from high unemployment.

A major disadvantage of government spending programs as a means of achieving economic objectives is that they take a long time to get under way. Highway construction and other public works programs require a considerable amount of planning time. Another disadvantage of government spending as a fiscal policy tool is the difficulty of reversing certain government spending programs. Indeed, it may be political suicide to try to eliminate certain programs. Moreover, certain projects, once in progress, cannot be abandoned without an immense waste of resources.

Problem 12-14

What are the advantages of changes in taxes over changes in government spending as a fiscal policy tool?

Requirement and Clue: *Changes in taxes have certain advantages over changes in government spending. You are to focus on these advantages.*

Solution

A tax cut designed to stimulate the economy is likely to be more favourably received than an increase in government spending. The tax cut will likely benefit more people directly as it increases their disposable income. Furthermore, people who believe that the government is already too big will resist increases in government spending.

Another advantage of using changes in taxes is that it may be easier and less wasteful to change taxes when economic conditions change. For example, if a tax cut is instituted to combat high unemployment, it may be easier to re-impose taxes when the situation improves than to cut certain government programs.

Yet another advantage of tax changes over changes in government spending is the relative speed with which tax changes can be implemented. In cases where a quick change is desired, tax changes may be preferable to changes in government spending.

Problem 12-15

How does fiscal policy affect the supply side of the economy?

Requirement and Clue: *Focus on how changes in government spending and taxes affect the economy's productive capacity.*

Solution

Anything that affects the productive capacity of the economy is a supply side factor. Let us focus first on government spending. If the government spends money on education and health, then such spending increases the economy's productive capacity. Likewise, government spending on capital goods, such as infrastructure (roads, rail systems, water systems, etc.) increases the economy's overall productivity. Such expenditures increase aggregate supply. A decrease in government spending can have a negative effect on the economy's production possibilities and hence can reduce aggregate supply.

Changes in taxes can also have supply-side effects. An increase in taxes reduces work incentives and causes people to save less. A reduction in saving reduces the funds available for productive investment purposes. Therefore, an increase in taxes reduces aggregate supply. A reduction in taxes, on the other hand, encourages work effort and increases saving. A reduction in taxes therefore increases aggregate supply.

Problem 12-16

How do supply-side considerations affect the conclusion that an expansionary fiscal policy will raise the price level?

Requirement and Clue: *A brief statement of the meaning of an expansionary fiscal policy is in order. Focus on the effects of an expansionary fiscal policy on the supply side of the economy.*

Solution

An expansionary fiscal policy refers to changes in government spending and taxes that increase aggregate expenditure. Considering only the demand-side effects of expansionary fiscal policy, an increase in government spending and/or a reduction in taxes will increase aggregate demand and raise the price level. However, when supply-side effects are considered, an increase in government spending and/or a reduction in taxes will increase aggregate supply and lower the price level. If the demand-side effects are stronger than the supply-side effects, then the price level will rise. If the demand-side effects are weaker than the supply-side effects, then the price level will fall. If the demand-side effects and the supply-side effects are equal, then the price level will not be affected.

Problem 12-17

Define each of the following lags:

(a) *Recognition lag*
(b) *Decision lag*
(c) *Implementation lag*
(d) *Impact lag*

Requirement and Clue: *This is a multi-part problem. Answer each part in order. You are required to state clearly and precisely the meaning of each concept.*

Solution

(a) It may take a while to recognise that a problem exists. The recognition lag is the time that elapses between the occurrence of a situation and the full recognition of that situation.

(b) The decision lag is the time that elapses between the recognition of the existence of a problem or situation and the decision to act on it.

(c) The implementation lag is the time that elapses between the decision to act on a problem or situation and the implementation of the decision.

(d) The impact lag (also called the effect lag) is the time that elapses between the implementation of a decision and its effects on the economy.

Problem 12-18

What are some of the limitations of fiscal policy?

Requirement and Clue: *Focus on three or four factors that adversely affect the effectiveness of fiscal policy.*

Solution

One of the limitations of fiscal policy is the existence of time lags. Before action can be taken, the problem must be recognized. Then it takes time to decide on the action to be taken. Once a decision is made, it takes time to implement the decision. Finally, after the decision is implemented, it takes time for the effects to be realized.

Another limitation of fiscal policy is the difficulty of varying government spending and taxes to suit economic conditions. Many expenditure items cannot be varied to any appreciable extent. For example, the salaries of civil servants cannot be varied as a means of stabilizing the economy. Similarly, the amounts spent on defence and as interest payments on the public debt cannot be varied in response to fluctuations in economic activity. Tax cuts are attractive to the government because voters like them. Tax increases are considerably less popular. So although it may be relatively easy to reduce taxes, it can be considerably more difficult to increase them when the economic situation warrants it.

The nature of the structure of government is another problem associated with fiscal policy. During a recession, an expansionary fiscal policy is appropriate, but the revenues of government decline during a recession. Government spending also tends to decline. Thus the actions of other levels of government can reduce the effectiveness of the fiscal policy being pursued by the federal government.

Another problem with the use of fiscal policy is that during periods of heavy national debt when the government is committed to reducing the deficit and to arresting the growth of the national debt, it may be difficult for the government to use expansionary fiscal policy to stimulate the economy.

Problem 12-19

Use the Keynesian 45-degree diagram to show the effect of each of the following on net domestic income.

(a) *The imposition of a lump-sum tax on income*

(b) *An increase in the tax rate.*

Requirement and Clue: *This is a two-part problem. Answer each part in order. In each case focus on how the tax will affect the consumption curve and thus the aggregate expenditure curve.*

Solution

(a) The equilibrium level of net domestic income is Y in the following diagram. The imposition of a lump-sum tax on income will reduce consumption and thus lower the aggregate expenditure (AE) line from AE to AE0 as shown in the diagram.

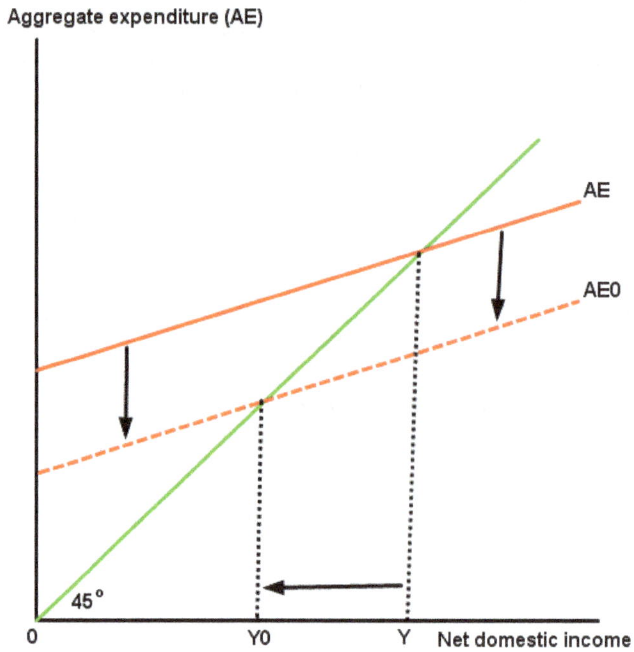

The level of net domestic income falls from Y to Y0.

(b) In the following diagram, the initial equilibrium level of net domestic income is Y. An increase in the tax rate causes the slope of the consumption line to change, and consequently, the slope of the aggregate expenditure (AE) line changes as shown in the diagram. The result is a fall in the equilibrium level of net domestic income from Y to Y0.

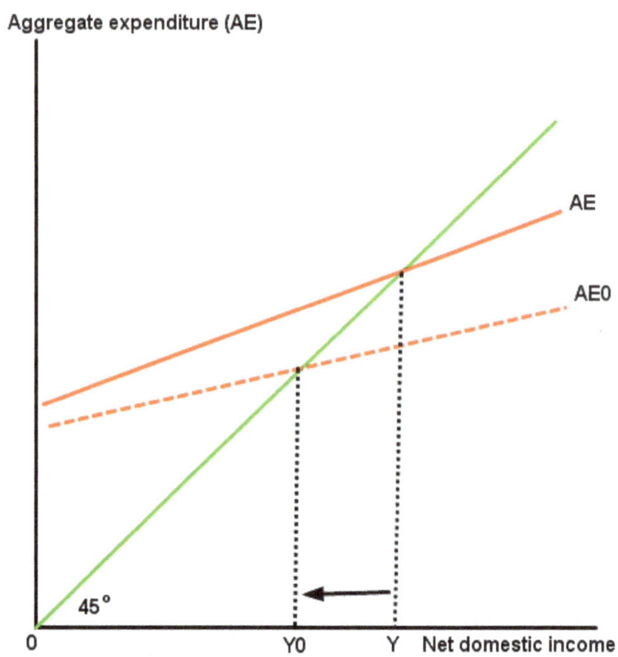

Problem 12-20

In the left-hand column of the following table are seven statements related to fiscal policy. Place each of the following terms in the right-hand column to match the statement in the left-hand column.

Misconception - Decision lag - Fiscal policy - Budget deficit - Taxes - Budget surplus - Fiscal drag

Statement	Matching term
(a) *Changes in government spending and taxes*	
(b) *A situation in which government spending is less then tax revenues*	
(c) *The view that government spending and taxes have no effect on the level of economic activity*	
(d) *This is an automatic stabilizer that prevents the economy from recovering from a recession*	
(e) *The time that elapses between the recognition of a problem and the time when a decision is made*	
(f) *This results when the government spends more than it collects in taxes*	
(g) *This, along with government spending, is used as a fiscal policy tool.*	

Requirement and Clue: *This problem is designed to test your knowledge of concepts and terms related to fiscal policy. Care and attention to detail are required.*

Solution

Statement	Matching term
(a) *Changes in government spending and taxes*	Fiscal policy
(b) *A situation in which government spending is less then tax revenues*	Budget surplus
(c) *The view that government spending and taxes have no effect on the level of economic activity*	Misconception
(d) *This is an automatic stabilizer that prevents the economy from recovering from a recession*	Fiscal drag
(e) *The time that elapses between the recognition of a problem and the time when a decision is made*	Decision lag
(f) *This results when the government spends more than it collects in taxes*	Budget deficit
(g) *This, along with government spending, is used as a fiscal policy tool.*	Taxes

Problem 12-21

Read the following statement carefully and point out any errors that you detect.

"The total effect of an increase in government spending of $100,000 is an increase in net domestic income of $100,000. The total of a tax cut of $100,000 is an increase in net domestic income of $100,000. As far as the total impact on net domestic income goes, it is immaterial whether the government increases its spending or reduces taxes by the same amount. They are equally expansionary."

Requirement and Clue: *You are expected to read the given statement critically. Mention any errors detected and offer a correction.*

Solution

An increase in government spending and a reduction in taxes of the same magnitude are both expansionary, but not equally so. An expenditure of $100,000 by the government is a direct injection of that amount into the economy. A tax reduction of $100,000 means that consumers' disposable income rises by $100,000, but it is likely that only a part of that amount will be injected into the economy, while a part will be saved, depending on the marginal propensity to consume (MPC). A part may also be spent on imported goods. Clearly the, an increase in government spending of a certain amount is more expansionary than an equal reduction in taxes.

Multiple-Choice

In each case, circle the letter that corresponds with the correct answer.

1. In a closed economy with government, income will be at its equilibrium level when:

a. saving equals investment
b. the sum of investment and government spending equals the sum of saving and taxes
c. government spending equals taxes
d. none of the above

Answer: c

Reason: *In a closed economy with government, injections are investment (I) and government spending (G). Withdrawals are saving (S) and taxes (T). Equilibrium occurs when the sum of the injections equals the sum of the withdrawals.*

2. If a closed economy with government spending and taxation is in equilibrium, then:

a. the budget must be balanced
b. the sum of consumption, investment, and government spending must be equal to aggregate output
c. aggregate expenditure is greater than aggregate output
d. none of the above

Answer: b

Reason: *In equilibrium, aggregate expenditure equals aggregate output.*

3. If government spending increases by X and taxes increase by X, then we know that:

a. the budget must be balanced
b. there is a balanced budget change in spending
c. there must be a budget surplus
d. there must be a budget deficit

Answer: b

Reason: *A balanced budget change in spending occurs when a change in government spending equals a change in taxes.*

Questions 4, 5, and 6 refer to the following diagram.

- *The full-employment output is $90 billion.*
- *G is government spending and T is taxes.*

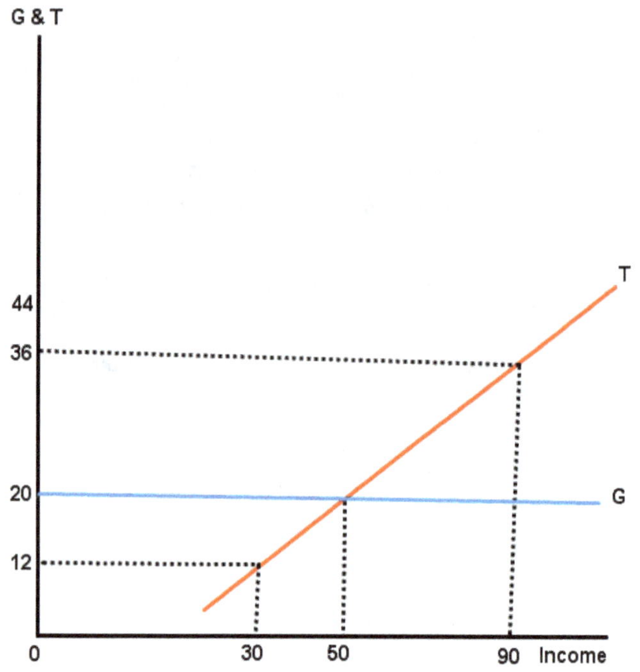

4. The full-employment budget:

a. has a deficit of $16 billion
b. has a deficit of $8 billion
c. is in balance
d. has a surplus of $16 billion

Answer: d

Reason: *At full-employment, T = 36 billion and G = 20 billion; therefore there is a surplus of $16 billion.*

5. At what level of output is the budget balanced?

a. $30 billion
b. $20 billion
c. $50 billion
d. $90 billion

Answer: c

Reason: *G = T at an output level of $50 billion*

6. Suppose that at an output of $90 billion, desired consumption is $50 billion, and desired investment is $10 billion. If full-employment is achieved by changing G, leaving the tax system unchanged, which of the following would result?

a. A reduced full-employment surplus
b. A full-employment deficit
c. A balanced full-employment budget
d. None of the above

Answer: a

Reason: *The increase in government spending with taxes remaining unchanged, would narrow the gap between taxes and government spending at full-employment.*

7. If government spending and taxes both increase by $50 million, other things being equal, net domestic income will:

a. increase by $50 million
b. remain constant
c. increase by less than $50 million
d. none of the above

Answer: a

Reason: *This is the balanced budget theorem.*

8. Fiscal policy:
   a. refers to changes in government spending and taxes
   b. refers to changes in exchange rates to improve the terms of trade
   c. changes in the money supply to achieve economic stability
   d. is conducted by the central bank

Answer: a

Reason: Fiscal policy is the manipulation of government spending and taxes to regulate economic activity.

9. Automatic stabilizers include:
   a. progressive taxes
   b. employment insurance benefits
   c. government assistance to agriculture
   d. all of the above

Answer: d

Reason: Choices a, b, and c are fiscal policy measures that are built into the economic system.

10. A built-in stabilizer that prevents the economy from recovering from a recession is called:
    a. recession stabilizer
    b. fiscal drag
    c. recession lag
    d. none of the above

Answer: b

Reason: The fiscal drag is an automatic (built-in) stabilizer that inhibits economic recovery.

11. Any fiscal policy measure that results in an increase in aggregate demand is said to be:
    a. demand specific
    b. expansionary
    c. aggregate intensive
    d. restrictive

Answer: b

Reason: An expansionary fiscal policy is one that results in an increase in aggregate demand.

12. A contractionary fiscal policy is any fiscal policy measure that:
    a. causes inflation
    b. increases employment
    c. reduces aggregate spending
    d. increases GDP

Answer: c

Reason: Any fiscal policy measure that reduces aggregate spending is said to be contractionary.

13. Other things being equal, a reduction in income taxes can:
    a. cause the aggregate demand curve to shift to the right
    b. cause the aggregate supply curve to shift to the right
    c. cause national income to rise
    d. all of the above

Answer: d

Reason: A reduction in income taxes, other things being equal, causes consumption to rise, thus increasing aggregate demand. A reduction in income taxes also causes workers to exert greater work effort, thus increasing aggregate supply. Both increase national income.

14. In order to combat an inflationary situation, the government could:
    a. increase its spending and reduce taxes
    b. increase its spending and increase taxes
    c. reduce its spending and increase taxes
    d. none of the above

Answer: c

Reason: In an inflationary situation, the appropriate fiscal policy is a contractionary one. This is consistent with choice c.

15. In general, advantages of using government spending rather than taxes to regulate economic activity include:
    a. government spending is more powerful
    b. government spending can be focused on specific regions
    c. neither a nor b
    d. both a and b

Answer: d

Reason: The government spending multiplier is greater than the tax multiplier and government spending can be more easily targeted to specific areas.

16. Which of the following is a limitation of fiscal policy?
    a. The presence of time lags
    b. The inflexibility of government spending and tax measures
    c. Poor coordination between various levels of government
    d. All of the above

Answer: d

Reason: Choices a, b, and c all reduce the effectiveness of fiscal policy.

17. The full-employment budget is:
    a. a budget that guarantees full-employment
    b. the position of the budget when it is in balance
    c. a budget that is designed to produce economic stability
    d. none of the above

Answer: d

Reason: The full-employment budget is the position of the budget if the economy were at full employment.

18. Fiscal policy affects:
    a. the demand side of the economy only
    b. the supply side of the economy only
    c. neither the demand side nor the supply side
    d. none of the above

Answer: d

Reason: Fiscal policy affects both the demand side and the supply side of the economy.

True-False Questions

Determine whether each of the following statements is true or false.

1. Government spending cannot affect economic activity unless there are also tax changes.

Answer: False

Explanation: *Changes in government spending, with no changes in taxes, can affect aggregate expenditure and thus the level of economic activity.*

2. The government's fiscal policy is conducted by the central bank under the direction of the Finance Department.

Answer: False

Explanation: Fiscal policy is conducted by the government.

3. Other things being equal, an increase in government spending will increase equilibrium income.

Answer: True

4. To increase aggregate expenditure, the government may reduce its spending, or increase taxes.

Answer: False

Explanation: *These measures will reduce (not increase) aggregate expenditure.*

5. The government spending multiplier is larger than the investment multiplier because the government has more power than firms do.

Answer: False

Explanation: *The government spending multiplier and the investment multiplier are the same. Each of the reciprocal of the marginal propensity to save.*

6. An increase in taxes, other things being equal, reduces the equilibrium level of income.

Answer: True

7. A balanced budget means that, by definition, the government's budget always balances.

Answer: False

Explanation: *A balanced budget means that government spending and tax revenues are equal, but the budget is not always in this position.*

8. A budget deficit exists when government spending exceeds tax revenues.

Answer: True

9. If the budget is in a deficit position, a balanced budget change in spending will leave it in a deficit position.

Answer: True

10. Automatic stabilizers are the mechanisms built into the tax and transfer system that automatically stabilize the economy.

Answer: True

11. The fiscal drag refers to the tendency of automatic stabilizers to reduce the impact of expansionary fiscal policy.

Answer: True

12. The balanced budget theorem states that an increase in taxes followed by an equal increase in government spending will leave the level of income unchanged.

Answer: False

Explanation: *The balanced budget theorem states than an increase in government spending accompanied by an equivalent increase in taxes will cause equilibrium income to increase by an amount equal to the increase in government spending.*

13. Functional finance refers to attempts by the government to maintain a balanced budget at all times.

Answer: False

Explanation: *Functional finance is the intentional use of budget deficits and surpluses to achieve desired economic objectives.*

14. If the economy is in a recession, the appropriate fiscal policy is an increase in government spending and/or a decrease in taxes.

Answer: True

15. If an economy is at full employment, an increase in government spending, other things being equal, will increase aggregate expenditure and cause the price level to rise.

Answer: True

16. Changes in the budget do not necessarily indicate changes in fiscal policy. Changes in the full-employment budget, however, do indicate changes in fiscal policy.

Answer: True

17. Fiscal policy can shift the aggregate supply curve.

Answer: True

18. Greater coordination between the various levels of government could conceivably increase the effectiveness of fiscal policy.

Answer: True

Completion

(Fill in the blanks)

Use each word or combination of words from the list exactly once.
*(**Hint**: Proceed by elimination)*

Word list

Automatic — Decrease — Deficit — Drag — Fiscal — Full-employment — Impact or effect — Increase — Inflation — Reduce — Reduces — Spending — Stabilizers — Surplus — Taxing — Unemployment

Questions

1. Fiscal policy is the use of government __________ and __________ powers to regulate economic activity.
2. If the government currently spends more than it collects in taxes, then it has a budget __________. If it currently spends less than its tax revenues, then it has a budget __________.
3. An increase in government spending, other things being equal, will result in a(n) __________ [increase, decrease] in net domestic income. An increase in taxes, other things being equal, will result in a(n) __________ [increase, decrease] in net domestic income.
4. Fiscal policy measures that are built into the economic system, and that operate automatically to promote economic stability are called __________ __________.
5. The __________ __________ is an undesirable built-in stabilizer that prevents the economy from recovering from a state of high unemployment and low economic activity.
6. A contractionary or restrictive fiscal policy is appropriate if the economy is experiencing __________ without __________.
7. Changes in the budget do not necessarily indicate changes in fiscal policy, but changes in the __________ budget indicate changes in fiscal policy.
8. The lag that elapses between the implementation of a policy and its effects on aggregate expenditure is the __________ lag.
9. The existence of time lags __________ [increases, reduces] the effectiveness of fiscal policy.
10. Poor coordination between various levels of government may __________ [reduce, increase] the effectiveness of fiscal policy.

Solutions

1. (spending (and) taxing)
2. (deficit, surplus)
3. (increase, decrease)
4. (automatic stabilizers)
5. (fiscal drag)
6. (inflation, unemployment)
7. (full-employment)
8. (impact or effect)
9. (reduces)
10. (reduce)

13 MONEY

LEARNING OBJECTIVES

In connection with this module, you should be able to:

1. explain the concept of money
2. discuss the functions of money
3. distinguish between money and money substitutes
4. explain how the money supply is measured
5. explain the meaning of the value of money
6. discuss the relationship between the money supply and inflation, and between the money supply and unemployment

DEFINITIONS & CONCEPTS

You should be able to define the following terms and concepts:

medium of exchange	unit of account
store of value	barter
double coincidence of wants	liquidity
currency	demand deposits
notice deposits	legal tender
fiat money	Gresham's law
near money	payments system
automatic teller machines	debit card
electronic funds transfer system	

SYNOPSIS

Money is anything that is generally accepted by members of a society as payment for goods and services or as settlement of a debt. The most important function of money is to serve as a **medium of exchange**. Other functions served by money are the **unit of account** and **store of value**.

The use of money avoids the exchange problems associated with the **barter system** which requires a **double coincidence of wants**. It also reduces the costs of making transactions and promotes economic efficiency.

The three kinds of money in common use are coins, notes, and checking accounts. Although these three items constitute the stock of money available for spnding in the economy, there are **near monies** and **money substitutes**.

The **payments system** refers to the set of arrangements whereby the exchange of goods and services is carried out. The payments system in many countries is quite advanced. Through the use of computers and telecommunications technology, the system is highly automated. For example, **the electronic funds transfer system (EFTS)** allows for the instantaneous transfer of deposit of funds.

The value of money refers to its purchasing power. If a given sum of money can buy fewer goods and services than previously, then the value of money has fallen. If it can buy more goods and services than previously, then its value has increased. In other words, the value of money is inversely related to the price level.

Excessive increases in the money supply can result in inflation. Inadequate growth or reductions in the money supply can result in economic recessions with the attendant increase in unemployment.

13 Money

Concepts, Definitions & Problems

Problem 13-1

What is money? How does money differ from near money?

Requirement and Clue: *This is a two-part problem. Answer each part in order. The first part is definitional. You are expected to state clearly and precisely what money is without writing an essay on money. For the second part, you must focus on the difference between the two concepts.*

Solution

Money is anything that is generally accepted as final payment for goods and services. It includes demand deposits, paper currency, and coins. Money is 100% liquid. Near money is any highly liquid asset that can be quickly converted into the medium of exchange—demand deposits or currency. A savings account is a good example of near money.

Problem 13-2

What are the economic functions of money in a modern economy?

Requirement and Clue: *Money performs different functions for different people. It might confer social status, it may make one feel powerful or secure, and just having it might make some people happy or miserable. You are not concerned here with these functions. Your concern is with the "economic" functions of money.*

Solution

The most important economic function of money is to serve as a medium of exchange. Money performs this function when we use it to buy goods and services or to settle debts. When you use money to pay for a course, to pay for a taxi ride, to buy a restaurant meal, etc. you are using it as a medium of exchange.

Besides functioning as a medium of exchange, money also serves as a measure of value or as a unit of account. Money gives information about the value of goods and services in terms of dollars and cents. If we are looking at two items with price tags of $200 and $500, we can conclude that the item with the $500 price tag is more valuable than the one with the $200 price tag. Prices are an example of money serving as a measure of value.

Finally, money serves as a store of value. When we get our paycheques, we do not immediately go out and spend it all. We often save a portion of it to purchase goods and services in the future. Money functions as a store of value when we deposit it in a savings account at a bank.

Problem 13-3

What are the major items that serve as money in a modern economy?

Requirement and Clue: *Focus on things that are used to pay for goods and services or to settle debts.*

Solution:

The major items that serve as money in a modern economy are coins, notes, and chequing accounts.

Coins include pennies, nickels, dimes, quarters, fifty cents, dollar coins, and two-dollar coins. These are used to make small purchases and to make change.

Notes or paper currency are issued by the central bank, and come in denominations of $1, $2, $5, $10, $20, $50, and $100 depending on the country.

Chequing accounts or demand deposits are deposits on commercial banks that can be transferred by writing cheques. They constitute the largest share of the money supply in a modern economy.

Problem 13-4

Define each of the following terms:

(a) *Token money*

(b) *Fiat money*

(c) *Legal tender*

Requirement and Clue: *This is a three-part problem. Answer each part in order. You are expected to state clearly and precisely the meaning of each term without embarking on a lengthy discussion.*

Solution

(a) Token money is money whose face value exceeds its commodity value. A $1 coin will purchase a dollar's worth of goods and services. That is its face value. If it is sold on the market as metal, it would fetch much less than its face value. It is token money.

(b) Fiat money is legal tender money that is not backed by gold or any other precious metal. It is money because the government has declared that it is money. Paper currency is fiat money.

(c) Legal tender money is money that must legally be accepted if offered as payment to settle debts. Fiat money is legal tender.

Problem 13-5

State and explain Gresham's law.

Requirement and Clue: *This is a two-part problem. Answer each part in order. You are expected to give a clear and precise statement of Gresham's law. Then you are to explain why the law holds.*

Solution

To state and explain Gresham's law, we use the concepts of "good money" and "bad money". Good money is money whose face value equals its commodity value. Bad money, on the other hand, is money whose face value exceeds its commodity value. Gresham's law is often stated as: "Bad money will drive good money out of circulation" or even more briefly as: "Bad money drives out good."

The law is explained as follows: If good money and bad money were circulating at the same time, people would tend to hold on to the good money because of its intrinsic value and spend the bad money instead. The good money would quickly disappear from circulation as people hoard it.

Problem 13-6

Credit cards have been called plastic money. Are credit cards money?

Requirement and Clue: *A simple "yes" or "no" answer will not suffice. You are expected to support or defend your answer. Focus on the main function of money.*

Solution

Credit cards should not be confused with money because they are not money. When money is used in a transaction, the payment is final in the sense that no further payment has to be made. When a credit card is used in a transaction, the owner of the credit card receives a bill requesting that payment be made by a specific date. No such request is made when payment is made with money. It is quite clear, then, that credit cards are not money. Credit cards are temporary substitutes for money because they enable buyers to obtain goods and services without immediately using money.

Problem 13-7

Is there any relationship between the value of money and the price level?

Requirement and Clue: *A simple "yes" or "no" will not suffice. If a relationship exists between the two concepts, then you should state that relationship.*

Solution

The value of money is what money can buy. If a given sum of money can buy more goods and services today than it could have bought a year ago, then prices have fallen and the value of money has risen. Conversely, if a given sum of money can buy fewer goods and services today than it could have bought a year ago, then prices have risen and the value of money has fallen. Thus, the value of money depends on the price level. During periods of high inflation, a given amount of money buys less this year than it did last year and more this year than it will next year. The value of money is inversely related to the price level.

Problem 13-8

Explain the effects of inflation on the "store of value" function of money.

Requirement and Clue: *It's probably a good idea to start with the meaning of the "store of value" function of money. Focus on how inflation affects money serving as a store of value.*

Solution

People may store up money now to be able to buy goods and services in the future. In this way, money serves as a store of value. It may be possible to store some commodities, but others are difficult to store because of prohibitive storage costs, or because they are bulky, or because their value diminishes rapidly. Money is a convenient form in which to store up purchasing power.

During an inflation, money loses its value. A given sum of money will be able to buy a smaller quantity of goods and services. Individuals who have saved up a large amount of money may be disappointed at finding that their money is actually worth much less when they are ready to spend it. Realization of this fact causes people to rely less on money as a store of value during an inflation. Any item that is losing its value will not perform the store of value function very well.

Problem 13-9

Define each of the following terms:

(a) *Double coincidence of wants*

(b) *Barter*

(c) *Liquidity*

Requirement and Clue: This is a three-part problem. Answer each part in order. Remember that in defining terms and concepts you are expected to state clearly and precisely the meaning of the term or concept, not to write an essay.

Solution

(a) Double coincidence of wants is a situation where trader A has exactly what trader B wants, and trader B has exactly what trader A has to trade. It is a necessary condition for barter to take place.

(b) Barter is the direct exchange of one good for another without the use of money.

(c) Liquidity is the ease with which an asset can be converted into cash without much capital loss.

Problem 13-10

In the left-hand column of the following table are situations involving different functions of money. In the right-hand column, fill in the function of money that is indicated by the situation.

Situation	Function of money
(a) *You purchase a set of books from a bookstore and pay $275.00.*	
(b) *You put $1500 in a savings account.*	
(c) *You are told that the price of a cell phone is $350.00*	
(d) *You use $60.00 to purchase a gift*	
(e) *Someone writes you a cheque for $150.00*	
(f) *Your friend says to you, "That company is worth millions of dollars."*	

Requirement and Clue: *Focus on the functions of money and think of the situations in the left-hand columns as examples of the different functions.*

Solution

Situation	Function of money
(a) *You purchase a set of books from a bookstore and pay $275.00.*	Medium of exchange
(b) *You put $1500 in a savings account.*	Store of value
(c) *You are told that the price of a cell phone is $350.00*	Measure of value
(d) *You use $60.00 to purchase a gift*	Medium of exchange
(e) *Someone writes you a cheque for $150.00*	Medium of exchange
(f) *Your friend says to you, "That company is worth millions of dollars."*	Measure of value

Multiple-Choice

In each case, circle the letter that corresponds with the correct answer.

1. Money is defined as:

a. major credit cards such as Visa and Master Card used to obtain goods and services
b. gold and other assets that contribute to wealth
c. anything that is generally accepted as final payment for goods and services
d. all of the above

Answer: c

Reason: Neither a nor b qualify as a medium of exchange and there cannot be money. Choice c does qualify.

2. The major functions of money are to serve as:

a. medium of exchange c. unit of account
b. store of value d. all of the above

Answer: d

Reason: Money serves as a medium of exchange, a unit of account, and as a store of value.

3. A price tag of $45.00 on an item is an example of money functioning as a:

a. medium of exchange c. measure of value
b. store of value d. none of the above

Answer: c

Reason: Money functioning as a measure of value gives information about the value of things. This is consistent with choice c.

4. A money economy is superior to a barter economy because:

a. it makes everyone happy
b. it does not require a double coincidence of wants for exchange to occur
c. it requires a double coincidence of wants for exchange to occur
d. none of the above

Answer: b

Reason: Barter exchange requires a double coincidence of wants; money exchange does not.

5. Which of the following represents money serving as a store of value?

a. $500.00 used to purchase a suit
b. $500.00 indicated as the price of a suit
c. $500.00 indicted as the balance in a savings account
d. All of the above

Answer: c

Reason: A store of value represents stored up purchasing power, such as the balance in a bank account.

6. Money should be:

a. generally acceptable c. divisible
b. portable d. all of the above

Answer: d

Reason: Choices a, b, and c are all desirable characteristics of money.

7. To say that an item is highly liquid means that:

a. it will maintain a stable value over time
b. it can be quickly converted into money with little or no loss of value
c. it can be quickly converted into money but only with a substantial loss of value
d. it can be converted into a soluble state.

Answer: b

Reason: The liquidity of an item is directly related to the ease with which it can be converted into the medium of exchange without much capital loss.

8. Which of the following is the most liquid asset?

a. Crude oil c. Gold bars
b. A Visa credit card d. A $50 bank note

Answer: d

Reason: Money, such as a $50 bank note, is the most liquid of all assets.

9. Which of the following is likely to be the least liquid?

a. Legal tender money
b. Canada savings bonds
c. A savings account
d. A bridge

Answer: d

Reason: A bridge is not easily converted into cash without much capital loss.

10. Paper currency today is:

a. fiat money
b. backed by gold
c. backed by the country's resources
d. none of the above

Answer: a

Reason: Paper currency is money because the government decrees it to be so.

11. Gresham's law states that:

a. money corrupts people
b. good money will drive bad money out of circulation
c. bad money will drive good money out of circulation
d. legal tender money is the best type of money

Answer: c

Reason: People will hoard the good money and spend the bad money.

12. Demand deposits are:

a. another name for savings accounts
b. not transferable by cheques
c. chequing accounts at commercial banks
d. none of the above

Answer: c

Reason: Demand deposits are deposits on commercial banks on which cheques can be written.

13. Near monies refer to:

a. money substitutes such as credit cards

b. money items that are backed by gold

c. assets such as savings deposits in banks which fulfil the store of value function but not the medium of exchange function of money

d. assets that can be converted into precious metals

Answer: c

Reason: Near monies are highly liquid assets that can be easily converted into cash without much capital loss.

14. The single largest component of the money supply in advanced economies is:

a. coins c. gold bars

b. currency d. none of the above

Answer: d

Reason: The single largest component of the money supply is demand deposits.

15. The narrow definition of the money supply includes:

a. coins c. currency

b. notes (paper money) d. all of the above

Answer: d

Reason: The narrow definition of the money supply is the monetary aggregate that includes currency (notes and coins) and demand deposits.

16. Which of the following has serves as money at some place or time?

a. Wampum c. Animal skins

b. Gold d. All of the above

Answer: d

Reason: At some time in history a variety of items have served as money, including those mentioned in the question.

17. The value of money is:

a. inversely related to the price level

b. directly related to the price level

c. independent of the price level

d. constantly rising because of inflation

Answer: a

Reason: When the price level rises, the value of money falls, and vice versa.

18. Rapid increases in the quantity of money may result in:

a. unemployment

b. inflation

c. an increase in the value of money

d. none of the above

Answer: b

Reason: Increases in the money supply may cause money to lose its value. When this happens, people tend to spend money more quickly. This tends to accelerate price increase, leading to inflation.

True-False

Determine whether each of the following statements is true or false.

1. Money serves as a medium of exchange, a store of value, and as a measure of value.

Answer: True

2. Money performs its most important function when it serves as a store of value.

Answer: False

Explanation: The most important function of money is to serve as a medium of exchange.

3. Because a barter system of exchange in simpler than a money system, it is much more efficient.

Answer: False

Explanation: A barter system is inefficient because it requires a double coincidence of wants.

4. Money is usually defined in terms of the functions that it performs.

Answer: True

5. Barter is the direct exchange of one good or service for another good or service without the use of money.

Answer: True

6. Barter cannot take place in a money economy.

Answer: False

Explanation: Even in an economy where money is used predominantly in trading, barter may still occur on a limited basis.

7. Exchange with the use of money involves a higher search cost than does exchange by barter.

Answer: False

Explanation: Under a barter system, a great deal of time must be spent in searching for a trading partner to satisfy the double coincidence of wants. Hence, the search cost is relatively high.

8. A modern money economy requires a double coincidence of wants for exchanges to occur.

Answer: False

Explanation: Exchange by barter requires a double coincidence of wants, but exchange with money does not.

9. Money is a good store of value during periods of inflation because of its liquidity.

Answer: False

Explanation: During an inflation, money is not a good store of value because it loses purchasing power.

10. The same item that performs the medium of exchange function can also perform the measure of value function.

Answer: True

11. Prices are an example of money serving the measure of value function.

Answer: True

12. Money in a modern society is backed by public confidence in the monetary system rather than by gold or any other precious metal.

Answer: True

13. Once an item becomes money, it will always remain money.

Answer: False

Explanation: *Money items change over time.*

14. Gresham's law states that good money always drives bad money out of circulation.

Answer: False

Explanation: *Gresham's law states that bad money drives good money out of circulation since people will hoard the good money.*

15. The largest component of the money supply in most modern economies is paper currency.

Answer: False

Explanation: *The largest component of the money supply is demand deposits or chequing accounts.*

16. Credit cards are not money because they cannot be used for the final settlement of debts.

Answer: True

17. Debit cards are money because they can be used to settle debts.

Answer: False

Explanation: *It is not the debit cards that are used to settle debts, it is the account to which they allow access.*

18. There is a connection between the money supply and the level of economic activity in a country.

Answer: True

Completion

(Fill in the blanks)

Use each word or combination of words from the list exactly once.
*(**Hint**: Proceed by elimination)*

Word list

Barter — Currency x 2 — Demand — Demand deposits — Fiat — Gresham's — Inflation — Legal tender — Liquidity — Measure of value — Medium of exchange — Money x 3 — Near monies — Notice — Store of value x 2 — Token money — Unemployment — Unit of account

Questions

1. Anything that is generally accepted as final payment for goods and services is regarded as __________.
2. __________ is the direct exchange of goods and services without the use of money.
3. The use of __________ in a transaction discharges the debt.
4. Money performs three basic functions. These are __________, __________, and __________.
5. A balance of $2,000 in a savings account is an example of money functioning as a(n) __________.
6. A vacation trip with a price tag of $1,500 is an example of money functioning as a(n) __________. (measure of value)
7. Coins and paper money are referred to as __________.
8. Money that is declared to be __________ must be accepted if offered in payment of a debt.
9. The ease with which an asset can be converted into the medium of exchange without much loss in value is called __________.
10. __________ is the most liquid of all assets.
11. Money that circulates by government decree is called __________ money.
12. __________ law states that bad money will drive good money out of circulation. (Gresham's)
13. Money whose face value is greater than its commodity value is known as __________.
14. Savings accounts are an example of __________ [notice, demand] deposits.
15. The monetary aggregate M1 (the narrow definition of money) consists of __________ outside banks, plus __________ deposits in commercial banks.
16. Liquid assets that perform the store of value function, but do not immediately perform the medium of exchange function are called __________.

17. Quantitatively, the most important type of money is __________.

18. Rapid increases in the quantity of money may cause __________ [inflation, unemployment]; rapid reductions in the quantity of money may cause __________ [inflation, unemployment].

Solutions

1. (money)
2. (Barter)
3. (money)
4. (medium of exchange, store of value, unit of account)
5. (store of value)
6. (measure of value)
7. (currency)
8. (legal tender)
9. (liquidity)
10. (Money)
11. (fiat)
12. (Gresham's)
13. (token money)
14. (notice)
15. (currency, demand)
16. (near monies)
17. (demand deposits)
18. (inflation, unemployment).

14 THE BANKING SYSTEM

LEARNING OBJECTIVES

In connection with this module, you should be able to:

1. describe the banking system
2. state The objectives of a central bank
3. identify the major items on the balance sheet of a central bank
4. discuss the origins of modern banking
5. discuss the services provided by commercial banks
6. discuss the main items on the balance sheets of commercial banks
7. explain the process of multiple deposit expansion by commercial banks
8. discuss the role of near banks in the financial system

DEFINITIONS & CONCEPTS

You should be able to define the following terms and concepts:

banking system	near banks
lender of last resort	fractional reserve banking system
balance sheet	reserve requirement
asset	liability
primary reserve	capital (owners' equity)
commercial bank	secondary reserve
unit banking system	branch banking system
money (deposit) expansion multiplier	

SYNOPSIS

The banking system consists of a **central bank** and a number of **commercial banks**. Their behavior influences the supply of money in the economy. **Near banks** are financial institutions other than commercial banks that accept deposits from the public.

The central bank is responsible for conducting the country's monetary policy. It controls the money supply, serves as banker to the commercial banks, acts as financial adviser to the government, and supports the financial system.

Modern banking owes its origin to the 17th century when goldsmiths accepted gold deposits and issued paper receipts. The goldsmiths' receipts became money once they were generally accepted as a medium of exchange.

The most important asset of the banks is loans while deposits constitute the major component of their liabilities. An examination of the banks' balance sheet gives us an idea of the types activities in which they are involved.

Banks operate on the basis of the **fractional reserve banking system** by which they keep in cash a fraction of the total amount of deposit liabilities. The ratio of cash reserves to total deposits is called the **reserve ratio**. Commercial banks can increase the money supply by granting loans.

14 THE BANKING SYSTEM

Concepts, Definitions & Problems

Problem 14-1

Briefly describe the banking system. How does the banking system differ from the financial system?

Requirement and Clue: *This is a two-part problem. Answer each part in order. For the first part, do not ignore the word "briefly". State what constitutes the banking system. For the second part of the problem, your solution should make the distinction between the two systems clear.*

Solution

The banking system is a network of financial institutions consisting of a central bank and a set of commercial or chartered banks. These commercial banks may or may not have branches.

The banking system may be considered a subset of the financial system which is a network of financial institutions consisting of a central bank, a set of commercial banks, and other financial institutions that provide a variety of financial services to their customers. The financial system is more inclusive than the banking system.

Problem 14-2

What are the functions of a central bank?

Requirement and Clue: *Acknowledging that not all central banks perform all the functions of a central bank, it is well to mention typical central bank functions.*

Solution

The following are the basic functions of a central bank.

Controller of the money supply

Excessive increases in the quantity of money may cause inflation; an inadequate supply of money may result in unemployment. The central bank issues bank notes (currency) and controls the quantity of money.

Manager of the country's monetary policy

The central bank controls the country's monetary policy. My adjusting the quantity of money and interest rates in the country, the central bank exerts a great deal of influence on economic activity within the country.

Banker to the commercial banks

The central bank serves as banker to the commercial banks. They keep deposits on the central bank, and they ca n also borrow from the central bank.

Banker and financial adviser to the government

The central bank serves as fiscal agent and financial adviser to the government. The government typically keeps a chequing account with the central bank, and can borrow from the central bank. The central bank possesses expertise in financial matters and is well equipped to advise the government on such matters.

Supporter of the financial system

Modern monetary systems are confidence-based. We accept paper currency from other people in exchange for valuable goods and services mainly because we are confident that others will, in turn, accept it from us. The central bank supports the financial system and prevents the loss of confidence that might cause panic and bank failures.

Problem 14-3

What is the lender of last resort function of a central bank?

Requirement and Clue: *Focus on the functions of a central bank and consider which of those functions would qualify as lender of last resort.*

Solution

One of the functions of a central bank is to serve as a lender of last resort. This lender of last resort function is related to the central bank's function of being banker to the commercial banks. If a commercial bank or a near bank finds itself without sufficient cash to meet its depositors' demands, such a financial institution could borrow, as a last resort, from the central bank. This function of extending loans to certain financial institutions is the lender of last resort function.

Problem 14-4

What are the main assets and liabilities of a central bank?

Requirement and Clue: *Considering the functions of a central bank will help to figure out its main assets and liabilities.*

Solution

The following are the main assets of a central bank:

- Foreign currency deposits
- Investments in treasury bills and securities
- Bank premises

The following are the main liabilities of a central bank:

- Bank notes in circulation
- Government deposits
- Commercial banks' deposits

Problem 14-5

What are the functions of a commercial bank? How to these functions differ from those of a credit union?

Requirement and Clue: *This is a two-part problem. Answer each part in order. Focus on the services that commercial banks provide. Think of what commercial banks do that credit unions don't do.*

Solution

The following are the functions that commercial banks perform:

Commercial banks establish chequing accounts for their depositors and honour cheques drawn on those accounts. They thus provide the most important component of the money supply in a modern economy. Commercial banks also establish savings accounts where customers can safely deposit money to serve as a store of value.

Another very important function that commercial banks perform is to lend money to businesses, consumers, individuals, and governments by purchasing their bonds.

Other functions performed by commercial banks include the provision of foreign exchange services, safe keeping of valuables, automatic teller machine (ATM) services, transfer of funds between accounts, telephone and internet banking, bill payment services, credit card and debit services, and selling money orders and traveller's cheques.

Unlike demand deposits on commercial banks, deposits on credit unions are not a part of the narrow definition of the money supply. Like commercial banks, credit unions accept savings deposits, engage in mortgage lending, and grant personal cash loans, but their scope of operation is much narrower than that of commercial banks.

Problem 14-6

In what sense is commercial banking a "balancing act"?

Requirement and Clue: *Focus on the thin line that commercial bankers must walk between liquidity and profitability.*

Solution:

As privately owned financial institutions, commercial banks want to earn a profit for their shareholders. Commercial banks, however, must keep sufficient funds on hand to meet the needs of their depositors. The problem that the commercial banker faces is the realization that assets that yield high earnings tend to be non-liquid. On the other hand, liquid assets tend to yield little or no earnings. For example, if a commercial bank keeps all of its assets in cash, the most liquid of all assets, it will be 100 per cent liquid, but it will earn nothing for its shareholders. If it keeps all of its assets in loans and long-term securities, which have high interest earnings, it will have a major liquidity problem and may not survive. Commercial banks therefore face conflicting needs for profitability on the one hand and liquidity on the other. Good banking consists of being able to use bank funds profitably while at the same time having due regard for liquidity and safety. It is in this sense that commercial banking can be considered a balancing act.

Problem 14-7

What are the main assets and liabilities of commercial banks?

Requirement and Clue: *Focus on the main sources and uses of the banks' funds. This will give you an idea of the banks' liabilities and assets.*

Solution

The main assets and liabilities of commercial banks are listed below. The assets indicate the main uses of funds while the liabilities indicate the main sources of funds.

Main Assets

Liquid assets:

- Central bank deposits, notes and coins
- Treasury bills
- Government securities

Less liquid assets:

- Loans
- Securities

Foreign currency assets

Main Liabilities

Personal savings deposits

Non-personal and term deposits

Government deposits

Shareholders' equity

Problem 14-8

Arrange the following items as they may appear on a commercial bank's balance sheet. Briefly explain each item.

Requirement and Clue: *This is a two-part problem. Answer each part in order. For the first part of the problem, determine which items are asset items and which are liability items. For the second part of the problem, statement clearly the meaning of each item with a "brief" discussion.*

Solution

A balance sheet indicates the assets and liabilities of an entity. The assets represent anything the entity owns, while the liabilities represent the indebtedness of the entity. The following table illustrates how the items in the problem may appear on the balance sheet of a commercial bank.

Assets	Liabilities
Cash reserves	Deposits
Loans	Capital

The term "deposits" refers to funds deposited in accounts at commercial banks. These may be demand deposits or notice deposits. Since deposits in a bank account represent amounts that the bank owes its depositors, these deposits are listed as liabilities on the bank's balance sheet. These deposits are of vital importance to the bank because they enable it to make loans and profitable investments from which it derives most of its earnings.

Commercial banks extend loans to households and firms. The difference between the interest the banks charge on loans and the interest that they pay to their depositors is a part of the banks' earnings. A loan is obviously an asset to the bank since the borrower has to repay the loan plus interest charges.

The establishment of a commercial bank requires a huge amount of capital. The bank raises this capital by issuing shares. The capital contributed by the shareholders represents a liability to the bank since it represents the bank's indebtedness to its shareholders.

Commercial banks keep a certain amount of money as cash reserves. This is necessary so that they can accommodate their customers who wish to withdraw funds from their accounts. The cash reserves are held as deposits at the central bank and in the form of notes. Banks keep some reserves. These are called desired reserves. Cash reserves are a part of the assets of a commercial bank.

Problem 14-9

Explain how commercial banks create money. What factors limit the amount of money that banks can create?

Requirement and Clue: *This is a two-part problem. Answer each part in order. For the first part of the problem, you are to explain the process of multiple deposit expansion. For the second part of the problem, focus on restrictions on the money creation process.*

Solution

Commercial banks create money in the form of bank deposits by making loans which enable them to create deposits. When a customer borrows money from a commercial bank, the bank deposits the amount in an account for the borrower. This deposit is money which the bank has actually created. The bank is likely to keep a certain fraction of its deposits as reserves. Any amount over its desired reserves can be lent out, thus creating new deposits. The process can be illustrated with an arithmetic example. Let's assume that a bank gets a new deposit of $1,000 and that its desired reserve is 10%. The bank keeps $100 as reserves and makes a loan of $900 to a customer. The bank deposits the $900 in a chequing account for the customer. This new deposit enables the bank to make an additional loan of $810 after keeping $90 as desired reserves. A new deposit of $810 is thus created. So far, the bank has created $(900 + 810) = $1,710. The process can continue until the bank's excess reserves have been exhausted.

The banks' ability to create money depends on the amount that customers deposit in bank accounts, the demand for loans and on the amount of desired reserves.

Customers' deposits

The greater the amount of money that customers deposit, the greater will be the banks' ability to extend loans and thus create money. The public's desire to hold cash will affect the amount of money deposited in bank accounts. If the public decides to hold a larger amount of money in the form of cash, then the ability of the banks to create money will be reduced.

The demand for loans

If customers do not borrow, the banks cannot lend; and if no loans are made, no money creation can take place.

Desired reserves

The larger the amount of money that banks desire to keep as reserves, the less will be available for loans and thus the less will be the amount of money created.

Problem 14-10

It has been said that banks create money by lending out their excess reserves. Is this true?

Requirement and Clue: Focus on the details of the money (deposit) creation process and determine the extent to which the statement is true.

Solution

The statement is false. Although it is possible for a bank to lend out its excess reserves, it is not in its best interest to do so. Instead, the bank grants a loan by creating a deposit for the borrower and keeping the excess reserves to meet its reserve requirement. By so doing, the bank can extend a great deal more loans on which it can earn interest income. The bank does not lend out its excess reserves but it does lend out an amount equivalent to its excess reserves.

Problem 14-11

Describe the balance sheet of a commercial bank.

Requirement and Clue: *Focus on what a balance sheet consists of. Describing a commercial bank's balance sheet is in fact describing the items that constitute that balance sheet.*

Solution

A bank's balance sheet is a statement of the bank's assets (what it owns), its liabilities (what is owes) and its net worth or capital (the difference between its assets and its liabilities). Thus we find that assets = liabilities + net worth.

The assets of a commercial bank are mainly deposits at the central bank, the loans that it makes to borrowers, investments that it has made in the form of treasury bills and securities, and its property and equipment.

The liabilities of a commercial bank consist mainly of customers deposits, and deposits by government and government agencies.

Problem 14-12

Define each of the following terms or concepts:

(a) *Fiduciary monetary system*

(b) *Branch banking system*

(c) *Fractional reserve banking system*

(d) *Deposit expansion multiplier*

Requirement and Clue: *This is a multi-part definitional problem. Answer each part in order. State clearly and precisely the meaning of each term or concept.*

Solution

(a) A fiduciary monetary system is one that is based on trust or confidence. People accept currency in a fiduciary system, not because of its intrinsic value, because they are confident that others will accept it from them.

(b) A branch banking system is a banking system in which there are relatively few individual banks with many branches.

(c) A fractional reserve banking system is a banking system in which banks keep only a fraction of their deposits in cash reserves.

(d) The deposit expansion multiplier, also called the money multiplier, is the number by which an initial deposit is multiplied to arrive at the resulting total deposits. The deposit expansion multiplier is the reciprocal of the reserve ratio.

Problem 14-13

Suppose a group of investors decide to open a bank and issue \$5,000,000 of capital stock to set it up. They use \$100,000,000 of this to buy the building from which they will operate. The remaining \$4,000,000 is kept as cash.

(a) *Show the original balance sheet.*

(b) *How will the balance sheet be affected if customers deposit \$500,000 in demand deposits in the bank?*

(c) *How will the balance sheet be affected if the bank now buys \$100,000 of government securities?*

Requirement and Clue: *This is a multi-part problem. Answer each part in order. You are required to demonstrate familiarity with the balance sheet of a commercial bank.*

Solution

(a) The following table shows the balance sheet of the bank.

	Assets (\$)	Liabilities & net worth (\$)	
Cash	4,000,000	Capital stock	5,000,000
Property	1,000,000		
Total	5,000,000	Total	5,000,000

(b) The deposit of \$500,000 in demand deposits will increase the bank's cash by \$500,000. But the bank now has a new obligation of \$500,000 to its customers. The following table shows how the bank's balance sheet will be affected by this deposit transaction.

	Assets	Liabilities and net worth	
Cash	4,500,000	Demand deposits	500,000
Property	1,000,000	Capital stock	5,000,000
Total	5,500,000	Total	5,500,000

(c) The purchase of \$100,000 of government securities means that the bank now has investments of \$100,000 in the form of government securities (an asset). But it loses cash assets of \$100,000. The transaction will affect the bank's balance sheet as shown below.

	Assets	Liabilities and net worth	
Cash	4,400,000	Demand deposits	500,000
Government securities	100,000	Capital stock	5,000,000
Property	1,000,000		
Total	5,500,000	Total	5,500,000

Problem 14-14

The following balance sheet summarizes the financial position of a hypothetical bank which we will call the ABC Bank.

Balance Sheet of the ABC Bank

	Assets	Liabilities and Net Worth	
Cash in Bank vault:	$500	Demand deposits	$2,500
Deposits w/ central bank:	$400		
Securities:	$300	Net worth	
Total Assets:	$2,700	Total liabilities & Net worth	$2,700

From the balance sheet information, calculate:

(a) *Cash reserve ratio*

(b) *The total amount of bank loans*

(c) *The bank's net worth*

Requirement and Clue: *This is a multiple-part problem. Answer each part in order. Answers require a knowledge of the relationship between the items on the bank's balance sheet.*

Solution

(a) The cash reserve ratio is the ratio of desired reserves to total deposits. From the asset side of the balance sheet, we note that desired reserves are \$(500 + 400) = \$900. From the liabilities side we note that deposits total \$2,500. Therefore, the cash reserve ratio is

$$\frac{900}{2500} = \mathbf{0.36 \text{ or } 36\%}$$

(b) Total bank loans = Total assets – (total cash reserves + securities)

= \$2700 – (\$900 + \$300) = **\$1500**

(c) Net worth = (Total assets – total liabilities)

= \$2700 - \$2500 = **\$200**

Problem 14-15

Use T-accounts to illustrate the effects of each of the following transactions on a bank's balance sheet.

(a) *Customer Jack Anderson deposits \$500 in his chequing account.*

(b) *Customer Sandra Black withdraws \$100 from her savings account.*

(c) *Customer David Simon makes a cash payment of \$250 on his loan account.*

(d) *Jennifer Reid writes a cheque for \$350 on her demand deposit account and the cheque is cashed.*

Requirement and Clue: *This is a multiple-part problem. Answer each part in order. T-accounts show changes in the balance sheet following a transaction. The problem requires familiarity with balance sheet items—asset items and liability items.*

Solution

(a) Jack's deposit of \$500 in his chequing account increases the bank's cash assets by \$500, but also increases its liabilities by the same amount. This is shown as follows:

	Assets	Liabilities and net worth	
Cash	+ \$500	Deposits:	
		Chequing account	+ \$500

(b) Sandra's transaction results in a reduction of cash assets for the bank and at the same time, a reduction in the bank's savings account liability. This is shown as follows:

	Assets	Liabilities and net worth	
Cash	- \$100	Deposits:	
		Savings	- \$100

(c) David's payment of \$250 on his loan account increases the bank's cash assets by \$250, but also reduces the bank's loan assets by the same amount. The transaction does not affect the bank's liabilities because no liability items are involved. The effect of this transaction is shown as follows:

	Assets	Liabilities and net worth
Cash	+ \$250	
Loan	- \$250	

(d) Jennifer's transaction affects the bank's liabilities as well as its assets. The bank's deposit liabilities will decrease by \$350, but its cash assets will decrease by the same amount. This is shown as follows:

	Assets	Liabilities and net worth	
Cash	- \$350	Deposits:	
		Demand	- \$350

Problem 14-16

Daniel Peters deposits \$500 in his chequing account at the KN Commercial Bank. The bank holds 20% of its deposits as cash reserves.

(a) *Complete the following table showing the maximum amount of money that the KN bank can create.*

The Money Creation Process

	Deposits	*Cash Reserves*	*Excess Reserves*	*Loans*
	\$500	*\$100*	*\$*	*\$*
Total	*\$_____*	______	______	______

(b) *Calculate the simple money expansion multiplier.*

(c) *What are the major assumptions in this simple model of bank money creation?*

Requirement and Clue: *This is a three-part problem. Answer each part in order. Familiarity with the multiple deposit creation process is required.*

Solution

(a) The Money Creation Process

	Deposits	Cash Reserves	Excess Reserves	Loans
	\$500.00	\$100.00	\$400.00	\$400.00
	400.00	80.00	320.00	320.00
	320.00	64.00	256.00	256.00
	256.00	51.20	204.80	204.80
	204.80	40.96	163.84	163.84
	.	.	.	.
	.	.	.	.
	.	.	.	.
Total	\$2,500.00	\$ 500.00	\$2,000.00	\$2,000.00

(b) The money expansion multiplier is the reciprocal of the cash reserve ratio, which is 20%. Thus, the money expansion multiplier is 1/20% = 5.

(c) The major assumptions of the model are: (1) all deposits are demand deposits; (2) the bank invests in loans only; and (3) the bank lends out the maximum amount possible.

Problem 14-17

Draw up a hypothetical balance sheet of a commercial bank, and itemize its major assets and liabilities.

Requirement and Clue: *This requires knowledge of a commercial bank's major assets and liabilities.*

Solution

Hypothetical Balance Sheet of a Commercial Bank as of December 31, 20___.

Assets	Liabilities
Cash Reserves	Deposits
Loans	Shareholders' Equity (Net Worth)

The major assets of a commercial bank are its cash reserves and different categories of loans that it makes to its customers. Its major liabilities are public and government deposits and shareholders' equity.

Problem 14-18

Suppose there is only one kind of deposit account—demand deposits—with a desired cash reserve of 10%, no currency drain, and ultimately, full lending (zero excess reserves) by the chartered banks. Suppose the central bank writes a cheque for $100,000 to a securities dealer. He deposits the cheque in his account at Bank A. Record the changes in Bank A's T-account at this stage.

Bank A

Assets	Liabilities & Net Worth
Reserves	Deposits
$_______	(b) $_______

Now, excess reserves are (c) $_______ and given that the money expansion multiplier is the reciprocal of the cash reserve ratio, the value of the multiplier is (d) $_______.

Bank A lends out an amount equal to the excess reserves of (e) $_______ to Bryson, a carpenter. Bryson uses the money to purchase some raw materials from T. Suppliers who banks at Bank B. Bank B credits Suppliers' account and clears the cheque through the central bank. The central bank transfers reserves from Bank A's account to Bank B's. After the reserves transfer, the T-account for Banks A and B look like this:

Bank A

Assets	Liabilities & Net Worth
Reserves (f) $_______	Deposits (h) $_______
Loans (g) $_______	

Bank B

Assets	Liabilities & Net Worth
Reserves	Deposits
(i) $______	(j) $______

Bank B now has excess reserves of (k) $______. If this amount is lent out, spent by the borrower, and ultimately deposited on Bank C, Bank C will find that it has acquired (l) $______ it could lend out. The process ends when (m) $_______ of new deposits have been created and the total amount of (n) $______ becomes reserves for the entire banking system.

Requirement and Clue: *This problem deals with the process of multiple deposit expansion. You must be able to show changes in the bank's balance sheet following certain transactions, using T-accounts. Focus on which side of the balance sheet will be affected and how.*

Solution

Bank A

Assets	Liabilities & Net Worth
Reserves	Deposits
(a) $100,000	(b) $100,000

Now, excess reserves are (c) $90,000 and given that the money expansion multiplier is the reciprocal of the cash reserve ratio, the value of the multiplier is (d) 10.

Bank A lends out an amount equal to the excess reserves of (e) $90,000 to Bryson, a carpenter. Bryson uses the money to purchase some raw materials from T. Suppliers who banks at Bank B. Bank B credits Suppliers' account and clears the cheque through the central bank. The central bank transfers reserves from Bank A's account to Bank B's. After the reserves transfer, the T-account for Banks A and B look like this:

Bank A

Assets	Liabilities & Net Worth
Reserves (f) $10,000	Deposits (h) $100,000
Loans (g) $90,000	

Bank B

Assets	Liabilities & Net Worth
Reserves	Deposits
(i) $90,000	(j) $90,000

Bank B now has excess reserves of (k) $81,000. If this amount is lent out, spent by the borrower, and ultimately deposited on Bank C, Bank C will find that it has acquired (l) $72,900 it could lend out. The process ends when (m) $1,000,000 of new deposits have been created and the total amount of (n) $100,000 becomes reserves for the entire banking system.

Problem 14-19

Identify any errors in the following passage.

"It is easy to see how commercial banks create money. Let's assume that a customer deposits $5,000 in her account at a bank. If I borrow $4,500 of that money from the bank, the bank creates a deposit of $4,500 in my account. That deposit is money. It is important to note, however, that this banking system cannot create any more money than the amount that I borrow. If it holds no reserves at all, the maximum amount that it will be able to create as a result of the deposit and any loans granted will be $5,000."

Requirement and Clue: *You should read the passage very carefully, noting any inaccuracies. In your solution, point out any mistakes that you may find and offer a correction.*

Solution

The passage suggests that commercial banks can create only as much money as is deposited with them, less any amount held as reserves. This is erroneous. In the example given, since the bank creates a deposit for the borrower, it has excess reserves from which further loans can be made, and new deposits created. Thus, a multiplier process is operative, and the total amount of money created will be several times the original deposit.

Problem 14-20

Define each of the following terms:

(a) *Initial deposit*

(b) *Secondary deposit*

(c) *Deposit expansion multiplier*

(d) *Excess reserves*

Requirement and Clue: This is a multiple-part problem. Answer each part in order. You are required to state clearly and precisely the meaning of each term, without offering lengthy explanations. Note that all the terms relate to the multiple deposit expansion process.

Solution

(a) Initial deposit or primary deposit is a deposit that a deposit-taking institution such as a commercial bank sells for cash. For example, if you deposit a cheque or $500 cash in a chequing account at a commercial, it is considered an initial or primary deposit.

(b) Secondary deposit or a derivative deposit as it is also called, is a deposit that is created by a bank when it extends a loan.

(c) Deposit expansion multiplier is the number my which an initial deposit is multiplied to arrive at the resulting total deposits. It is also called the money multiplier and is the reciprocal of the reserve ratio. Thus, if the reserve ratio is 20%, then the deposit expansion multiplier is 1/20% = 5.

(d) Excess reserves are cash reserves held in excess of the desired cash reserves. For example, if a bank receives a deposit of $500, and it keeps a cash reserve of 10%, i.e., $50, then it has excess reserves of $450.

Problem 14-21

Carefully describe how a loan repayment can lead to deposit destruction.

Requirement and Clue: *You are required to show how a loan repayment results in a reduction in the money supply. Balance sheets will be helpful.*

Solution

Let us assume that the bank's position before the loan repayment was as shown in the balance sheet below. The bank keeps cash reserves of 10%.

Bank's Balance Sheet

Assets		Liabilities & Net Worth	
Desired cash reserves	$300,000	Demand deposits:	
Excess reserves	0	Previous	$885,000
Government securities	100,000	Additional	2,115,000
Loans:		Capital stock	500,000
Previous	485,000		
Additional	2,115,000		
Property	500,000		
Total	$3,500,000	Total	$3,500,000

Suppose now that some of the bank's creditors repay a total of $150,000 of their loans. The creditors do this by writing cheques for a total of $150,000 drawn on their accounts at the bank. The bank's loan assets will fall by $150,000, and its deposit liability will fall by an equivalent amount. Other things being equal, this implies a reduction of $150,000 in the money supply. The following table illustrates the situation.

Bank's Balance Sheet after Loan Repayment

Assets		Liabilities & Net Worth	
Desired cash reserves$	285,000	Demand deposits:	
Excess reserves	15,000	Previous	$3,000,000
Government securities	100,000	Current	2,850,000
Loans:		Capital stock	500,000
Previous	2,600,000		
Current	2,450,000		
Property	500,000		
Total	$3,350,000	Total	$3,350,000

Multiple-Choice

In each case, circle the letter that corresponds with the correct answer.

1. The banking system consists of:

a. all the commercial banks and their branches in the economy only
b. the central bank and its relationship with the commercial banks
c. only the most important commercial banks in the country
d. none of the above

Answer: b

Reason: The banking system describes the association between the central bank and the commercial banks, which interact to provide banking services to customers. Choice b fits this bill.

2. The financial system:

a. consists of a network of banks and other financial institutions that provide a variety of financial services to their customers
b. is a network of commercial banks and central banks also referred to as the banking system
c. includes banks but excludes near banks
d. includes near banks but excludes banks

Answer: a

Reason: The financial system consists of the central bank, commercial banks, near banks, and other financial institutions.

3. A central bank is:

a. a collection of commercial banks
b. a collusion of financial institutions whose objective is to control the wealth in a country
c. a country's main monetary authority, whose principal function is to regulate money and credit in the country.
d. all of the above

Answer: c

Reason: A central bank is responsible for the country's money supply and for conducting its monetary policy.

4. Which of the following is a near bank?

a. A credit union
b. A trust company
c. A savings and loans association
d. All of the above

Answer: d

Reason: Near banks are financial institutions that perform many of the functions of banks but do not offer demand deposit accounts.

5. The Bank of England, the Bank of Canada, and the Federal Reserve System in the United States are all:

a. commercial banks c. near banks
b. central banks d. none of the above

Answer: b

Reason: They are all central banks because they control their country's money supply and conducts its monetary policy.

6. The objectives of a central bank include:

a. economic stability c. viable balance of payments
b. economic growth d. all of the above

Answer: d

Reason: Most central banks in advanced countries pursue the objectives listed.

7. Which of the following is ***not*** a function of most central banks?

a. To control the country's money supply
b. To accept deposits from the public
c. To conduct monetary policy
d. To support the financial system

Answer: b

Reason: It is not a typical function of a central bank to accept deposits from the public.

8. A central bank serves as banker to the commercial banks when it:

a. conducts the country's monetary policy
b. keeps the government's accounts
c. administers the country's fiscal policy
d. keeps their cash reserves

Answer: d

Reason: Commercial banks keep a fraction of their deposits in accounts as reserves at the central bank.

9. Usually, the major asset of a central bank is:

a. notes in circulation
b. foreign currency deposits
c. government securities
d. none of the above

Answer: c

Reason: Central banks typically carry large amounts of government securities in their portfolios.

10. Usually, the major liability of a central bank is:

a. notes in circulation
b. foreign currency liabilities
c. government securities
d. cash deposits from the public

Answer: a

Reason: The paper currency that countries use is issued by the central bank which is actually a liability. In most cases it's the major liability.

11. A branch banking system differs from a unit banking system in that:

a. a unit banking system consists of a number of independent banks without branches, while a branch system does not
b. a branch banking system consists of independent banks without branches, while a unit banking system

does not

c. a unit banking system consists of banks with several branches all over the country whereas a branch banking system does not

d. all of the above.

Answer: a

Reason: *In a branch banking system, the banks have many branches; in a unit banking system, the banks are independent and typically do not have branches.*

12. Commercial banks perform a variety of functions including:

a. the granting of loans, the establishment of convenient chequing accounts, and the establishment of savings accounts

b. the formulation of monetary policy for the country

c. the safekeeping of valuables, foreign exchange services, and bill payment services

d. a and c

Answer: d

Reason: *The operation of commercial banks include the items listed in choices a and c.*

13. The main asset item of commercial banks is:

a. loans c. personal savings deposits

b. treasury bills d. none of the above

Answer: a

Reason: *Commercial banks make their earnings mainly through profitable loans and investment. This accounts for the primacy of loans in their asset portfolio.*

14. Among the assets of a commercial bank are its:

a. reserves and loans c. deposits

b. loans and deposits d. net worth and reserves

Answer: a

Reason: *Deposits and net worth are on the liabilities side of the balance sheet.*

15. A commercial bank's deposits are:

a. reserves c. net worth

b. assets d. liabilities

Answer: d

Reason: Deposits are liabilities because they represent the bank's indebtedness to its depositors.

16. When a commercial bank grants a loan:

a. its assets increase

b. its liabilities decrease

c. its assets and liabilities remain the same

d. its assets decrease

Answer: a

Reason: *Loans are assets to a commercial bank.*

17. Commercial banks are able to affect the money supply because of:

a. the fractional reserve banking system

b. their ability to create new deposit accounts as a by-product of their profit-seeking activities

c. their ability to make profits for their shareholders

d. a and b

Answer: d

Reason: *Commercial banks create money (deposits) because they keep only a fraction of the money deposited with them. They use their excess reserves to extend loans and in the process, they create new deposits.*

18. When a cheque written on a bank for $500 is collected, the bank's loss of reserves is:

a. some part of the $500 c. a multiple of $500

b. zero d. $500

Answer: d

Reason: *When the cheque is cleared, the bank's reserves will fall by the amount of the cheque.*

19. The simple money expansion multiplier may be defined as:

a. the cash reserve ratio

b. the ratio of the change in the money supply to the change in actual cash reserves that brought it about

c. the reciprocal of the desired cash reserve ratio

d. b and c

Answer: d

Reason: *The simple money expansion multiplier is the number by which an initial bank deposit is multiplied to arrive at the resulting total deposits. This is consistent with choices b and c.*

20. If the desired reserve ratio is 20%, then:

a. the maximum deposit expansion multiplier is 5

b. desired reserves equal 20% of total reserves

c. the maximum deposit expansion multiplier is 2

d. none of the above

Answer: a

Reason: *The maximum deposit expansion multiplier is the reciprocal of the desired reserve ratio.*

True-False

Determine whether each of the following statements is true or false.

1. The banking system consists of commercial banks, and near banks such as trust companies.

Answer: False

Explanation: *The banking system consists of the central bank and the chartered banks.*

2. The financial system does not include the central bank.

Answer: False

Explanation: *The central bank is an important part of the financial system.*

3. The financial system consists of banks and other financial institutions that provide a variety of financial services to their customers.

Answer: True

4. All central bank are owned by commercial banks.

Answer: False

Explanation: *Central banks are generally owned by the government.*

5. Commercial banks are financial institutions that accept funds from the public, establish demand deposits and other accounts, and grants loans.

Answer: True

6. Near banks are financial institutions other than commercial banks that accept deposits from the public. They include institutions such as credit unions, mortgage loan companies, and trust companies.

Answer: True

7. Near banks are a part of the financial system, but not a part of the banking system.

Answer: True

8. Central banks usually control the country's money supply, act as banker to the commercial banks, conducts the country's fiscal policy, manages the country's monetary policy, and regulates the country's imports and exports.

Answer: False

Explanation: *Central bank do not conduct fiscal policy and they do not regulate international trade.*

9. Central banks are not permitted to make loans to commercial banks.

Answer: False

Explanation: *Central banks are authorized to make loans to commercial banks. They do so in their role as lender of last resort.*

10. Commercial banks maintain an account at the central bank.

Answer: True

11. A fiduciary monetary system is one that is based the soundness of the economy as measured by the gross domestic product.

Answer: False

Explanation: A fiduciary monetary system is one that is based on trust.

12. The main asset item of central banks is deposits by the public.

Answer: False

Explanation: *The public does not maintain deposits with the central bank. The main asset item of central banks is government securities.*

13. Bank notes in circulation are the main liability of central banks.

Answer: True

14. One of the functions of a central bank is to conduct the country's fiscal policy.

Answer: False

Explanation: *The central bank conducts monetary policy, not fiscal policy.*

15. The major asset item on a central bank's balance sheet is government securities.

Answer: True

16. The main liability of a central bank is foreign currency deposits.

Answer: False

Explanation: *Foreign currency deposits appear as assets on a central bank's balance sheet. The main liability is notes in circulation.*

17. A branch banking system is one in which all banks are obliged to have at least one branch.

Answer: False

Explanation: *A branch banking system is one in which relatively few banks have many branches.*

18. A unit banking system is one in which only one commercial bank is allowed to operate in the country, and it is not allowed to have branches.

Answer: False

Explanation: *A unit banking system is one in which there is a large number of independent banks without branches.*

19. Commercial banks must strike a balance between profitability and liquidity.

Answer: True

20. The largest asset item on commercial banks' balance sheets is personal savings deposits.

Answer: False

Explanation: *Personal savings deposits are liabilities, not assets, of commercial banks.*

21. Commercial banks' funds are used mainly to purchase government securities.

Answer: False

Explanation: Commercial banks' funds are used mainly to grant loans to businesses and individuals.

22. The reserve ratio is the ratio of reserves to deposits.

Answer: True

23. Secondary reserves include highly liquid assets such as currency, day-to-day loans, and treasury bills.

Answer: True

24. Only central banks can create money, because they are the only institutions that can legally print money.

Answer: False

Explanation: Commercial banks create money in the form of deposit money. This happens in the process of extending loans.

25. Commercial banks are able to create money because of the fractional reserve banking.

Answer: True

Completion

(Fill in the blanks)

Use each word or combination of words from the list exactly once.
*(**Hint**: Proceed by elimination)*

Word list

Assets x 2 — Balance — Bank — Banks — Branch — Cash — Central x 2 — Commercial — Debentures — Demand — Deposit — Deposits x 2 — Desired — Government — Last — Lender — Liabilities x 2 — Loans x 2 — Money — Near x 2 — Notes — Primary or initial — Reserves — Resort — Sheet — Unit — Vault

Questions

1. The banking system consists of the ________ ________ and a number of ________ ________.
2. A banking system in which independent banks have branches is called a ________ banking system; a banking system with a large number of independent banks without branches is called a ________ banking system.
3. Financial institutions other than commercial banks that accept deposits from the public are called ________ ________.
4. The central bank function of lending money to commercial banks is referred to as ________ of ________ ________.
5. A statement of a bank's assets, liabilities, and net worth is called a ________ ________.
6. Notes in circulation represent ________ [assets, liabilities] of a central bank.
7. The desired cash reserve ratio is the ration of the amount of ________ ________ a bank desires to keep to their ________ liabilities.
8. Commercial banks keep their desired cash reserves as ________ cash and as deposits at ________ banks.
9. The most important asset item on the balance sheet of a central bank is ________ securities.
10. The most important liability item of a central bank is ________ in circulation.
11. The largest earnings of commercial banks come from their ________.
12. Notes and deposits with central banks, loans, mortgages, and treasury bills constitute ________ of commercial banks.
13. A commercial bank's ________ tell us about its sources of funds, while its ________ tell us about its uses of funds.
14. ________ are bonds secured by the creditworthiness of the borrower rather than by specific assets.
15. The target reserve ratio is the fraction of ________ ________ that commercial banks hold as cash reserves.
16. A deposit that a deposit-taking institution sells for cash is called a ________ deposit.
17. Excess reserves equal actual reserves minus ________ reserves.
18. Banks increase the money supply when they create ________ in the process of extending ________.
19. The reciprocal of the desired reserve ratio gives the ________ multiplier.
20. Savings and loans associations are examples of ________ banks.

Solutions

1. (central bank, commercial banks)
2. (branch, unit)
3. (near banks)
4. (lender (of) last resort)
5. (balance sheet)
6. (liabilities)
7. (cash reserves, deposit)
8. (vault, central)
9. (government)
10. (notes)
11. (loans)
12. (assets)
13. (liabilities, assets)
14. (debentures)
15. (demand deposits)
16. (primary or initial)
17. (desired)
18. (deposits, loans)
19. (money)
20. (near)

15 MONETARY THEORY & MONETARY POLICY

LEARNING OBJECTIVES

In connection with this module, you should be able to:

1. explain the Quantity Theory of money
2. explain the Keynesian theory of money
3. explain the liquidity preference theory of interest
4. discuss the relationship between the money supply and national income
5. discuss the instruments of monetary policy
6. explain how monetary policy works
7. discuss the effectiveness and limitations of monetary policy

DEFINITIONS & CONCEPTS

You should be able to define the following terms and concepts:

quantity theory of money	liquidity preference curve
velocity of circulation of money	monetary policy
equation of exchange	open market operations
monetarism	bank (discount) rate
transactions demand for money	deposit
speculative demand for money	liquidity trap
liquidity preference	redeposits

switching (drawdowns and precautionary demand for money)

SYNOPSIS

Most people establish some kind of relationship between money and the economy. **Monetary theory** deals with the demand for and supply of money, and how they affect income, output, employment, and the price level. **Monetary policy** refers to changes in the money supply and interest rates by the central bank, designed to achieve some economic objective.

The **crude quantity theory of money** states that changes in the quantity of Money cause direct and proportional changes in the price level. The **new quantity theory (monetarism)** predicts that increases in the quantity of money will increase national income, while reductions in the quantity of money will reduce national income.

The velocity of circulation is the number of times, on average, that a unit of money is spent during a year. It may be calculated by dividing the GDP by the money supply.

The desire to hold wealth in the form of money rather than in the form of interest-earning assets is called liquidity preference. Keynesian theory cites three reasons

for holding money: (1) the **transactions motive**, (2) the **precautionary motive,** and (3) the **speculative motive**. The need to hold money for all these purposes is called the total demand for money. The main determinants of the quantity of money demanded are income and the rate of interest.

Other things being equal, an increase in the money supply causes the rate of interest to fall; and a decrease in the money supply causes the rate of interest to rise. Since changes in interest rates affect investment and total spending, they affect economic activity.

Monetary policy is designed to bring about changes in the money supply, the availability of credit, and the level of interest rates in order to influence general economic conditions.

If the economy is experiencing unemployment, the central bank may use an expansionary monetary policy to stimulate spending, and hence, economic activity. If the economy is experiencing inflation, the central bank may pursue a contractionary monetary policy to relieve the inflationary pressure.

Monetary policy will be ineffective if the economy is in a **liquidity trap,** or if investment is insensitive to changes in the rate of interest. Monetary policy is used quite frequently.

15

MONETARY THEORY & MONETARY POLICY

Concepts, Definitions & Problems

Problem 15-1

Define each of the following terms:

(a) *Quantity theory of money*

(b) *Velocity of circulation*

(c) *Equation of exchange*

(d) *Monetarism*

Requirement and Clue: *This problem is definitional with multiple parts. Answer each part in order. Lengthy discussions are not required. You are to state clearly and precisely the meaning of each concept.*

Solution

(a) The quantity theory of money is the theory that states that changes in the price level are due to changes in the quantity of money. In its crude form, the theory states that the quantity of money is directly proportional to the price level.

(b) The velocity of circulation (of money) is the number of times, on average, that a unit of money is spent per year. To say that the velocity of circulation of money is 9 means that on average, each dollar will buy $9 worth of goods and services in a year.

(c) The equation of exchange is an expression that equates the product of the quantity of money and the velocity of circulation with the product of the price level and real output. Thus, if M represents the quantity of money, V, the velocity of circulation, P the price level, and Q, real output, then the equation of exchange can be expressed as:

$$MV = PQ$$

(d) Monetarism is the school of thought that claims that changes in the money supply are the major cause of economic fluctuations and that macroeconomic stability can be achieved by a steady increase in the money supply.

Problem 15-2

Explain the logic behind the quantity theory of money.

Requirement and Clue: *It's a good idea to begin with a brief statement of the quantity theory. Then explain why it makes sense.*

Solution

The quantity theory of money states that changes in the price level are due to changes in the quantity of money. The logic behind the quantity theory of money is that any increase in the quantity of money will cause households and firms to end up with more money than they want to hold for transaction purposes only. Households and firms tend to keep some portion of their wealth in the form of currency and demand deposits so that they can pay for the goods and services they want. The classical economists saw no reason for holding more money than was required for this purpose. They based their argument on the fact that assets held in the form of currency and demand deposits earn little or no interest. Because of the assumption of full employment, output cannot increase in response to the increase in total spending. The quantity of money therefore forces prices up.

Problem 15-3

What are the limitations of the crude quantity theory?

Requirement and Clue: *A brief statement of the crude quantity theory of money is in order. For weaknesses, focus on the assumptions and the predictive capability of the theory.*

Solution

The crude quantity of money, also called the naive quantity theory, states that the quantity of money is directly proportional to the price level. If the quantity of money doubles, then the price level will double also. The assumption that the economy always operates at full employment so that output is constant is one of the weaknesses of this theory. The economy is quite often operating at less than full employment. Consequently, the output of goods and services is subject to some degree of variation. With output varying, the possibility arises that an increase in the quantity of money may lead to an increase in output, rather than to an increase in the price level. It is also possible for an increase in the quantity of money to affect both the price level and real output. The increase in the price level may not then be proportional to the increase in the quantity of money.

Another limitation of the crude quantity theory is that it assumes the velocity of circulation to be constant. The velocity of circulation may be fairly constant under certain circumstances. However, in times of rapid inflation, households and firms will be unwilling to hold money because its value will decrease. Thus, the velocity of circulation tends to increase sharply during periods of inflation as people try to spend money whose value is falling.

Problem 15-4

What is the equation of exchange?

Requirement and Clue: *State/write the equation of exchange and explain its meaning.*

Solution

The equation of exchange is an expression that equates the product of the quantity of money and the velocity of circulation with the product of the price level and real output. Thus, if the quantity of money is denoted by M, the velocity of circulation by V, the price level by P, and real output by Q, the equation of exchange may be written as the following:

$$MV = PQ$$

The left side of the equation (MV) is the amount of money spent in purchasing goods and services. If the quantity of money is \$100 billion, and each dollar is spent 8 times a year on average, then total spending must be \$800 billion. The right side of the equation is gross domestic product (GDP). Because the total amount spent on the economy's output of goods and services must equal the value of that output, the equation of exchange is an identity.

Problem 15-4

How can the equation of exchange be converted into a theory of money?

Requirement and Clue: *Consider that the equation of exchange is an identity, not a theory. Think of assumptions that could result in a cause-effect relationship between the variables of the identity.*

Solution

The equation of exchange is an identity, meaning that it is true by definition. It is not a theory at all. However, by making certain assumptions about the variables in the equation of exchange, it is possible to convert the identity into a theory. Consider the equation of exchange in the form:

$$MV = PQ$$

where M = the quantity of money, V = the velocity of circulation, P = the price level, and Q = real GDP.

Let us now assume that the quantity of money (M) is fixed by the monetary authorities, that the velocity of circulation (V) is determined by institutional factors such as payment practices and the frequency of receipt of income, that would make V a constant, and that real GDP (Q) is fixed at the full-employment level of output. Thus, the price level (P) is the only variable to be determined.

If we divide the equation through by V, we obtain

$$M = Q/V \times P$$

Since Q and V are constants, then Q/V is a constant, then M is directly proportional to P.

The equation of exchange has now been converted into a theory that states: ***"Changes in the quantity of money cause proportional changes in the price level."*** This is the quantity theory of money.

Problem 15-5

What is the difference between the transactions demand for money and the asset demand for money?

Requirement and Clue: *You must be familiar with both concepts. Focus on the motives behind both reasons for retaining money.*

Solution

The transactions demand for money is the quantity of money that people are willing to retain for transaction purposes. Households and firms will hold a part of their wealth in the form of currency and demand deposits so that they can carry out certain transactions. The amount of money that will be demanded for this purpose depends on the level of income. The greater the level of income, the greater the number of transactions people will want to make and the greater will be the amount of money demanded.

The asset demand for money considers money as an asset rather than as a medium of exchange as is the case with the transactions demand. The asset demand for money expresses a relationship between the amount of money retained as an asset and the rate of interest. Because money is the most liquid of all assets, many people find it convenient to hold a part of their financial assets in this most liquid form. The quantity of money that people will be willing to hold as an asset is inversely related to the rate of interest. Whereas the quantity of money that will be held for transaction purposes depends on the level of income, the amount of money held as an asset depends on the rate of interest.

Problem 15-6

Is there any relationship between the transactions demand for money and people's lifestyles?

Requirement and Clue: *Focus on the nature of the transactions demand for money and how such a demand may be influenced by people's habits.*

Solution

The transaction demand for money is the demand for money to hold in anticipation of the expenditures that they make. People's lifestyles will severely influence the amount and varieties of transactions that they make. For example, a typical full-time student with a part-time job will have a different lifestyle than a thirty-five year old man with a family, a full-time job, car payments and mortgage payments. Similarly, a very conservative family who spends a great deal of time at home will display a different expenditure pattern than one that is extravagant and out-going. The difference in lifestyle will dictate, to a large extent, the amount of money demanded for transaction purposes.

Problem 15-7

List five types of financial assets whereby wealth may be held.

Requirement and Clue: *There are many forms in which people may hold financial wealth. Think about these types and select any five of them.*

Solution

(Any five of the following will suffice)

1. Currency, that is, notes (paper money) and coins. These are the most liquid but earn no interest.
2. Demand deposits. These are accounts on banks which are subject to withdrawal on demand. Funds can be withdrawn by writing cheques on such accounts.
3. Deposits in savings accounts at commercial banks or at other deposit-taking financial institutions such as credit unions and savings banks. These deposits earn interest for their holders.
4. Government bonds. These also earn interest to their holders.
5. Corporation bonds. These, like government bonds, are interest-earning assets.
6. Common stock. These yield dividends to their owners.
7. Life insurance policies and pension funds are other financial assets whereby wealth may be held.

Problem 15-8

How can the equation of exchange be derived from the velocity of circulation?

Requirement and Clue: *Familiarity with the equation of exchange and the velocity of circulation is required. Start with an equation expressing the velocity of circulation and manipulate it to arrive at the equation of exchange.*

Solution

The equation of exchange is the identity expressing the fact that the product of the quantity of money and the velocity of circulation must equal the product of the price level and real GDP. Such an identity may be written as:

$$MV \equiv PQ$$

where M = quantity of money, V = velocity of circulation, P = price level, and Q = real GDP.

Now, the velocity of circulation (V) can be expressed as the ratio of GDP to the quantity of money. Thus,

$$V = \frac{GDP}{M} = \frac{P \times Q}{M}$$

By multiplying both sides of the equation above by M, we obtain the following:

$MV = PQ$, which is the equation of exchange.

Problem 15-9

Given that the GDP is \$300 billion and the velocity of circulation is 7.5, what is the quantity of money?

Requirement and Clue: *Use the equation of exchange and express the quantity of money (M) in terms of the other variables.*

Solution

We know that GDP = PQ = \$300 billion. From the equation of exchange, we have MV = PQ where V is the velocity of circulation, P is the price level, and Q is real GDP.

This means that M = PQ/V = GDP/V

= 300 billion/7.5 = **\$40 billion.**

Problem 15-10

You are told that the total value of all transactions within an economy is \$500,000 and the quantity of money is \$50,000. Calculate the velocity of circulation.

Requirement and Clue: *Focus on the meaning of the velocity of* *circulation. Basically, you are being asked to determine the number of times, on average, that a dollar must be spent to finance all transactions in the economy.*

Solution

The velocity of circulation is the number of times, on average, that a dollar is spent in financing transactions. If the value of all transactions is $500,000 and the quantity of money in the economy is $50,000, then on average, each dollar would have to be spent a total of 500,000 ÷ 50,000 = 10 times. Thus, the velocity of circulation is 10.

Problem 15-11

In a certain year, the GDP of an economy was $700 billion and the quantity of money was $160 billion. What was the velocity of circulation of money?

Requirement and Clue: *Use the equation of exchange or the formula for the velocity of circulation to calculate the velocity of circulation.*

Solution

The equation of exchange can be written as MV = PQ where M is the quantity of money, V is the velocity of circulation, P is the price level, and Q is real GDP. From this equation, we get

V = PQ/M. But PQ is GDP, so V = GDP/M = 700/160 = 4.375. The velocity of circulation is **4.375.**

Problem 15-12

In a certain economy, real GDP was $300 billion, the quantity of money during the same period was $100 billion, and the velocity of circulation was 4. On the basis of this information, what was the price level?

Requirement and Clue: *Use the equation of exchange to calculate the price level.*

Solution

The equation of exchange is MV = PQ where M is the quantity of money, V is the velocity of circulation, P is the price level, and Q is real GDP. From this equation, we arrive at the following formula for P.

$$P = MV/Q$$

$$P = \frac{100 \times 4}{300} = 1.33$$

The price level was 1.33

Problem 15-13

Explain the new quantity theory of money.

Requirement and Clue: *You are required to demonstrate an understanding of the new quantity theory. Focus on what is "new" about this theory, compared with the "old" quantity theory.*

Solution

The new quantity theory, also referred to as monetarism, maintains that output is variable because the economy may be operating at less than full employment. The velocity of circulation is assumed to vary only slightly over time, and such variations are considered to be predictable. Whereas the crude quantity theory stressed the relationship between the quantity of money and the price level, the new quantity theory emphasizes the relationship between the quantity of money and nominal income. This relation is expressed in the following form:

$$M = (1/V)P \times Q$$

where M = quantity of money, V = velocity of circulation, P = price level, and Q = real GDP. If V were assumed to be constant, 1/V (which we can denote by k) would also be a constant. The product of P and Q is simply GDP or total income, which we denote by Y. We can rewrite the equation above as

$$M = kY$$

It is clear that if k is a constant, the quantity of money will be proportional to total income. But because V is assumed to vary slightly over time, k is not a constant. The new quantity theory predicts, therefore, that increases in the quantity of money will increase nominal income, while reductions in the quantity of money will decrease nominal income.

Problem 15-14

Briefly explain the transactions demand for money.

Requirement and Clue: *You are required to demonstrate some understanding of the concept of transactions demand for money. In addition to defining the concept, you should illustrate with an example.*

Solution

Households and firms will retain a part of their wealth in the form of currency (paper money and coins) and demand deposits so that they can carry out certain transactions. This is referred to as the transactions demand for money. The amount of money that will be retained for transaction purposes will depend on the number of anticipated transactions, which, in turn, depends on the level of income. If the annual income of a family increases from $80,000 to $100,000, we can expect the family to hold more money for transaction purposes. In the same way then, if total income in the economy increases, we expect the demand for money for transaction purposes to increase.

Problem 15-15

Explain the speculative demand for money.

Requirement and Clue: *You are required to demonstrate some understanding of the concept of speculative demand for money. An illustrative example will be helpful in the explanation.*

Solution

The speculative demand for money is the desire to retain money in anticipation of movements in the prices of financial assets. When the purchasing power of money is rising (prices are falling), people will t end to retain more money. By so doing, they hope to obtain a financial gain by purchasing goods at lower prices in the future. When money is losing its value (prices are rising), people will tend to convert their money into goods to avoid incurring a loss. People also hold money in anticipation of a decrease in the prices of financial assets. If they expect the price of financial assets to decrease in the future, or the rate of interest to increase, they will hold more money balances.

Here is an illustrative example. Let us assume that the public can hold its wealth in two forms only: (1) money that earns no interest and (2) bonds that do earn interest. Suppose you received reliable information that interest rates on bonds were going to rise appreciably in the near future. You would likely buy bonds, thereby holding less money. But you would need money to purchase the bonds. It would be an opportunity to profit from an anticipated movement in the rate of interest. In this situation, the money held would be for speculative purposes.

The amount of money that people will be willing to hold for speculative purposes is inversely related to the rate of interest.

Problem 15-16

Do you think that credit cards have had any effect on the precautionary motive for holding money?

Requirement and Clue: *It's a good idea to define the precautionary motive for holding money. Focus on how the existence of credit cards might affect behaviour in relation to the precautionary motive.*

Solution

People hold money for unforeseen emergencies. This is the precautionary motive for holding money. The existence of credit cards is likely to reduce the amount of money that people will hold for this purpose. In an emergency, it will often be possible to use a credit card instead of money.

Problem 15-17

Explain the liquidity preference theory of interest.

Requirement and Clue: *First state the theory then present and explain the model of interest rate determination.*

Solution

The liquidity preference theory of interest states that the rate of interest is determined by the demand for and supply of money. The diagram below helps to explain the theory.

The demand for money is shown by the downward-sloping liquidity preference curve (L). The curve is downward-sloping showing that at higher rates of interest, people will hold a smaller quantity of money. The money supply curve (QM) is vertical because we assume that the quantity of money is fixed by the monetary authorities and will not be affected by changes in the rate of interest.

At an interest rate of R1 the quantity of money demanded is 0M1, but the quantity supplied is 0M. The interest rate is too high for the quantity of money demanded to equal the quantity supplied. There is a surplus of money on the money market; so the rate of interest must fall. At a rate of interest of R2, the quantity of money demanded is 0M2, but the quantity supplied is 0M. The excess quantity demanded (shortage) will exert an upward pressure of the rate of interest. Now, consider a rate of interest of R. At this rate of interest, the amount of money that the public wants to hold (the quantity of money demanded) is 0M, which exactly equals the quantity supplied by the monetary authorities. Therefore the equilibrium rate of interest is R.

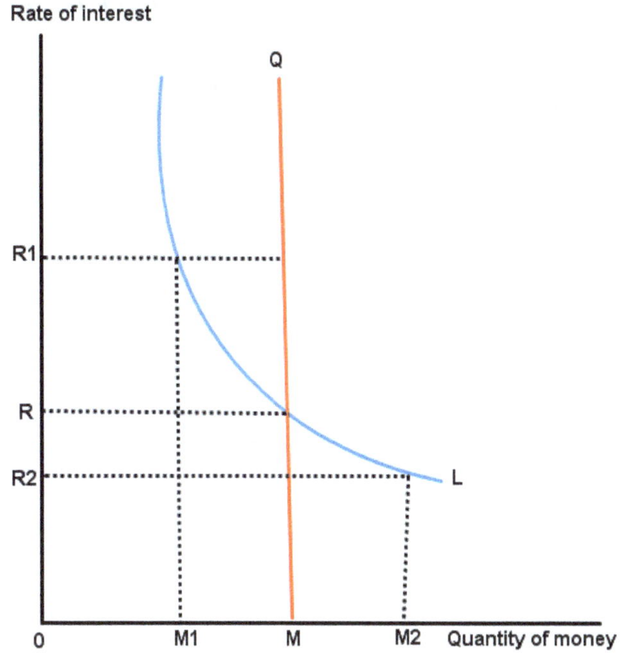

Problem 15-18

What is the significance of a vertical money supply curve?

Requirement and Clue: *Consider the variables that are on the vertical and horizontal axes of the diagram showing the money supply curve.*

Solution:

A vertical money supply curve means that the quantity of money will not be affected by changes in the rate of interest. In the following diagram, whatever the rate of interest, the quantity of money remains unchanged.

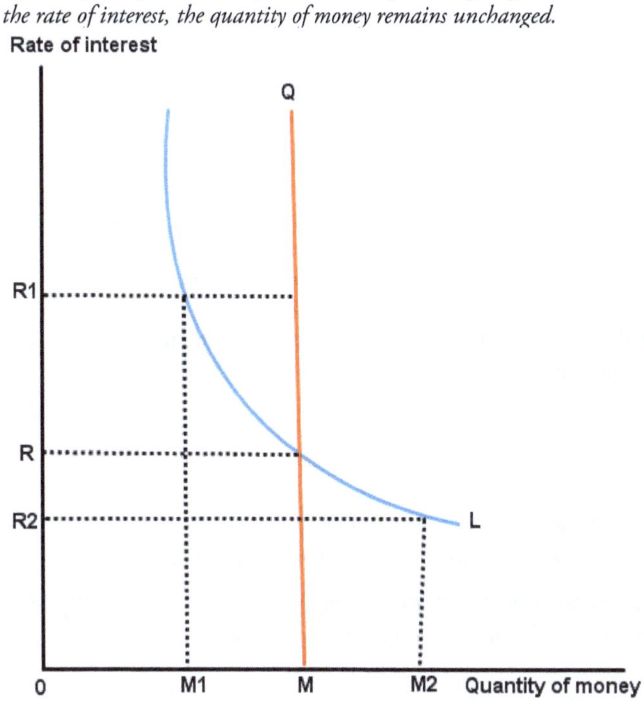

Problem 15-19

What effect will a fall in total income, such as in a recession, have on the equilibrium rate of interest? Illustrate with a graph.

Requirement and Clue: *Consider the effect of a fall in total income, such as in a recession, on the demand for money. Use a graph to show the effect of this change in the demand for money on the rate of interest.*

Solution

A fall in total income will reduce the demand for money. With lower income, people will be undertaking fewer transactions; hence a smaller quantity of money will be demanded for transaction purposes at any rate of interest. The quantity of money demanded for precautionary purposes will also fall. It is assumed that the quantity of money demanded for speculative purposes will be affected more by changes in interest rates than by changes in income. Thus, at any rate of interest, the demand for money curve will shift to the left as a result of a fall in income. With no change in the supply of money, the equilibrium rate of interest will fall.

The following graph illustrates the point.

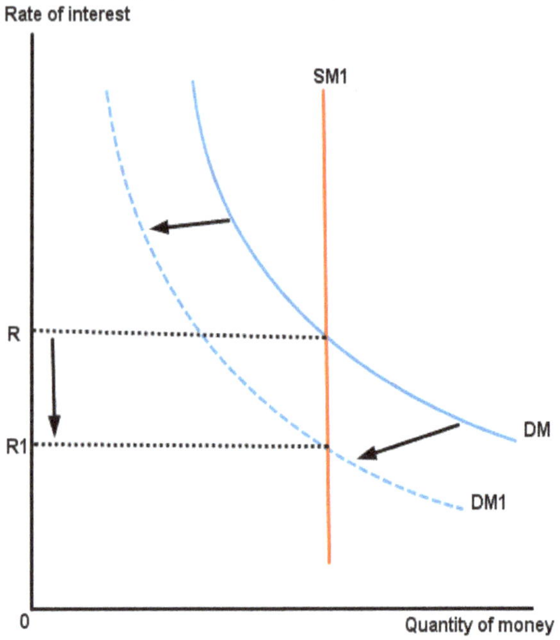

The demand for money curve is shown as DM in the diagram. The money supply curve is shown as SM1. The initial nominal interest rate is R. The fall in income shifts the demand-for-money curve to the left from DM to DM1 as shown in the diagram. This causes the interest rate to fall from R to R1. Thus, it can be concluded that a fall in income, other things being equal, will result in a fall in the equilibrium rate of interest.

Problem 15-20

Use a graph to show the effect of a decrease in the money supply on the rate of interest, other things being equal.

Requirement and Clue: *A graph of the money market (liquidity preference and supply of money) will be appropriate.*

Solution

The following diagram will illustrate the effect of a decrease in the money supply on the rate of interest.

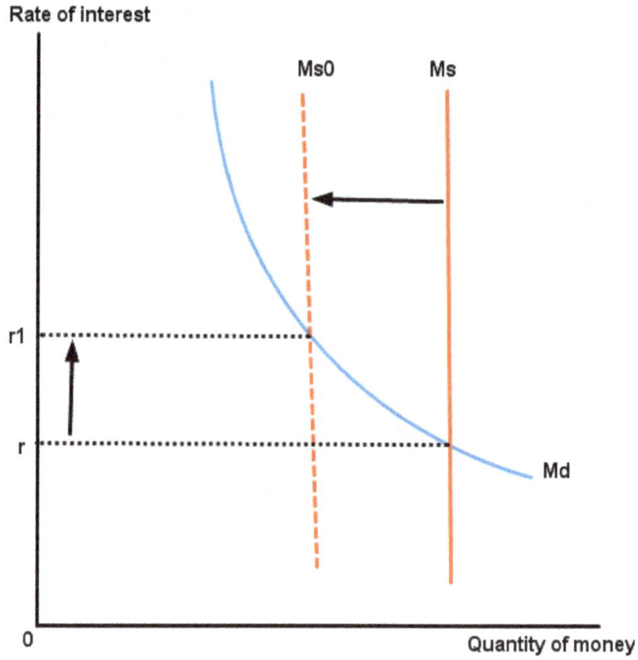

The demand for money curve is *Md* and the initial supply of money curve is *Ms*. The equilibrium rate of interest is *r*. A decrease in the money supply is shown by shifting the money supply curve from *Ms* to *Ms0*. This results in a shortage of money in the money market that forces the interest rate up from *r* to *r1* as shown in the diagram.

Problem 15-21

What is monetary policy and what are its objectives?

Requirement and Clue: *This is a two-part problem. Answer each part in order. The first part is definitional. State clearly and precisely the meaning of the term without attempting a lengthy discussion. For the second part, state what monetary policy hopes to achieve.*

Solution

Monetary policy refers to actions taken by the central bank in terms of changing the money supply and interest rates to bring about desired economic conditions.

The objectives of monetary policy are high employment, stable prices, a high rate of real output, and stability in the external value of the country's currency. A high rate of employment (a low rate of unemployment) is desirable because it means that the economy is making use of its resources to produce goods and services for the population. Maintaining stable prices means that inflation is kept under control to enable a more efficient economy. Economic growth is desirable because it facilitates a higher standard of living; and stability in the external value of the country's currency is necessary for the health of the foreign sector.

Problem 15-22

List the specific tools that are available to a central bank for conducting monetary policy?

Requirement and Clue: *The solution to this problem requires knowledge of the instruments of monetary policy. Only a listing is required.*

Solution

1. Open-market operations: buying and selling securities by central banks to the public.
2. Central bank advances and the bank rate: Loans by central banks to commercial banks can augment the reserves of the commercial banks. Changing the bank rate can affect other interest rates.
3. Switching government funds between commercial banks and the central bank: redeposits and drawdowns can affect the money supply.
4. Purchase and resale agreements: these affect the reserves of commercial banks.
5. Moral suasion: this tactic results in cooperation of commercial banks with the central bank.

Problem 15-23

Define each of the following terms:

(a) *Monetary base*

(b) *Bank rate*

(c) *Redeposit*

(d) *Moral suasion*

Requirement and Clue: This is a multi-part problem. Answer each part in order. State clearly and precisely the meaning of each term.

Solution

(a) The monetary base (also called high-powered money) is paper money, coins, and banks' deposits at the central bank.

(b) The bank rate is the rate of interest that the central bank charges on loans to banks and other financial institutions.

(c) Redeposit (also called deposit switching) is the act of transferring government funds from the central bank to the commercial banks.

(d) Moral suasion refers to any persuasive tactic by the central bank to secure the cooperation of the commercial banks.

Problem 15-24

How do open-market operations affect the quantity of money?

Requirement and Clue: *It's a good idea to define open-market operations. Focus on how the buying and selling of government securities by the central bank affect the monetary base and the money supply.*

Solution

Open-market operations refer to buying and selling securities by the central bank. Government securities are a central bank's major assets, while its major liabilities are currency held by the public and bank reserves, which are the main components of the monetary base.

If the central bank wants to increase the quantity of money, it can purchase government securities on the open market. Holders of government securities will exchange their securities for money from the central bank. The assets and liabilities of the central bank will increase, and the monetary base will increase. The operation of the money creation multiplier then causes the total money supply to increase even more than the increase in the monetary base. Open-market sales of government securities by the central bank have the opposite effect. By selling government securities, the central bank reduces its assets and liabilities at the same time, thus reducing the monetary base. Through the operation of the multiplier, the reduction in the monetary base causes an even greater reduction in the total quantity of money.

Problem 15-25

How do open-market operations affect interest rates?

Requirement and Clue: *Focus on how buying and selling securities affect the prices of securities and make the connection with interest rates. Remember the inverse relationship between bond prices and interest rates.*

Solution

Open-market operations affect interest rates in this way. When the central bank purchases securities in an attempt to increase the money supply, other things being equal, security prices will rise, which means that interest rates will fall. Similarly, when the central bank sells government securities on the open market, other things being equal, security prices will fall and interest rates will rise.

Problem 15-26

What is the liquidity trap and what is its implication for monetary policy?

Requirement and Clue: *This is a two-part problem. Answer each part in order. The first part is definitional. State the concept clearly and precisely. For the second part of the problem, focus on the effect of an increase in the money supply on interest rates when the economy is in a liquidity trap.*

Solution

The liquidity trap is a situation in which the rate of interest is so low that people prefer to hold large amounts of money over other forms of liquid assets. In that case, the demand for money curve becomes perfectly elastic as shown in the diagram by the curve L, and an increase in the money supply from Ms to Ms1 has no effect on the rate of interest (r).

In the case of a liquidity trap, monetary policy will be ineffective in stimulating economic activity. When the central bank increases the money supply, interest rates do not fall, and consumption and investment spending are not stimulated. Thus, monetary policy will be ineffective.

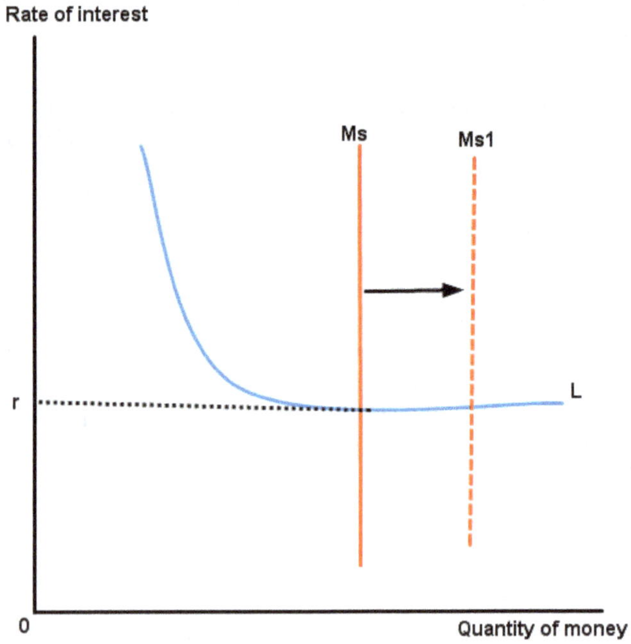

Problem 15-27

What monetary policy can a central bank use to move an economy from a situation of low output to the full-employment level of output?

Requirement and Clue: *Remember what monetary policy is. A graph, such as an aggregate demand/aggregate supply graph, can be used to illustrate an appropriate monetary policy.*

Solution

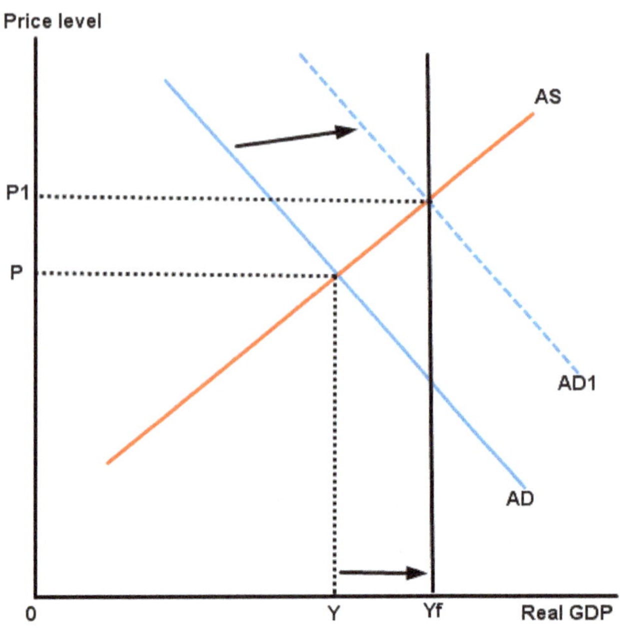

Monetary policy refers to changes in the money supply and interest rates by the central bank to achieve some desirable economic objective. The diagram above shows that the economy is in equilibrium initially at Y where the aggregate demand (AD) and the aggregate supply (AS) curves intersect. This is far below the full-employment level of Yf.

To move the economy closer to the full-employment level of output, a central bank can increase the money supply and/or reduce interest rates. This will increase both consumption and private sector investment, shifting the aggregate demand curve from AD to AD1 as shown in the diagram. The economy is now in equilibrium at the full-employment level of output. Such a policy is an expansionary monetary policy.

Multiple-Choice

In each case, circle the letter that corresponds with the correct answer.

1. Monetary theory deals with:

a. the factors affecting the demand for money
b. the effect of the money supply on the rate of interest
c. the effect of the money supply on the level of income
d. all of the above

Answer: d

Reason: Monetary theory deals with the demand for and the supply of money and with the effects of changes in these variables on income, output, and the price level.

2. According to the crude quantity theory of money:

a. there can be no monetary theory because money is too complex
b. the money supply is directly proportional to the price level
c. the money supply is inversely related to the level of income
d. none of the above

Answer: b

Reason: The crude quantity theory states that changes in the quantity of money will cause directly proportional changes in the average level of prices.

3. According to the crude quantity theory of money, an

increase in the money supply will result in:

a. a decrease in the level of total spending
b. a directly proportional increase in the price level
c. a directly proportional decrease in price
d. none of the above

Answer: b

Reason: The theory states that the quantity of money and the price level are directly proportional.

4. The velocity of circulation is:

a. the rate at which the price level rises
b. the speed with which banks increase the money supply
c. the number of times, on average, that a unit of money is spent per year
d. the number of times that people buy the same items each year.

Answer: c

Reason: Velocity of circulation is the speed with which money changes hands. It represents how much a dollar can buy in a year.

5. If M = money supply, V = velocity of circulation, P = price level, and Q = real output, the equation of exchange can be written as:

a. MV = PQ
b. M = PV/Q
c. MP = VQ
d. none of the above

Answer: a

Reason: MV represents total spending and PQ represents nominal GDP. They are identical.

6. The velocity of circulation of money can be computed by:

a. multiplying the price level by GDP
b. subtracting real GDP from nominal GDP
c. dividing GDP by the quantity of money
d. none of the above

Answer: c

Reason: Dividing the GDP by the quantity of money will give the number of times that a dollar is spent in purchasing the GDP. That is the velocity of circulation.

7. According to the new quantity theory:

a. the economy's output will always be at its equilibrium level
b. there is no relation between the money supply and the price level
c. variations in the velocity of circulation will be slight and predictable
d. none of the above

Answer: c

Reason: Choice c is one of the assumptions of the new quantity theory.

8. The new quantity theory of money is most closely associated with:

a. Irving Fisher
b. Adam Smith
c. John Maynard Keynes
d. Milton Friedman

Answer: d

Reason: Milton Friedman was the prominent developer of the new quantity theory and monetarism.

9. Which of the following is true of the crude quantity theory?

a. It was developed by Keynes
b. It assumes that the velocity of circulation is constant
c. It assumes that output fluctuates wildly and is always below the full-employment level
d. All of the above

Answer: b

Reason: The theory assumes that the velocity of circulation is determined by institutional factors which tend to be quite stable.

10. According to Keynes, which of the following is a motive for holding money?

a. Transactions motive
b. Speculative motive
c. Precautionary motive
d. All of the above

Answer: d

Reason: Choices a, b, and c are reasons given by Keynes for holding money.

11. The transactions demand for money:

a. is independent of the level of income
b. varies directly with the rate of interest
c. varies directly with the level of income
d. none of the above

Answer: c

Reason: The greater the level of income, the greater the number of transactions that will be made and hence the greater the quantity of money that people will want to hold.

12. Retaining money for unforeseen contingencies is the:

a. transactions motive
b. speculative motive
c. precautionary motive
d. asset motive

Answer: c

Reason: The precautionary motive/reason for holding money is to meet emergency situations.

13. Monetarists and Keynesians agree that:

a. changes in the money supply to not affect interest rates
b. interest rates have no effect on total spending
c. there is only one reason for holding money
d. increases in the money supply will increase net domestic income.

Answer: d

Reason: Whether increases in the money supply increase the price level or income, they will increase net domestic income.

14. According to the transactions demand for money, a change in income will cause:

a. people to think that prices will remain unchanged
b. a corresponding drop in transactions demand
c. transactions demand to remain unchanged
d. a corresponding change in transactions demand, given other determinants of the demand for money.

Answer: d

Reason: A change in income, other things being equal, will cause a change in the transact ions demand for money.

15. The liquidity preference curve shows:

a. an inverse relation between the level of net domestic income and the rate of interest

b. an inverse relation between the rate of interest and the quantity of money demanded
c. that the demand for money is unaffected by changes in income
d. none of the above

Answer: b

Reason: If the rate of interest rises, the quantity of money demanded will fall, and vice versa.

16. New quantity theorists are known as:

a. monetarists
b. empiricists
c. Keynesians
d. none of the above

Answer: a

Reason: The new quantity theory of money and monetarism have so much in common that they are considered to be the same.

17. According to monetarists, an increase in the quantity of money tends to:

a. have a neutral effect on net domestic income
b. bring about a direct increase in national income
c. bring about an indirect increase in national income via interest rates
d. bring about a direct decrease in national income

Answer: b

Reason: Monetarism claims that there is a direct relation between the quantity of money and income.

18. Both Keynesians and monetarists agree that:

a. an increase in the quantity of money results in an increase in net domestic income
b. an increase in the money supply, in a situation of less than full employment, causes real output to increase
c. in a situation of full employment, an increase in the money supply causes the price level to increase
d. all of the above

Answer: d

Reason: Choices a, b, and c are views held in common by monetarists and Keynesians.

19. In most advanced economies, a country's monetary policy is conducted by:

a. all commercial banks in the country without any input from the central bank
b. the central bank with input from the commercial banks
c. the finance department of the government
d. the major corporations in the country

Answer: b

Reason: Monetary policy is the responsibility of the central bank, but its effectiveness depends on the cooperation of the commercial banks.

20. Monetary policy refers to:

a. changes in government spending and taxes to achieve desired economic objectives
b. a set of prudent practices that each of us ought to follow in managing our money
c. changes in the money supply and interest rates by the central bank designed to achieve economic stability
d. none of the above

Answer: c

Reason: A country's monetary policy is generally conducted by the central bank and it involves changes in the money supply and credit conditions.

21. Which of the following is an objective of monetary policy?

a. To raise funds for the government to carry out public projects
b. To achieve economic stability
c. To achieve income equality
d. All of the above

Answer: b

Reason: The objectives of monetary policy are high employment, low inflation, and equilibrium balance of payments.

22. Which of the following is an instrument of monetary policy?

a. Open-market operations
b. Moral suasion
c. The bank rate/discount rate
d. All of the above

Answer: d

Reason: The central bank uses choices a, b, and c to regulate the quantity of money and interest rates.

23. A central bank may increase the money supply and credit by:

a. purchasing government securities
b. lowering the bank rate/discount rate
c. persuading commercial banks to lower interest rates
d. all of the above

Answer: d

Reason: Choices a, b, and c are instruments that a central bank may use to increase the money supply and to make credit more easily available by lower interest rates.

24. A central bank may reduce or eliminate a recessionary gap by:

a. increasing the money supply
b. decreasing the money supply
c. raising the bank/discount rate
d. raising interest rates

Answer: a

Reason: Increasing the money supply will reduce interest rates which will stimulate consumption and investment, thus increasing total spending. This will tend to reduce or eliminate a recessionary gap.

25. The economy is in a liquidity trap if:

a. the liquidity preference curve is vertical
b. the liquidity preference curve is horizontal
c. interest rates are very high and people prefer not to hold money
d. none of the above

Answer: b

Reason: The economy is in a liquidity trap when increases in the money have no effect in reducing interest rates. This means that the liquidity preference curve is flat.

True-False

Determine whether each of the following statements is true or false.

1. Monetary theory deals with actions taken by the central to bring about certain economic conditions.

Answer: False

Explanation: The statement defines monetary policy, not monetary theory.

2. An explanation of how changes in the money supply affect interest rates is an example of monetary theory.

Answer: True

3. According to the crude quantity theory of money, the velocity of circulation is constant.

Answer: True

4. The velocity of circulation may be expressed as: M/GDP where M is the quantity of money.

Answer: False

Explanation: Velocity is GDP/M.

5. The velocity equation and the equation of exchange are closely related.

Answer: True

6. The equation of exchange is not really a theory about money; it is just an identity.

Answer: True

7. A conclusion of the crude quantity theory is that changes in the quantity of money will not affect the price level.

Answer: False

Explanation: The theory concludes that changes in the money supply cause proportional changes in the price level.

8. The crude quantity theory states that an increase in the money supply will increase national income.

Answer: False

Explanation: The theory states that an increase in the money supply will cause a proportional increase in the price level.

9. One of the weaknesses of the crude quantity theory is the assumption that the velocity of circulation is constant.

Answer: True

10. In the new quantity theory, there is no link between the money supply and nominal GDP.

Answer: False

Explanation: On the contrary, the new quantity theory establishes a strong link between the money supply and nominal income.

11. In the Keynesian theory, the transactions demand for money depends mainly on the rate of interest.

Answer: False

Explanation: The transactions demand for money depends on the level of income, not the rate of interest.

12. The speculative demand for money depends on the rate of interest.

Answer: True

13. The asset demand for money is the desire to hold money as an asset.

Answer: True

14. There is no way to estimate the opportunity cost of holding money.

Answer: False

Explanation: The interest that could have been earned if the funds were invested in an interest earning asset such as a bond is the opportunity cost of holding money.

15. An increase in the money supply can result in lower interest rates, greater investment, and greater output and employment.

Answer: True

16. The major difference between the crude quantity theory and the new quantity theory is that the crude quantity theory predicts the effects of changes in the quantity of money on the level of net domestic income, while the new quantity theory considers the effects on the price level.

Answer: False

Explanation: The crude quantity theory predicts the effects of changes in the money supply on the price level, while the new quantity theory relates the money supply to net domestic income.

17. The economy is said to be in a liquidity trap when the demand for money curve is horizontal.

Answer: True

18. Keynesian monetary theory predicts that the interest rate will fall as the money supply falls over time.

Answer: False

Explanation: As the money supply falls, the rate of interest will tend to rise.

19. Main instruments of monetary policy include open-market operations, changes in the bank/discount rate, deposit switching, and moral suasion.

Answer: True

20. A central bank may use an expansionary monetary policy to reduce or eliminate a recessionary gap.

Answer: True

21. Time lags present a problem for fiscal policy but not for monetary policy.

Answer: False

Explanation: Time lags affect both fiscal policy and monetary policy.

22. Monetary policy will be effective if the liquidity preference curve is steep and the marginal efficiency of investment curve is flat.

Answer: True

Completion

(Fill in the blanks)

Use each word or combination of words from the list exactly once.
*(**Hint**: Proceed by elimination)*

Word list

Bank or discount — Buy — Circulation — Deflationary — Equation — Exchange — Gdp or nominal income — Increases — Inflationary — Interest — Level — Liquidity — Market — Monetarism — Monetary x 2 — Money — Moral — More — Open — Operations — Policy — Preference — Price — ate — Reduce — Right — Sell — Speculative — Suasion — Supply — Theory — Transactions — Velocity

Questions

1. __________ __________ deals with the effects of the demand for and supply of money on income, output, and the price level.
2. The crude quantity theory states that the money supply is directly proportional to the __________ __________.
3. The __________ of __________ is the number of times, on average, that a unit of money (such as a dollar) is spent per year in purchasing goods and services.
4. If M = money supply, V = velocity of circulation, P = price level, and Q = real GDP, then the equation MV = PQ is usually referred to as the __________ of __________.
5. The velocity of circulation can be determined by dividing the GDP by __________.
6. The new quantity theory predicts that increases in the money supply will increase __________.
7. __________ is the school of thought that claims that changes in the money supply are the major cause of economic fluctuations.
8. The opportunity cost of holding wealth in the form of liquid money balances is the __________ foregone.
9. __________ __________ is the desire to hold money rather than less liquid interest-earning assets.
10. A sum of $1,000 retained each month to pay bills represents the __________ demand for money.
11. Money set aside by a family to take advantage of changing interest rates (changing bond prices) represents the family's __________ demand for money.
12. An increase in income causes the demand for money curve to shift to the __________.
13. An increase in the money supply __________ [increases, decreases] net domestic income.
14. Changes in the money supply and interest rates by a central bank to achieve some national economic objective is called __________ __________.
15. If the central bank wants to increase the money supply, it can __________ [buy, sell] securities on the open market. If it wants to reduce the money supply, can __________ [buy, sell] securities on the open market. Such purchases and sales of securities are called __________ __________ __________.
16. The interest rate that the central bank charges on loans or advances to chartered banks is called the __________ __________.
17. An attempt by the central bank to get the commercial banks to cooperate with its monetary policy is called __________ __________.
18. The central bank can use an expansionary monetary policy to reduce or eliminate a(n) __________ [inflationary, deflationary] gap, and it can use a restrictive or tight monetary policy to reduce or eliminate a(n) __________ [inflationary, deflationary] gap.
19. Time lags __________ [reduce, increase] the effectiveness of monetary policy.
20. Monetary policy will be __________ [more, less] effective when the marginal efficiency of investment curve is relatively flat.

Solutions

1. (Monetary theory)
2. (price level)
3. (velocity [of] circulation)
4. (equation [of] exchange)
5. (money supply)
6. (GDP or nominal income)
7. (monetarism)
8. (interest)
9. (liquidity preference)
10. (transactions)
11. (speculative)
12. (right)
13. (increases)
14. (monetary policy)
15. (buy, sell, open market operations)
16. (bank rate or discount rate)
17. (moral suasion)
18. (deflationary, inflationary)
19. (reduce)
20. (more)

16 BALANCE OF PAYMENTS & EXCHANGE RATES

SYNOPSIS

The **balance of payments (BOP)** is a record of international economic transactions. It is divided into two main sections: the **current account** and the **capital account**. The current account contains all current sales and purchases of goods and services to or from the rest of the world. The difference between exports and imports of goods and services is the **balance of trade.** A positive balance of trade (i.e., a **trade surplus**) results in a payment to the country from the rest of the world. A negative balance of trade (i.e., a **trade deficit**) results in a payment from the country to the rest of the world.

The capital account contains any transaction not recorded in the current account. It contains long-term capital flows, short-term capital flows, and changes in official reserves. **Long-term capital flows** include **direct foreign investment** and **portfolio investment. Short-term capital flows** include financial assets with maturities less than a year. **Official reserves** consist mainly of gold, U.S. dollars, other foreign currencies, and Special Drawing Right.

The **exchange rate** is the price of foreign currency. Exchange rates may be fixed or they may be left to be determined by demand and supply. Under a flexible exchange rate system, an increase in the value of a country's currency is called an **appreciation** of the currency, while a decrease is called a **depreciation** of the currency. Under a fixed exchange rate system, a raising of the value of the currency is called a **revaluation**, while a lowering of the value of the currency is called a **devaluation**.

The advantages of a freely fluctuating exchange rate regime are automatic external balance and protection from foreign inflation. The disadvantages are impediment to international trade and possible reduction in income and employment. The great advantage of fixed exchange rates is that they provide a certain amount certainty to international traders. A serious disadvantage is that they limit the scope of monetary policy.

Under a fixed exchange rate system, foreign exchange transactions affect the money supply in a manner similar to open-market operations. International repercussions affect the effectiveness of monetary and fiscal policies.

LEARNING OBJECTIVES

In connection with this module, you should be able to:

1. explain the balance of payments
2. explain exchange rates and how they are determined
3. explain the relationship between inflation and exchange rates
4. discuss fixed and flexible exchange rates
5. explain the relationship between foreign exchange transactions and the money supply
6. explain the international repercussions of monetary and fiscal policies

DEFINITIONS & CONCEPTS

You should be able to define the following terms and concepts:

balance of payments	official reserves
current account	capital account
balance of trade	direct foreign investment
portfolio investment	special drawing rights(SDR)
exchange rate	appreciation (of currency)
depreciation (of currency)	devaluation (of currency)
revaluation (of currency)	dirty float

16

BALANCE OF PAYMENTS & EXCHANGE RATES

Concepts, Definitions & Problems

Problem 16-1

What is the meaning of the balance of payments?

Requirement and Clue: *This problem is definitional. State clearly and precisely the meaning of balance of payments.*

Solution

International economic transactions are recorded in accounts called the balance of payments accounts. The balance of payments is a summary statement of international economic transactions. The balance of payments is divided into two main sections: (1) the current account which is a record of sales and purchases of currently produced goods and services to or from other countries, and (2) the capital account which is a record of international capital flows.

Problem 16-2

Define each of the following concepts:

(a) *Current account*

(b) *Balance of trade*

(c) *Short-term capital flows*

(d) *Direct foreign investment*

Requirement and Clue: *This is a multi-part problem. Answer each part in order. In defining each concept, simply state its meaning clearly and precisely.*

Solution

(a) The *current account* is a record of sales and purchases of currently produced goods and services to or from the rest of the world.

(b) The *balance of trade* is the difference between the value of a country's exports and its imports. For example, if the country exports \$500,000 of goods and services and imports \$450,000 of goods and services, then its balance of trade is \$500,000 – \$450,000 = \$50,000.

(c) *Short-term capital flows* refer to the movement of financial assets internationally whose term to maturity is less than one year.

(d) *Direct foreign investment* is the ownership or control of a business in a foreign country.

Problem 16-3

List the major items in a country's current account.

Requirement and Clue: *The first thing to note is that only a listing of the items is required. It is a good idea to first define the current* *account.*

Solution:

A country's current account is a record of sales and purchases of currently produced goods and services to or from the rest of the world. The major items in the current account are listed below:

1. Exports of goods and services
2. Imports of goods and services
3. Travel
4. Transportation
5. Investment income
6. Transfers

Problem 16-4

What is the relationship, if any, between a country's the balance of payments and its GDP?

Requirement and Clue: *Consider the expenditure approach to measuring the GDP and make a link with the balance of payments.*

Solution

There is a relationship between a country's balance and payments and its GDP. To see this relationship, let us express the GDP as follows:

$$GDP = C + I + G + (X - M)$$

Where C = consumption, I = investment, G = government purchases, X = exports, and

M = imports.

The last term (X – M) in the equation above is often referred to as net exports and it defines the balance of trade. Clearly, changes in the balance of trade will affect the GDP. If the balance of trade increases, other things being equal, GDP will rise. If the balance of trade decreases, GDP will fall.

Also, if the GDP of a country rises, its imports are likely to rise as citizens with a higher income buy more foreign goods. This means that the balance of trade will fall, other things being equal.

Problem 16-5

Explain why the balance of payments account always balances.

Requirement and Clue: *Focus on how deficits and surpluses in the overall current and capital accounts are dealt with.*

Solution:

If there is a deficit in the overall current and capital accounts, then the inadequacy must be made up by using reserve assets. Conversely, if there is a surplus in the overall current and capital accounts, the excess foreign exchange is added to the country's foreign exchange reserves. The double-entry system of bookkeeping used in recording the entries in the balance of payments means that the sum of all the credit items in the current and capital accounts, as well as the official settlements, must equal the sum of all the debit items. But because of estimation errors, there will be a discrepancy. The item in the balance of payments termed "statistical discrepancy" is designed to equalize the totals of credits and debits. Therefore, the balance of payments account always balances.

Problem 16-6

Enter "current account" or "capital account" at the end of each of the following to indicate under which section of the balance of payments it should be entered.

(a) *An importer pays freight and shipping charges for goods imported from a foreign country. (____________)*

(b) *A corporation establishes a subsidiary in a foreign country. (____________)*

(c) *A domestic bank takes over a bank in another country. (____________)*

(d) *A country sends $2 million aid to a foreign country. (____________)*

(e) *Domestic farmers sell wheat to a foreign country. (____________)*

(f) *A group of travelers from a foreign country takes a trip to your country and spends two weeks there. (____________)*

(g) *Foreign investors buy a major corporation in your country. (____________)*

(h) *A major foreign corporation spends $5 million to upgrade its plant in your country. (____________)*

(i) *Immigrants to your country send money to their relatives in the countries from which they emigrated. (____________)*

(j) *Non-residents of country A pay income tax to country A, totalling $1.5 billion. (____________)*

Requirement and Clue: *Focus on whether the item relates to currently produced goods and services or not.*

Solution

(a) An importer pays freight and shipping charges for goods imported from a foreign country. (current account)

(b) A corporation establishes a subsidiary in a foreign country. (capital account)

(c) A domestic bank takes over a bank in another country. (capital account)

(d) A country sends $2 million aid to a foreign country. (current account)

(e) Domestic farmers sell wheat to a foreign country. (current account)

(f) A group of travelers from a foreign country takes a trip to your country and spends two weeks there. (current account)

(g) Foreign investors buy bonds of a major corporation in your country. (current account)

(h) A major foreign corporation spends $5 million to upgrade its plant in your country. (capital account)

(i) Immigrants to your country send money to their relatives in the countries from which they emigrated. (current account)

(j) Non-residents of country A pay income tax to country A, totalling $1.5 billion. (current account)

Problem 16-7

During a certain year, the following transactions were made between Country A and the rest of the world (ROW).

	$million
Exports of goods from Country A	*150*
Imports of goods from ROW	*120*
Exports of services from Country A	*50*
Imports of services from ROW	*40*
Purchases of securities by Country A from ROW	*70*
Sale of securities to ROW	*60*
Funds taken to Country A by immigrants from ROW	*30*
Gold import by Country A	*10*
Funds sent by immigrants to ROW	*50*

Using the information above, construct Country A's balance of payments.

Requirement and Clue: *You are required to be able to demonstrate familiarity with current account and capital account items in the balance of payments account. Determine whether or not each item relates to currently produced goods and services.*

Solution

	Current receipts (+)	Current payments (-)	Balance
	(millions of dollars)		
CURRENT ACCOUNT			
Merchandise	150	120	30
Services	50	40	10
Immigrants' funds	30	50	-20
Total current account	230	210	20
CAPITAL ACCOUNT			
Investment in ROW			-70
Investment in Country A			60
Balance on capital account			-10
Gold import			-10

Problem 16-8

Write a short note on the item "Official international reserves" in the balance of payments account.

Requirement and Clue: *In your short note should be a definition of the concept. You should also mention what they consist of. In your solution, do not ignore the word "short".*

Solution

The item, official international reserves, appears in the Capital Accounts section of the balance of payments account. Official international reserves are reserves held by a central bank to make international payments. They consist of gold, U.S. dollars, euro, other major foreign currencies, and special drawing rights (SDRs). Special drawing rights are deposits with the International Monetary Fund (IMF) and can be used as international money to settle indebtedness among nations.

Problem 16-9

Define each of the following concepts.

(a) *Foreign exchange market*

(b) *Foreign exchange rate*

(c) *Flexible exchange rate system*

(d) *Fixed exchange rate*

Requirement and Clue: *This is a multi-part problem. You should answer each part in order. The problem is definitional. You are required to state the meaning of each concept clearly and precisely.*

Solution

(a) The *foreign exchange market* is the market in which foreign currencies are traded.

(b) The *foreign exchange rate* is the value of a country's currency in terms of another country's currency.

(c) A *flexible exchange rate system* or regime is a system in which a country's exchange rate is determined by market forces of demand and supply.

(d) A *fixed exchange rate* is an exchange rate that is fixed by the government at some specified level. It is also called a pegged exchange rate.

Problem 16-10

Explain how the exchange rate is determined in the foreign exchange market.

Requirement and Clue: *A demand/supply graph will be helpful in explaining how the exchange rate is determined.*

Solution

The following diagram will be used to explain how the exchange rate is determined in the foreign exchange market.

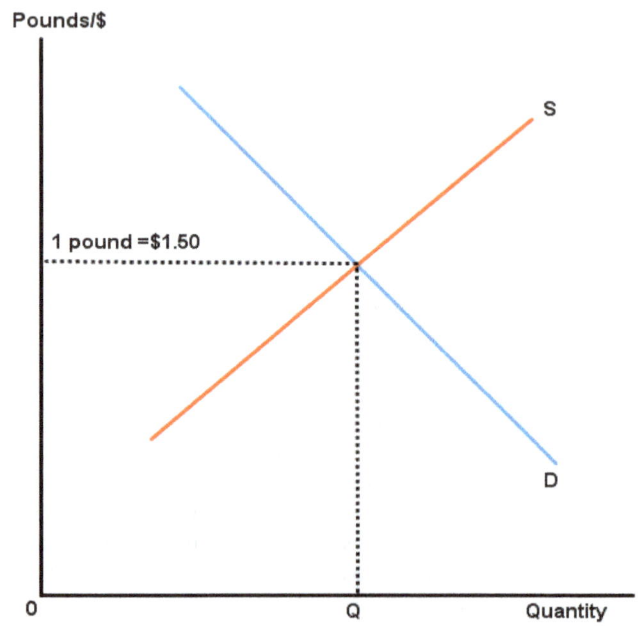

We assume that the trading countries are Britain and the United States. The demand for pounds (£) represented by the downward demand curve D, comes from Americans who might want to buy British goods or who might want to invest in Britain, or who might want to hold British pounds for speculative purposes. The greater the number of dollars that have to be given up by Americans, the fewer pounds will be demanded by the Americans. Thus, the demand curve slopes downward as shown in the diagram.

The supply curve S in the diagram, shows the supply of pounds by the British. British residents supply pounds to the foreign exchange market for the same reasons that the Americans demand British pounds. If British residents want to purchase American goods, or make investments in the United States, or increase their holdings of American dollars for speculative purposes, they will require U.S. dollars for these transactions. If the price of pounds rises (in terms of dollars), the British will offer more pounds (buy more dollars). Therefore the supply curve slopes upward, as shown in the diagram.

The foreign exchange market is in equilibrium when the demand and supply curves for pounds intersect. This gives an exchange rate of £1 ($1.50) as shown.

Problem 16-11

Distinguish between the following pairs of concepts:

(a) *Appreciation and revaluation of currency*

(b) *Depreciation and devaluation of currency*

Requirement and Clue: *Focus on the exchange rate regime within which each occurs.*

Solution

(a) Appreciation is a market determined increase in the value of a country's currency in terms of another country's currency, while revaluation is the raising of the value of a country's currency in terms of another country's currency. The distinguishing feature is that appreciation takes place within the context of a freely fluctuating exchange rate regime whereas revaluation takes place within the context of a fixed exchange rate regime.

(b) Depreciation is a market-determined decrease in the value of a country's currency in terms of another country's currency, while devaluation is the lowering of the value of a country's currency in terms of another country's currency. The distinguishing feature here is that depreciation takes place within the context of a flexible exchange rate regime whereas devaluation takes place within the context of a fixed exchange rate system.

Problem 16-12

Explain the law of one price.

Requirement and Clue: *It's a good idea to state the law first; then explain why the law would hold.*

Solution

The *law of one price* states that the prices of internationally traded goods should be the same everywhere after allowing for transportation, customs duties, and other transaction costs. Consider two neighbouring countries, A and B. According to the law of one price, the price of a TV set in country A should be the same as an identical TV set in country B. The reason is as follows: If the price were lower in country B, residents of country A would purchase their TV sets in country B instead of in country A. Some traders might even find it profitable to buy TV sets in country B and sell then in country A. Such actions would raise the price of TV sets in country B and lower it in country A until the price was the same in both markets.

Problem 16-13

What is purchasing power parity?

Requirement and Clue: *This problem is definitional. You are required to state clearly and precisely the meaning of the concept. An illustrative example will be helpful.*

Solution

The purchasing power parity theory is a method of determining exchange rates between nations. The purchasing power parity theory is the hypothesis that the exchange rate between two countries is that rate that equalizes the purchasing power of the currencies. For example, if the price of a certain item in Britain were £500 while it was US$600 in the United States, then because of the law of one price, the price of the item must be the same in both countries. That means £500 = $600 dollars. Thus £1 = $1.2.

The exchange rate between Britain and the United States should be

1 British pound for 1.2 U.S. dollars.

Problem 16-14

A particular item in Germany costs €500, whereas in Japan it costs ¥50,250. If the law of one price holds, what will be the exchange rate between Germany and Japan?

Requirement and Clue: *You must be familiar with the law of one price. Use the purchasing power parity hypothesis to arrive at the solution.*

Solution

According to the law of one price, we have the information that 500 Euros = 50,250 yen.

Therefore, 1 Euro = 50,250 ÷ 500 = 100.5 yens.

Problem 16-15

The following table shows various values of the Australian dollar in terms of the U.S. funds.

Value of $AUD in $U.S.	Value of $U.S. in $AUD
$0.90	
0.85	
0.80	
0.75	
0.70	

(a) *Calculate the value of the $U.S. in terms of $AUD at the exchange rates given, and then complete the table.*

(b) *Suppose Australia has a flexible exchange rate, and that when the Australian dollar is worth $0.80 U.S., American residents import 10,000 units of lumber from Australia. Assume that Australian lumber is sold at $2 per unit. If the elasticity of demand for Australia's lumber in the United States is 0.9, and the value of the $AUD falls to $0.75 U.S., how many units of lumber will the United States import from Australia?*

(c) *How much will the American importers have to pay (in $U.S.) for their Australian lumber?*

Requirement and Clue: *This is a multi-part problem. Answer each part in order. Be careful not to make mathematical errors in your calculations.*

Solution

(a)

Value of $AUD in $U.S.	Value of $U.S. in $AUD
$0.90	1 ÷ 0.90 = 1.11
0.85	1 ÷ 0.85 = 1.18
0.80	1 ÷ 0.80 = 1.25
0.75	1 ÷ 0.75 = 1.33
0.70	1 ÷ 0.70 = 1.43

(b) Elasticity (E) is

$$\frac{\Delta Q}{Q} \div \frac{\Delta P}{P}$$

where Q is quantity demanded and P is price. Substituting we get

$$0.9 = \frac{\Delta Q}{10{,}000} \div \frac{5}{80}$$

ΔQ = 4500/8 = 562.5

New quantity = 10,000 + 562.5 = **10,562.5**

(c)Value in Australian dollars = $(2 × 10,562.5) = $21,125

Value in $U.S. = $21,125 × 0.75 = **$15,843.75**

Problem 16-16

What are the shortcomings of the purchasing power parity theory?

Requirement and Clue: *Focus on cases or situations in which the theory will break down.*

Solution

The following are the shortcomings of the purchasing power parity theory.

1. The theory applies only to goods that are traded internationally, mobile, and standardized.
2. It applies only when transportation and transaction costs are not substantial.
3. The theory works only if there are no barriers to trade.
4. If markets are not competitive in the trading countries, the law of one price will break down, and the purchasing power parity theory will not work.

Problem 16-17

Can a country improve its balance of trade by changing its exchange rate?

Requirement and Clue: *Consider the effects of changes in exchange rates on a country's exports and imports.*

Solution

A country can indeed improve its balance of trade by changing its exchange rate. Suppose that a country has a large deficit in its balance of trade. It can improve the situation by devaluing its currency. Such an act will make the country's goods less expensive to foreigners. At the same time, it will make foreign (imported) goods relatively more expensive. Thus, by devaluing its currency, a country can stimulate its exports and discourage imports. This improves its balance of trade and may generate income and employment within the domestic economy.

Problem 16-18

What effect do changes in the exchange rate have on the price level?

Requirement and Clue: *Focus on how changes in the exchange rate affect the buying behaviour of residents of the countries concerned.*

Solution

Let us consider this problem with respect to Canada and the United States. When the value of the Canadian dollar falls in terms of the U.S. dollar, the prices of American imported goods rise. Canadian residents have to pay more for consumer goods imported from the United States. Moreover, a depreciation of the Canadian dollar in terms of the U.S. dollar raises the prices of imported inputs from the United States and this forces up production costs in Canada. The Canadian price level will therefore tend to rise when there is a depreciation of the Canadian dollar in terms of the U.S. dollar.

Changes in the exchange rate can affect the price level in another way. When the value of the Canadian dollar falls in terms of the U.S. dollar, Canadian goods become relatively cheap. Residents of the United States will tend to increase their purchases of Canadian goods and thus exert upward pressure on the Canadian price level. At the same time, the fall in the value of the Canadian dollar makes foreign goods more expensive. It is therefore likely that Canadian residents will substitute domestic goods for the relatively more expensive imported goods, thus putting further upward pressure on domestic prices.

Problem 16-19

What are the advantages and disadvantages of flexible exchange rates?

Requirement and Clue: *This problem is straight forward. Remember to discuss both advantages and disadvantages.*

Solution

An exchange rate that is left to be determined by market forces is said to be flexible. Flexible exchange rates have both advantages and disadvantages. First, the advantages. Under a flexible exchange rate system, equilibrium in the in the foreign exchange market is achieved without any direct intervention by policymakers. The exchange rate will adjust automatically to changes in demand and supply and thus maintain equilibrium. There is therefore no need to maintain foreign reserves in order to peg the exchange rate. This means that a flexible exchange rate system frees monetary policy so that it can be used in conjunction with fiscal policy to keep the economy operating at a high level of employment with relatively stable prices.

In addition to the automatic achievement of equilibrium, a flexible exchange rate system helps to insulate a country against foreign inflationary pressures. Suppose there is inflation in the United States while Canada is experiencing a period of of price stability. Canadian exports to the United States will rise as residents of the United States switch to relatively cheaper Canadian goods. Also, Canadian imports from the United States will fall as Canadian residents reduce the quantity of the relatively expensive U.S. goods demanded. The resulting increase in demand for Canadian goods will tend to increase prices in Canada. But the exchange rate will rise and thus prevent Canadian prices from rising.

One disadvantage of a flexible exchange rate system is that it causes uncertainty which will tend to discourage international trade. It is important for international traders to know what they will pay for their imports and what they will receive for their exports. International trade is unlikely to flourish in an environment of uncertainty.

Another disadvantage of flexible exchange rates is that it may affect the economy adversely. For example, an appreciation of the Canadian dollar means that foreign goods become less expensive to Canadians. Lower-priced imports will then compete with Canadian-made goods, and con summers may buy foreign products instead of made-in-Canada products. That in turn may lead to reductions in income and increases in unemployment.

Problem 16-20

Discuss the advantages and disadvantages of fixed exchange rates.

Requirement and Clue: *This problem is straight forward. Remember to discuss both advantages and disadvantages.*

Solution

A fixed exchange rate is one that is fixed by the government at some specified level. Fixed exchange rates have the great advantage of certainty and security. International traders can confidently arrange their transactions, knowing that prices and costs will not change in the interim. A serious disadvantage of a fixed exchange rate is that a country may be forced to adopt a monetary policy with undesirable domestic effects just to be able to maintain the exchange rate at its fixed level. For example, a restrictive monetary policy with high interest rates may be necessary to maintain the official level of the exchange rate. Such a policy, however, may result in high unemployment and low economic growth.

Problem 16-21

Discuss the international repercussions of an expansionary monetary policy under a fixed exchange rate regime.

Requirement and Clue: *Focus on how increases in the money supply affect interest rates and the response of the central bank to maintain the exchange rate at its desired level.*

Solution

If the central bank increases the money supply under a system of fixed exchange rates, interest rates will fall. The central bank will enter the foreign exchange market and sell foreign currency. This sale of foreign currency by the central bank reduces the money supply. Thus, the net increase in the money supply will be less than the initial increase. Furthermore, the expansionary monetary policy may push the domestic price level upward, resulting in a fall in the country's exports and an increase in its imports. Hence, aggregate expenditure falls.

Problem 16-22

Study the following passage and then point out any errors that it may contain.

"The rate at which one country's currency exchanges for that currency of another country (i.e., the exchange rate) is the best measure of the countries' relative economic performance. For example, if the Canadian dollar is valued at 15% below the U.S. dollar, it means that the Canadian economy is 15% less efficient than the U.S. economy. If it is valued at 10% more than the U.S. dollar, it means that the Canadian economy is 10% more efficient than the U.S. economy; and if the Canadian dollar is at par with the U.S. dollar, then one can safely conclude that the Canadian and the U.S. economies are equally efficient."

Requirement and Clue: *Make sure you read the passage critically, looking for mistakes in relationships, illogical conclusions, and other flaws. Point out any errors and offer corrections.*

Solution

The relationship between exchange rates and economic efficiency is not as close as the passage suggests. In the first place, the exchange rate may be fixed, and the level at which it is fixed might have little or nothing at all to do with economic efficiency. But even if the exchange rate is market determined, it may bear little relationship to economic performance or efficiency. For example, the number of American visitors to Canada might increase, and other things being equal, this increase in the number of visitors will cause an increase in the demand for Canadian dollars, and thus increase the value of the Canadian dollar relative to the U.S. dollar. Such an increase in the exchange value of the Canadian dollar would hardly be attributed to any increase in the relative efficiency of the Canadian economy.

Multiple-Choice

In each case, circle the letter that corresponds with the correct answer.

1. The balance of payments is:

a. the balance owing to foreign countries after imports have been paid for

b. the balance due from foreign countries after partial payment has been made for imports

c. a record of economic transactions with the rest of the world

d. all of the above.

Answer: c

Reason: *The balance of payments is a record of international economic transactions.*

2. The two main sections into which the balance of payments is divided are:

a. the revenue account and the capital account

b. the domestic account and the foreign account

c. the current account and the personal account

d. the current account and the capital account.

Answer: d

Reason: *The balance of payments account is divided into the current account and the capital account.*

3. Which of the following is recorded in the current account?

a. Imported goods

b. Direct investment

c. Portfolio investment

d. Official reserves

Answer: a

Reason: *Options b, c, and d are recorded in the capital account.*

4. Assume that the United Kingdom exports £50,000 worth of potatoes to Hong Kong and imports £60,000 worth of hand bags from Hong Kong. Then:

a. the United Kingdom will receive a net payment of £10,000 from Hong Kong

b. the United Kingdom will make a net payment of £10,000 to Hong Kong

c. neither the United Kingdom nor Hong Kong has to make any payment because exports pay for imports

d. none of the above

Answer: b

Reason: *Exports do pay for imports, but there will be a balance of £10,000 that the United Kingdom must pay to finalize the transaction.*

5. Which of the following is recorded in the capital account?

a. Exports of goods and services

b. Immigrants' funds

c. Direct investment in a country by foreigners

d. Withholding taxes

Answer: c

Reason: *Options a, b, and d are recorded in the current account.*

6. Which of the following statements is correct?

a. The balance of payments need not balance because exports and imports of goods and services may not be equal

b. The current account always balances even if imports and exports of goods and services are not equal

c. Exports are recorded with plus (+) signs in the capital account

d. Imports of goods are entered with minus (–) signs in the current account.

Answer: d

Reason: *Imports relate to currently produced goods and services and result in payment to other countries. They are recorded as debit.*

7. The foreign exchange rate is:

a. the ratio of a country's exports to its imports

b. the amount of money a country has to pay for a unit of foreign currency

c. how much goods and services a unit of a country's currency will buy

d. none of the above

Answer: b

Reason: *The foreign exchange rate is the price of foreign currency.*

8. If $1.00 Canadian = $0.73 U.S., then $1.00 U.S. equals:

a. $1.36 Canadian

b. $1.27 Canadian

c. $1.73 Canadian

d. $0.64 Canadian

Answer: a

Reason: *1/0.73 = 1.36*

9. The demand curve for foreign currency slopes downward because:

a. exports increase as the rate of inflation falls

b. the higher the price of foreign currency, the less will be the quantity demanded

c. the higher the price of foreign currency, the greater the amount of foreign currency that will be put on the market

d. none of the above

Answer: b

Reason: *Inverse relationships are depicted by downward sloping curves.*

10. The equilibrium exchange rate of the Canadian dollar occurs where:

a. the foreign demand for Canadian dollars equals the supply of Canadian dollars by Canadians

b. the value of the Canadian dollar equals the value of the foreign currency

c. the quantity of Canadian dollars demanded by foreigners equals the quantity of Canadian dollars supplied by Canadians

d. all of the above.

Answer: c

Reason: *Choice c defines the condition for equilibrium of the foreign exchange rate.*

11. The *law of one price* states that:

a. once the equilibrium exchange rate is determined, it

cannot be changed

b. each internationally traded item can have only one price

c. once allowance is made for certain costs associated with trade, the price of an internationally traded item will be the same everywhere

d. none of the above

Answer: c

Reason: The law of one price is the hypothesis that the prices of traded goods should be the same everywhere the good is traded after allowing for transportation and other transaction costs.

12. The law of one price is most closely related to:

a. a fixed exchange rate

b. a flexible exchange rate

c. the purchasing power parity theory

d. a managed flexible exchange rate

Answer: c

Reason: The purchasing power parity theory is based on the law of one price.

13. If the Canadian dollar depreciates in terms of the U.S. dollar, we expect:

a. exports from Canada to the United States to fall

b. imports to Canada from the United States to increase

c. exports from Canada to the United States to increase

d. Canada to have a trade deficit.

Answer: c

Reason: Because of the relatively cheaper Canadian dollar, U.S. residents will buy more Canadian goods.

14. A country can reduce a large trade deficit by:

a. revaluing its currency c. encouraging imports

b. discouraging exports d. devaluing its currency

Answer: d

Reason: This will encourage exports and discourage imports.

15. An increase in the average incomes of New Zealanders is likely to:

a. increase imports and lower the exchange value of the New Zealand currency

b. increase imports and raise the exchange value of the New Zealand currency

c. lower imports and raise the exchange value of the New Zealand currency

d. lower imports and lower the exchange value of the New Zealand currency

Answer: a

Reason: With increased incomes, New Zealanders will tend to import more goods and services. The increase in demand for foreign currency will raise the value of foreign currency (lower the value of the New Zealand currency)

16. Under a flexible exchange rate system, a balance of payments deficit can be eliminated by:

a. a fall in the exchange value of the currency

b. an increase in the exchange value of the currency

c. an increase in imports into the country

d. none of the above.

Answer: a

Reason: A fall in the exchange value of the country's currency will make its goods cheaper to foreigners and thus increase its exports.

17. Under a flexible exchange rate regime, a sale of foreign currency:

a. increases the domestic money supply

b. reduces the domestic money supply

c. may increase or reduce the domestic money supply

d. has no effect on the domestic money supply

Answer: d

Reason: The central bank does not intervene so the domestic money supply is not affected.

18. If a country is on a fixed exchange rate system, the effect of an increase in the money supply, with international repercussions considered, will be:

a. amplified c. zero

b. dampened d. uncertain

Answer: b

Reason: This is because of the impact of the intervention of the central bank.

True-False

Determine whether each of the following statements is true or false.

1. The balance of payments refers to the net indebtedness of the government.

Answer: False

Explanation: The balance of payments is a record of international economic transactions.

2. The two major sections into which the balance of payments id divided are the current account and the capital account.

Answer: True

3. If immigrants take money with them when they move to a new country, the money is recorded in the capital account under short-term capital flows.

Answer: False

Explanation: Immigrants' funds are recorded in the current account.

4. Profits of American subsidiaries in Canada which are sent to the United States appear as a credit item in the Canadian balance of payments.

Answer: False

Explanation: This is a payment from Canada to a foreign country and is therefore recorded as a debit item.

5. Even if the current account and the capital account do not balance, the balance of payments will always balance.

Answer: True

6. If an Australian dollar is worth $0.86 U.S., then $1.00 U.S. is worth $1.16 Australian.

Answer: True

7. The law of one price is the hypothesis that the prices of internationally traded goods should be the same everywhere after allowing for transportation and other transaction costs.

Answer: True

8. Purchasing power parity theory is the theory that the exchange rate between two countries will reflect the difference in prices between them.

Answer: True

9. If New Zealand is on a flexible exchange rate system, an increase in demand for New Zealand goods by Japanese, other things being equal, will cause the value of the New Zealand dollar is terms of the Japanese yen to increase.

Answer: True

10. A depreciation of the Canadian in terms of the U.S. dollar causes Canadian goods to be more expensive to Americans.

Answer: False

Explanation: A depreciation of the Canadian dollar in terms of U.S. funds means that the value of the U.S. dollar has increased relative to the Canadian dollar. Hence, Canadian goods are less expensive to Americans.

11. If Britain has a balance of payments surplus, its foreign exchange reserves will decrease.

Answer: False

Explanation: A surplus will increase its foreign exchange reserves.

12. Inflation in a country that is on a flexible exchange rate regime may cause a depreciation of its currency.

Answer: True

13. Foreign currency transactions affect the money supply only if the central bank is involved in the transaction.

Answer: True

14. Under a fixed exchange rate system, international repercussions amplify the effects of fiscal policy.

Answer: True

Completion

(Fill in the blanks)

Use each word or combination of words from the list exactly once.
*(**Hint**: Proceed by elimination)*

Word list

Amplified — Appreciate — Balance of merchandise [visible] trade — Balance of trade — Capital x 2 — Current x 2 — Deficit — Depreciate — Devalue — Direct — Exchange rate — Flexible — Gold — Law of one price — Make — Managed exchange rate or dirty float — Other foreign currencies — Portfolio — Special drawing rights [SDRs] — Surplus — To — U.S. Dollars

Questions

1. The balance of payments is divided into two main parts: the __________ account and the __________ account. The __________ account contains sales and purchases of currently produced goods and services. The __________ account contains long-term and short-term capital flows.
2. The difference between total exports of goods and total imports of goods is called the __________. The difference between exports of goods and services and imports of goods and services is called the __________.
3. If a country has a balance of trade deficit, that country will __________ [receive, make] a net payment __________ [to, from] the rest of the world.
4. Ownership or control of a business in a foreign country is __________ foreign investment. The purchase of bonds in a foreign country is __________ investment.
5. Official foreign exchange reserves include __________, __________, __________, __________, and __________.
6. The rate at which one country's currency exchanges for another country's currency is called the __________.
7. The __________ states that if we ignore transportation costs, customs duties, and other transaction costs, and if competition prevails, then the price of a good that is traded internationally will be the same wherever the good is traded.
8. A country may __________ [revalue, devalue] its currency in an attempt to stimulate its exports and discourage imports. This action will tend to reduce its trade __________ [deficit, surplus] or increase its trade __________ [deficit, surplus].
9. Assume that both Canada and Great Britain have freely fluctuating exchange rates. If Canada has a surplus

in its trade with Great Britain, then the value of the Canadian currency in terms of the British currency will ________ [appreciate, depreciate], and the value of the British currency in terms of Canadian currency will ________ [appreciate, depreciate].

10. If a country manages its currency so that its value on foreign exchange markets fluctuates only within certain limits, then the country is said to have a ________ system.
11. Under a ________ exchange rate regime, foreign exchange transactions do not affect the domestic money supply because the central bank does not intervene.
12. If a country is on a flexible exchange rate regime, the effects of monetary policy will be ________ [amplified, dampened] by international repercussions.

Solutions

1. (current, capital, current, capital)
2. (balance of merchandise [visible] trade, balance of trade)
3. (make, to)
4. (direct, portfolio)
5. (gold, U.S. dollars, other foreign currencies, special drawing rights [SDRs])
6. (exchange rate)
7. (law of one price)
8. (devalue, deficit, surplus)
9. (appreciate, depreciate)
10. (managed exchange rate/dirty float)
11. (flexible)
12. (amplified)

About the Author

Elijah M. James is a professor in the Department of Economic at Dawson College in Montreal, Quebec, Canada. He has also taught at McGill University, John Abbott College, and Concordia University. Dr. James studied economics at Memorial University of Newfoundland, University of Western Ontario, Concordia University (Montreal), University of Toronto, and California Western University. Professor James has published extensively in the area of economics and his textbooks on microeconomics and macroeconomics are well-known to Canadian students.

Professor James won the Teaching Excellence award in 2009-2010 at Dawson College and has been awarded the *Association québécoise de pédagogie collégiale (AQPC) Honourable Mention 2017.* He has been recognized for his contribution to education.

www.ingramcontent.com/pod-product-compliance
Lightning Source LLC
LaVergne TN
LVHW060033210926
848481LV00013B/3851
9781926716459